THE COMPANION GUIDE TO

Normandy

THE COMPANION GUIDES

GENERAL EDITOR: VINCENT CRONIN

*It is the aim of these Guides to provide a
Companion, in the person of the author,
who knows intimately the places and
people of whom he writes, and is able to
communicate this knowledge and affection
to his readers. It is hoped that the text
and pictures will aid them in their prep-
arations and in their travels, and will help
them to remember on their return.*

LONDON · THE SHAKESPEARE COUNTRY · EAST ANGLIA · KENT AND SUSSEX
DEVON AND CORNWALL · NORTHUMBRIA · NORTH WALES · SOUTH WALES
THE WEST HIGHLANDS OF SCOTLAND
THE SOUTH OF FRANCE · SOUTH WEST FRANCE · BURGUNDY
THE ILE DE FRANCE · THE LOIRE
ROME · VENICE · FLORENCE
MADRID AND CENTRAL SPAIN
TURKEY · JUGOSLAVIA · MAINLAND GREECE · THE GREEK ISLANDS
THE SOUTH ISLAND OF NEW ZEALAND
THE NORTH ISLAND OF NEW ZEALAND
SYDNEY · SOUTH AFRICA

Certain of these guides are also available in limpback

In preparation
OUTER LONDON · NEW YORK · OXFORD AND CAMBRIDGE
EDINBURGH AND THE BORDER COUNTRY

THE COMPANION GUIDE TO

Normandy

NESTA ROBERTS

COLLINS
8 Grafton Street, London WI

William Collins Sons & Co Ltd
London · Glasgow · Sydney · Auckland
Toronto · Johannesburg

First published 1980
© Nesta Roberts 1980
Second edition 1986

ISBN 0 00 216552 10

Set in Times Roman by Inforum Ltd, Portsmouth
Maps drawn by Brian and Constant Dear
Made and printed in Great Britain by
Robert Hartnoll (1985) Ltd, Bodmin

Contents

❧

Illustrations

Maps

❧

Acknowledgments

To attempt to catalogue the many agencies and individuals whose co-operation has made possible the writing of this book would be to risk invidiousness. Instead I would record my warmest thanks to all of them, and in particular to the librarians, local historians and busy parish priests who so readily gave their time to an unheralded and importunate stranger. Such encounters remain among my happiest memories of Normandy.

Introduction

'EVERYBODY knows Normandy, and therefore Normandy is hardly known at all,' said a travel writer of eighty years ago. Normandy, he went on, suffered from being too readily accessible, so that it was remembered 'for its fashionable watering places and for one or two of its historic towns'.

Today, when modern transport has changed our ideas of accessibility, it suffers from being a staging post. Travellers pass through Normandy at speed on their way to the Mediterranean sun, often with no time to spare even for its historic towns. To do so is to disregard a province which, for the variety of its scenery and the splendours of its architecture, is one of the most attractive of France. Also, it is to miss an opportunity of finding the other half of our own past, of suddenly understanding the meaning of the term 'Anglo-Norman'.

An accident of geography, the Channel, cut in two what was one region. An accident of history, the Conquest, united politically over nearly four hundred years two peoples who shared the same Scandinavian stock. Small wonder that English travellers landing in Normandy have a sense of being on familiar ground; almost, indeed, on home ground. Here are the white cliffs they have left behind; here, often enough, is the English weather that can change within hours from a blue shimmer of heat to a grey sea banging on pebbles. Most familiar of all, here are no volatile Latins, but farmers and sailors as steady and cautious and penny-wise as their equivalents in Yorkshire or Lincolnshire.

It was the Scandinavian invasions of the ninth and tenth centuries which gave the province its name of Terra Northmanorum, or Northmannia, which, over the centuries, evolved into Normandy. There had been earlier invasions. Between 58 and 51 B.C. the Romans conquered and colonized a Celtic people who were already trading regularly with England and Ireland. Rome gave them three centuries of peace, civilization and material prosperity – in Normandy, as in England, the Roman roads can still be traced – and an

11

imprint which was to prove enduring. Christianity came during the latter part of the epoch, penetrating by way of the Cotentin and of Rouen, where Saint Mellon founded a see in about A.D. 300; and, after the collapse of the Empire before the waves of Germanic invaders, it was the structure of the Church which took over from the Roman administration.

Though many of the Gallo-Romans were driven westward by the barbarians, outposts, mostly in the towns, held out, sometimes with garrisons made up largely of German mercenaries, who set their army loyalty above their race. The last of the barbarians, the Franks, were themselves already partly 'Romanized' and were soon to become Christian. It was under their rule that Normandy experienced the first flowering of monastic civilization, with the founding during the sixth and seventh centuries of the great abbeys of the Seine Valley. The Merovingian and Carolingian kings fostered the movement, granting land to the new communities.

Once more there was a period of peace and order, lasting for more than 400 years, before the next invasion. This had momentous consequences: the Vikings, mostly from Denmark, who came as sea-robbers, sacking and burning towns, pillaging abbeys and driving out the monks, stayed as settlers. Within a century of their first appearance in the Seine Valley in 820, their leader, Rollo, had been baptized in the name of Robert, and had concluded with Charles le Simple at Saint-Clair-sur-Epte in 911 a treaty which gave him the dukedom of Normandy. Much of the territory was already occupied by the Vikings, and now that their position was legally established, there was an influx of Scandinavian settlers who became assimilated with remarkable speed. Rollo's son, Guillaume Longue-Épée, the second duke, set the pattern. His father's conversion may have been politically inspired; the sincerity of his own belief was not to be questioned. It was he who began the refounding of the monasteries so recently destroyed by his ancestors.

Longue-Épée's son, later Duke Richard I, had to be sent to Bayeux to learn the Norse language, which had already died out at Rouen. The Norman nobles who, little more than a century later, sailed for England with Richard's great-grandson, William the Conqueror, were Frenchmen; their Norse kinsmen who, over approximately the same period, had settled in England, still retained many of their Scandinavian characteristics. William himself can hardly be said to have assimilated into his new kingdom; he never succeeded in learning its language and he treated it as a colony rather than a settlement.

It was a profitable colony. England in the tenth and eleventh centuries was one of the richest countries in western Europe and, during William's reign, English money flowed into Normandy as Norman knights and nobles flowed into England. The influx during the first ten years after 1066 has been estimated at between five and ten thousand, a number which would have included retainers, in a population set, even more approximately, at between one and two million. But the union was mutually fruitful. The Normans were passionate, almost compulsive builders. With the creamy Caen stone of which Canterbury Cathedral and the Tower of London were built, they introduced the 'Norman' style of architecture, which elsewhere than in this country, is known as Romanesque. The Anglo-Norman kingdom prospered and so greatly enlarged its borders that when, in 1204, the kings of France reconquered mainland Normandy, their northern limit was the Scottish border, their southern the Pyrenees.

Though it lost its independence by the union with France, the dukedom kept its administrative autonomy and enjoyed almost a century and a half of peace, unbroken until 1346, when Edward III landed in the Cotentin to pursue his claim to the French throne. For the next hundred years sporadic warfare was the norm, with Normandy living under English occupation from 1418 to 1450, when the invaders were finally turned out.

Once more there was a century or so of peace and restoration before the duchy was again ravaged, this time by the Wars of Religion, which continued from 1562 to the end of the century and left their mark in damage to a number of churches and cathedrals. The Protestant Reformation came early to Normandy, which, like all coastal areas with busy ports, was readily open to outside influences, and it developed a considerable Protestant population.

Norman autonomy ended with the Revolution, which brought the division of France into new administrative units. Politically speaking, there is today no such entity as Normandy, but the human and historic foundations of the modern province, made up of the departments of the Seine-Maritime, Eure, Orne, Calvados and Manche, are solid enough. The Vikings who settled here have left their colouring and physique to many of the people; the boundaries of today's departments follow closely those of the ecclesiastical dioceses, which were themselves based on the Roman administrative areas, the *civitates*.

Physically the province is highly disparate; there can be few regions of comparable size which offer such contrasts of landscape.

It is customary to speak of two Normandies, the granite country to the west, the chalk to the east, though the division does less than justice to the diversity to be found on either side of the rather blurred frontier between them, running south-east from Valognes in the Cotentin Peninsula. For a good deal of its length that frontier marks also the division between Haute Normandie and Basse Normandie. The former centres on Rouen, and more and more feels the influence of Paris. Basse Normandie, harsher, remoter, still largely undefiled, turns away from rather than towards Caen in its south-east corner.

Common to both is some of the richest agricultural land in Europe, where the cream comes straight from the cow and, it used to be said, a farmer's stick planted in the ground at night will have broken into leaf by the morning. It is a country as green as Ireland, garlanded rose and white with flowering orchards in the spring, brocaded with the russet and gold of oak and beech forests in the autumn.

Such prosperity, coupled with a ready supply of building stone, has made it an area of fine churches and country houses as well as of cathedrals and châteaux. The manor houses, so integral to their background that they seem less artefacts than natural growths, add greatly to the charm of many prospects. Not long since, this was an area also of towns whose ancient timbered houses took one back to the Middle Ages. Most of them went in the havoc of World War II. Some survive, and there have been commendable restorations, as at Rouen, but a great many have been three-quarters rebuilt since 1945, often enough in reinforced concrete. Like the results or execrate them as you will, to bypass such places and to ignore the life-style they express is to treat a province and its people as a folk museum, an attitude even more impoverishing to the traveller than insulting to the residents.

In this book, to simplify the planning of itineraries, I have divided Normandy into three parts. Working from west to east they may be labelled 'rock', 'woodland' and 'plain and plateau', though this indicates only their dominant aspects.

It is the eastern section which, for many of the English, represents quintessential Normandy, partly, perhaps, because its coast, from Étretat to Le Tréport, supported an appreciable English colony during much of the 19c. and early 20c. Its seaside resorts, most of them having beaches of pebble and shingle, with sand uncovered at low tide, are sufficiently varied to suit most tastes and budgets. Inland there is a country of large-scale farming, with vast fields of corn and beet and the unexpected cool blue of flax, studded with even more unexpected clumps of trees. There are historic towns – Eu, Gisors, Les Andelys – in addition to Rouen, which, for those seriously interested in art and architecture, could well occupy one week of a holiday, even if Michelin does say you can see the old centre of the town in two-and-a-half hours.

This section is bounded on the south by the Seine Valley, where the scenery is enchanting and there are a number of small riverside resorts as an alternative to the coast. Between Rouen and the estuary are three of the abbeys, St-Georges-de-Boscherville, Jumièges and Saint-Wandrille, which contributed so much to the life of Normandy.

The central section has the best-known seaside area of northern France in the Côte Fleurie, the coastal strip between the estuaries of the Seine and the Orne. Beaches here are sandy, and the immediate hinterland almost extravagantly beautiful. There are smaller and less sophisticated places than Cabourg and Trouville-Deauville, but those planning family holidays should bear in mind that this is not an inexpensive area.

Inland is the lush country of the Pays d'Auge, wooded and undulating, the land of cider and noble cheeses. In the south is the horse-breeding area of the Perche, to the west the crag and river landscape of the Suisse Normandie, to the east and south the Abbey of Le Bec-Hellouin, nursery of English bishops, and the old frontier with France fortified by the Anglo-Norman kings. It is excellent country for walking and riding (*see* Appendix), also for church-crawling beyond the starred items. Some of the lesser-known towns in this area, Conches-en-Ouche, Verneuil-sur-Avre, Orbec, Bernay, are most rewarding, with the added attraction of not being too tourist-ridden. Technically, central Normandy has two cathedrals, Évreux and Sées; aesthetically speaking, it has five. Saint-Pierre, at Lisieux, which was demoted from cathedral status at the end of the 18c., remains one of the finest Gothic buildings in Normandy, and the abbeys of St-Étienne and La Trinité, at Caen, eclipse many cathedrals. Caen is the one town in the province whose post-war rebuilding has been wholly successful, thanks largely to the use of local stone.

With the west, 'Breton Normandy', we are in another country: the Cotentin Peninsula still keeps many of the virtues of its relative remoteness, though Bayeux and Mont Saint-Michel, to the south-east and south-west respectively, inevitably attract their hordes. Both are worth any amount of jostling, and, for compensation, you are likely to have peace, if not solitude, when visiting the exquisite cathedral of Coutances, the ruin of Hambye and the Romanesque abbey church of Lessay.

In contrast to the arable land of the east, farming here means dairying – as in most of Normandy there is still, by English standards, a surprising amount of hand-milking – and animal husbandry, including horse-breeding. The markets have an enormous vitality. Flaubert would be at home in many of them.

On the west and east coasts there are sandy beaches with resorts which, on the whole, are simpler than those farther east and have not lost their character of fishing ports. The north-eastern tip of the peninsula has a wild majesty of cliff and ocean that is unforgettable. 'Always declare an interest' – in case the fact is not by now self-evident, the west is the part of Normandy which I find the most exhilarating.

Itineraries

This book sets out three round tours starting and ending respectively at Dieppe, Le Havre and Cherbourg, all of which have regular car ferries from England. Each itinerary includes a coastal strip and all cover attractive inland areas. For historic and artistic interest, any choice between them can be only subjective.

ITINERARY I

Dieppe and environs.
Puys and coast to Le Tréport — Eu — Bures-en-Bray — Mesnières-en-Bray — Neufchâtel — Forges-les-Eaux — Gisors. Vernon — Les Andelys — Écouis — Lyons-la-Forêt — Fontaine-Guérard. Rouen, centre and environs. St-Georges-de-Boscherville — Duclair — Jumièges — Saint-Wandrille — Caudebec-en-Caux — Villequier — Yvetot — Lillebonne. Tancarville — Filières — Étretat — Fécamp — Saint-Valéry-en-Caux — Bourg-Dun — Coast to Varengeville and Pourville — Dieppe.

ITINERARY 2

Le Havre — Graville — Montivilliers — Harfleur — Pont de Tancarville — Pont-Audemer. Val de Risle — Brionne — Le Neubourg — Beaumont-le-Roger — Louviers — Évreux — Nonancourt — Tillières — Verneuil-sur-Avre — Conches-en-Ouche — Bernay — L'Aigle — Mortagne. Alençon — Sées — Argentan — Haras du Pin — Vimoutiers — Livarot — Orbec — Lisieux — Saint-Pierre-sur-Dives — Falaise. Caen. Environs of Caen — landing beaches and coast to Ouistreham — Douvres — La Délivrande — coast to Cabourg — Dives — Côte Fleurie — Pont l'Évêque — St-Hymer — Deauville — Trouville — Honfleur — Quillebeuf.

ITINERARY 3

Cherbourg and region
Flamanville — Barneville-Carteret — Bricquebec — Saint-Sauveur-le-Vicomte — Coutances — Coutainville. Hambey — Villedieu-les-Poêles — Granville — Îles de Chausey — Granville to Avranches — Mont Saint-Michel. Bocage: Val de Sée — Mortain — Domfront — Lonlay — Bagnoles. Flers — Condé-sur-Noireau — Vire — Saint-Michel-de-Montjoie — Torigni — St-Lô. Bayeux and region. Longues-sur-Mer — Port-en-Bessin — Colleville-sur-Mer — Formigny — Vierville-sur-Mer — Isigny — Carentan — Sainte-Mère-Église — Valognes — Cherbourg.

ITINERARY ONE

Dieppe, Arques-la-Bataille, Miromesnil,
Offranville, Puys,
Le Tréport, Eu, Bures-en-Bray, Mesnières-en-Bray,
Neufchâtel, Forges-les-Eaux, Gisors, Epte Valley,
Vernon, Gaillon, Les Andelys, Écouis, Mortemer,
Lyons-la-Forêt, Fontaine-Guérard, Rouen,
Saint-Martin-de-Boscherville, Duclair, Jumièges,
Saint-Wandrille, Caudebec-en-Caux, Villequier, Yvetot,
Lillebonne, Tancarville, Filières, Étretat, Fécamp,
Bailleul, Valmont,
Saint-Valéry-en-Caux, Bourg-Dun,
the coast to Varengeville, Pourville

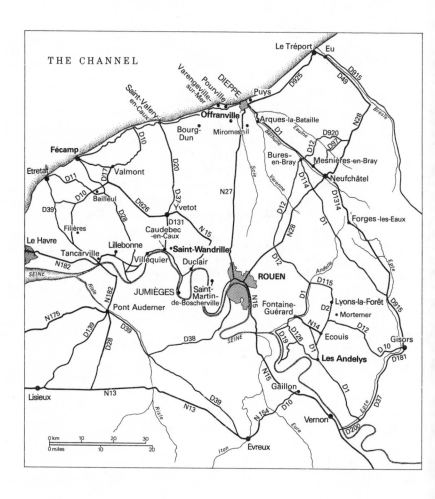

THE CHANNEL

Le Tréport
Eu
DIEPPE
Puys
Saint-Valéry-en-Caux
Pourville
Varengeville-sur-Mer
Offranville
Bourg-Dun
Miromesnil
Arques-la-Bataille
Mesnières-en-Bray
Fécamp
Bures-en-Bray
Neufchâtel
Etretat
Valmont
Baîlleul
Yvetot
Forges-les-Eaux
Filières
Caudebec-en-Caux
Le Havre
Lillebonne
Saint-Wandrille
Tancarville
Villequier
Duclair
ROUEN
SEINE
JUMIÈGES
Saint-Martin-de-Boscherville
Lyons-la-Forêt
Pont Audemer
Mortemer
Fontaine-Guérard
Gisors
Ecouis
Les Andelys
Lisieux
Gaillon
Vernon
Evreux

D10 D11 D17 D20 D37 D926 D131 D39 D28 N15 N27 Scie Bethune Eaulne Varenne D1 D12 D920 D97 N28 Bresle D925 D49 D915 D114 D1314 D1 N28 D12 D115 D2 D1 N14 D126 D19 D1 N15 N154 D10 D38 D39 N13 N175 D139 D28 D39 N182 Risle SEINE N182 N13 Risle Iton Eure Andelle Epte Epte D12 N15 D10 D1 D37 D200 D181 D915

0 km   10   20   30
0 miles   10   20

CHAPTER ONE

Dieppe — Arques-la-Bataille — Miromesnil — Offranville

🦂

APPROACHING **Dieppe** towards the end of the crossing from Newhaven, one has a panorama of the town and its hinterland which is a microcosm of Upper Normandy. West and east rise the chalk cliffs which, from the milky tint of the sea at their foot – eating away the soft rock and earth at the rate of three million cubic metres a year – have earned for the area the name of the Alabaster Coast. Here and there the crescent of the cliffs is broken by small bays like Puys and Pourville, on either side of Dieppe, more often by hanging valleys. The town itself is at once market and port, fishing, industrial and passenger, with an industrial area to give a foretaste of Normandy's enormous post-war development. Its buildings, of which the crown is the 14c. lantern tower of the church of St Jacques, illustrate, if unevenly, most of what has happened architecturally between that period and the era of curtain walling and ferro-concrete brutalism.

There was a settlement on the cliffs 3 kilometres to the north-east in Gallo-Roman times; excavations on the site of the Cité de Limes, above the beach at Puys, have uncovered flint axe-heads suggesting a much earlier occupation. By the 9c., a small town named Bertheville, after the mother of Charlemagne, had grown up near the mouth of the River Arques. It was the Norse raiders who gave it its present name, deriving from the Germanic word for 'deep', an allusion either to the valley or to the water inshore. Dieppe remains one of the deepest and safest harbours on the English Channel.

By the end of the 12c. it had entered on its first period of prosperity, which lasted until the end of the 17c. despite savagely destructive wars, foreign, civil and religious. Philippe Auguste (1180-1223), during his campaign against Richard Lionheart, burned the town with all the ships in the harbour; after Agincourt it was captured by the English, who held it in a mailed fist until 1435, when the Dieppois, who had failed to learn submission during more than a century of occupation, rose under Charles des Marets and bundled them out. For two hundred years that victory, which took place on the eve of the Feast of the Assumption (15 August), was commemorated in mystery plays, and later by a fair which English visitors patronized happily, unaware of its origins.

At that period Dieppe, like St-Malo, was a walled city with the sea beating against its ramparts. Like St-Malo also it was the home of sailors who were pirates or explorers as occasion arose, as well as fishermen who cast their nets off the Icelandic and Norwegian coasts. The great century was the sixteenth, when the ships built for Jehan Ango ranged the seas of the world.

Ango, whose fleet, over a few years, captured more than three hundred Portuguese ships, was the type of Renaissance man in every particular, from the magnificence of his life to the near tragedy of his end. He entertained François I, to whom he was marine adviser, and lent the monarch large sums of money; he built a palace on the present Quai Henri IV and a country house at neighbouring Varengeville whose elegance testifies to his role as patron of the arts; he was banker and Governor of the town and castle as well as sailor and shipowner. He died poor and abandoned.

From the 16c. Dieppe played an important part in the colonizing and evangelizing of Canada, and later in the defence of the colonists against both English and Indians. During the last thirty years of the 17c., heaven, Louis XIV and the British Navy – the order is chronological – dealt Dieppe a series of blows from which it did not recover for more than two hundred years. From 1668 to 1670 it suffered an outbreak of plague in which the death toll is estimated at somewhere between five and ten thousand. The revocation of the Edict of Nantes, in 1685, which deprived the Protestants of their already eroded rights, caused the emigration of many of the bourgeois and craftsmen who constituted the human resources of the town. And in 1694 the English bombed it from the sea for three days, totally destroying two thousand buildings. Lord Berkeley, commanding the English fleet, reported: 'if we had been in the town, nobody hindering us, we could not have burned it better'.

The ferry berths in the heart, if not the geographical centre, of Dieppe; from the **Gare Maritime** we step on to the busy Quai Henri IV. In the past the station would have been virtually home territory, for Britain established a monopoly of the Channel Packet Service in the 18c., when three shipmasters, John Chapman and Samuel Barton, senior and junior, ran their vessels between Brighton and Dieppe during the Revolution, providing an escape route for many

priests and aristocrats during the Terror. There was much indigna-
tion when, in 1872, two French-built steamers were introduced,
though they continued to be manned by British seamen until 1894.

Turn left along the **Quai Henri IV**, then bear right up the **Grande
Rue**, which is even more attractive now that it has been barred to
motor traffic. It shares with the Quai Duquesne (*see* pages 33, 34)
the characteristic of being a pleasant area for idling, with the diver-
sion of shop-gazing and, on the right-hand side going up, has a
couple of teashops where one can experience at the outset of one's
stay in Normandy the difference which the lavish use of fresh butter
makes to the local *pâtisserie*. The centre of the town, through which
it drives a diagonal, is the result of the rebuilding ordered by Louis
XIV after the British bombing; the harmony of its tall brick houses
remains a monument to early 18c. town planning and to the abilities
of the town engineer of the period, M. de Ventabren.

On the left the **Place Nationale** opens on to the splendid church of
St Jacques, a building whose exterior embodies elements from five
centuries, from the buttresses of the 12c. church beside the south
door to the opulence of the 16c. choir. The first St Jacques, though
not the first church on the site, which was a chapel dedicated to St
Catherine, in the Romanesque style, was still in building when all
but the south transept was destroyed during Philippe Auguste's
burning of the town in 1195. It was almost a hundred years before
work was restarted, and the lower part of the nave was not completed until the end of the 13c. The triforium, the great west door, the
airy flying buttresses and the lantern tower are 14c. Gothic; the two
features which, for many, are the most distinctive of the church, the
lavishly decorated Perpendicular of the north-west tower and the
apse, are respectively 15c and 16c. Marks of the fire which followed
the bombardment of 1694 can still be seen on the north side.

The interior has undergone a series of restorations since the 14c.,
when the transept was remodelled after the collapse of the central
tower, but the north and south windows of the transept are those of
the 13c. church. The lower part of the choir, as of the nave, is 13c.,
the clerestory late 14. Later still is the luxuriant decoration, which is
a legacy of Dieppe's prosperity, when its wealthy shipowners were
ready to pay for the adorning of their parish church. Its peak is the
apsidal chapel, as ornate as a reliquary, with Flamboyant and
Renaissance carving mingling in a lovely riot of fruit and foliage,
animals and flowers. Ango's chapel and oratory, a damaged masterpiece, are to the right of it as one faces east.

Of the chapels of the south transept, that of the Saint Sépulcre merits attention for the carving of its 15c. doorway. In the so-called Scots chapel (third from the west end) a tablet commemorates Robert Reid, Bishop of Orkney, who represented Scotland at the marriage of Mary Stuart, and died at Dieppe in 1558. The outer wall of the treasury in the north transept includes in its abundance of carving a frieze of Brazilian natives, monkeys and wild beasts. It is said to have come from Ango's palace, destroyed in 1694; whatever the truth, it is proof that by the 16c. the citizens of Dieppe knew something of the New World. The Treasury, now used as a sacristy, has a Renaissance stairway of carved oak.

The *place*, the scene of a Saturday market when the wealth of the Pays de Caux spills over into the Grande Rue, is dominated by a statue of one of Dieppe's most illustrious sailors, Abraham Duquesne (1610-88), whose victorious career began when, as a seventeen-year-old captain, he defeated the Dutch at Stromboli, Agosta and Palermo. Louis XIV denied him a marshal's baton because he refused to abjure his Calvinist faith, but, alone among French Protestants of the period, he avoided exile and was allowed to keep his titles.

Continue up the Grande Rue to the **Place du Puits Salé**, a natural centre and meeting place for the town, which is overlooked by one of the most typically Norman of Dieppe's 18c. buildings, the *Café des Tribunaux*, topped by a small belfry. A modern wellhead at the road junction recalls the day in 1858 when, after twenty-three years' work by the Rouen railway engineer, Toustain, Dieppe was assured a supply of pure water. The town sang *Te Deum*: Toustain went bankrupt and was imprisoned for taking so long over the job, which had involved building an aqueduct.

Beyond the *place*, which marks the beginning of the Rue de la Barre, the Rue des Bains, on the right, leads to the church of **St Rémy**, built between 1522 and 1645, with a central tower added in 1756 and a rather lumbering classical façade which was remodelled at the end of the 19c. The inside is more appealing, with a successful marriage of Gothic architecture and Renaissance decoration in the choir. There is an unexpected detail in the gilded woodcarving of some of the east end pillars, which is an 18c. addition. St Rémy has one of the finest organs in France, an 18c. instrument by Parisot and Paul. Saint-Saëns, whose father was a farmer in the neighbouring commune of Rouxmesnil, was once its organist.

The **Protestant church**, set back from the road at No. 71 Rue de la Barre, was once the chapel of the Carmelites, who came to Dieppe with the Counter-Reformation. Farther along, the Rue des Chastes, on the right of the Place des Martyrs, leads up to the **château**.

Bearing in mind the amount of rebuilding and addition it has known, almost the most striking feature of the great mass dominating the west cliff and giving a superb bird's-eye view of the town is its homogeneity. Only the great west tower and an *arc brisé* doorway opening on to the rear court remain of the castle built by Duke Richard I, which was probably enlarged by Henry II of England, and then burned by Philippe Auguste. The 14c. north-west tower, which was originally free-standing, was incorporated into the 15c. building, and the whole was enlarged in the 16c. and again in the 17c., when the squat south tower, that of the old parish church of Ste Marie, was taken into it. Wind and weather having done their work on flint and sandstone and the tiles and slates of the roofs, the total impression remains that of a medieval fortress. Once the residence of the governors of Dieppe, the château was a prison during the Revolution, and later a barracks. Chateaubriand served in its garrison when he was a junior officer in the Regiment of Navarre. It continued to be manned until 1898; today, having survived a threat of destruction in the early years of the present century, it is one of the most majestically housed museums in France. (Open daily, 10–12, 14–18; closed on Tuesdays from 15 September to 15 June.)

The unique feature of the **museum** is its collection of local ivories. The art of ivory carving developed during the 16 and 17c., when tusks from India and Africa were landed here. Before the revocation of the Edict of Nantes scattered many of them, three hundred and fifty artist-craftsmen worked in Dieppe, making, to quote from an early prospectus, 'every kind of curio in ivory: carved, engraved, fluted and fretworked cases; openwork snuff boxes and other snuff boxes worked in all manners; shuttles and bobbins for Ladies; knives, ear-picks, baskets, reels and trumpets; ordinary crucifixes and fine crucifixes of all sizes; figures of saints mounted on pedestals and other figures to decorate chimney-pieces; all sorts of fans, cut and carved in every style; snuff boxes with the customer's own arms or initials; beads and billiard balls, dice-boxes, backgammon pieces, chess and domino sets . . .' All are here, from the marvels of ingenuity – it would be unjust to say 'mere' ingenuity, though ivory is a medium which encourages intricacy run mad – to the noble simplicity of the best portrait medals, and the work of the remarkable Pierre-Antoine Grillon (1807-72), who found his models and his inspiration among the humble folk of Dieppe much as Millet found them among the Norman peasants. The two local craftsmen still practising are both the sons and grandsons of ivory carvers.

The marine section has, among much else, an ivory model of Verrazano's *Dauphine* and a facsimile of the planisphere made in 1546 by Pierre Desceliers, the father of French hydrography, who was a priest at Arques-la-Bataille, six kilometres south-east of Dieppe. The department of painting is less remarkable than might have been expected in a town which, since the first years of the 19c., has attracted painters, British and French, from Bonington and Turner to Braque and Picasso, but it is rich in works by Sickert and Jacques-Émile Blanche, the former a Dieppois by adoption, the latter for years a resident, who, between them, evoke turn-of-the-century Dieppe very vividly. A collection of manuscripts, letters, furniture and pictures left to the town by Saint-Saëns includes the composer's first piano.

From the château a path leads down, by way of the little green Square du Canada, to the sea front. Turn left into the Rue Alexandre Dumas and walk towards the west cliff, at the foot of which there are several old cave dwellings. One of a row of fairly recently built red-brick houses near the beginning of the road, the **Villa Olga**, perpetuates a royal association. An earlier Villa Olga, hereabouts, was regularly visited by the Prince of Wales, later King Edward VII. The occupant, the Duchesse de Caracciolo, daughter of a French diplomat of Portuguese extraction named Sampayo, and an American mother, had left her Neapolitan husband at the church door, having married him solely to escape from her parents, and later had a liaison with Prince Poniatowski, equerry to Napoleon III.

The Duchess had lived in England and her only daughter, Olga Alberta, was the Prince of Wales's god-daughter – also, reputedly, his natural daughter. Either way, she was the ostensible reason for the visits of the Prince, who came ashore in a launch from his yacht, the sight of which, moored offshore, caused Lord and Lady Cecil, if they were in residence at their villa at Puys, to show their disapproval by non-attendance at the Anglican church at Dieppe during the Prince's stay. Olga Alberta, who married the Baron Adolphe de Meyer Jackson and lived to be a photographer for Hearst Press and *Vogue*, had a privileged seat in Westminster Abbey for Edward VII's coronation.

Turning, you face the gentle curve of the *plage*, which, at Dieppe, means not the beach of firm sand below pebbles worn smooth by the waves but the ten hectares of lawn which separate it from the buildings along the promenade. The Empress Eugénie, coming here in 1853 with her husband, Napoleon III, is usually credited with having prepared a plan for laying it out as an English garden, with winding paths and flower beds and trees. Was she inspired by her husband, who was an amateur landscape gardener and, during the years he spent in England, had learned to love lawns? Perhaps it was because, in the following year the Empress deserted Dieppe for Biarritz, that the plan was carried out only in part; the trees were never planted.

By that time Dieppe's new prosperity, which grew from the 19c. fashion for sea-bathing, born at Brighton, was well established. In fact the beginnings of sea-bathing at Dieppe went back some two-and-a-half centuries, when the practice was purely medicinal. Salt water was believed to be sovereign against hydrophobia, and the suspects who were immersed as a prophylactic included, during the 17c., three princesses of the French Royal House, who were towed astern from a small boat, naked and kicking and screaming.

Though Queen Hortense brought her family, including the future Napoleon III, to Dieppe in 1812, it was the arrival, a few years later, of English visitors in increasing numbers that opened the new era. The happily disorganized fashion in which they enjoyed their sea-bathing horrified French officialdom and alerted French commercial acumen. In a surprisingly short time the beach was tidied up and a promenade built. A supervised *Établissement des Bains*, which was as much concerned with segregating the sexes as with preventing both from drowning, and a casino whose three white pavilions, linked by covered promenades, had a hint of Regency elegance, were opened in 1822. A couple of years later, the first visit of the ebullient Marie-Caroline of Bourbon, Duchesse de Berry, ensured Dieppe's future as a fashionable resort. The little casino was renamed *Les Bains Caroline* and embellished with her coat of arms. In the 1840s it was providing a wide range of amenities. A visitor of the period describes 'a spacious hall for the gentlemen', containing a library and a reading room furnished with French and English periodicals, and another for the ladies where 'a pianoforte and several collections of the most amusing lithographic prints are destined to kill time with decency'. There was even a project for building a chain pier on the Brighton model as a landing-stage for Channel packets, fortunately abandoned because it was thought that it would mar the sweep of the beach.

Meanwhile the English invasion was becoming a peaceful occupation. The comparison with Anglo-Indian life is irresistible. The colonists were amiable towards the natives while avoiding – or being denied – intimacy with them; they imported tea, kippers and English mustard along with the Church of England and, though they might choose a French education for their young, they never came within hailing distance of assimilation. Towards the end of the century they included Lady Blanche Hozier and her three children. One of them was to become Lady Churchill, and it was to those early years at Dieppe that she owed the command of French which was to delight General de Gaulle. According to Jacques-Émile Blanche, her mother was a beauty, with a characteristic and stately Victorian elegance – and 'an impenitent gambler'.

The fluctuations of taste over a century-and-a-half have been faithfully reflected in the **casino** at the western end of the *plage*, now in its fifth incarnation. After the charming *Bains Caroline* came, in 1857, a 'vaste et coquet palais thermal', known as Versailles-on-sea, but owing more in its inspiration to the Crystal Palace. Its fortunes waned with the craze for glass houses: within twenty years it was steadily losing money. Its successor, opened in 1886, a Moorish confection of red and buff brick, with green copper domes and twin minarets, cost more than a million francs, and included among its amenities a magnificent concert hall upholstered in red plush. Older residents still speak of it as being 'vraiment beau' and regret its replacement in 1928 by a new building conforming to the seemly lines of the current fashion. That, the fourth casino, was blown up by the Germans when they were strengthening their coastal defences.

Today's sleekly functional building, opened in 1961, is, unlike its predecessors, set back from the sea front, in line with the other buildings of the Boulevard Verdun. It is open the year round for boules, roulette and baccarat: there are a theatre, cinema and restaurant as well as dancing and bowling. Next to it is the only surviving fragment of the old fortifications, the much restored Porte du Port-d'Ouest, with its pepperpot towers. Otherwise there is little enough to lift the heart in the remaining buildings of the boulevard, which was rebuilt after the devastation of World War II. Only here and there a front of stone-faced brick, a wide bay window, an ample balcony, recalls the Dieppe of the 'nineties, when Madeleine Lemaire, who was one of the models for Proust's Madame Verdurin and contributed something to his Madame Villeparisis, had her summer house at No. 32 Rue Aguado, as the boulevard was then named, where she held court and entertained the young Proust and his cousin, Reynaldo Hahn.

The games area is near the casino. There is an open-air Olympic swimming pool, with sea water heated to 23°C, and, the wheel having come full circle, an establishment for France's latest fad, thalassotherapy, or cure by sea water, which, these days, is effected by more complicated means than merely getting into it.

Further along the sea front are two monuments to the officers and men, respectively of the Royal Hamilton Light Infantry and the Montreal Fusiliers, who were killed during the Dieppe raid of 19 August 1942, which was one of the most murderous, as it remains one of the most controversial, episodes of World War II.

The plan involved dawn landings at eight points along the coast, from Sainte-Marguerite-Varengeville in the west to Berneval in the east, of a force of 6,000, most of them Canadians. The essence of the plan was tactical surprise, and success depended upon hairline timing, with the prior destruction by commando units of the enemy batteries on the flanking headlands which commanded the central beaches. That done, the main force, between one tide and the next, would attempt to destroy enemy defences, equipment and transport facilities, to appropriate to their own use invasion barges known to be in the harbour, and to seize secret documents believed to be at Divisional Headquarters at Arques-la-Bataille, besides taking prisoners.

In the event, while the commando operation at Sainte-Marguerite-Varengeville was wholly successful, that at Berneval was only partly so, and the landing at Puys was a disaster. The strength of the enemy defences concealed in the eastern headland proved to have been grossly underestimated: the beaches on which the main landings took place were swept by withering fire, while the landing forces were cruelly lacking in supporting fire. Canadian casualties alone amounted to 3,379, of whom 1,000 were killed and 600 wounded, out of a total force of 5,000. Crews of the landing craft lost proportionately even more heavily. Also, despite its definite superiority, the R.A.F. lost 113 pilots killed and missing, and 40 wounded.

Viewed as a raid, the operation was both a costly failure and a gift to German propaganda, which inevitably represented it as an invasion attempt hastily mounted under Russian pressure upon the Western Allies to open a second front. The fact that tanks were landed lent credibility to this. Viewed as what Churchill at the time called 'a reconnaissance in depth', in fact a rehearsal for the later Normandy landings, it was held to have justified the losses. The Prime Minister, in his *Memoirs*, wrote: 'Until an operation on that scale was undertaken no responsible General would take the responsibility of planning for the main invasion'. Even the Canadians, in their *War History*, called the casualties of the raid 'part of the price paid for knowledge that enabled the great operation of 1944 to be carried out at a cost in blood smaller than even the most optimistic had ventured to hope for'.

Towards the east end of the Boulevard de Verdun, on the landward side of the *plage*, the Rue de la Rade leads to the old fishermen's quarter of **Le Petit-Veules**, where a handful of Dieppe's original red-tiled, half-timbered houses, which survived Lord Berkeley's bombardment, have been or are being restored. Continue down the Rue de la Rade to the Avant Port, turn right along the Quai Henri IV, then cross the Pont Jean-Ango, on the left, for Le Pollet, a suburb largely peopled by fishermen who are still to some extent a self-contained community. Up to the 19c. it was almost another country, its people keeping their own speech, which was as far removed from the Norman *patois* of the other side of the river as from standard French. There was a legend that they had come originally from Venice, which was made more credible by the red hair common among them and by the southern character of the traditional costume which they wore on feast days. This included, for the men, red or blue coats decorated with white or pale blue silk, flowered waistcoats, silk stockings and buckled shoes, and a black velvet toque; for the women, short skirts when those of the French were ground length. Both men and women sparkled with ornaments of marcasite, made locally from the iron pyrite found in the cliffs. The quarter has retained its old streets, with the red-roofed houses piled one above the other up the hill. The former cave dwellings in the cliff face were occupied by Dieppois made homeless after the bombardment of 1694.

From the Grande Rue du Pollet veer left into the Rue de la Cité de Limes. If you prefer to visit the site now rather than taking it in on the way to Eu, continue along the road for some three kilometres, then turn left for Puys. The path for the Camp de César, as the **Cité de Limes** is often erroneously called, leads up from the beach to a grassy plateau studded with burial mounds, where the boundary walls of the fortified settlement can be traced clearly. Limes was inhabited until the Middle Ages.

Otherwise, turn left uphill for the clifftop chapel of **Notre-Dame de Bon Secours**. Its curiously proportioned façade gives the impression of a solid tower flanked by minute pepperpots, with a slightly inconsequential church attached. The usual canons do not apply here; this is a sailors' church, a place for prayer and a daymark before it is a work of architecture. It was built in 1874-6 by the *Société de Secours Mutuel de la Marine*. The walls are lined with ex-votos and, more grimly, with a memorial to every sailor from

Dieppe lost at sea during the past hundred years. Their number, and the extreme youth of many, is a sharp corrective to the notion that smoothness is the universal norm of contemporary life.

Retrace your steps and turn left into the Rue Charles Blound, running past the prison which, from the 17c. until the Revolution, was a Capuchin convent. Notre-Dame des Grèves, beside it, another sailors' church, with votive ships in the side chapel, was consecrated in 1849.

A right-hand turn leads to the inner harbour, busy with small shipyards. The docks that extend further inland handle 800,000 tons of cargo a year, notably bananas from the West Indies – Dieppe is France's foremost banana port – citrus fruit from Morocco and early vegetables from the Canaries. The industrial zone stretching south-east, discreetly removed from the tourist's Dieppe, houses activities ranging from a Renault factory to an outpost of the ready-to-wear end of the *haute couture*.

Turn right over the footbridge and right again on the other side, then follow the Quai du Tonkin. The railway station on the left, which was opened in July 1848, was built with British bricks, and the Dieppe extension of the Paris–Rouen railway, started in 1846, was built largely by British navvies. They were, we are told, 'of uncouth size, manners and habits' and wielded spades, mattocks and pick-axes of a size never seen in France. Ahead is the **Parc Jehan Ango**, which has a Japanese garden with a pretty cascade. The strictly contemporary Hôtel de Ville and administrative centre set in it was built in 1967. Lavish with space, as with glass and marble, it is the most ambitious building of post-war Dieppe. The Syndicat d'Initiative is here: in the summer there is also a branch on the *plage*. Over the way from the park, on the corner of the Boulevard du Général de Gaulle and the Quai Duquesne, the statues of Jehan Ango and Pierre Desceliers look out from either side of the door-way of the 19c. Chamber of Commerce at the monument to Verrazano which faces it.

From the Hôtel de Ville take the Boulevard Maréchal Joffre and cross the Rue Claude Groulard into the Rue Victor Hugo, then turn down the Rue d'Écosse on the right. A plaque on the building which now occupies the site of the old Hôtel-Dieu recalls the departure from Dieppe in 1639 of three nuns who left to found an Hôtel-Dieu in Quebec. The road leads to the Quai Duquesne, with its café tables looking out at the green and blue hulls swaying with the tide in the fishing harbour, and the **Halle aux Poissons** on the far side of it.

The history of fishing in Dieppe is believed to go back to the 7c. By the 13c. there were royal ordinances regulating the size of the mesh of fishing nets and the method of salting herring. Over the centuries, fishing in this port has meant everything from cod off Newfoundland, or even whaling, to inshore fishing, the former being the speciality of Dieppe proper, the latter of the 'little men' of Le Pollet. The rivalry between them persists.

Before the coming of the railways, Dieppe, as the nearest seaport to Paris, supplied the capital with fresh fish daily; every night a cart loaded with the best of the day's catch, packed in seaweed, covered the 285 kilometres to the capital, changing horses at regular staging posts, and arriving in time for the morning market at Les Halles. That monopoly ended with the development of France's train services.

Turn left to regain the Gare Maritime, passing the arcaded building of the retail fish market facing the opening of the Grande Rue, whose glittering set pieces, laid out fresh after every landing, are a reminder of the due place of fleshly pleasures.

Two diametrically different châteaux in the neighbourhood of Dieppe, the remains of the 12c. fortress, Arques-la-Bataille, 6 kilometres to the south, and the 17c. magnificence of Miromesnil, with its wooded setting and its association with the novelist and short-story writer, Guy de Maupassant (1850-93), may be seen during a day's excursion.

Arques, built between 1038 and 1083, by an uncle of the Conqueror, another Duke William, was reconstructed by Henry Beauclerc during the following century. It changed hands several times before the English were turned out for good in 1449, but the battle commemorated in its name is that of 1589, when Henri de Navarre defeated the Duc de Mayenne and the troops of the League, despite being outnumbered by five or six to one. Later, Napoleon was to say that Henri did not deserve to win because his tactics were faulty.

Time, the 'cannibalizing' of the stone, chiefly during the 18c. and the bombardments of a later war have reduced the once impregnable fortress to a romantic ruin, in whose walls the brick glows through the facing like old Sheffield plate. It is set on a spur of rock surrounded by an immensely deep fosse: the footpath which runs along the outside of the latter gives an unequalled view over the valley and the forest of Arques. The massive towers guarding the entrance gate were built in the early 16c., and apart from some additions made to the keep in 14c., the rest is 12c. work.

The little town below is charming, with old houses of pale brick and a church, once in the possession of the Abbey of Saint-Wandrille, which, though its building continued for more than a century from 1515, remains Flamboyant Gothic. The interior has a superb Renaissance *jubé* (or rood-screen) and a choir screen of almost equal quality. There is 16c. glass in the five windows of the apse.

For **Miromesnil**, 5 or 6 kilometres to the west as the crow flies, take the road for Saint-Aubin-sur-Scie and turn left a kilometre before reaching the village. The château (open daily, 1 May – 15 October, 14 – 17.30), where Guy de Maupassant may or may not have been born (*see* under Fécamp), but where he certainly spent the first three years of his life, stands among glorious avenues of beeches. One's first impression is of the splendid pilastered façade, decorated with urns and garlands, which dates from 1640. The garden side, the oldest part of the house, which is late 16c., is equally attractive in the simplicity of its brick and stone, with flanking pepperpot towers. The tiny chapel in the park, built in 1583, has admirable wood carving and a fine grille of wrought iron.

Return to Dieppe by way of **Offranville**, less than 2 kilometres west of Saint-Aubin. Its 11c. church has an unusual war memorial in a painting of a soldier's burial by Jacques-Émile Blanche. The artist, who spent his summers here, has included portraits of the citizens among the mourners.

CHAPTER TWO

Puys and the coast to Le Tréport — Eu —Bures-en-Bray —Mesnières-en-Bray —Neufchâtel —Forges-les-Eaux — Gisors

❧

THE 31 kilometres of coast road between Dieppe and Le Tréport – the main road cutting across the plateau between the valleys of the Béthune and the Bresle has little but speed to recommend it – give glimpses of the pleasant little resorts, all of them suitable for quiet family holidays, which break the line of the cliffs.

Puys, the first of them, was made fashionable by Alexandre Dumas the younger, whose father died there in 1870. In the same year Lord Salisbury bought a holiday house at Puys, where he and his family spent part of every summer for the next twenty-five years. Queen Victoria's Prime Minister thought the simple life was good for the children after the luxury of Hatfield, but the simplicity of Chalet Cecil seems to have been relative. There were draughts, and japanned ware instead of silver, and the service was exiguous, but the household bills still came to £84 a week. Lady Salisbury found the French, almost without exception, 'dirty, brutal, liars and cheats'. Worse, they were almost all radicals and free-thinkers.

Puys was badly damaged during the Dieppe raid; there is a memorial on the beach to the men of the Royal Regiment of Canada who landed there, to be killed or taken prisoner almost to a man. Beyond, the road climbs to the clifftop, with little valleys running down to the various *plages*. Belleville-sur-Mer's church has a 13c. tower; Berneval-le-Grand has been almost wholly rebuilt since 1944. Its companion village, Berneval-sur-Mer, at the easternmost point of the Dieppe landings, has another beach memorial.

In the early 19c. **Biville-sur-Mer**, 6 kilometres further on, was the scene of another landing which, in spite of the fate of the chief protagonists, has an operatic rather than a tragic flavour. In August 1803, a small group of Royalist conspirators, who had formed a plan to assassinate Napoleon and restore Louis XVIII, were rowed ashore from a Spanish brig with an English master and scaled the

36

30-metre cliff with the aid of a knotted rope left in place by an accomplice. The assassination had been decided on after an earlier attempt to blow up the First Consul had failed. The architect of the plan, Georges Cadoudal, the Vendéen leader, had for some time run a camp near Romsey where French Royalists were trained in guerrilla warfare: it was financed by the British Government, who gave Cadoudal a letter of credit for one million francs when he crossed to France. Before the assassination, which was to have taken place during a military parade in the Place du Carrousel, could be attempted, he was recognized and captured, and was later executed.

Criel-sur-Mer has a hospice, originally intended for sailors' orphans, housed in the 16c. Château of Briançon, which was founded in 1685 by the Duchesse de Montpensier, 'la Grande Mademoiselle', niece of Louis XIII. The last 6 kilometres from **Mesnil-Val** to Le Tréport is a panoramic way along the cliffs, dotted with viewpoints and parking places. It culminates in **Les Terrasses**, above the town, where, from the foot of the Calvary, one can look down a hundred metres to the harbour and out to a view extending as far as the mouth of the Somme to the north-east and, to the south-west, to Saint-Valéry-en-Caux, beyond Dieppe. Les Terrasses is linked with the town by a cable car and a 300-step stairway as well as by road.

Le Tréport, sheltering beneath dramatic cliffs at the mouth of the Bresle, is, with Dieppe, the nearest point on the coast to Paris, and, largely for that reason, is the most popular resort in Normandy, if not in the whole of France. In spite of all that implies in the way of noise, crowds, candy floss and, at the height of the season, a smell of *frites* that is almost palpable, I am rather fond of it. It is the kind of lethally healthy seaside place where the Anglo-Saxon race tends to send its young to prep school, but the sun can shine, and the bathing is good, off the pebble ridges into deep water for swimmers, in the sandy shallows for children and dabblers. The town has character and a busy, warlike buccaneering past. It can even claim royal patronage. Improbably, it was launched as a seaside resort by King Louis Philippe, who built the first villa here when he was staying at the Château d'Eu. Its commercial history goes back two thousand years. Then Le Tréport was Ulterior Portus, the outport of the Roman city of Augusta. In the 13c. Henri II, Comte d'Eu, gave it the privilege of free trade. The English occupation of Calais for two centuries, from 1347, added to its prosperity but also to its misadventures; well into the 16c. it suffered continual devastating attacks from the English. The corsairs who harried British ships in the Channel during the Revolution had many old scores to pay off. The later invasions were German. Le Tréport was occupied in 1870 as well as in 1940. Much of the defensive work of the latter occupation remains.

The activity of the port, which is divided between shipping cereals from the fertile plain of the Caux and coastwise fishing whose landings add to the daily hubbub of the waterfront, is concentrated on the **Quai François I**, on the left of the harbour. To reach the shore, continue along the quay, past the Place de la Batterie, to the casino which, in season, houses the Syndicat d'Initiative – out of season it is at the *mairie* – and turn left along the promenade.

The upper town rises above the Quai François I where the rock juts out in a promontory still known as the *Musoir* – jetty or pier-head – though it is long since the tide lapped its foot. A double ramp leads up on either side of it to the Rue de Paris and a little market place which has a granite Calvary of 1618, with a Crucifixion on one side and a Virgin and Child on the other.

At the end of the Rue Abbé Vincheneux, leading off on the left, there is a Renaissance house embellished by a small Mannikin Pis, older and more battered than his brother in Brussels; but the real justification for climbing to the *Ville Haute* is the church of **St Jacques** at the end of the street. The first church on the site collapsed when the base of the cliffs crumbled after a great storm in 1360, and a vital part of the restoration was the beginning of the great supporting wall on the seaward side. English raiders badly damaged the new church; the building we see today, strikingly diapered in sandstone and silex, with statues of St Peter, St John the Evangelist and St James crowning the unfinished tower, is largely 16c. Its glory is the roof of the nave, with pendent bosses, which are beautiful as well as remarkable. The four F's, the initial of François I, on that nearest the organ gallery show that the bosses date from the first half of the 16c.

The 15c. carved wooden canopy over the choir organ and a black marble plaque in the chapel of St Nicolas in the south aisle are relics of the Benedictine abbey of St Michel, which ceased to exist in 1791. It was founded in 1036 by Robert I, Comte d'Eu, and his wife, Béatrice, and was a dependency of the greater abbey in the Bay of Mont St-Michel. Lacking the defences of the island abbey, it was attacked by the English intermittently from the 13c. to the 16c., restored from a state of moribund disorder by the 17c. Maurist reform and extinguished by the Revolution.

There is a small 13c. chapel of banded brick and stone, dedicated to St Julian, at the end of the Rue Papin, which leads on from the east end of the church (if it is locked the key may be obtained from the hospital near by). The ends of the roof beams grotesque carvings; the black stone font is 12c. From St Jacques a staircase leads back to the *Musoir*, passing, in a little *place* on the left, the brick and flint Hôtel de Ville, built partly on an archway which is all that remains of a François I tower. On the other side of the harbour is the companion resort of **Mers-les-Bains**, which is effectively part of Le Tréport, though technically in the department of the Somme, but rather quieter, with a sandy beach which makes it popular for children's holidays.

At **Eu**, only 4 kilometres to the east, we are in another hemisphere. This was the ancient Auga, or Augum, once the river port, as Le Tréport was the outport of Augusta. The first fortress here was built in the 10c. by Rollo the Dane, who died in it five years after abdicating from the dukedom of Normandy which he had acquired when the Treaty of Saint-Clair-sur-Epte, in 911, and the baptism which followed it had transformed him from a Viking raider into a Christian ruler. It was here that Duke William, the future Conqueror, married Matilda of Flanders and, two years before Hastings, received Harold. In 1475 château and town were burned by the order of Louis XI, who feared that if the English, under Edward IV, invaded France, Eu, which they had held from Agincourt to the end of the Hundred Years War, might once more become an enemy stronghold. Only the churches were spared.

Eu centres on the Place Carnot – the Syndicat d'Initiative is here – with the collegiate church of **Notre-Dame et St Laurent** filling one side of it and the largely modern château and park adjoining to the west. The church, built between 1186 and 1230, is one of the great religious buildings of Normandy. It owes its double dedication to the death there in 1181 of the saintly Archbishop of Dublin, Laurence O'Toole. Legend says that he presented himself at the monastery as an old and penniless beggar, saying: 'Here I shall rest for ever' ('Haec requies mea in saeculum saeculi'). More probably he was on a diplomatic mission: either way his relics remain in the church; and the pilgrims who flocked there even before his canonization in 1218, and the income that accrued from them, contributed to its splendour. The typically Norman sobriety of the façade and transepts contrasts with the exuberant Flamboyant of the east end, whose profusion of pinnacles and flying buttresses and delicate balconies was added or refashioned during the 15c. The ambulatory

39

chapels were built at the same time, except for that in the apse, which was added in 1825.

Inside, the detail delights as much as the general light and harmony, even if there are items, such as the vast and magnificent churchwardens' pew, with a *baldacchino* supported by caryatids, on the north side of the nave, which jar in their setting. It was carved by Adrien the Younger, of neighbouring Abbeville, in 1731. By contrast the famous *colonne torse*, its stone seemingly living and growing like a tree, adorns the south transept as well as holding up its gallery. The first ambulatory chapel on this side, entered down five steps beneath an arch surmounted by a 16c. wooden statue of God the Father, crowned like Charlemagne, contains the major marvel of the church. This is a late 15c. Entombment, its big polychromatic figures sheltered by a finely carved canopy, the whole lavishly gilded. The head of Christ on the wall facing it is also 15c., but curiously distant in spirit from the Entombment.

In the apsidal chapel there is a wooden statue of the Virgin which is believed to be the work, and also the gift, of François Anguier, the elder of two sculptor brothers born at Eu early in the 17c. The four funerary columns of coloured marble topped with bronze, which were set up in the crossing during the 18 and 19c., are, like the churchwardens' pew, objects which are historically interesting but which, visually, one might wish elsewhere. The two nearest the nave commemorate respectively Louis-Auguste de Bourbon, Prince de Dombes, the grandson of Louis XIV and Madame de Montespan, and Catherine de Clèves, Duchesse de Guise, who, 'tirant son origine de la race de St Louis, s'envola aux cieux' ('tracing her birth to the race of St Louis, took flight to heaven') at the age of eighty-four; her heart is buried in the church.

A series of slabs in the floor of the choir marks the sites of tombs whose figures have been removed to the crypt. This (normally open daily: apply to sacristan) is not to be missed. It was restored in 1828 by the Duc d'Orléans, soon to become King Louis Philippe, who assembled there the effigies of the princes and princesses of the House of Artois, Comtes d'Eu during the 14 and 15c. whose graves were desecrated during the Revolution. They make up a remarkable collection of Gothic sculpture, much of it in white marble, displayed in a building which succeeds in being at once a perfectly lit museum and a church. The statues, all of them contemporary with the burial of their subjects, include one of St Laurence, happy and holy on his bier.

The **Château** of stone-faced pinky brick, set in a park designed by

Le Nôtre, though something fallen away from its first fair state, is rich in the gossipy kind of history which the French call *la petite histoire*. (Open daily, 1 April – 30 October, 10–12, 14–18.) Only the right wing and the chapel remain of the building started in 1578 by Henri, Duc de Guise, ten years later to be assassinated at Blois on the order of Henri III. La Grande Mademoiselle, who bought it in 1661 as a refuge from the pleasures of the court – it was fortunate that she found it congenial, for it became the place of her enforced exile for eighteen months after she had refused to marry the King of Portugal – enlarged and improved it, filling the house with royal portraits. Pictures and furniture were burned or hacked to pieces during the Revolution; under the Empire, when the property passed to the senators of Rouen, the process continued with the building.

It was the Duc d'Orléans who, after the Restoration, restored and embellished the château, which became one of his favourite homes. The style of decoration was 19c. historic, Renaissance and Louis XIII. Every available surface was carved or painted or draped or covered according to its nature, and sometimes in defiance of it. 17c. tapestries were chopped up to be stuck in wall panels. The whole was as rich as a Victorian trifle, and the Queen was twice received here, in 1843 and 1845. On her first visit, according to a contemporary account, the King held her in his arms 'as if he had found a long-lost daughter'. After the Revolution of 1848 there was another period of decline for the château. It now belongs to the town of Eu, but it is still Louis Philippe's presence which is most strongly felt.

The contents include a gallery of sporting trophies, the skins and skulls and antlers of creatures great and small, not shot but acquired during his travels by Prince Henri d'Orléans. The staircase is lined with portraits of the thirty-four Comtes d'Eu, the last of whom was the grandfather of the present Comte de Paris, Pretender to the French throne. On the first floor we see La Grande Mademoiselle's room, with the original décor, that of Louis Philippe, with his toilet set – so much glory and so little water – and the Grand Salon, where the Gobelin tapestries and the plethora of gold leaf are less impressive than the wonderful parquet of exotic woods.

In the park, behind the chapel, is a stone table on which Louis Philippe caused to be inscribed: 'C'est à l'ombre de ces hêtres que les Guises tenaient leur conseils au XVIme siècle'. In fact they did not. Beeches there may once have been here: today the trees surrounding the table are mostly ash, sycamore and chestnut, with the occasional yew.

From the Place Carnot the Rue du Collège leads to the old Jesuit college, now the Lycée Anguier, which Henri de Guise, le Balafré, founded as a defence against the advance of Protestantism. The chapel (closed for restoration at the time of writing), built after Henri's death by his wife, Catherine de Clèves, contains two mausoleums which she ordered, according to one opinion, from a Genoese sculptor, according to another from the French royal sculptor, Germain Pilon (c. 1537–90). Le Balafré was not buried at Eu; his wife's grave was violated during the Revolution. The mausoleums remain, superb in white, red and black marble, with the Duke and Duchess in court dress; on the top, each kneeling at a prie-dieu, below, each reclining on one elbow, relaxed as in life.

The neighbouring streets have a number of attractive old houses: No. 8, in the Rue de Verdun, with carved heads, is Louis XIII; No. 4, in the Rue de la Grande Mademoiselle, brick and stone with a pedimented doorway, is 13c. Better still, because more surprising, is the early 16c. doorway of the old Ursuline convent in the Rue de la République, beyond the crossing of the Rue de Verdun. The wide portal, carved with cherubs and surmounted by a coat of arms, leads now to a garage.

South-east of the town the Forest of Eu, a strip of woodland interspersed with farming country and alive with game, extends for 30 kilometres. On its outskirts (leave Eu by the Rue d'Aumale, beyond the Champ de Mars and turn right after the level crossing) is what is believed to be the site of the city of Augusta. Aerial photographs show it to have covered some forty hectares and to have included a huge defensive enceinte. So far a theatre and a group of temples have been uncovered.

The way from Eu to Neufchâtel, 41 kilometres to the south, passes through the best of the rolling, well-wooded farmland of the Pays de Bray. A departure from the main road after **Londinières**, which lengthens the journey by scarcely three kilometres, will give you a sight of the most superb château in this part of Normandy, as well as taking in several interesting churches. That of Londinières itself counts among them, less for the building, of which only two 16c. bays on the north side of the choir survived World War II, than for its troop of statues, of which the most ancient, a St Benoît, is 13c.

Leave the main road here to follow the D12 through the Forêt du Hellet. **Bures-en-Bray**, where it joins the D1, has a 12 – 13c. church with an extraordinary latticed spire, which is both twisted and tilted out of true. The interior still has much of its 14 – 15c. flooring of glazed terracotta tiles, and a tablet in the north wall of the choir records the consecration of the church in 1168 by Rotrou of Warwick, Archbishop of Rouen. There are a number of 16c. statues and a grisly rarity from the same period in the form of a wooden coffin containing a realistically decomposing corpse, also of wood, once used during what must have been the least consolatory of obsequies. Continue by the D114 to **Fresles,** where the little 13c. church (key at the house next to the churchyard) has traces of early frescoes in the crossing and the south transept. Here too there is a rich collection of 14 – 16c. statues, also a wooden retable of the 15c., its five panels carved with scenes from the Passion.

Fork left into the D97, which crosses the river Béthune to **Mesnières-en-Bray.** To those who know the Loire Valley the Renaissance château will recall Chaumont, a likeness probably explained by the friendship between Louis and Charles de Boissay, the father and son who built Mesnières, and the Cardinal d'Amboise, Archbishop of Rouen, the owner of Chaumont. Building began in the late 15c. and ended near the middle of the 16c.; the Gothic chapel was consecrated in 1546.

After the Boissays the **Château** passed through many hands, including, briefly, those of Louis XV, who promptly swopped it with the Marquis de Poutrincourt for three houses to be used as stables for the Tuileries. Since 1848 it has been a college directed by the Pères du Saint Esprit, who have reconciled most admirably their duty to their pupils with their duty to a magnificent building. Visits are on Sundays only, normally by previous appointment and for groups, but the exterior view of the château, with its magnificent double staircase leading to a *cour d'honneur* flanked by massive, machicolated towers, is impressive enough to justify the 6-kilometre run out from Neufchâtel, let alone a wayside halt. The guided visit allows one to enjoy in detail the splendid classicism of the *cour d'honneur*, with its superimposed orders and busts set between the first floor windows. In the gallery opening on to it a line of stone stags, each topped by antlers taken from a beast killed in the park, was set up against the wall, just above eye level, in 1660. It sounds rather nasty but looks remarkably effective.

Neufchâtel, celebrated for its cheeses, is one of the many enormously vital market towns in Normandy which have kept their character through wartime destruction and post-war rebuilding. Its history goes back to the Merovingian period, when it was known as Driencourt; the change of name came in 1106, when Henry I of England built here a castle which was demolished by order of Henri IV of

France in 1595. The church of **Notre-Dame** – the Syndicat d'Initiative is in the *place* near by – has been triumphantly restored from its wreckage: the radiant light of the high, white interior enhances the impact of the 13c. choir, which has a notably beautiful triforium and three tiers of windows in the apse. Only parts of the lantern tower survive from the original church of 1130; the rest of the fabric ranges from the 14c. of the north transept to the 16c. of the nave and the unfinished Flamboyant tower. There is an impressive Entombment of 1491, in polychromatic stone, in the south transept, and, of the same period but in a far different mood, a Coronation of the Virgin, in polychromatic wood, on a pillar of the crossing; this has four little cherubs, gay as putti, two setting the crown in place, two kneeling, the whole blazing with gold and altogether enchanting.

It is sad not to be able to like the new **theatre** in the upper town when it is so obviously full of the enthusiasm of post-war reconstruction, but neither the drum tower building, of harsh red brick with disconcerting insets of blue and yellow, green and purple, nor the fountain in its cobbled forecourt, a lamentable lattice of iron piping, inspires affection. The town's **folk museum**, another war casualty, has been reassembled and installed most felicitously in a timbered house at the junction of the Rouen road and the Place du Mai (open 14–17, Saturdays, Sundays and public holidays). The exhibits include a 12c. enamelled processional cross.

The slightly faded charm of the bourgeoisie clings to **Forges-les-Eaux**, 17 kilometres south of Neufchâtel. Iron was worked here from Gallo-Roman times until the 15c.; then, after the industry had dwindled, Forges found a new vocation as a spa, thanks to the discovery of a chalybeate spring in 1573. The town, open and tranquil, with forest on its borders and all the amenities of a peaceful, rather middle-aged holiday resort, centres on the Place Brévière. On one side of it the **Hôtel de Ville** occupies the site of the house where Louis XIII and Anne of Austria, still childless after eighteen years of marriage, stayed for some weeks during the summer of 1632, accompanied by Cardinal Richelieu, in the hope that the waters would make the Queen fertile. The hope was long deferred – Louis XIV was not born until six years later. Two charming little pavilions of brick and timber behind the house commemorate the visit. That on the right, with a needle-fine gable, now the Syndicat d'Initiative, was the Queen's oratory, that on the left the *corps de garde*.

In the small **museum** of the Hôtel de Ville (apply at the Syndicat d'Initiative) there is an attractive collection of local pottery, the development of which was largely due to an English immigrant, George Wood, who, arriving in the town in 1797, used the local white clay to make finer ware than the peasant pottery which was then the only local product. He even produced porcelain. Much of his factory's output was akin to Newcastle and Staffordshire ware; the Hôtel de Ville collection includes the nearest thing to an indigenous Toby jug which one is likely to see in France.

From the *place* the Rue de la République and the Avenue des Sources lead to the **thermal park**. The late 17c. or early 19c. façade on the left comes from the church of the Carmelite convent at Gisors; it was set up here in 1954. There is a similar *remontage*, this time the front of a graceful 18c. house, opposite the park gates. The park itself is cool and sylvan, with a lake formed by the Andelle, a casino open the year round for roulette, baccarat and boules, and a statue of Richelieu, reclining and apparently moribund. To this day the three springs are known as the Royale, the Reinette and the Cardinale, after the visit of 1632.

Between Forges and Gisors, 45 kilometres to the south-east, there is more fat farmland, lit with orchards and rich in butter and cheese. **Gournay-en-Bray** is the home of the soft, white Petit Suisse, which has become popular all over the country since a French farmer's wife and a Swiss cowherd, between them, hit on the idea of mixing fresh cream with curds. The church of **St Hildevert** survived the bombing of 1940, the latest incident in its life of nearly eight centuries. It has been much restored, though the nave and the western end of the crossing remain essentially Romanesque, but it is of outstanding interest for the capitals on the south side of the nave and choir. Among the traditional formal motifs of Romanesque sculpture in Normandy they have human figures, misshapen to the point of grotesquerie. Crude, truncated, grossly disproportionate, these mannikins represent the earliest efforts of Norman sculptors to rediscover the ability to portray the human form which was to flower in Gothic architecture.

Gisors, once a frontier fortress, now a bustling market town threaded by streams, has a main street climbing up to a **château** (free entry to enceinte; guided visits to buildings hourly, 9, 10, 11, 12, 15, 16 from 1 May to 30 September; 10, 11, 14, 15, 16 from 1 October to 30 April; closed Tuesdays) which was built by William Rufus on the site of a 10c. fortress. Henry Beauclerc surrounded it with the enormous enceinte, Henry II added two storeys to the polygonal donjon and strengthened the walls with massive buttresses. After his death, when his heir, Richard Lionheart, was in a German prison, the castle was taken by Philippe Auguste. Richard responded by building the Château Gaillard at Les Andelys.

The donjon, facing the gate in the Rue de Penthièvre, remains basically the strongpoint of Rufus and Henry II, which seems the more remarkable when you learn that its foundations are less than one metre deep. From the summit, reached by 101 steps, there is a sensational view over the valley of the Epte, with, at one's feet, the few remaining old houses in the centre of Gisors.

We visit also the vaulted hall of the Governor's Tower, built by Philippe Auguste, and the Prisoner's Tower, a majestic three-storey cylinder with walls four metres thick, which is linked to it by a curtain wall. In the dungeon here two prisoners, held respectively during the 15c. and the 16c. have embellished the walls with carvings and inscriptions incised in the soft stone. There are scenes from the Passion, St George slaying the dragon, a tournament, a ball, and, above a Crucifixion and a carving of St Martin, a poignant: 'Mater Dei, memento mei'.

After leaving the château, make the round of the promenade, planted with splendid trees, before crossing the main street to the church of **St Gervais et St Protais**, a composite building which makes up a most satisfying whole. Part of the base of the central tower is the only remaining fragment of the church which was consecrated in 1119, in the presence of Pope Calixtus II, formerly Archbishop of Vienna, who was the son of Count William of Burgundy. The choir was rebuilt in the second quarter of the 13c. and the ambulatory chapels added between 1498 and 1507. The transept and the nave of five aisles, much higher than the choir and looking even loftier because of the straight upward thrust of the clustered shafts without capitals, were added during the 16c. At the same time the amalgam of early and Flamboyant Gothic was given a Renaissance west front with a splendidly ornate north tower, topped by a little cupola in the style of François I, which was completed in 1536, and a purely classical south tower, left unfinished in 1591.

Without and within, the detail is sumptuous, a good deal of it the work of three generations of local sculptors, the Grappin family of Beauvais. They worked on the west front, where, in the low relief of the Dream of Joseph over the doorway, small angels go up and down a ladder like an escalator. The north porch, with its prophets and sibyls and labours of the seasons, and a ravishing frieze of angel musicians, has been compared, with justice, to the west front of Rouen cathedral. See the Renaissance panels, carved with an Annunciation and an Epiphany, and mourn for those of the west door, burned in 1940.

The interior lives up to the expectations aroused. Entering by the south porch you are struck by the series of ornamented pillars in the south aisle, notably that of the Corporation of Tanners, hexagonal, and carved with low reliefs in which scenes from the life of St Claude are interspersed with those from the working life of 16c. craftsmen. St Claude figures again in the window of the corporation in the fifth chapel, counting from the west, which is the work of Engrand Leprince of Beauvais. Glowing with opulent reds and blues, it is one of the finest examples of the church's 15 – 16c. glass, surpassed only by the grisaille window with scenes from the life of the Virgin in the south choir aisle.

Among the wealth of statues and carvings, the 14c. Virgin and Child in polychromatic stone beside the altar of the Assumption, the great low relief of the Virgin, with the attributes of her litanies and angel musicians above it – disregard the kneeling line of donors, they were a 19c. afterthought – and the stone figures of St John, St Mary Magdalene and a holy woman, also on the north side of the choir, stand out.

The whole merits a leisurely visit. When you leave, cross the bridge over the Epte on the south side of the church for the Hôtel de Ville, with the Syndicat d'Initiative near by. The Rue de Paris continues south to another bridge spanning the shallow and sluggish Troësne. Once it must have been a more impressive stream, for Philippe Auguste, thrown into the water when an earlier bridge collapsed under him as he was fleeing from Richard Lionheart, was in danger of drowning. He was saved by invoking the Virgin, the patron of Gisors, whose statue stood on the parapet of the bridge, and, in gratitude, placed a golden mantle on her shoulders and gilded the bridge. The corporation cannot afford to maintain the latter splendour but there is still a golden Virgin on the parapet. The present statue, set up with due solemnity by the Archibishop of Rouen, is said to have been found in a cupboard in the church tower in 1856.

CHAPTER THREE

Epte Valley to Vernon — Gaillon — Les Andelys — Écouis — Mortemer — Lyons-la-Forêt — Fontaine-Guérard

TO follow the course of the Seine from Vernon to the sea is to take one of the most historic highways in France. Bronze Age traders were using the estuary four thousand years ago. The Romans built a road along the river; in the 3c. A.D. Christianity came up it, and after the missionaries, the Vikings. Today the pipeline taking petrol from Le Havre to Paris symbolizes the enormous industrial development in the lower part of the valley, which has justified Napoleon's pronouncement that Le Havre, Rouen and Paris were a single town whose main street was the Seine.

From Gisors the D37 for Vernon follows the Epte, once the frontier between Normandy and France, hence the ruins of medieval fortresses which command the peaceful valley. The first of them, at **Neaufles Saint-Martin**, was built by Henry II in 1192, only to be captured by Philippe Auguste soon afterwards. **Dangu**, on a hillside, has two châteaux in one, both modern or modernized. A 13c. building was virtually reconstructed in the 19c. except for three towers. Beside it the Count Pozzo di Borgo, a diplomat who contributed to the downfall of Napoleon, set up an 18c. château, transported laboriously from Saint-Cloud. The church has a curious west front, with a Romanesque window rising above a stone porch added in 1560.

Saint-Clair-sur-Epte saw the birth of Normandy when, in A.D. 911, Rollo the Viking met Charles le Simple of France to conclude the treaty which established the borders of the duchy. The donjon on high ground across the river a couple of kilometres further on is all that remains of a château built by William Rufus in 1087.

The road to Vernon passes through **Giverny**, where Claude Monet lived and painted from 1881 until his death in 1926. His grave is behind the apse of the 12c. church of **St Radegonde**. The water garden which he created in the grounds of his house standing back from the D5 has been recreated; to walk beside the lake starred with water-lilies and spanned by Japanese bridges is to have the illusion of having stepped into the great series of murals: Les Nymphéas, in the Orangerie Museum in Paris, which Monet painted here. Nearer the house the flower garden which he designed is blooming once more. The house itself is a Monet museum. There are no original paintings, only reproductions and Japanese prints, but the interiors, including the artist's studio and the splendid kitchen, glowing with copper pans, are enormously evocative.

Vernon keeps the peace of woods and water in spite of its dangerous accessibility from Paris. Its coat of arms, three bunches of watercress on a field argent, is exquisitely appropriate. The gold fleurs-de-lis which complete the device are said to denote that the arms were bestowed by St Louis, who enjoyed the local cress when he stayed here, but Vernon's history predates him. It claims Rollo as its founder and, until the end of the 12c., was ruled by its own counts.

One of them, Guillaume I, in 1160, founded a college of canons to serve the church of **Notre-Dame** which had been dedicated at the end of the 11c., though it was not to be completed until the 17c. The façade, Flamboyant Gothic in all its intricate grace, has a rose window flanked by octagonal towers whose airy flying buttresses and elaborate turrets contrast with the sturdy Romanesque of the central tower.

Inside, the narrow height of the nave is enhanced by the extreme elegance of the triforium and the high windows. The furnishings and statues are lavish, with the splendid Renaissance organ loft carved with a low relief of SS. David and Cecilia, with angel musicians and figures of the cardinal virtues outstanding among them. The tapestries hung below the gallery are 17c. Flemish. There are 16c. windows with scenes from the Passion and the life of John the Baptist, in the second chapel of the south aisle. In the fifth a grisaille painting of St Vincent, patron of *vignerons*, is a reminder that, up to the Revolution, there were vineyards on the slopes near Vernon.

The Louis XVI style high altar of marble and stone, remarkable in its fashion but startlingly inappropriate in its surroundings, came from the Chartreux of Gaillon. One of its two reliquaries contains a reputed glove of St Thomas of Canterbury.

Most of the timbered houses which survived the war are near the church. That immediately north of it is 15c.; there is another of the same period, with carved figures on the angle post, at the corner of the Rue Carnot and the Rue de Pont. The massive Tour des Archives on the left of the Rue Carnot was part of a castle built by Henry Beauclerc in 1123.

Turn down the Rue Potard – No. 6 is a splendid timbered house with four carved heads – to the river and follow the Avenue de Mail beside it. The donjon with pepperpot corner towers on the far side once formed part of the defences of a 12c. bridge, fragments of which can be seen downstream of the modern bridge. The Rue d'Albuféra leads back to the Rue Carnot and the church.

Two kilometres south-west of the town, on the edge of the Forest of Bizy (leave Vernon by the Rue d'Albuféra and take the N181 for **Pacy-sur-Eure**) is the château of **Bizy** (visits Easter to All Saints, 10–13, 14–18; closed Tuesdays and Wednesdays). It has been radically reconstructed since it was built during the mid-18c. for the Maréchal de Belle-Isle, grandson of Louis XIV's disgraced finance minister, Fouquet, but the pillared façade, style Louis XVI of 1855, is imposing. Only the *cour d'honneur* behind the house keeps its quietly graceful 18c. buildings. The park is charming, with baroque statues and fountains near at hand and the distances merging into the forest. King Louis Philippe, who inherited the property from his mother, the Duchesse d'Orléans, was largely responsible for laying it out. The interior has some good 18c. furniture and woodwork.

From Vernon, the road on the right bank skirts the Forêts de Vernon and Andelys. That on the left bank passes through **Gaillon**, which has the sad remnants of the once magnificent château of the Archbishops of Rouen. Cardinal Georges d'Amboise, Louis XII's minister, after a visit to Italy, transformed what had begun as a 12c. fortress, later developed and enlarged, into a palace which was the first Renaissance building in Normandy. A contemporary writer called it 'the most beautiful, splendid and pleasant house in France'. The cardinal's nephew, another Georges d'Amboise, who succeeded him as both cardinal and archbishop, continued the work. Later, when Jacques-Nicolas Colbert, son of Louis XIV's great minister, was archbishop, Hardouin-Mansart and Le Nôtre respectively further enlarged the building and laid out the garden. Fénélon of Cambrai, an archbishop of a different sort, was horrified. Shepherds with the charge of so many sheep should not have time to beautify their houses, he said.

After the Revolution the château was sold to a speculator who took it methodically to pieces. The façade of the main entrance went to Paris, to be placed first in the Musée des Monuments Français, later in the court of the *École des Beaux Arts*, where it still stands. Today, behind the splendid gatehouse with richly carved pilasters and flanking polygonal towers (the access ramp is on the right at the top of the N13 *bis* heading for Rouen) little remains of the château but a single block with the chapel in one of its towers and the so-called *chambre du Cardinal* in the other.

Les Andelys is one of those great scenic set pieces of the Seine Valley which, unlike many set pieces, never falls short of expectation. The broad curve of the river between its wooded banks and the flaunting castle above, its walls echoing the flash of the chalk cliffs downstream, are at their best seen against the clear green and blue of early summer, or in the autumn, with burnished trees and mist drifting off the water like tulle. There are a couple of pleasant hotels looking over the river. Altogether, Les Andelys is a good spot at which to spend a few days.

The **Château Gaillard** (visits 15 March – 15 October, 10–12, 14.30–17.30, daily except Tuesday and Wednesday mornings) is one of the most remarkable examples of feudal military architecture in Normandy. Visitors who are understandably dismayed by the common rendering of its name as 'saucy castle' may like to remember that 'gaillard' can equally well mean 'bold' or 'strong'.

Astonishingly, it was completed a year after Richard Lionheart, in 1196, decided to fortify this keypoint of his eastern frontier. In view of the scale of the building and the depth of the fosse which was excavated without mechanical aids, the feat was prodigious. Richard claimed that his castle was impregnable, and under his command it might have remained so. After John Lackland had succeeded his brother, Philippe Auguste took the castle by establishing his forces on the high ground to the south-east of it, filling the fosse before the *châtelet* and sapping the wall of the forecourt. The siege before the final assault had lasted five months and was marked by the brutal treatment of the old men, women and children who had taken refuge in the castle. The governor turned them out as idle mouths to feed, trusting in the mercy of Philippe Auguste: the king exercised it only after most of the pitiful couple of hundred had died of starvation and exposure.

In the 14c. the castle served as a prison for two queens, both convicted of adultery. Marguerite de Bourgogne, whose fate inspired Dumas the elder to his *Tour de Nesle* was strangled in her cell by order of her husband, Louis X. Her sister-in-law, Blanche de la Marche, wife of Charles le Bel, lived to end her days in a nunnery. More happily, David Bruce, King of Scotland, lived at Château Gaillard when he fled to France in 1334. During the Hundred Years War the English held the castle for thirty years. It was demolished in 1603 on the orders of Henri IV.

For a true appreciation of the site, take the footpath leading up the hillside from **Le Petit Andely**. By car, leave the Avenue du Général de Gaulle (the Syndicat d'Initiative is here) in Le Grand Andely by the Rue Louis Pasteur, turn left into the D1, then right into the Allée du Roi de Rome for the parking place, to finish the journey on foot. Only one of the original five towers, that by which Philippe Auguste's men entered, now remains of the triangular *châtelet*, a fortress in itself, which covered the castle from the north. A footbridge crosses the moat to the fort proper, with outer and inner baileys. The northward-facing wall of the latter consists of a succession of arcs linked by curtain wall to give the largest possible number of angles of fire. The walls of the donjon, which originally had three storeys, are five metres thick and sloped at the bottom, so that projectiles thrown from above would ricochet and cause the maximum damage. The Crusaders are believed to have brought back this defensive technique from the East. From the footpath that rings the castle one can study its foundations on the one hand and enjoy stunning views over the Seine Valley on the other.

Back in Le Petit Andely, take a stroll downstream along the grassy waterfront. The vestigial ruins on the Île du Château are the remains of an octagonal fort built by Richard Lionheart to complete his defence of the valley. The sleek dome further along is that of the Hospice Saint-Jacques, founded in 1784 by the Duc de Penthièvre, once the owner of the château of Bizy.

Return to the **Place Saint-Sauveur**, which has some of the town's best timbered buildings: see particularly No. 19, opposite the east end of the church, a 16c. house with a richly carved door and overhanging upper storey. The column in the *place* commemorates Jean-Pierre Blanchard (1753–1809), the pioneer aeronaut, who invented the parachute and was the first to cross the Channel by balloon in 1785. His wife, who is not commemorated, sometimes accompanied him on his flights. The tradition seems native to this part of Normandy. A distinguished resident of Lyons-la-Forêt, who is a well-known balloonist, and his wife regularly fly *à deux*.

St Sauveur is a completely simple and completely successful Gothic church which was built in two stages, the lower parts between 1220 and 1240, the upper at the beginning of the 14c. The spire was destroyed by lightning in the early 1970s. The porch of stone and timber, which is early 15c., has a 13c. statue of Christ blessing. Inside, the eye is drawn at once to the elegant lines of the choir and polygonal apse; there are traces of a 15c. fresco on the triforium. In the high windows the glass is 16c. but much restored. In the transept chapels there are two 18c. altars from the abbey of Mortemer. The Adoration of the Shepherds on the retable of that on the south side has been attributed to Philippe de Champaigne. In the north transept there are more remains of a fresco, this time 16c., and an exquisite 15c. Virgin.

St Sauveur's organ is known among musicians far beyond Les Andelys. It was built by Ingout of Rouen in 1674 for Adrienne des Courtils, Abbess of the Abbey of Trésor-Notre-Dame-en-Vexin. Confiscated during the Revolution, it was bought by the municipality in a moment of enlightenment and placed in the church in 1926. Apart from the pedal, which was modernized during a restoration in that year, all the registers are as they left the maker.

From the church the tree-lined Avenue de la République leads to **Le Grand Andely**. Its centre, now rebuilt rather pleasantly, was destroyed by fire in 1940, when the most notable loss among the buildings was the Hôtel du Grand Cerf, a 16c. timbered house which had been an inn since 1749. Early in the 19c. a remarkable *patron* and a collection of *objets d'art* made it almost a museum. Guests at this period included Victor Hugo and Walter Scott, who signed the visitors' book:'Gautier l'Écossais'.

The **Nicolas Poussin Museum** – the artist was born at the hamlet of Villers, 3 kilometres south-east of Les Andelys – is in one of the remaining old houses of the Rue Sainte Clotilde, behind the Hôtel de Ville (open Monday, Thursday and Saturday, 14.30–18.30; Sundays and public holidays, 10–12, 14.30–18.30). Its major item is Poussin's *Coriolan fléchi par les larmes de sa mère*, ('Coriolanus moved by the tears of his mother') which is hung in a room with a magnificent roof beam.

Further along the street the **Fountain of St Clotilde** is shaded by an enormous lime tree, reputedly six hundred years old. The widow of Clovis turned its water into wine for the benefit of some weary and recalcitrant workmen who were building for her a Benedictine convent which was to be revered beyond France before it was destroyed by the invading Norsemen in the 9c. Ever since, it has been credited with healing properties, and well into the present century there was an annual pilgrimage on the Vigil and Feast of the saint, 2–3 June, when her relics were dipped in the water and the sufferers then plunged in. At worst they must have been temporarily numbed as the water is paralysingly cold. Nowadays the healing fount has degenerated into a wishing well into which tourists drop coins to be salvaged by local children, but ex votos record cures as late as 1962–63.

The church of **Notre-Dame**, set on wide green lawns and as imposing as a cathedral, is a monument of contrasted styles. Building went on from the second quarter of the 13c., the date of the west front, the nave (without transepts) and the choir, to the third quarter of the 16c., which saw the addition of the north transept with its flanking chapels. The chronology still does not prepare one for the shock of surprise that comes when, starting from the opulently Flamboyant south transept and rounding the more restrained west front, with its twin towers and turrets, one is faced with the stately Renaissance of the north side, round arches, superimposed orders and the full decorative repertoire of urns and caryatids, cartouches and garlands and foliage.

Apart from the magnificent organ case and gallery of 1673, the former carved with figures of Old Testament kings and prophets, the latter with figures representing the Christian virtues, pagan gods and the sciences and liberal arts in amiable juxtaposition, the glory of the interior is the glass. The best of it, all 16c., is in the south aisle and the high windows of the south side of the nave. Starting from the west end, the first two windows, telling the story of St Clotilde at Les Andelys, are fascinating for their contemporary landscapes and buildings. The fourth, where a window depicting the Annunciation and the Assumption incorporates the legend of Theophilus with a particularly bizarre devil, red and hairy, with cow's horns and a bear's snout, has a painting of the Regina Coeli by Quentin Varin, Poussin's first teacher. (There are two more paintings by him on the north side of the church, a martyrdom of St Clair in the transept and a martyrdom of St Vincent in the chapel to the west of it.) The window in the fifth chapel has been attributed to Arnoult de Nimègue.

Beginning at the east end, the nave windows trace the Old Testament story from the Creation to Moses. The Creation window was the gift of the Confrérie du Saint Sacrement; the brethren, in hooded blue cloaks, are shown at the bottom of the window walking in a funeral procession. The *confréries*, whose regalia and costumes, banners and torch-holders, embroidered hoods worn crosswise over the shoulder and *soutanelles*, short, black, sleeved garments, are often displayed in Norman churches and museums, are charitable bodies, akin to the *Misericordia* of Florence, whose members are pledged to help the priest at ceremonies, and especially to succour the dying and give seemly burial to the poor. The oldest documents relating to them date from the 14c., but oral traditions go back to the 11c. – the *confrérie* of La Trinité de Mesnil Josselin (now La Trinité de Réville) is said to have sent a delegation to the Conqueror's funeral. They flourished chiefly from the end of the 14c. to the end of the 17c., the plague period, hence the pairs of little bells worn by the *tintellier*, warning people to keep clear. But the *confréries* are not mere folk lore: suppressed in 1792, along with all other charitable and pious associations, they were restarted early in the 19c. Today they are active in more than a hundred parishes of the Eure Department. An inquiry in 1972 revealed that eighty professions were represented in their membership, among them artisans and students, lorry drivers and civil servants, a barrister, a retired colonel, a banker, a former deputy, four *presidents-directeurs généraux* (managing directors) and sixty mayors.

Of the many statues, almost all are interesting, the most outstanding being the 16c. Entombment at the foot of the south tower and the stark figure of the dead Christ, 13c. or 14c., beside it, a most beautiful wooden Virgin and Child in the south transept and a 14c. wooden St Anne in the north choir aisle. There are spirited misericords on the 15c. choir stalls: see the mermaid on the north side and the joiners at work on the south.

Les Andelys is within comfortable striking distance of the Forêt de Lyons, as well as being an ideal base from which to explore the Seine Valley. The section downstream to the great locks of Amfreville, which divide the fluvial from the tidal Seine, is ravishing, the river flowing first between chalk cliffs, then through parkland. Five kilometres from Amfreville-sous-les-Monts (take the D200) is the height of the Côte des Deux Amants, a 138-metre spur of rock with lordly views over the valleys of the Andelle and the Eure as well as the Seine. The lovers were Caliste, only daughter of Rulphe, Baron of Saint-Pierre, and Raoul, a youth of lowly birth but noble bearing. Rulphe decreed that they could marry only if the young man could run, non-stop, to the summit, with Caliste in his arms. Raoul achieved it, but fell dead from exhaustion at the top. Whereupon Caliste, in the true romantic tradition, died beside him.

Lyons-la-Forêt is an equally attractive centre for a short stay; the choice is purely subjective, governed by whether one prefers river or forest scenery. The D2 from Les Andelys passes through **Écouis**, which is an imperative during any stay in this part of Normandy. Its collegiate church of **Notre-Dame** is a museum of sculpture which the visitor stands a fair chance of being able to enjoy alone. Both church and much of its contents are owed to Enguerrand de Marigny, Finance Minister and favourite of Philippe le Bel, who was born at Lyons-la-Forêt. He it was who, in 1310, founded at Écouis a college of twelve canons and embellished with statues the great church which he built for them. His enlightened patronage is thought to have been responsible also for the number and quality of early 14c. statues found in the village churches in and around the Forêt de Lyons.

Enguerrand's church has changed little since it was completed – it is indicative of the chanciness of life in the 14c. that, two years later, Philippe le Bel having died, its founder was hanged – except that a chapel was added to the south side of the nave in 1528 and the west door was remodelled in 1792. The broad, plain exterior, cruciform, with two square towers flanking the west front, prepares one for the simplicity of the interior, a nave without aisles, shorter than the immense choir. It is conventional to deplore the brick and stone vault which, in 1768, replaced the original roof timbers, except in the choir chapels. I must confess to greatly liking its clean, pale sweep.

The statues are astonishing: to single out a few is to particularize among masterpieces. Two of the most famous, Notre-Dame d'Écouis, beside the chapel on the south side of the nave, and an Annunciation against the opposite wall, reflecting respectively the beginning and the end of the 14c., are a fascinating contrast. The first is all sweet repose; the Virgin of the Annunciation is so imbued with life and movement that you expect to see the folds of her robe flutter in the draught as the door opens. The pedestal on which she stands is supported by three small angels poring over one book.

In the south transept the effigy of Jean de Marigny, Archbishop of Rouen and brother of Enguerrand, who died in 1351, is a Clouet in stone. At the east end of the transept a very different stone statue shows Margaret, or Marina, of Antioch, a saint whose existence is dubious in the extreme, emerging from the back of a dragon, the form assumed by the devil, which had swallowed her. The woodwork here, as in the north transept, is 17 – 18c. at its finest.

There are four remarkable statues in the north transept, where the unforgettable 15c. *Ecce Homo*, in wood, looks across to the grave, 14c. Virgin, in marble touched with gold, over the altar. In the other corners are two 14c. stone statues, a St Veronica with the Holy Face in low relief on her napkin, and a standing figure, her nakedness covered only by the rippling cloak of her hair, which is usually identified as St Agnes, but who may be the Magdalene.

The choir stalls have 14c. seats and back panels showing the skill of a Norman wood-carver whose imagination had been fired by the Italian Renaissance. The doorway behind the altar once formed part of the Louis XIV *jubé*. As we leave the church, we pass a reminder of Enguerrand de Marigny. The statue of a woman with the folds of a veil falling over her brow is that of Alips de Mons, his second wife.

The D2 continues past the Cistercian abbey of **Mortemer** (guided visits: 1 April – 15 November, weekdays 14–18, Sundays and public holidays, 11–18). Founded in 1134 by Benedictines who came from Beaumont-le-Perreux, near Gisors, it was received into the order of Cîteaux four years later, and prospered so exceedingly, particularly by the acquisition of land, that by the end of the century it was known throughout France and entertained kings, among them Henry Beauclerc and Richard Lionheart, also, later, Philippe Auguste and Charles le Bel. It was at Mortemer that Beauclerc ate his fatal dinner of lampreys, though, a considerate guest, he got as far as Lyons before dying of it. Little remains today of the 12c. and 13c. monastery: the domestic block added in the 17c. has been restored and is now used for social events. There is a small museum in the 12c. cellar beneath it.

By contrast, the 12c. gatehouse and a fine dovecot of the same period are virtually intact. For monasteries, which continually had to provide for unexpected guests, a dovecot was the medieval equivalent of a deep-freeze. Some visitors may find the park, with its woods and farmland and lake teeming with waterfowl on the surface and fish below it, more evocative than the remaining buildings of the worldly power and wealth of a great religious house in the Middle Ages. A train of wagons which circulates it regularly will give them an opportunity of seeing it in detail.

Lyons, a calm little town with a population of less than a thousand, is set in 10,600 hectares of the finest beech forest in France – 70 per cent of the trees are beeches, the rest mostly oak and hornbeam. In the 11 and 12c. this was the favourite hunting ground of the dukes of Normandy, and the stag is still hunted here between 15 September and 15 April, with the formality of the French *chasse à courre*, which makes an English hunting field, with its rag, tag and bobtail of followers by motor car and on foot, look like democracy in action. During the Hundred Years War, when the area was occupied by the English, the forest was the refuge of French guerrillas; during World War II it was a centre of the Resistance, particularly valuable for parachuting and clandestine landings in the clearings deep among the trees. A number of adequate roads traverse the forest, and it is seamed with footpaths and bridleways. A map of them is available at Lyons.

The town itself has a history going back long before the dukes of Normandy. Excavations carried out over many years on a private property have uncovered the foundations of a fair-sized Roman theatre, also with those of houses. Lyons today is known for its timbered buildings, many with their original charm restored by the removal of the disfiguring plaster with which they were covered in the 19c., and particularly for its splendid market hall, dating in its present form from the 18c. Isaac de Benserade, a court poet of Louis XIV, was born in a 17c. house next to the Hôtel du Grand Cerf, and, in another Norman-style house in the Rue de la République, Maurice Ravel composed *Le Tombeau de Couperin* in 1917, and, five years later, orchestrated Mussorgsky's *Pictures at an Exhibition*.

The late 18c. brick Hôtel de Ville on the Menesqueville road is more interesting inside than out. It possesses a Primitive *Descent from the Cross* bearing the arms of the King of France and of Renée de France, daughter of Louis XII, who held the viscounty of Lyons in 1528, and a portrait of Benserade attributed to Mignard. The fact that, at the beginning of the Revolution, the local *curé*, the Abbé Lebrun, was a deputy of the États Généraux and the Constituent Assembly of 1789, probably earned for Lyons the model of the Bastille, carved from one of its stones, which was originally kept in the church and is now at the head of the staircase in the Hôtel de Ville. The church, on the eastern edge of the town, is 12c. with 15–16c. additions. Among a number of interesting statues it has a notable 16c. wooden St Christopher in the north choir aisle.

Those who have, or who find they are acquiring, a taste for this intimate, divinely domestic art can spend an absorbing day or two hunting out other statues in churches in the near neighbourhood of Lyons. **Beauficel**, to the north-east, has a polychromatic stone Virgin and Child of the late 12c., **Lisors**, due south, a 14c. Crowned Virgin, also stone, found in 1936; in the little 12c. church of **Menesqueville**, to the south-west, there are several 13c. and 14c. statues. The most interesting though by no means the shortest way back to the Seine is to follow the valley of the Andelle, joining it at **Vascœuil** (the 's' is not sounded) north-west of Lyons. Here the Château de la Forestière, whose oldest parts are 14c., has been restored, and is now an international cultural centre where exhibitions are arranged each summer (visits daily 1 July – 31 October, 10–12, 14–18.30; open until 19.30, Sundays and public holidays). It was here that Jules Michelet (1798-1874), the liberal historian – so liberal that he was twice suspended from the Collège de France – wrote part of his *Histoire de France*.

Below Vascœuil the valley has a certain amount of industry, but it is not oppressive. **Charleval**, 8½ kilometres downstream, takes its name from Charles IX who began to build a château there, but never finished it. **Radepont** has the ruins of a 12c. fortress, once defended by the Conqueror, and an existing château which was built in 1895. The miniature antique temple in its park was set up as a gesture of gratitude to his host, the Marquis de Radepont, by the Duc de Penthièvre, who was offered hospitality here during the Revolution. The church, 13–16c., done up during the 19c., gives a foretaste of the ruined abbey of Fontaine-Guérard, which lies a short distance to the right of the main road, 1½ kilometres further on. The church has a 16c. retable, among other items, which came from the abbey.

Fontaine-Guérard, idyllically set among trees, its walls reflected in still water, was founded probably during the decade 1180–90 by Robert aux Blanches Mains, Earl of Leicester (visits 14–18 weekdays, 19 Sundays). During its first years almost all its nuns were daughters of the Norman nobility. Of the 13c. abbey there remain the roofless church and a restored building which has on the ground floor the vaulted chapter house and the nuns' parlour and workroom, above the dormitory, lit by narrow lancets. The square chapel of St Michel, in the foreground to the left of the church, was built in the 15c. by Guillaume de Léon, lord of Hacqueville, in expiation for the murder of his wife, whom he had pursued to the abbey where she had fled to escape from his ill-treatment.

Pont St Pierre, 3½ kilometres down the valley, with the height of Les Deux Amants overhead, is distinguished by a huge, 12c. church, to which a west tower and two apsidal chapels to flank the original *cul-de-four* were added in the mid-19c. The interior has been impressively enriched from Fontaine-Guérard: the Louis XIV high altar and a series of panels in carved oak came from the abbey. The statues include a 14c. Virgin on the south side of the choir, rare for Normandy in its decoration; the robe is encrusted with *cabochons* and small plaques of glass.

For a closer view of the great barrage of **Amfreville**, at the mouth of the Andelle valley, turn left off the D19 into the *chemin des écluses* as you enter Amfreville-sous-les-Monts. There is a footbridge from which one can get the full impact of the immense dam. The road goes on through **Pitres**, once the seat of Carolingian kings, with an 11–13c. church, and Alizay, where the N13 *bis* leads right to Rouen. At **St Adrien-du-Becquet**, just short of 9 kilometres along it, a chapel niched in the chalk cliff above the Seine was, during the 16c., an oratory for the Augustinian priory at Rouen.

CHAPTER FOUR

Rouen (1) — Centre

FOR Ruskin, **Rouen** was '*the* place of north Europe, as Venice is of south Europe', though the cities of south Europe which he listed with it as constituting 'the three centres of my life and thought' were Geneva and Pisa (for him, Geneva meant Chamonix, which makes it less unlikely). Since he wrote, his 'labyrinth of delight, its grey and fretted towers misty in their magnificence of height' has been a focus for modern industrial development as well as modern warfare. Thanks to the superb restoration of its outstanding buildings and an enlightened programme of conservation for the timbered houses which were not devastated by bombing, it remains the most interesting town in Normandy.

Its charter goes back to the first half of the 12c. and was to be the model for those of communes as distant as La Rochelle and Bayonne. Its history began far earlier. By the time of the Roman conquest, a Bronze Age settlement on the river had grown into Ratumagos, capital of the Celtic Véliocasses. The Romans changed its name to Rotomagus and installed a garrison and a prefect.

The 9c. saw the beginning of the invasion, and of the warfare and pillage which was to punctuate Rouen's history over more than a thousand years. In 841, Ogier the Dane sacked the city; after the Norman conquest of Britain it suffered in the long struggle between the dukes of Normandy and the French crown. During the Hundred Years War it was starved into submission after a seven months' blockade by Henry V in 1419 before, in 1431, becoming the scene of the ignoble trial of Joan of Arc; during the Wars of Religion it was ravaged by both Catholics and Huguenots. The combined destruction of a thousand years did not approach the devastation of World War II. Rouen today, a regional capital and the focus of an impressive complex of industries, with a modern administrative quarter grafted on to its ancient centre, has risen from a hundred hectares of ruin.

In a city so large and so rich in history, art and architecture, the

60

first principle of enjoyable sightseeing, if time is short, is to decide what one is *not* going to look at. For the benefit of those hell-bent on filling every moment of a single day's visit I have nevertheless laid out an itinerary which covers all the major monuments in the heart of the city; also the places associated with Joan of Arc. It was at Rouen that the peasant girl who inspired the French to turn out the invading English was tried on charges of heresy, convicted and burned at the stake. The other suggested routes, dividing the area into digestible sections, presuppose a fairly leisured stay. Museums are described separately, but their whereabouts are indicated in the various itineraries.

The **cathedral**, built on the site of Rouen's first Christian church, that raised by St Victrice in 393, which itself stood near the crossing of the two great Roman roads traversing the town, is the starting point. It is hard to think of any other in France which better repays time devoted to its exterior, time spent in the kind of apparently idle gazing which can bring the reward of a permanently imprinted visual memory as well as in systematic looking.

The west front of the cathedral is a handbook of Gothic architecture, from its birth in the second half of the 12c. to its last flowering in the 16c. Its earliest sections are the 12c. lateral doorways, that on the north side dedicated to St John the Baptist, that on the south to St Stephen. The carving in the embrasures has been compared to that of the cathedral of Monreale, in Sicily, which shows Arab influence. It is a reminder of the medieval cross-fertilization of east and west in which crusaders, merchants and marauding Vikings all played their part. The little colonnades above the arches of the two doors are of the same period; the tympanums, carved respectively with the dance of Salome before Herod and the stoning of Stephen, are 13c. Above the relative sobriety of these porches the early Flamboyant of a rebuilding between 1370 and 1420 rises in tall blind bays, ornamented with statues and surmounted by pierced gables.

The centre of the façade, which offers a similar contrast between the massive central doorway and the delicacy of the upper storey, with its elegant narrow gable and openwork galleries, is the work of the architects Jacques and Roulland Le Roux. The Stem of Jesse, in the tympanum, was restored in 1626, after it had been mutilated by the Huguenots, who may have been responsible also for the damage to the figures of patriarchs and prophets and sibyls in the embrasures of the flying buttresses. The embrasure of the arch has a multitude of tiny figures – reputedly 356 – sacred and profane.

Topping the skyline of the façade are four elaborate turrets, of which only the first on the north side is of the period, the rest being modern restorations.

The Tour Saint-Romain, on the north side, which was originally free-standing, has a remarkable unity, though its early 12c. base is the oldest part of the fabric and the top storey was not added until the late 15c. The Tour de Beurre, on the south side, was so called, according to one account, because it was built with the money paid for dispensations to eat butter during Lent. According to another, it derived its name from the colour of the new stone. It is a masterpiece of Flamboyant, the decoration becoming progressively richer as the six storeys rise to the octagonal crown. Both are bell towers. The Butter Tower has a carillon of fifty-five bells, St Romain has the single Jeanne d'Arc, weighing 9,500 kilograms.

North of the cathedral a 15c. gateway opens on to the *Cour des Libraires*, so called because it was once crowded with booksellers' stalls, leading to the *Portail des Libraires* in the north transept. The sculpture here is late 13c. and early 14c., remarkable for its life and fantasy: a Last Judgment in the tympanum, a low relief of the Resurrection, and a company of apostles and martyrs in the arches are set off by a veritable bestiary in the lower part of the doorway. The corresponding door in the south transept, the *Portail de la Calende*, is flanked by square towers built at the turn of the 13–14c. Many of the big statues of apostles and deacons are restorations or replacements. The rest of the carving is 13–14c., and as remarkable as that of the *Portail des Libraires*.

This side of the cathedral gives a striking view of the 15c. central tower, whose continued existence, as indeed that of the whole cathedral today, is due to the heroic devotion of a team of workers who, at great personal risk, shored up one of the piers which was shattered by the bombing of 1944. Originally the lantern was topped by a timber spire. Destroyed by lightning in 1822, it was replaced by the present cast-iron structure; its 151 metres makes it the tallest in France. It has been called one of the greatest trials that the massy buttresses of the central tower have to bear. Straining charity, one may say that it is tolerable in a far, misty view: at close quarters it adds nothing to the building. For compensation there is a charming lead figure of the Virgin and Child by the 16c. Rouen sculptor, Nicolas Quesnel, on the roof of the Lady Chapel.

In its clarity and unity the interior, which, except for the apse, was completed during the 13c., is the antithesis of the façade. The four storeys of the nave, main arches, false tribune – the plan for building a gallery was never carried out, but the aisles still have the clusters of shafts which would have supported it – triforium and high windows soar to the 28 metres of the roof.

A massive 16–17c. organ case fills the west end; the 17c. glass in the great rose window above it portrays God the Father surrounded by the hosts of heaven. The nave is divided from the choir by the magnificent lantern tower, its four supporting pillars, 13 metres in circumference, each girded by thirty-one *colonnettes*, rising unbroken to the arches supporting the octagonal vault 50 metres overhead.

The elaborately decorated wall of the south transept, which is the reverse side of the *Portail de la Calende*, has low reliefs which equal and closely resemble it. In the chapel of St Joseph, on the left of the door, the brilliant series of windows devoted to the life of St Romain, patron of the city, date from 1521. The Pentecost window, with the Holy Spirit seen descending in its upper part, is 13c.; so is the remarkably beautiful stone *Ecce Homo* in the transept.

In the north transept the famous library staircase, screened by a Flamboyant casket of a *loge*, is 15c. only in its lower part, which was built by Bishop Guillaume Pontis, to the order of Cardinal d'Estouteville. It leads to the old chapter library. The upper part, which leads to the old archives room, is an 18c. pastiche. There is a striking *Pietà* of 1591 in the north-east corner chapel. The almost effaced gravestones include that of Canon Denis Gastinel, one of Joan of Arc's judges.

The choir, the most perfect part of the cathedral, lost the greater part of its furniture during the bombing of 1944 – it had already lost a good deal by the aberrant taste of the 18c. authorities, followed by Revolutionary vandalism. Happily the stalls, carved between 1457 and 1469, at the expense of Cardinal d'Estouteville, have survived. Their misericords portray, along with the customary fabulous beasts, the daily life of the period, providing a record of the tools and trades and costumes of the 15c., as authentic as is that of the Bayeux tapestry for the 11c. There is 15c. glass in the three upper windows of the east end. The lead figure of Christ over the high altar was made by the Nancy-born sculptor, Claude Michel (1738–1814), called Clodion, for the classical rood screen with which the authorities of the period misguidedly replaced the Gothic rood. The flanking angels, which came from the neighbouring church of St Vincent, destroyed in 1944, are by the Paris-Italian sculptor Jean-Jacques Caffieri (1725–92).

A grille cuts off the choir ambulatory and the Lady Chapel, with their great tombs and exquisite glass. Do not leave the cathedral without passing it, even if fitting a conducted tour into your timetable, or possibly contracting with a verger for a private one, involves some inconvenience. During the Easter and summer holidays there are guided visits, which include the 11c. crypt, at 10, 11, 14.15, 15, 16, 17, on weekdays, afternoons only on Sundays and public holidays. Out-of-season visits are on Saturday and Sunday afternoons only.

The crypt was found during excavations in 1934–5: its horseshoe vault with apse and ambulatory upset the prevailing theory that in the 11c. Norman churches were built without ambulatories. It has been further opened out since the war; the well in the centre, still giving forth living water, has been cleared and the apse altar reconstructed. The most interesting discovery has been that of the heart of Charles V. It was known to have been buried in the crypt, but only after 1944 was the lead casket containing it found built into a wall.

The ambulatory was the burial place of the first dukes of Normandy. On the south side are the tombs of Rollo and Richard Lionheart, on the north those of Guillaume Longue-Épée, Rollo's son, and Henri Court-Mantel, Richard's elder brother. Except for that of Rollo, which is a replica, the life-size effigies are all 13c. Near Henri's tomb, on the north side, a plain slab marks the grave of the Duke of Bedford, younger brother of Henry V and Regent of France during the 15c.

There are five superb 13c. windows in the ambulatory, one devoted to St Julian the Hospitaller (this inspired a story by Flaubert), two to St Joseph and one each to the Passion and the Good Samaritan. The intensity of the blue, remarkable even in so sumptuous a range of colour, recalls that of Chartres, and the Joseph windows are indeed signed by Clément, glass painter of Chartres.

In the Lady Chapel there are 14c. windows with portraits of twenty-four Archbishops of Rouen. There is also some 16c. glass brought from St Vincent, and, on the 17c. retable, an admirable Nativity by Philippe de Champaigne (1602–74), who, though he was Belgian by birth, made his reputation, notably as a portrait painter, in France. All take second place to the splendour of the two 16c. tombs, that of Cardinal Georges I d'Amboise and his nephew, Georges II, on the south side, and on the north that of Louis de Brézé, Sénéschal of Normandy and husband of Diane de Poitiers.

Georges I (1460–1510) was a minister of Louis XII, much involved in the diplomatic manoeuvres which followed the king's claim to the dukedom of Milan, as well as a prelate who was a

eppe: a view past the
stle to the beach

The Château of Miromesnil stands among glorious avenues of beeches

Rouen Cathedral –
the west front

The old part of Rouen
with its typically
Norman buildings

benefactor to Rouen. He is credited with having improved the water supply as well as having been, with Cardinal d'Estouteville, one of the builders of the Bishop's Palace. The great tomb, built between 1518 and 1525, at the command of Georges II, is one of the triumphs of French Renaissance architecture, marked by the Italian influences which Georges I helped to introduce into the country. It was designed by Roulland Le Roux; originally its alabaster-like marble was gilded and coloured. The two cardinals, their capes trailing behind them, kneel beneath an elaborate canopy decorated with statues of prophets, apostles and sibyls. In the niches behind them are six more statues, including St John the Baptist and St Romain, and a low relief of St George and the Dragon. The base has exquisite little figures of six of the cardinal virtues — Hope is on the higher level — separated by those of monks in the attitude of prayer. The statue of Georges II was added twenty years after that of his uncle: its head is attributed, rather doubtfully, to Jean Goujon (c. 1512–c. 1566), the Norman architect and sculptor who worked on the decoration of the Louvre.

Goujon certainly designed the tomb of Louis de Brézé, in alabaster and black marble. Above, the Great Sénéschal rides his war horse in full armour; below, in the tradition of the period, he is shown as a corpse in his winding sheet. The alabaster figure was made from an impression taken after his death. On the left, Diane de Poitiers, in widow's weeds, sheds pious tears, shortly to be wiped away when she became the mother-mistress – her lover was twenty years her junior – of the Dauphin, later Henri II.

The treasury (apply to the sacristan) contains the 12c. reliquary of St Romain, of gilded bronze, which was exposed during the Ascension Day ceremony of La Fierté de Saint-Romain (*see* below). The other items are mainly 17c. and 18c.; among them are twenty-four Aubusson tapestries which used to hang on the pillars of the cathedral on feast days. Since 1944 the treasury has been housed in one of the upper rooms of the Tour Saint-Romain.

Leave the cathedral by the west door. The Syndicat d'Initiative is at No. 25 in the *place*, a splendid Renaissance house which was once the Bureau des Finances. Its building was begun in 1509, the same year as the west front of the cathedral: its architect also was Roulland Le Roux, who was able to employ in a secular building the new style which could have no place in the Gothic façade.

The **Rue Saint-Romain** runs along the north side of the cathedral with, on the left of its opening, what remains of another Renaissance building, the old Cour des Comptes, which was devastated during 1944. The ungracious forced marriage, suffered by its ruins, with the glass and reinforced concrete of the new *Palais de Congrès* seems to have been the continuation of a well-established trend. At the turn of the century Percy Dearmer was lamenting that the 16c. building had been 'entirely engulfed in the huge buildings of the Mutuelle Vie, which seem to have been designed to dwarf the unfortunate cathedral'. The Chambre des Comptes, which had two presidents, ten masters and eight auditors among other officials, was suppressed at the Revolution.

On the right side, just beyond the Cour d'Albane, which was once the cathedral cloister, the 'vieille maison' of 1466, which is now the headquarters of the craftsmen who maintain the cathedral, is only one among its peers in the Rue Saint-Romain. The overhanging upper storeys of a number of the fine timbered houses testify to their age; an ordinance of 1525 forbade this style of building.

Beyond the *Cour des Libraires* are the pepperpot towers of the Archbishop's Palace, an enormous 15c. building, incorporating elements of earlier palaces, respectively from the 13c. and the 11c., which was extensively remodelled during the 18c. The wall bordering the street is all that remains of the medieval chapel where, on 29 May 1431, Joan of Arc was condemned to death by burning. Here too, on 7 July 1456, a second tablet records, her rehabilitation was proclaimed. On the opposite side of the street, beneath the ochre and timber façade of No. 76, there are 13–14c. cellars where exhibitions are staged (open daily, 10–20).

Cross the Rue de la République for what is perhaps the most spectacular example of Flamboyant architecture in France, the church of **St Maclou**. Maclou was Malo, a 7c. missionary saint, born probably in south-west Wales, who ministered and established foundations in Brittany. Built between 1437 and about 1520, the church is a supreme example of a style pushed to its limits, with elaboration of ornament allied to daring balance and tension producing a building whose apparent fragility is in fact steely delicacy. Five narrow gables above the arches forming the convex west porch rise to the gable of the nave; the whole culminates in a central tower surmounted by a pierced stone spire. This last was set up in 1868 in place of one of lead and timber which had been pulled down in 1735.

The three central doors of the porch have decorated panels attributed to Jean Goujon. On the *Porte des Fonts*, on the left, which is dedicated to the Good Shepherd, the wolves driven from the sheepfold are symbolized as religious error, represented by

Islam, Egypt and pagan Greece.

The restoration of the church after bomb damage has called for skills almost equivalent to those employed in its building, and has included the embedding of reinforced concrete girders in the walls to ensure the stability of the tower. Only the nave is likely to be open to the public in the foreseeable future, but this contains a notable Renaissance organ gallery which is supported by two pillars of black and white marble, the work of Jean Goujon. The Flamboyant spiral staircase leading up to it was originally that of the rood.

There is a group of 15c. houses, admirably restored, in the cobbled **Place Barthélemy**, before the church. The elaborate façade of the presbytery, No. 5 in the Rue Eugène Dutuit, on the south side of the church, is a transplant; it was formerly in the Rue Malpalu. On the north side a battered Renaissance fountain, filled by a cherubic Mannikin Pis, marks the opening of the **Rue Martainville**. The houses here, which range from the 15c. to the 18c., vary widely in height and style, with façades and tiles and timbers warmly glowing or blanched and weathered, the whole achieving a harmony which is more appealing than unity.

Between Nos. 184 and 186 is the entrance to the remarkable **Âtre Saint-Maclou**. The low, galleried buildings set round a tree-lined court might be almshouses. In fact this is one of the few remaining medieval charnels, and the only one of Rouen's historic monuments which escaped war damage. From the time of the Black Death until 1780 the central court was the parish cemetery; as it filled, older graves were opened and the bones were stored in the surrounding buildings, which are carved with skulls and crossbones and the tools of the gravedigger's trade. Three sides of the square were built between 1526 and 1533, that on the south side dates from 1640. At present the buildings are used by the École des Beaux Arts.

Return to Saint-Maclou and turn right into the ancient **Rue Damiette**, with the crown of Saint-Ouen rising at the end of it. There are 15c. cellars, used as art galleries and open during the day, beneath Nos. 7 and 11. The former Hôtel de Senneville, or d'Aligre, where Lord Clarendon, Charles I's Chancellor, died in 1674, is at No. 30. On the same side the strait, sunless Impasse des Hauts-Mariages, lets one sense the realities of medieval living. There are two outstanding 17c. houses off the Place du Lieutenant-Aubert at the end of the street: on the left, the Hôtel d'Étancourt, whose façade, decorated with statues of the Elements and gods and goddesses, was brought from a court off the Rue aux Ours; on the right, at No. 83 Rue d'Amiens, the carved front of the house known as the Havre d'Écosse.

This area, one of the first sectors of Rouen chosen for restoration and conservation, typifies the magnitude of the task undertaken by the municipality, in co-operation with the *Monuments Historiques*. Architecturally the houses were glorious; most of them were also slums, lacking every normal amenity. Making them habitable while preserving their character involves training craftsmen as well as a prodigal spending of time and money. Inevitably, it involves also changing the composition of a quarter traditionally inhabited by the less fortunate.

From the Rue Aubert the Rue des Boucheries Saint-Ouen leads to the garden of the Hôtel de Ville, once that of the abbey, which, as a tablet at the entrance recalls, was the scene of the odiously contrived abjuration of Joan of Arc (*see* p.66). The reproduction of the runic stone of Jelling, set up at Jutland in 970 by Harald Bluetooth, and a rather Tennysonian statue of Rollo, recall a more ancient past; the bust of the Belgian Symbolist poet, Émile Verhaeren, is here only because he met his death by being run over by a train at Rouen in 1916.

Start your visit to the church by walking round it anti-clockwise, so that your first impression is the view from the garden of the pinnacles and double flying buttresses of the east end rather than the 19c. sham Gothic of the west front. The latter's banality is the sadder when one knows that in the 18c. there was a brilliantly original plan for a concave façade with the flanking towers projecting diagonally, so that the side doors faced inwards.

Saint-Ouen is the oldest of the great abbeys which existed in Normandy long before the Viking invasions. A Merovingian foundation, originally dedicated to SS. Peter and Paul – it changed its patrons for St Ouen when the relics of the saintly Bishop of Rouen were lodged there late in the 7c. – the church was rebuilt by St Ouen in the mid-7c. That church was succeeded by a basilica dedicated in 1126, which was almost wholly destroyed by fire ten years later. The present church, which is slightly larger than either the cathedral of Rouen or Notre-Dame de Paris, was started in 1318 and was two hundred years in the building, which makes its unity the more remarkable.

Walking eastward along the south side of the cathedral, you pass first the *Porte des Ciriers*, Flamboyant-type only, since it is an addition of 1774, then the glorious *Portail des Marmousets*, leading into the south transept. The gable above is the 14c. at its richest and most daring. Statues of saints, and of the kings and queens of Judea people it, fourteen more saints frame the tympanum, which is carved with scenes from the Golden Legend. St Ouen is on the *trumeau*, above forty medallions carved with scenes from his life. The daring enters with the vault of the porch, whose ribs, instead of being supported by pillars, fall on to two pendants.

Rounding the apse, with a memorable view of the diadem of the tower, you pass the old meridian, the work of the 18c. Flemish sculptor, Slodtz, which was once in the Bourse. The 18c. buildings, now occupied by the Hôtel de Ville, were formerly part of the abbey. At the point where they join the north transept of the church is the only surviving fragment of the Romanesque basilica, the little two storey *Tour des Clercs*.

Walk through the hall of the Hôtel de Ville to the Place du Général de Gaulle, which is dominated by a statue of Napoleon, cast from the bronze of cannon captured at Austerlitz, and turn left to enter the church.

The interior of Saint-Ouen is sometimes criticized for being 'correct' to the point of being cold. It is a subjective reaction. There are temperaments which find perfection forbidding, and this soaring church, its faultless lines their own adorning – added ornament is almost wholly absent – is the very perfection of Gothic. The windows are magnificent in scale as well as quality. The plan was fixed at the outset by the Abbé Jean Roussell – known as Marc d'Argent, who began the rebuilding of the church in 1318 – and was executed during the 14c. and 15c. In the nave, the clerestory windows, with patriarchs, prophets and sibyls on the north side, apostles, saints and bishops on the south, are 15c. and 16c. The west window dates from 1575; before it a 17c. gallery supports one of the finest organs in France. In the transepts the rose windows, a blue-and-gold Stem of Jesse in the south, the Hierarchy in the north, were designed respectively by Alexandre de Berneval, architect of the cathedral, and his son, Colin de Berneval.

The choir is closed by 18c. wrought iron gates whose luxuriance fits perfectly into this elegant austerity. All the glass here is 14c., except for the Crucifixion in the east window, which is by the contemporary glass painter Max Ingrand. The carved choir stalls are from 1615.

There is more 14c. glass in the ambulatory chapels, most of which have 18c. wrought iron gates. Alexandre and Colin de Berneval are buried in the chapel of St Cecilia; their tombstones show them respectively designing the south transept rose window and working on a geometric drawing. Marc d'Argent's grave – the tomb is not the original – is in the Lady Chapel.

On leaving the church, cross the *place* diagonally left into the Rue de l'Hôpital and turn left into the Rue des Carmes. The Rue aux Juifs, on the right, leads to the **Palais de Justice**, one of Europe's great public buildings, now successfully restored from the wreckage of 1944. We are back with Roulland Le Roux: it was he who, with Roger Ango, built the central block for the Parliament of Normandy between 1508 and 1526.

The façade increases in splendour as it rises above a ground floor which was once used as a prison. Try to see it under floodlighting; the fretwork of dormers and pinnacles against the steep-pitched roof is then even more breathtaking than by day. The statues date only from 1840.

A classical wing, added during the 18c., collapsed in 1812; the existing Gothic replacement built during the ten years 1842–52 is by Grégoire, the architect who was responsible for the west front of St Ouen. In the west wing of 1499, the noble Gothic *Salle des Pas Perdus* has been successfully restored. Continue along the Rue aux Juifs, through the Place du Maréchal Foch into the Rue Rollon, leading to the **Place du Vieux Marché**, which was the scene of Joan of Arc's execution. She was brought to Rouen some months after her capture at Compiègne by the Burgundians in May 1430. Realizing that, if her execution was not to set France aflame, she must first be discredited before a church court, the English caused her to be handed over to Pierre Cauchon, Bishop of Beauvais, whose diocese covered Compiègne. Cauchon had her brought to Rouen and imprisoned in a tower, now vanished, of the castle occupied by the English commander, the Earl of Warwick, while the farrago of charges accusing her of heresy and witchcraft was prepared. Preliminary questioning, which took place in the surviving donjon (*see* p.77) began on 21 February 1431; the trial took place at the end of March. Throughout Joan steadfastly denied the charges.

On 24 May she was taken to the cemetery of St Ouen (*see* pp.68-9) to hear the reading of the sentence which abandoned her to the civil power for execution. Here, for the first time, she faltered, signed a form of abjuration which was ready and waiting, and was condemned to perpetual imprisonment. Two or three days later she declared that SS. Catherine and Marguerite had blamed her for the 'treason' of the abjuration and she was abandoned to the English as a relapsed heretic, to be condemned to death by burning.

Her sentence was annulled by Pope Calixtus III after a thorough investigation of the trial had been made by Guillaume d'Estoute-ville in 1452. She was canonized and declared the patron of France in 1920.

Since the removal of the wholesale market the medieval ground-level of the *place* has been restored and the site of the stake at which Joan was burned has been uncovered, as has the ancient pillory and the foundations of the church of Saint Sauveur, from which Brother Isambard de la Pierre fetched the cross which he held out to her. The 20-metre cross which now marks the spot, is a national monument. Louis Arretche, Rouen's consultant architect, who designed post-war St. Malo, was responsible for the lay-out of the *place*, with market buildings and a Gallery of Remembrance radiating from the new church of Sainte-Jeanne d'Arc. Modern in its use of materials, wood and concrete, brick and glass, in form it harks back to the old tradition of building a church like the unturned hull of a ship. There is a hint of Honfleur about the sweeping curve of its roof. The glorious 16c stained glass came from the church of Saint Vincent, destroyed during the raids of 1944; the statue of Joan outside the church is by Real del Sarte.

The **Joan of Arc museum** on the south side of the *place*, which is housed in a 15c. cellar (open daily), is worth seeing for a single item, and that a reproduction. Among the waxworks and books and documents there is a sketch taken from the margin of a page from the register of the Parliament of Paris, dated 10.5.1429. It depicts a young woman with her hair tied back, a banner in her right hand, a sword in her left; it is the scribble of a bored clerk. The entry beside it refers to reports in Paris that on the previous Saturday Orléans had been delivered. Few relics give so vivid a sense of actuality.

Walk back towards the Rue Rollon and turn right into the Place de la Pucelle d'Orléans for the sumptuous **Hôtel de Bourgthéroulde**, a building on the watershed between Gothic and Renaissance. The *porte cochère*, which was restored in the mid-19c. gives a foretaste of the inner court (open during business hours, otherwise apply to the concierge). The Flamboyant block facing the entrance is covered with 16c. carvings in low relief. Even more remarkable are the panels above and below the windows of the Renaissance gallery on the left. The upper series shows the Triumphs of Petrarch, a favourite subject of the period. Below is the meeting of François I and Henry VIII at the Field of the Cloth of Gold. Worn as the carvings are, Cardinal Wolsey has been distinguished in Henry's retinue, and the papal legate among the cardinals accompanying the French king.

71

Return to the market and turn right into the **Rue du Gros Horloge**. As a commercial thoroughfare this street is as old as the city which, in its admirable post-war programme, has turned it into a pedestrian precinct and restored the splendid timbered façades. If some of the work is cosmetic only, in the sense that the upper storeys remain untenanted, a soft light through curtains and a vase of flowers in the window being so much amiable camouflage, the shops and cafés thrive and the street is an open-air common room. There is a 15c. house at No. 80, and a 14c. one at Nos. 139–141. On the opposite side, the house at Nos. 148–150 is late 15c.

The Gros Horloge itself, now handsomely gilded and repainted, is Rouen's best-loved monument. Since 1527 it has occupied a Renaissance clock house which bridges the street in a wide arch, with a steep, mansarded roof crowned with the arms of Rouen. Beneath the arch there are high reliefs of the Good Shepherd among his flock. The two faces of the clock, each with a single hand, look east and west; they tell, besides the time of day, the day of the week and the phases of the moon.

Originally the clock was housed in the adjoining belfry tower, built in 1489 to replace an older one. The latter had been demolished by order of Charles VI because its bells had given the signal for the revolt of *La Harelle*, in 1382, a peasant rising which had much in common with Wat Tyler's rebellion in the previous year. The belfry is now a small museum (open daily except Tuesday, from Palm Sunday to the second Sunday in September, 10–12, 14.30–15.30). To climb to the platform at the summit (the cupola dates only from 1707, when it replaced a lead spire) is to be rewarded by a memorable view of the city, and particularly of the cathedral, as well as by a sight of the works of the clock of 1389 and of the two 13c. bells, Rouvel and Cache-Ribaud, which rang for the Harelle. Rouvel is now cracked; Cache-Ribaud still sounds a symbolic curfew at nine o'clock each evening.

Tucked into the angle between the belfry and the clock house is a little Renaissance loggia, now an antique shop, which once housed the keeper of the clock. The charming Arethusa fountain which backs on to it was put up in 1732 to celebrate the good relations between the city and the royal governor of the period, François Montmorency, Duke of Luxembourg.

On the far side of the archway, the early 17c. building with Italianate bosses at the corner of the Rue Thouret, whose architect was Jacques Gabriel, was once the Hôtel de Ville. Beyond it, the street opens on to the west front of the cathedral.

CHAPTER FIVE

Rouen (2) — with Museums

THE sections of the city outside the immediate centre can be visited comfortably in three itineraries, for which the respective starting points are the Vieux Marché, the Place du Général de Gaulle and the Place de la Cathédrale. Their attractions include a number of churches of major interest – there were thirty-five parish churches within the walls of the old city – and the donjon, which is all that remains of Rouen's castle.

<u>Musée Corneille – Musée Flaubert – St Gervais – St Patrice.</u>

From the south-west corner of the Vieux Marché, turn into the **Rue de la Pie**. At No. 4, the house where the dramatist Pierre Corneille (1606–1684) was born and lived for fifty-six years, a museum has been set up (open daily, 10–12, 14–18, except Tuesday and Wednesday mornings). The façade has been restored to its original condition; the interior preserves faithfully the domestic ambiance of a professional man of the 17c. Corneille was a lawyer as well as a poet and dramatist. His birth certificate and several autographs are among the exhibits, which are complemented by sketches and engravings of old Rouen. The Corneille library on the second floor is rich in first editions and has an impressive collection of translations.

Continue to the Rue de Fontenelle and turn right, then left into the **Rue de Crosne**. It owes its handsome *hôtels particuliers* to an abortive town planning scheme of the 18c., which was to have involved building an Hôtel de Ville in the Vieux Marché, renamed the Place Royale. This got no further than the foundations, which are still visible on the north side of the Rue Thomas Corneille, named after Pierre's brother, who was also a dramatist, though a lesser one, but the prospect inspired some impressive building in the Rue de Crosne.

Cross the Boulevard des Belges into the Avenue Gustave Flaubert. The **Musée Flaubert et d'Histoire de la Médecine** occupies part of the Hôtel-Dieu, a house built in 1755 to lodge the surgeon of the hospital. From 1816 to 1882 it was occupied successively by the novelist's father, Achille Cléophas Flaubert, who was first surgeon, later principal of the hospital's School of Medicine, and his elder brother, another Achille, who was surgeon in his turn. Gustave Flaubert was born here in 1821 and lived here with his parents until 1846.

The statues of the healing saints, Roche, Mathurin, Elizabeth of Hungary, in the first ground floor room are accompanied by a 16c. St Anthony in polychromatic wood. In the next, an assembly of instruments dating from the heroic period of surgery, and of the irons used to restrain the mentally disturbed, are a reminder that, even in the so-called age of reason, patients might have had good cause to invoke them. There is a good collection of 18c. pharmaceutical jars of Rouen faïence. Upstairs, an atmosphere of domesticity has been successfully recreated (after 1882 the rooms were used as doctors' quarters). It is difficult to envisage a more propitious early environment for a realistic novelist than this apartment where the dining room opened on to one of the wards and the mortuary and anatomy theatre adjoined the garden wall, which Gustave and his sister, Caroline, would climb to gaze at the ranked corpses.

Walk along the Rue de Lecat to the right and turn into the Rue du Contrat Social for the **Place de la Madeleine**. The church which looks down on it, its calm classical façade topped by a fine slate dome, was consecrated in 1781 for the Augustinian canonesses, who were then nurses at the Hôtel-Dieu. The high relief of Charity over the central porch, like the low reliefs of Faith and Hope in the transept, are by the Rouen sculptor, Jaddoulle.

Retrace your steps along the Rue de Lecat, of which No. 18 was the birthplace of Gide's cousin, Madeleine Rondeaux, later to be his wife, whom he used as the model for three of his heroines, including Emanuelle of *Si le Grain ne meurt* (If It Die . . .), and continue by the Rue du Renard and the Rue Jean Revel to the Place Jean Baptiste de la Salle. Just beyond the opening of the Rue Chasselièvre is the site of the priory of **St Gervais**, where the Conqueror was brought to die after he had been fatally injured at the sacking of Mantes-la-Jolie, not by the sword but by falling aginst the iron pommel of his saddle. The 19c. Romanesque of the church which now occupies it is typical of the rather uninspired ecclesiastical architecture of Normandy at that time, but the crypt beneath it is a relic of the Gallo-Roman necropolis where St Mellon was buried. Some coffins of the period, found in the neighbourhood, are in the church above.

From the *place* take the Rue St Gervais to the Place Cauchoise and turn diagonally left into the **Rue St Patrice**. This is a quietly elegant street of splendid 17c. and 18c. houses, mostly hidden behind heavy *portes cochères*. At No. 29, a pink brick house with pretty balconies, the Abbé Cochet (*see* under Le Havre) died in 1878. The church of St Patrice, built in 1535 and enlarged rather more than a century later, owes its dedication to the fact that the parish was originally populated largely by Irish who had commercial interests in the town.

The well-mannered simplicity of the interior – single columns with capitals *en bague*, no transept, double choir aisles – is an admirable setting for the glorious series of windows, mostly dating from between 1538 and 1625. The most remarkable glass is in the choir, with a late 16c. Passion and Resurrection and the wonderful Triomphe de la Loi de Grâce in the Lady Chapel. There is some 19c. glass in the windows of the south aisle, but that of the Woman taken in Adultery dates from 1549 and the windows of St John the Baptist, the Adoration of the Kings and the story of Job (again) are partly or wholly 16c. Of the numerous paintings, the *Christ au Prétoire* (Christ in the Judgment Hall) and the St Cecilia (alternatively described as St Justine) are attributed respectively to Bassano and Mignard.

This part of the town is so rich in old houses that it is worth making a rather circuitous return to the Vieux Marché. Continue beyond the church as far as the opening of the **Rue du Sucre** on the right, where, at Nos. 5–7, there is a particularly fine Flemish-type brick and stone façade, inaptly named the Hôtel Vilain. Turn and walk back to the **Rue Étoupée**. The sagging black-and-white house at No. 19 was probably standing when Joan of Arc passed through the quarter on her way to the stake; No. 4, the house called the City of Jerusalem, built in 1580, has a low relief of the Holy City. There are more 15c. houses in the **Rue des Bons Enfants** on the right. The building now numbered 100–102 was the birthplace of Corneille's nephew, Le Bovier de Fontenelle, one of the earliest popularizers of scientific ideas, whose life spanned the century 1657–1757.

The Gothic building in the **Rue Ste Croix des Pelletiers**, further along on the left, is the church of the same name, built at the end of the 15c., or beginning of the 16c., and now transformed into a concert hall. Continue to the end of the street and turn at the acute angle of the Rue Cauchoise, which leads back to the Vieux Marché. There are more 17c. houses here, notably at Nos. 68–70 and 45–49.

Place du Général de Gaulle – Rue Eau de Robec – St-Vivien – St. Niçaise – Lycée Corneille – Place de la Rougemare – Musée des Antiquités – Musée d'Histoire Naturelle – St Romain – Donjon – Musée des Beaux Arts – St Godard – Secq-des-Tournelles.

From the south side of the church take the Rue des Boucheries St-Ouen and turn left into the **Rue Eau de Robec**, which was once threaded by a stream, so that the houses on the north side were approached by small bridges. It was a district of rich merchants, clothiers and dyers, whose noble 17c. and 18c. houses can be identified by their open lofts, where the cloth was dried. Flaubert made his Charles Bovary, as a medical student, take a room on the fourth floor of one of them, where, on summer evenings, he leaned on the window sill to look down on the 'rivière, qui fait de ce quartier de Rouen comme une ignoble petite Venise', ('the river which makes this part of Rouen into a shabby little Venice'). Since the beginning of the present century the street has degenerated materially and socially; the restoration now in hand is a daunting enterprise, but enormously worth while. Look for the low relief, on the 17c. house at No. 186, of the horse who saved his master; he is shown advancing through a wooded landscape at a dignified Spanish trot. The **Salle des Mariages** at the corner of the Rue de Ruissel – it was once a restaurant specializing in wedding receptions – is a 1475 house, tottering but magnificent, crying out for speedy consolidation. Beside it, the enchanting **Pavillon des Vertus**, of 1530, is an inspiring example of what can be achieved. Until 1967 it was slowly disintegrating in the court of the *Salle des Mariages*; now, refurbished and reassembled, with one of the stone columns of the portico replaced, it is a delight.

Half-way along its length the street opens into the **Place St Vivien**, with its 15c. church, foursquare, with a rather squat spire. It has a 15c. *Pietà* in the south aisle and an 18c. carved wood *poutre de gloire*. The massive sanctuary retable, framed in pillars of red marble, is by the 18c. Rouen sculptor, Millet-Deruisseau.

The Rue Orbe leads to the Rue Bourg l'Abbé, with, on the right, the vast baroque chapel of the old **Jesuit College**, whose foundation stone was laid by Marie de Médicis in 1614. Her son, Louis XIII, provided the succeeding ones from the ruined Château Gaillard. The college, now the Lycée Corneille, is round the corner in the Rue Louis Ricard, with a statue of the dramatist, by Duparc, in the cobbled 17c. courtyard. Pierre Corneille was a pupil from 1615 to 1622: others include his brother Thomas, Flaubert, Maupassant and André Maurois.

The Rue Bourg l'Abbé continues into the Place de la Rougemare, which might have been lifted complete from a small provincial town. The 'sea of blood' refers to the battle of 949 between the victorious Richard I, Duke of Normandy, and the combined armies of France, Flanders and Germany. There is another disused chapel here, that of the old Benedictine convent of St Louis, dating from 1683. Restoration has given back the glowing, pristine gold to the stone of the façade, with its immensely luxurious decoration of cherubs, garlands, grapes and roses. Ironically, the building owes its relative structural soundness to its use as a store by the corporation highways department.

Turn uphill into the **Rue Beauvoisine**, where once the old road from Rouen to Flanders, by Beauvais, began. There are 15c. houses at Nos. 132, 181 and 202. The Musée des Antiquités and the Musée d'Histoire Naturelle are on the right at the top of the street.

From the Place Beauvoisine, just above it, turn left into the Boulevard de l'Yser. The church of **St Romain**, the 7c. bishop who is the patron of Rouen, remembered for his struggle against paganism, is in the Rue du Champ des Oiseaux on the right. It was once the chapel of the Carmelite convent. The rather unprepossessing 17–18c. building, its lead tower reconstructed in 1877, gives no hint of the white and gold splendour within. St Romain's tomb, red marble of the 7c., is beneath the altar. The church is a repository for treasures from churches in Rouen which have been demolished over the past two centuries, notably a superb 17c. font cover, with scenes from the Passion in low relief, and a number of 16c. windows, including a Stoning of St Stephen.

Opposite the opening of the Rue du Champ des Oiseaux, turn down the Rue Bouvreuil for the **Tour Jeanne d'Arc**, (open daily, 10–12 and 14–17, closed Wednesday and during November), the donjon which is all that remains of the castle which Philippe Auguste ordered to be built in 1204. Only by good fortune has it survived. After it had suffered many vicissitudes, including the common one of being a quarry, the land on which it stood passed into the ownership of an Ursuline convent whose nuns wanted to pull down the tower and lay out a garden for their pupils on the site. Salvage and restoration – the upper part was rebuilt by Viollet-le-Duc – took more than thirty years. The vaulted room where Joan of Arc was brought before her judges and shown the instruments of torture remains unchanged. (*see* p.70). Five hundred years later its narrow windows looked down on other scenes of torture. During World War II the Gestapo had their headquarters near the donjon, which they used as an air-raid shelter.

Walk down the main Rue Jeanne d'Arc to the green oasis of the **Square Verdrel** before the **Musée des Beaux Arts**. The 15–16c. church of **St Godard** at the end of the Rue du Baillage, which runs beside it, has splendid glass, particularly the Stem of Jesse window of 1506, which is by Arnoult de Nimègue, and the mid–16c. St Romain window at the end of the south aisle.

South of St Godard a spectacular Flamboyant tower, completed in 1501, signals the Church of **St Laurent**. The 20c. has justified the faith of the builders who, in the 16c., carved in the balustrade on the south side of the nave the inscription: 'Post tenebras spero lucem'. Deconsecrated in 1791, the church was bought by the state in 1920, and now houses a world-famous wrought iron museum, Le Secq-des-Tournelles.

Regain the Place du Général de Gaulle by the Rue Thiers.

Cathedral – La Fierté – Quai de Paris – Left Bank – Jardin des Plantes – Pont Jeanne d'Arc – Théatre des Arts – Tour St André et St Vincent – Rue aux Ours.

From the south porch of the cathedral walk through the Place de la Calende and bear left for the **Place de la Haute Vieille Tour**. The elegant little Renaissance loggia backing on to the restored 16c. market hall is the chapel of La Fierté de Saint-Romain, built in 1542 to stage the annual ceremony of the Privilege. This, which originated in the 12c. and continued until 1790, gave the chapter of the cathedral on each Ascension Day the right to release a criminal who had been condemned to death. When he had been chosen by vote of the Chapter, the relics of St Romain were carried in procession to the chapel, where the prisoner climbed the steps to the lantern over the loggia and raised the reliquary three times before the citizens crowding the *place* below. He was then free, and, crowned with flowers, helped to carry the reliquary back to the cathedral.

Walk through the *place* to the Quai de Paris. To the left, past the opening of the Rue des Maillots Sarrasins, is the **Porte Guillaume Lion**, the Louis XV gateway which is all that remains of the old city wall. The river here is exhilarating, as much for the activity of its shipping as for the space and light and air it brings into the city. Rouen is the boundary between the seaport and the river port, the point to which ocean-going vessels come upstream and barges come down. Turn your back on the old gateway and the Île Lacroix, transformed since World War II from an industrial into a residential and recreational area, and walk along the **Quai Pierre Corneille** and the **Quai de la Bourse**, for an impression of the docks which stretch for eighteen kilometres downstream. Rouen's imports and exports are about evenly balanced. It is France's first port for the import of wood-pulp and paper and the export of cereals. Beyond that, phosphates, coal, petroleum, chemical products and fruit, particularly citrus fruit and bananas, come in, and petrochemicals, building materials and mechanical and electrical engineering products, among a good deal else, go out. The walk along the *quais* can be prolonged as far as the curve in the river at the Presqu'île Rollet, but a better option for those seriously interested in the port is to join one of the river excursions which operate during the summer (details from the Syndicat d'Initiative).

The *quais* of the Right Bank offer the best viewpoint for the administrative city which has been built on the Left Bank in place of the old complex of factories, which are now farther out of the town. The Préfecture in particular, an arc flanked by a daringly slender 80-metre tower, has quality. Cross the river by the **Pont Boïeldieu**, reconstructed since 1940 and adorned by four monumental sculptural groups, the arrival of the Vikings in Normandy and the Departure of the Conqueror and his army for England on the Right Bank, the Seine and the Atlantic on the Left. It was from the Pont Mathilde, which formerly crossed the river at this point, that the ashes of Joan of Arc were thrown into the Seine. On the far side the **Rue St Sever**, which becomes the Rue de la Résistance, runs due south to the 10-hectare **Jardin des Plantes**, (if you are walking this itinerary take a No. 12 bus at this point – it is a long, dull trudge), whose collection of tropical plants is celebrated. The runic stone in the gardens was a gift from Norway when Normandy celebrated the thousandth anniversary of its founding.

There are two churches on the Left Bank which were founded by King Henry II. The first, the old chapel of the **Priory of Grandmont** at the end of the Rue de Lessard (second left off the Rue St Sever), is now being restored for worship after having served as a powder magazine from 1770 until our own day. It was rebuilt in the 15c., but the apse retains bays from the 12c. church.

The second, in the sad industrial suburb of Le Petit-Quevilly, (if driving, follow the Rue St Julien from the Place St Sever and bear right into the Rue Ursin Scheid, otherwise take a No. 6 bus and, from the terminus, turn left along the Rue Lucien-Vallée) is the chapel of **St Julien**. The small Romanesque church was built in 1160 as the oratory of the king's hunting lodge. In 1183 Henry founded on his lands a lazar house for nobly born women, and the oratory became its chapel. It has a remarkable series of 12c. paintings of the Childhood of Christ.

Return to the Right Bank by the Pont Jeanne d'Arc, next downstream from the Pont Boïeldieu, and walk up the street of the same name, past the diginified **Théatre des Arts**, which is one of the unqualified successes of post-war Rouen. The bronze statue of Corneille in the *place* before it is by the 19c. sculptor David d'Angers (1788–1856). An early 16c. doorway on the right side of the street is all that remains of the church of St Vincent, destroyed in 1944. Fortunately, the glass for which the church was renowned had been removed: some, as we have seen, is now in other churches in the city. By contrast, the late Gothic **St André**, farther up on the left, was wantonly demolished when the **Rue Jeanne d'Arc** was built. Before the bombardment, the 15c. tower in its green square, which marks the site of the church, was surrounded by the façades of old buildings from various parts of the city which had been set up here.

For the cathedral, turn right along the **Rue aux Ours**. This is rich in old houses, many recently restored. Nos. 59 and 39 have 15c. black-and-white façades. No. 61 was the birthplace of Boïeldieu (1775–1834), a composer whose operatic career included directing the Royal Opera at St Petersburg besides scoring successes with *La Dame Blanche* and *Le Calife de Bagdad*.

Museums

<u>Musée des Beaux Arts.</u> Open daily, 10.30–12, 14–18, except Tuesday and Wednesday mornings. Ticket admits also to the **Musée Le Secq des Tournelles** and the **Beffroi**.

This is a major collection of painting, sculpture and ceramics, widely representative, but particularly strong in 17c. and 20c. work. It possesses a handful of unquestionable masterpieces, a larger number of outstanding pictures and certain items which cannot be paralleled elsewhere. If time is short, it would be wise to concentrate on these, and wise also to start with the first floor, continue with the second and end with the ground floor. The pictures are mentioned here under their respective schools rather than by the numbers of the rooms in which they are likely to be hung, as the gallery may be rearranged for temporary exhibitions.

The position of the supreme masterpiece remains constant. One enters the department of painting on the **first floor** by way of a skilfully lit alcove in which Gérard David's *Virgin and Saints* is

The Abbey of Fécamp,
once the most important
pilgrimage centre in
Normandy

The spectacular cliff
scenery of Etretat

The Château of Bailleul.
'A visit is not simply
worthwhile: it is
imperative'

The little clifftop
church of St Valéry
at Varengeville

shown alone. In its serenity, its grave joy, its balance that satisfies as the resolution of a fugue satisfies, this is a picture that brings you in spirit to your knees. The Italian Primitives include a Perugino triptych from the church of St Peter in Perugia; among the later Italians are four paintings by Veronese and the wonderful Caravaggio *Flagellation*. Velázquez's *Man with the Map of the World* is outstanding in the Spanish school.

Among the peaks of the strong section of French painting, which is continued on the **second floor**, are François Clouet's *Diana at the Bath*, which may or may not be based on Diane de Poitiers, Poussin's *Venus and Aeneas*, four paintings by Claude, and Ingres's masterly portrait of *La Belle Zélie*.

Delacroix's great *Justice of Trajan* occupies the whole end wall of one room and should be seen from the **gallery** at the other end, when the line of vision passes over the drawings and engravings on the side walls. Another room is devoted to Delacroix's model and mentor, Théodore Géricault, born at Rouen in 1791, who, before his short life ended in 1824, had had a powerful influence on the Romantic painters of the time. The gallery has one of his best horse paintings, the 'Stallion Tamerlain', and the famous portrait of Delacroix, besides sketches for two well-known paintings in the Louvre, the 'Raft of the Medusa' and the 'Officier de Chasseurs de la Garde Impériale chargeant'. The four rooms devoted to the Impressionists witness to the importance of the landscape and seascape of Normandy to many of the painters of this school.

Also on the **first floor** is the admirably arranged collection of ceramics, one of the finest in Europe. The art in Normandy goes back to the tilemakers of the 13c. Between the 16c. and the late 18c., it produced a wide variety of household ware and ornamental pieces, first in blue and white, later with the addition of red, green and yellow in patterns in which the traditional motifs of the native lacemakers and wrought ironworkers are often discernible. The craft died not from any failure of inspiration, but because the French manufacturers could not stand up to the competition of English faïence, admitted after 1786. The masterpieces among the remarkable exhibits here are the pair of terrestrial and celestial globes of 1725.

Return to the **ground floor** for two collections in the 'unparalleled elsewhere' class. That consisting of work by members of the Duchamp family might, indeed, almost claim to be unique, since little of it is to be seen elsewhere in Europe. Marcel Duchamp (1887–1968), most of whose work was done in New York, was, with

Picabia and Arp, one of the founders of the Dada movement which preceded Surrealism; his brother, known as Jacques Villon (1875–1963) was a Cubist; another brother, Raymond Duchamp-Villon, a sculptor with Cubist sympathies.

The second, and far different, is that devoted to Jacques-Émile Blanche (1861–1942), whose portraits, of which the museum has seventy-six, present the literary, artistic and social life of Paris and its seaside annexe over several decades. It might be said that Blanche illustrated Proust, who was a patient of the artist's doctor father.

The Musée de Secq-des-Tournelles (opening times as for Beaux Arts) is remarkable alike for its range, and for the presentation of its contents. The height and the varying levels of the church make it possible to display in ideal conditions 19c. tradesmen's signs, a collection of keys showing the development of the locksmith's art from the 3c. to the 19c., kitchen utensils and corsairs' chests, surgical instruments of the 16c. and the exquisite altar railings from the 13c. abbey of Ourscamp. The metal objects are complemented by several windows from the church of St Vincent, lit with striking artifice. This is an imperative visit.

Musée des Antiquités (open daily, 10–12, 14–17, except Wednesdays), housed in the former convent of the Order of the Visitation.

A regional museum with interesting Gallo-Roman and Merovingian sections. In the first is the great mosaic of 'Apollo in pursuit of Daphne' from Lillebonne, once the Roman city of Juliobona, in the second are some notable jewellery and glass. The medieval section has a number of Nottingham alabasters, many of which found their way to Normandy during the English occupation. The gold and enamel and ivory from church treasuries in this section are sumptuous.

The term 'antiquities' is stretched to include fine furniture and silver from the Renaissance and the 17c. The 15c. allegory of the winged stags is perhaps the choice item in an admirable collection of tapestries.

Musée d'Histoire Naturelle (open daily 10–12, 14–18, except Mondays and Tuesdays).

This is a notable collection, particularly strong in ornithology and embracing ethnography and prehistory. It includes a section of comparative anatomy.

Finally there are two literary pilgrimages to be made on the outskirts of the town. Among the petrol refineries of Le Petit Couronne, 14 kilometres distant (leave the centre by the D13 and, once in Le Petit Couronne, take the Rue Pierre Corneille and bear right), the 17c. house, timbered and red-tiled, where, from boyhood till the end of his life, Corneille spent his summers, stands intact behind its protecting walls. The interior, furnished in period, is now a museum (open daily 10–12, 14–18.30 except Wednesdays), whose contents include the poet's translation into French verse of Thomas à Kempis's *Imitation of Christ*, with notes in his handwriting.

Nearer our day, and more poignant because seemingly even more precariously sited among the factories and the roaring traffic of Croisset, 5 kilometres out of Rouen by the D51, is the little summer pavilion which is all that now remains of the riverside house where Flaubert wrote *Madame Bovary* and *Salammbô*. This also is now a museum (open daily, 10–12, 14–18 except Tuesday and Wednesday mornings). He never, in fact, used the pavilion as a writing room, but his presence is curiously actual among the mementoes, the MSS, and, above all, a letter to a friend announcing the completion of *L'Éducation Sentimentale*, in which the ink scarcely seems dry on the triumphant splutter of the pen with which he wrote: 'Fini! mon vieux!'

Flaubert's library, at the *mairie* of Canteleu-Croisset, may be visited by appointment.

CHAPTER SIX

Rouen – Saint-Martin-de-Boscherville – Duclair – Jumièges – Saint-Wandrille – Caudebec-en-Caux – Villequier – Yvetot – Lillebonne

THE stretch of the Seine between Rouen and Lillebonne, the 'Road of the Abbeys' of the tourist brochures, is one of dramatic contrasts. The river moves in broad, serpentine curves, now passing through exquisite pastoral landscape, now through as intense a concentration of modern industry as France can show.

From Rouen the N182 climbs steeply to the hill of **Canteleu**. The so-called 'Cité Verte', its residential quarter, leaves an impression of sad grey slabs which the surrounding lawns and trees cannot do much to redeem, but it is worth stopping on the height for the sweeping backward view over the valley to the city. Canteleu's church has a 13c. choir.

The road goes on through the birch and pine of the Forêt de Roumare; as it drops down to the valley again you see on the left, just off the main road, the village of **St Martin-de-Boscherville**, with, at its heart, the most perfect Romanesque church in this part of Normandy, the abbey of St Georges-de-Boscherville. Its founder was Raoul de Tancarville, Chamberlain to William Duke of Normandy, not yet the Conqueror, who, some time between 1050 and 1066, replaced the little village church of St Georges by a large cruciform one, with accompanying monastic buildings, where he installed a college of Augustinian canons. They did not prosper. In 1112–13, Raoul's son, Guillaume, himself Chamberlain to King Henry I, replaced them by a group of Benedictines from St-Evroult, at the same time enlarging and improving the church built by his father. It remained, substantially, as we see it today, undamaged and virtually unaltered, though stripped of most of its original furnishings. Since, throughout its life, Boscherville was a monastery of only secondary importance – hard as it is to credit with the noble mass of the church before one's eyes, the average number of monks was between twelve and twenty, the absolute maximum thirty or thirty-five – it never knew the ambitious building schemes fostered by prosperity which have marred the unity of so many churches. It survived the Revolution because the village adopted it as their parish church, instead of the old church beside the river.

The simple, sufficient façade, with a blind gable above two tiers each of three windows, surprises by the contrast between the narrowness of the flanking towers and the breadth of the arch above the doorway. There is another contrast between the extreme sophistication of the geometric carvings on the mouldings of the vault and those of the capitals on which they fall. These speak of half-assimilated influences and something new struggling to be born. Note particularly the moving Primitive of the Flight into Egypt on the north side of the doorway. Before going inside, walk round the church to the east end, usually the most satisfying view of a Romanesque building. It is worth walking down the road on the south side of the church to get the full effect of the massive central tower, with its short, octagonal spire, rising above the apse.

The interior, a nave of eight bays with a blind triforium, suffused with light from the clerestory windows and with nothing to break the vista through crossing and choir to the semicircular apse, has the same unity and simplicity; the fact that the vaulted roof was not added until the 13c. does not detract from it. Those who think they are indifferent to architecture might do worse than sit for a while in a church like Boscherville, or Lessay, or Cerisy, and see what osmosis will do. There can be few better ways of kindling a response which may lead to a serious interest.

Having done so, notice how the monumental thickness of the pillars allows the clerestory gallery to be pierced through them before moving on to the transept, each of whose arms is occupied by an open gallery. The two decorated arches beneath each of them fall on to a central pillar, with a remarkable carving in the wall space above. On the north side, a bishop raises his hand in blessing, on the south side two warriors, crude and ill-proportioned – the knights are about two-and-a-half times too big for their horses – join combat. The east face of the capital beneath the latter has a carving of beasts which recalls the cave paintings of Lascaux. There is a superb 18c. confessional, overrun with cherubs, in this transept. In the centre of the choir Antoine Le Roulx, the last regular abbot, lies beneath a slab of slate and marble.

The 12c. chapter house adjoining the north transept survives, though it is now embedded in a 17c. building (for access, ring the bell on the south side of the church and have patience – the concierge may not be poised on the other side of the door, ready to respond instantly). The three arches of its west front once opened on to the cloister, now destroyed. Their carvings illustrate the whole repertoire of typical late Norman ornament. By contrast, the three statue-columns on the right are the only ones of their kind known in the province, except for a single example in the museum of St-Wandrille, and the capitals of the interior are carved with such elaboration and refinement that Lucien Musset, a leading authority on Romanesque art in Normandy, has compared them to Hispano-Moorish work. The tiled pavement dates from the 13c. Possibly because noble communications encourage good manners, the modern *mairie* across the village green is a most elegant little building.

After Boscherville, the road follows the curve of the river, with chalk cliffs rising on the right, to **Duclair**, one of several points along this route where a car ferry crosses the Seine. Duclair, long noted for the breeding of ducks, and so for dishes based on them, indeed for good eating in general, is an excellent base for those who object to spending their nights in a town. There are pleasant walks beside the river and on the height above it, and one is within easy striking distance of Jumièges and Saint-Wandrille, as well as Rouen. Do not expect it to be inexpensive, though. The small riverside resorts hereabouts are not rustic villages; the English equivalent is the Thames Valley.

Duclair's 14–15c. church was restored in 1860, but has kept its 12c. tower; the slate-hung spire was added in the 15c. or 16c. Inside are a series of early 13c. statues of the Apostles which came from Jumièges. At the entrance to the choir two marble columns ante-date the church by centuries. They came from a Gallo-Roman building, possibly that of the Merovingian monastic cell which once existed here.

The longer, riverside route to Jumièges is to be preferred for the sake of the lyrical landscape of woods and water, meadows and orchards through which it passes. Across the river from the ferry at **Yville-sur-Seine** is a fine early 18c. château, probably designed by Jules Hardouin-Mansart, which in 1780, just a year before his resounding bankruptcy, was acquired by John Law, founder of the Compagnie des Indes. At **Le Mesnil-sous-Jumièges**, a couple of kilometres further on, are the remains of a 13c. manor, now incorporated in a farmhouse, where Agnès Sorel, mistress and backbone of the feeble Charles VII, also the mother of four of his children, died in 1450.

Approached from the river, the church of the Benedictine abbey of **Jumièges** is like an annunciation, with the western towers dazzling against the sky – as always in memories of chalk country, one envisages it brilliantly white on blue. Coming up from Le Mesnil you realize earlier that the fortress is a shell. The first monastic community here was founded in 654 by St Philibert, who, according to the custom of the time, built three churches, dedicated respectively to Notre-Dame, St Peter and St Denis, and St Germain. The first was the most important, and is known to have been cruciform and to have had two towers.

The abbey, whose rule had elements drawn from those of St Columba and St Benedict, was soon renowned for practical works as well as piety and learning. The monks ran the ferry over the Seine and encouraged the local peasants in clearing the forest and cultivating the land. Its prosperity was ended by the Viking raiders who, from the 9c., devastated the Seine Valley. The monks fled from Jumièges in 851; it is a measure of the terror and unrest of that time that they carried the body of their founder to five temporary resting places before it was finally buried at Tournus, on the Saône.

A hundred years later the descendants of the Norsemen, settled and baptized, made restitution. An attempt at refounding the abbey about 935–942 was encouraged by Guillaume Longue-Épée, the second Duke of Normandy, but, though the small Carolingian church of St Peter was made sound and a cloister added, monastic life was slow to be re-established. The true restoration came during the 11c. Abbot Robert, later to be successively Bishop of London and Archbishop of Canterbury under Edward the Confessor, rebuilt the abbey church of Notre-Dame. It was dedicated in 1067, in the presence of the Conqueror, who endowed the abbey generously with properties in England. Later, Jumièges was to provide a number of abbots for English monasteries: three for Abingdon, others for Evesham and Malmesbury.

The history of the next hundred years was the classic one of growing prosperity up to the introduction in 1464 of the commendatory system, which gave the abbacy and the wealth of the monastery to an outsider who might be, and often was, an absentee landlord, of decline after it, arrested by the Maurist reform in 1616, then of another falling away. There were only fifteen monks at Jumièges when it was closed in 1790, though the abbey kept its reputation for charity which had earned it the title of 'Jumièges l'Aumônier'. The destruction of the buildings is particularly poignant here, because the villagers wanted to take over Notre-Dame as their parish church, in place of the dilapidated St Valentin. Had they succeeded, we might have had today another and even more majestic Boscherville. They were refused because the abbey had been designated as a refuge for eighteen monks from other religious houses closed under the constitution who, ironically, occupied it for only a year before it became a barracks. After its sale as a national property there was a period of systematic destruction, during which stone from the cloister found its way to Highcliffe Castle in Hampshire (*see* below). The first efforts to save what remained were hampered by the Romantics' taste for ruins, but in 1852 a new owner brought a more enlightened attitude.

Extensive as was the work of building and rebuilding that went on between the 11c. and the end of the 17c., it is Abbot Robert's church which remains at the heart of a visit to Jumièges today (open daily, 9–12, 14–18, from 1 May to 30 September; 10–12, 13.30–16, from 1 October to 30 April). Behind the façade, with its twin towers, square below, octagonal above, rising to 46 metres – they kept their spires until about 1830 – the walls of the nave are standing, though open to the sky. For the full impact of the church, stand midway up the nave, between the magnificent series of pillars, single shafts alternating with massive, rectangular piers with engaged columns, and look east to the arch incredibly supporting the one remaining wall of the lantern, with its narrow little stair tower, then back to the lower one above the west gallery.

Beyond the great eastern arch, all that remains of the transept are fragments of the north and south walls of the crossing, which were largely rebuilt in the 14c. The Romanesque choir, with an ambulatory, was replaced by a Gothic one in the second half of the 13c.; only the foundations survive. From the south transept a 14c. vaulted passage leads to the church of St Pierre. What remains of the façade and the first two arches on the north side of its nave are from the Carolingian church.

Between Notre-Dame and St Pierre, an ancient yew tree marks the centre of the now vanished cloister. There are still vestiges of the 12c. chapter house which opened on to it. West of the cloister is the 'grand cellier', a huge, vaulted store-room, probably from the late 12c., and more Gothic than Romanesque. Up to the beginning of the 19c. the arches over its main doorway and that opening on to the cloister were decorated with particularly rich geometric carving. Between 1825 and 1835 much of it was removed by Lord Stuart de Rothesay, then British Ambassador in Paris, for incorporation into his house at Highcliffe. The period, as Lucien Musset remarks tartly, was the heyday of 'Elginism'.

A small **museum**, made up largely of sculptures from the abbey, has been arranged in the former abbot's lodging (at the time of writing this was closed for rearrangement and the date of re-opening was indefinite). The contents include the funeral slab of Agnès Sorel, whose heart was buried in the north transept of the abbey. As the inscription records, the monks remembered her as 'piteuse entre toutes gens, et qui largement donnait de ses biens aux églises et aux pauvres'.

There are more relics from the abbey in the parish church of **St Valentin**, up the hill on the right as one leaves the grounds. This is very much worth a visit, both for the striking view of the abbey ruins from the churchyard and for the ungainly charm of the building itself. An austere 11–12c. nave, sloping quite steeply uphill to a triumphal arch, is joined in a summary fashion, stone and wood being used on no very obvious plan, to an ambitious Renaissance choir with ambulatory and side chapels. The building was started in 1537, but the outbreak of the Wars of Religion prevented its completion; the choir has a timber roof instead of the intended vault. There is some good 16c. glass. The first chapel (working from west to east) on the south side has fragments of 14c. grisaille which are believed to have come from a studio working for the Duc de Berry, whose craftsmen were inspired by their fellows of Florence and Siena. The 14c. font, a stone group of the Virgin and St Anne, which is from the 14c. or 15c., the lectern and pulpit, both 17c., and a glorious Louis-XIII confessional are among the items which came from Notre-Dame. In a different genre, but affecting in their ferv-our and their occasional *naïveté* of form and colour, are the poly-chromatic wooden statues, mostly of the 15 and 16c., in which rural craftsmen so often did better than they knew.

On the way back to the main road down the valley do not miss the tiny 11c. church of **Yainville**, with its rounded apse growing directly out of the squat mass of the tower. Here too there are statues worth seeing.

Le Trait's shipyards, in their unlikely rural setting, closed in 1971, but there are still metal works here. The 16c. church has a life-size Holy Sepulchre of the same period. There are alabaster low reliefs of the Adoration of the Kings and the Coronation of the Virgin on the bases of the statues at either side of the altar.

From **Caudebecquet**, 7 kilometres further down the valley, a turning on the right leads to the abbey of **Saint-Wandrille**, the third of the great abbeys along our route, and today a living religious community. It was founded in 649 by Wandrille, once a member of King Dagobert's court, and at that time was known as the Abbey of Fontenelle, after the stream beside which it was built. It was early renowned as a house of saints and scholars; the abbots during the Carolingian period included Eginhard, Charlemagne's secretary and biographer, and the chronicler Ansegis, author of the Capitularies of Charlemagne and begetter of the *Gestes des Abbés de Fontenelle*, compiled in 831, which is the first history of a monastery in the west and a precious source for the Merovingian and Carolingian periods.

Like Jumièges, Fontenelle was sacked by the Vikings, who burned the abbey in 852. It was after its rebuilding in 960, by the remarkable Abbot Maynard, who later, at the invitation of Richard I, Duke of Normandy, took a group of monks to re-establish the monastic life at Mont St-Michel, that the abbey was given the name of its founder.

After the Revolution, Saint-Wandrille, for a time, housed a spinning factory; at the end of the 19c. the Benedictines returned briefly, only to be evicted in 1901 under the law against associations. Between 1906 and their permanent return in 1931 the abbey at least had a worthy tenant. Maurice Maeterlinck the Belgian playwright, Nobel Prize winner and author of *Pelléas et Mélisande*, among much else, lived there.

The attractive wooded grounds, the ruins and the church may be visited freely; there are guided visits daily from 10.15 – 12 and 15 – 17, except during vespers.

The church whose outlines are marked by the bases of the nave pillars thrusting through the turf – only the north transept remains standing – was a 13–14c. Gothic building, more than 80 metres long, which succeeded earlier churches, destroyed either by the Vikings or by fire.

The monastic buildings round the courtyard are mostly 17c. and 18c.; the exception is a 12c. barn now used by the monks as a small factory for household products. The cloister, once the burial ground of the monks, as the occasional inscribed flagstones indicate, is 14c. on the south side, which backed on to the church, 15c. and 16c. as to the rest. There are some interesting carvings, notably a 14c. Virgin and Child on the south side and a Coronation of the Virgin in the tympanum of the doorway on the same side. Both were mutilated with systematic savagery during the Wars of Religion. Outside the chapter house there is a lavabo, dating from 1500 and alleged to be unique, carved with New Testament scenes. Above, a wholly secular jester holds a drinking vessel and a broken mallet; the carving is thought to be a warning against the perils of intemperance. The refectory, which is seldom shown to visitors, contains the oldest part of the building; the herring-bone patterned gable wall dates from about 1014–20.

To build a new church among all this would have been to court disaster. Instead of attempting it, the community took down a 13c. tithe barn at Canteloup, about 50 kilometres distant, and transported it, piece by piece, to Saint-Wandrille, where it was reassembled. The majestic simplicity of this building, whose roof is supported by single tree trunks from a 15c. forest, is unforgettable. Also the acoustics are superb. To hear the office sung here is a rare experience.

There is one older church which forms part of Saint-Wandrille. For the tiny, ancient **Chapel of St Saturnin**, turn right downhill on leaving the grounds, and, after about 150 metres, bear round to the right and take the path which runs alongside the wall of the abbey. The building, roofed with rosy tiles, has a short tower rising above the trefoil east end. St Germain, at Querqueville, near Cherbourg (*see* in Cotentin section) is the only other church in Normandy built on the same plan. As it stands, it is not earlier than the 10c., and the façade was rebuilt in the 16c. or 17c., but the foundations are almost certainly Merovingian.

Return to the main road – Caudebec-en-Caux is 3 kilometres along it. The new suspension bridge spanning this stretch of the river might, with that of Tancarville, be a response to the reproach of André Malraux, General de Gaulle's Minister for Cultural Affairs as well as novelist, that our civilization is the first which does not know how to build either a cathedral or a tomb. An age might have worse monuments than the audacious geometry of these skyborne roadways. A short distance past the bridge, a monument set against the cliff above the road commemorates the French and Norwegian aviators who perished with Amundsen in 1928, in an attempt to find the Italian, Umberto Nobile, whose dirigible had crashed on the ice north-east of Spitsbergen. Nobile and seven of his companions were later rescued by an ice-breaker, though seventeen of his crew were lost.

Caudebec, once the capital of the Pays de Caux and until World War II one of the most picturesque small towns in Normandy, was eighty per cent flattened in 1944. I wish I could like better the trim little riverside resort which has replaced the old streets of timbered houses, but I recognize this distaste for the well-barbered look of

91

the waterfront as an entirely personal foible. Many, perhaps most people, will find Caudebec a pleasant stopping place, well supplied with hotels. The site is charming, with the wide mouth of the valley of St Gertrude opening behind the town and the Forêt de Brotonne across the river. Before the process of damming and embanking the Seine, which has been intensified since the war, Caudebec offered a dramatic spectacle at the equinox, when, twice daily, the *mascaret* or tidal bore, rushed up the river to shatter in foam over its banks. Even today the sudden brimming and overflowing of the water can be impressive.

Miraculously, the exquisite Flamboyant church of **Notre-Dame** was not irreparably damaged. A first sight of the façade, with a triple porch whose extravagant delicacy recalls St-Maclou, and the intricately pierced and hollowed octagonal spire, justifies Henri IV's statement that it was the most beautiful chapel in his kingdom. Surprisingly, he added, 'Le bijou est mal enchâssé.'

A church consecrated on this spot in 1267 was abandoned during the English occupation of the Hundred Years War: in recompense, Henry IV helped the building of the present church, which began in 1426 and continued into the 15c. The curious little loggias with caryatids over the porch were a Renaissance afterthought. Before entering the church look at the parapet running round the building. The carving resolves itself into extracts from the Magnificat and the Salve Regina, in letters a metre high.

The interior is a treasure house, and the most exigent monarch could scarcely complain of this casket. The organ gallery, with angel musicians, is from 1559, and the instrument itself, the work of Antoine Josselyne, of Rouen, from 1542. It was restored between 1739 and 1750, but still has most of its original stops.

The splendid Louis XIII woodwork of the first ambulatory chapel on the south side of the choir came from St-Wandrille, the 17c. Holy Sepulchre in the chapel next to it from Jumièges. Near by is a 14c. *Pietà*. The Lady Chapel, in the apse, is remarkable for its tremend-ous pendant. Guillaume Letellier, nephew and pupil of Poussin, who planned the church and supervised the first thirty years of its building, is buried in this chapel; his tombstone, inscribed by his son, is under the south window. A number of 14c. and 15c. statues, of wood or stone, are disposed about the church – see particularly the 14c. stone Notre-Dame de Bon Secours, massive as a Giotto, and the affecting wooden Magdalen of the late 15c. – but there is nothing to rival the 15c. and 16c. glass of the windows. That over the north door, which was the gift of Fulke Eyton, Henry V's captain here in 1435–46, whose arms are incorporated in the design of St George, St Catherine, St Michael and the Virgin and Child, is one of the few specimens of English glass to be found in France. It is done in grisaille and pale, silvery gold on a background glowing with blue, red and yellow.

On the right as one leaves the church, three 15c. timbered houses are a sad indication of what has been lost. The other, and more remarkable, building which has survived from old Caudebec is the 13c. House of the Templars, in the Rue de la Boucherie, which turns down on the right beyond the apse of the church. This, a rare example of the secular building of the period, is now a museum of local history (open from 15–18 on Sundays and public holidays during June, July and August, otherwise on Tuesdays and Thursdays on application to the Lemoine printing house in the Place d'Armes).

For most of its length the 4½ kilometres of road from Caudebec to Villequier is a corniche above the river, with views which deserve to be taken slowly. **Villequier** is a pleasant waterside town, sheltered by wooded hills, but its attractions as a resort are overshadowed by its tragic notoriety as the scene of the boating accident in which Victor Hugo's nineteen-year-old daughter, Léopoldine, and her husband of six months, Charles Vacquerie, aged twenty-six, were drowned with two of their relatives. A statue of the poet has been set up at the foot of the chalk cliff on the road to Caudebec, facing the spot where the accident happened; the loss inspired a number of his *Contemplations*. The house belonging to the Vacquerie family, where Hugo often stayed with his friend and fellow writer, Auguste Vacquerie, is now a **museum** where sepulchral evocations of the young couple find a place along with assorted memorabilia of the poet's life.

Hugo, with his wife, his youngest daughter, Adèle, and members of the Vacquerie family, including the four victims of the accident, are buried in the churchyard, opposite the last window on the south side of the nave. The church itself, 16c. on a 12c. foundation, has kept most of its 16–17c. glass, including a window depicting a naval engagement, off the Azores in 1523, between three vessels from Normandy and what appears to be half the Spanish fleet.

Like Duclair and Caudebec, Villequier is a good base for pleasant pottering by car among the farms and villages of the Pays de Caux, where you find the French getting on with their own affairs in a fashion which can be refreshing after a spell in places geared to tourism. There are two towns in the area which are worth visiting if you are interested in sculpture or modern stained glass. **Barentin**, 10 kilometres north-east of Duclair by the D143, a small industrial town otherwise remarkable only for the 27-arch viaduct which the English engineer, Locke, built in 1846 to carry the Paris–Le Havre railway line over the Austreberthe Valley, has so many statues in its streets and squares that it is known as 'the town with the street museum'. They include Rodin's 'l'Homme qui marche' – this is on the edge of the town near the N13 *bis* for Saint-Valéry-en-Caux – a number of pieces by his pupil, Bourdelle, and a bust of Corneille by Caffieri. The 17c. fountain in the Place de la Libération is by Nicolas Coustou, one of a family of French sculptors who worked during the 17–18c. His brother, Guillaume, did the famous Marly horses at the entrance to the Avenue des Champs-Élysées in Paris.

Yvetot, 12 kilometres north-east of Caudebec, a busy little textile town, its centre rebuilt since the war, became known far beyond Normandy as the subject of a song by the 19c. *chansonnier*, Pierre-Jean de Béranger: 'Le Roi d'Yvetot'. It referred to the period between 1392 and the Revolution when, for reasons which remain obscure, the town was an independent territory, exempt from taxes and the duty of homage, whose lord had the title of king. Today its attraction is the church of **Saint-Pierre**, completed in 1956, a great drum, 20 metres high, 40 in diameter, with a free-standing belfry, in which ferro-concrete serves as a scaffolding for walls of glass by Max Ingrand, whose work is to be seen in so many of Normandy's post-war churches.

The road to Lillebonne passes two more 15c. churches, at **Norville** and **St-Maurice-d'Etelan**, with, between them, a glimpse on the left of the château of **Etelan**, the last word in Flamboyant, before reaching the pylons and refineries of Notre-Dame de Gravenchon. **Lillebonne**, the Juliobona of the Romans, was once a busy port with a population of some twenty-five thousand. The quantity and quality of Gallo-Roman antiquities found here testify to its importance in the ancient world. The Roman theatre, built early in the 2c. A.D. (to visit, apply to the Café de l'Hôtel de Ville, 35 Rue Gambetta) which is the most important monument of its period in Normandy, could seat the whole of the town's present population of ten thousand or so. Most of the stone seats have vanished, but some of the masonry of the upper parts survives, running courses of terracotta tiles banding small stones, with a flint core. A little **Archaeological Museum** has been arranged in the Hôtel de Ville (open daily, 10–12, 14–18). The striking 55-metre spire of **Notre-Dame**, which dominates the Place Sadi-Carnot, is 16c., as are the porch and part of the nave of the church.

After the Romans, the Conqueror made Lillebonne into a strongpoint. His **château** (take the narrow Rue Croy, first on the left after the *mairie*, then first right; visits daily except Sundays and public holidays) was rebuilt in the 12–13c., but the massive donjon is that of the original fortress. A plaque on a free-standing arch recalls that, on this spot, William gathered his barons before the invasion of England.

CHAPTER SEVEN

Tancarville – Filières – Étretat – Fécamp – Bailleul – Valmont – Saint-Valéry-en-Caux – Bourg-Dun – the coast to Varengeville and Pourville

✣

BETWEEN Lillebonne and Fécamp lies the calm, unemphatic landscape of the Pays de Caux. A detour at the start of the route will take in two widely contrasted châteaux.

Tancarville, dominating the Seine estuary from a spur of rock on the right of the N182, has 10c. origins, but the oldest surviving portion is the ruined 12c. donjon. Visits have been suspended for some time.

At the bridge, turn right into the N810, then branch left into the D39 and, beyond St Romain, turn right for **Commerville** and the **Château de Filières** (visits Easter to All Saints, 14–19, Thursdays, Saturdays and Sundays). Le Nôtre laid out the park, whose most celebrated feature is the beech avenue known as 'the Cathedral'. The house, an imposing 18c. building of Caen stone, with an inappropriate pendant in a modest 16c. left wing, illustrates the troubled history of France during the Revolution. According to tradition – and the moat supports the idea – there was a fortress on the site in the 14c. In the 16c. it was succeeded by a château which in the late 18c. the owner, the Marquis de Mirville, planned to replace by a more ambitious house. He is believed to have commissioned Victor Louis, the architect of Bordeaux's gracious theatre, to design it, but the Revolution halted the building, which was never completed. The five ground floor rooms which are shown include an 18c. Chinese drawing room with hand-painted wallpaper framed in panelling. There is some good Louis XV and Louis XVI furniture, royal mementoes among the bibelots and pictures which include lithographs by Fragonard and portraits by Nattier, Mignard and Carl Van Loo.

Continue past the château and take the first turn right to join the main road for **Bolbec**. The town, at the junction of four valleys, has in its public gardens, behind the Hôtel de Ville, two pieces of

96

sculpture – a *Diana* and a group, 'Les Arts relevés par le Temps' – which were once in the park of Marly, near Paris. For Étretat, take the road which runs north-west through Beuzeville-le-Grenier and Bréauté to **Goderville**, whose church, rebuilt during the 19c., has side altars adorned by four enchanting little angels which came from the abbey of Valmont, near Fécamp.

Étretat, with its theatrically beautiful cliff scenery and its beach of smooth pebbles, sloping steeply to the sea, ideal for swimming as opposed to dabbling in the surf, is perhaps the most agreeable of the many pleasant seaside resorts of the Pays de Caux. Relatively it is quiet (nowhere is quiet during August), or at least what the French call 'élégant' and the English 'select', but it is a far cry from today's promenade and casino and golf course and tennis courts to the village where, up to the mid-19c., the fishermen hauled up their boats on the beach. Disused boats were given a roof of thatch or timber and used as storage sheds, known as *caloges*. The two or three now on the beach have been reconstructed.

Isabey (1767–1855), the marine and landscape painter and chronicler of Louis Philippe's court, who was the first to discover Étretat, had the sense to keep his own counsel, as did his artist friends. The fashionable world, headed by Jérôme Bonaparte, ex-King of Westphalia, Marie-Christine, Dowager Queen of Spain, and the aged Marshal Grouchy, veteran of Waterloo, mounted its invasion when the novelist, Alphonse Karr (1808–90), made the place the setting for a couple of his books. In gratitude for the prosperity that followed, Étretat named one of the roads opening on to the sea front after him.

On either side of the beach, notably to the west, where the 70-metre Aiguille stands guard before the great arch of the Porte d'Aval, the **cliffs**, rising to 85 metres, have been fretted and pierced by the sea into vaults and spires and flying buttresses. There are good walks in either direction, both along the beach below the cliffs and by the paths on top of them. On the first, watch the tide; on the second, watch your feet. The paths are not all guarded by a rail, and steep grassy slopes, particularly when they are wet or very dry, can be perilous if you are not wearing studded soles. To the west, the path tops the peak of the Porte d'Aval, with sensational views along the coast, infinitely varied in the changing light, and goes on over the still more massive archway of the Manneporte. Between the two a rather sketchy path leads down to the tiny cove of Petit-Port, which is connected with the beach of Étretat; it is accessible also by road. The lighthouse on the headland is a replacement for that destroyed in 1944. Unhappily, there is no way of replacing the guillemots which once haunted and gave their name to a rock near by. Both footpath and road continue to the tiny resort of **Bruneval**, crammed into a breach in the cliffs, 2 kilometres distant on foot, 5 by car. The monument on the southern cliff, whose first stone was laid by General de Gaulle, commemorates the first raid made by British air and naval forces on European territory after 1940, which involved the successful destruction of an enemy radar post on the night of 27/28 February 1942.

The east cliff, the Falaise d'Amont – to drive up, take the Rue Jules Gerbeau and the Chemin Damilaville – is crowned by the memorial to the French aviators, Nungesser and Coli, the first to attempt a non-stop Paris–New York crossing, who were last seen over this spot on 8 May 1927, before disappearing in the Atlantic. The thrusting arrowhead of the present memorial, dedicated in 1962, replaces the original, which was destroyed by the Germans. There is a small museum on the site. The little chapel of **Notre-Dame-de-la-Garde**, built by the sailors of Étretat in 1854, which was also destroyed in 1944, was rebuilt in 1950. There is a nice view of its needle spire through the arch of the memorial. Don't miss the dolphin gargoyles. This side of the cliffs, too, offers the alternative of climbing down to the beach or walking 3 kilometres over the top to **Benouville**, where there is another rock pillar, the Aiguille de Belval.

The town of Étretat is slightly below sea level, protected from the tide by a natural ridge of pebble which is supported by the promenade. The rather effective market hall in the Place Foch is a reconstruction, like the *caloges*, but the church of **Notre-Dame**, to the north-east, is splendidly authentic, with massive drum pillars in the first six bays of the nave, which are 12c., and a transept, choir and lantern from the 13c.

From Étretat to Fécamp the coast road (leave the town by the Avenue Nungesser-et-Coli) is preferable to the rather dull main one further inland. There are a number of tiny resorts along it, or down byways a kilometre or so off it. The road drops to the shore at **Yport**, which is a good deal smaller and less sophisticated that Étretat, but much like it in character.

Fécamp is a splendid town, both a working port – the foremost in France for deep-sea cod fishing – and a resort with all the usual amenities, including an excellent yachting harbour. Its 'noble and royal' **abbey church** is the legacy to our age of a monastery which was once the most important pilgrimage centre in Normandy. The monks left us also the recipe for Benedictine, which continues to be manufactured in the town, though now by secular hands.

Nuns, not monks, first occupied the site. About 660 St Waneng, or Waninge, secretary and friend of King Clotaire III, founded a convent dedicated to the Holy Trinity, whose church possessed a priceless relic, a vessel containing a few drops of the blood which flowed from the wounds of Christ. According to legend, it had been concealed in the trunk of a fig tree at a time of persecution and cast into the sea by a nephew of Nicodemus, to be washed ashore at Fécamp. Monkish etymologists even made the name of the town derive from 'fici campus', the field of the fig tree, rather than the actual Celtic-Latin fiscamnum. When the convent was destroyed by the Vikings the relic survived to become the greatest treasure of the Benedictine monastery which replaced it in the 10c. This became one of the most important in the province, and town and port prospered with it.

The modern town centres on the church of **St-Étienne**, built about 1500, with a façade and tower, the latter having a most satisfying solidity, which date from a 19c. reconstruction. On the tympanum of the south door there is a much worn low relief of the martyrdom of the saint. Inside, see the equestrian statue of St Martin in the south transept. I know no livelier stone horse anywhere nearer than Venice. There are a number of wooden statues from the 17c. and 18c. On Saturdays, around the church, there is a zestful **market** where land and sea meet, a woman re-seating cane chairs and another inviting customers to taste her Reine de Reinettes before buying from neighbouring baskets of shrimps, live and flickering, and crabs crawling round their wooden boxes.

From the Place Adolphe Bellet before the church, with the Syndicat d'Initiative on its north side, walk up the **Rue Jacques Huet** to the Hôtel de Ville, which backs on to the side of the Church of the Trinity. Its dignified 18c. buildings in pale brick and stone were once the living quarters of the monks. When the monastery was suppressed at the Revolution thirty or so remained. Some were said to have been tainted by the ideas of the Enlightenment, a few even to be Freemasons. Even if the charges were true, they seem a doubtful warrant for pillaging the treasury and library of the monastery and melting down *le gros Fécamp*, the great bourdon of the church, which had been cast in 1533.

The massive square building diagonally left from the Hôtel de Ville, and, like it, 18c., was once the mill of the abbey. Other one-time monastic buildings border the *place*. Opposite the west front of the church are the ruins of the château built early in the 10c. by Guillaume Longue-Épée, son of Rollo.

The classical façade of **La Trinité** which replaced the 13c. façade in the mid-18c., is almost the only regrettable feature of an essentially thoroughbred building. As it stands, the church is neither that of the 10c., where the Conqueror often kept his Easters, and his daughter, Cécile, took the veil, nor, for the most part, its successor, the Romanesque building which was consecrated in 1106. The latter was destroyed by fire in 1168; only the chapels of St Pierre and St Nicolas, with a fragment of the ambulatory, survived to be incorporated in the great church which was built between 1175 and 1220. They are on the north side; the south, with its long row of flying buttresses, has a fair amount of ornament but the full-blooded Flamboyant of the Lady Chapel still comes as a surprise when one rounds the apse. The whole is dominated by the lantern tower, lopped now of its spire, which has been replaced by a mere pyramid, rising 60 metres above the crossing. Its mass is lightened by three tall windows on each face in the top storey, and blind bays alternating with windows below them, with a smaller blind arcade at the base.

The interior, high, narrow, gloriously light, has the majestic simplicity of early Gothic, made even more impressive by the fact that one surveys it from the height of a flight of twelve steps at the west end. From here, too, it is possible to disregard the 19c. Stations of the Cross, which are a disaster. By contrast, the ornaments and furniture are sumptuous, even though one of the most important features, the 15c. *jubé*, one of the finest in France, was removed in 1803. Fragments of it remain at the original site, the eighth bay of the nave.

In the south transept is the wonderful group of the Falling Asleep of Our Lady, a 15c. masterpiece. On the right of the group is the carved 15c. reliquary containing the stone marked with the 'angel's footprint', dating, we are told, from the consecration of Guillaume Longue-Épée's church in the 9c., when, as the bishops were pondering its dedication, an angel alighted briefly to order that it should be dedicated to the Holy and Indivisible Trinity. Richard I and Richard II, dukes of Normandy during the 10c. and 11c., are buried in the baptismal chapel near by. Popular belief holds that the two figures on a 17c. cenotaph in this chapel, wearing what look rather like World War I gas-masks, are the nuns of Fécamp who, when the Viking raiders appeared in 842, mutilated themselves in the hope of escaping violation. Actually they are ritually clothed mourners.

The choir has elements of four stages of building, from the 11c. to the end of the 13c. Theoretically, it is hard to think of a more certain recipe for disaster than to insert into so nobly austere a building a high altar which is part Renaissance, part 18c., overhung by an ornate gilded *baldacchino*. In fact, the result is a triumph. Behind the bronze crucifix and candlesticks of the Louis XV altar rises a white marble reredos of 1507 by the Genoese sculptor Girolamo Viscardo. The shrine above it is surmounted by an 18c. statue of the Risen Christ in gilded wood. The *baldacchino* floats above, its pale gold arcs and garlands seemingly weightless. Ironically, the abbot who commissioned it from the Rouen architect Defrance, who did the Arethusa fountain in the Rue du Gros Horloge, was the same Montboissier de Canillac who put up the ill-judged west front. The oak stalls are also by Defrance.

Exquisitely carved stone screens, Italian in feeling if not in work-manship, partition off the ambulatory chapels. Starting from the south side, the second chapel has another equestrian St Martin, noted for its faithful detail of 16c. harness, and the third a remark-able series of low reliefs below the window, which came from the tomb of Guillaume de Ros, abbot from 1082 to 1108. One of his successors, Thomas de Saint-Benoît (1297–1307) is buried in the fourth chapel, in a richly decorated tomb whose high reliefs repres-ent legends of the abbey. The head of the abbot is not the original. There is another splendid tomb, that of Abbot Guillaume IV de Putot, who died in 1297, on the left of the fifth chapel.

With the Lady Chapel we come to the luxuriant elegance of Flamboyant; only the first bay of the earlier chapel was preserved during the rebuilding at the turn of the 15–16c., though the crypt, still used as a sacristy (entrance in the next chapel) is 12–13c. Some of the glass is of the same period. The carved panels, among which that representing a veiled Christ is celebrated, are 18c. On the back of the choir altar, facing the entrance to the Lady Chapel, is the delicate white marble tabernacle, part of the work commissioned from Viscardo, which contains the relic of the Precious Blood.

The next two chapels belong to the Romanesque church. Abbot Richard d'Argences (1223) is buried in the second, the masterly simplicity of his tomb contrasting with that of the first abbot, Gulielmo de Volpiano, in the fourth chapel, which was erected by the Maurist reformers with all the elaboration of the later 17c. Dom Blandin, the last monk of Fécamp, who died in 1848, is commemorated in this chapel.

There are some figures from the *jubé* in the north transept.

Overhead, a 17c. clock tells the tides as well as the time.

Leave the church by the south porch – No. 10 in the Rue des Forts was once the abbey's guest house – and turn left for a memorable view of the east end from the courtyard of the former choir school at No. 23, which has an 11–12c. tower. Return to the west front and turn right into the Rue A.P. Leroux for the Rue Alexandre Legros. The **Municipal Museum and Arts Centre** at No. 2 (open 10–11.30, 14–17, closed Tuesdays) has a good collection of ceramics, from the Far East, Delft and Nevers as well as the more predictable Rouen, and, among the pictures, an interesting series of 16c. portrait drawings. There are documents relating to the abbey and, among the relics of it, a nice 15c. English alabaster. The unique attraction is the marine section on the second floor where, among the pictures and maps and models, you can learn a good deal about the daily life of the fishermen who, for four-and-a-half centuries, have sailed from Fécamp for the Grand Banks of Newfoundland, and of the folk lore and superstition which have gathered about their calling.

From the Municipal Museum, continue the line of the Rue Alexandre Legros along the Rue Félix Faure to the museum attached to the **Benedictine Distillery** (open daily, 3 April – 3 October, 9–11.30, 14–17.30; closed on Saturdays and Sundays during the rest of the year), beside whose preposterous buildings the utmost that Victorian Gothic can do would have a primitive simplicity. There are bits of Renaissance here, too.

It was the monk Bernardo Vincelli who, in 1510, found the secret of distilling a liquid which 'shines like gold and warms like sunlight'. It was given to the sick at the monastery as medicine and is likely to have been more beneficial than many of the remedies of the period. When the abbey library was dispersed at the Revolution the recipe came into the hands of a layman. Among the twenty-seven herbs that comprise it are hyssop, balm, angelica, nutmeg, clove, musk, thyme and, surprisingly, tea. Perhaps the most striking proof of its popularity is the fact that the distinctive bottle has been counterfeited the world over, from Iceland to Hong Kong. A display of eight hundred of these imitations is shown during the tour of the distillery.

The **museum** is of serious interest, as the founder of the firm, Alexandre Le Grand, was an enlightened amateur of the arts, with the means to gratify his tastes. Its bias is towards medieval *objets d'art* and its foundation, which came from the abbey, included a thousand books from the monks' library, also yet more portions of the *jubé*. On this, M. Le Grand built up a collection, ranging from gold and ivory and enamel, through sculpture and paintings and tapestries, to wrought ironwork, the intricately locked chests of the Norman corsairs and the enormous boots, weighing more than six kilos and fixed to the saddle, worn by the postilions of the abbey. See, in the Gothic room, a 16c. ivory triptych and a particularly beautiful Renaissance low relief of the Presentation in the Temple, in wood and ivory; in the dome, the 18c. carved wood panels; in the Oratory, a series of English alabasters of the 15c. and a Cologne polyptych of the early 16c. The *crêpes Bénédictines* served at the buffet near the exit are to be recommended. As an alternative, the neighbouring *pâtisserie* is considered to be the best in the district.

Continue along the Rue Théagène-Bouffart and the Rue Louis-Caron to reach the sea front, a shallow curve of sand below pebble, with the tide receding to expose a black rug of weed below the sheer chalk cliffs on the north-east. The **port**, where Charles II landed after his escape from the Battle of Worcester, opens between the beach and the cliffs. Fécamp builds distant-water trawlers as well as sending them out, these days to the Barents Sea and the Davis Straits as well as the Grand Banks. By applying to the Syndicat d'Initiative it is possible to go over a modern trawler. The usual supporting industries have grown up round the ship-building. Near-water fishing and general trade are, relatively, minor activities.

Cross the harbour by the bridge which leads from the Quai Bérigny (turn right at the yacht harbour) to the **Quai Guy Maupassant**. The novelist and short-story writer was born at No. 82. That he was recorded as having been born at the château of Miromesnil, some 8 kilometres south of Dieppe, which his parents were renting at the time, is due to his mother's determination that the birth should be registered from a good address. Almost immediately after it, she and the infant were hurried off to the château, where Maupassant lived until he was three years old.

A lane (steps) between No. 64 and No. 66 leads to the little sailors' oratory of **Notre-Dame-du-Salut** on the cliff top. There was a chapel here in the 11c.; rebuildings, the last after the damage of 1944, have been numerous, but the east end and crossing are 13c. and the north transept 14c. The chapel stayed open during the Revolution; it is said that, when a party of Republicans tried to close it, the congregation repelled them by force of arms, even pitching some of them over the cliff. It is possible to drive up to the oratory and the neighbouring semaphore by taking the left turn which winds uphill from the Dieppe road, though, by doing so, you will miss the sailors' Calvary beside the footpath, a crucifix with a gold figure mounted on the mast of a concrete boat, with the gulls riding the wind above it.

A leisurely day's outing from Fécamp will take in both the **Château of Bailleul** and the Abbey of Valmont. A visit to Bailleul (open Easter until 30 June, 10–12, 14–18; 1 July until 30 September, Sundays and public holidays only, 14–18; October to All Saints, 10–12, 14–16) is not simply worth while; it is imperative. Setting, building and contents unite in an almost unreal perfection.

Leave Fécamp by the Yvetot road and turn right off it into the D28, which follows the Ganzeville valley, then right again into the D11. The first right turn after Angerville passes the château gates. The house was built midway through the 16c. by a member of one of the oldest families in Normandy. A Bailleul fought at Hastings. Later the family established a branch in Scotland, where the name became Balliol. John de Baliol (d. 1268/69) founded Balliol College, Oxford. His son, another John, and his grandson, Edward, were kings of Scotland respectively from 1292 to 1296 and from 1329 to 1371, their claim to the throne being based on their kinship with Margaret of Norway, Queen of Scots.

The château has remained in the possession of the family. Set deep in a park where flowering shrubs embroider the magnificence of oak and chestnut, it stands foursquare in pale stone and slate, each corner marked by a rectangular building with the mitred roof, crowned with a leaden statue, and tall chimneys of the Renaissance. There is a superb entrance porch, with the arms of Bailleul in a luxurious low relief over the door, and the pillars rising in superimposed orders to a deliciously decorated lucarne, topped by another lead figure from the 16c. Each side has a dome and lantern, like a tiny temple, and Italianate loggias on either side.

The interior lives up to the promise of the exterior, which is not invariably true of French châteaux. In particular, the pictures are magnificent. A bedchamber in which a Hans Memling triptych stands out in the company of Rembrandt, Frans Hals and Hobbema is a fair indication of what to expect. Unreality reaches its climax when, from a gallery, visitors look down on the sumptuous tapestries and Renaissance furniture of the *grand salon*. It is tranced; drop a ballpoint over the balustrade and you feel that the whole will vanish into thin air.

The chapel near by, built in 1543, has an attractive relief of the Adoration of the Magi of about the same period and a wrought iron grille which is remarkable even by the standards of Normandy.

Continue along the D10 to the main road from Fécamp to Fauville-en-Caux, cross it and continue diagonally left to **Valmont**, where the majestic ruin of a church, with one exquisite chapel surviving, stands on the left bank of the river of the same name, with, on the right bank, the donjon of the seigneurs of Estouteville.

The family which was to play so large a part in the history of Normandy owned the land at the beginning of the 11c. Robert I went to Hastings with the Conqueror and is represented in the Bayeux tapestry. The brick donjon which stands today was built by Nicolas's father, Robert II, who died in an English prison. The so-called 'old château', of which the building of banded brick and stone on the right of the donjon is a relic, was built for Jacques d'Estouteville, grandson of Louis, the heroic defender of Mont Saint-Michel (*see* pp.246-7). Half-way through the following century the 'new château' was added to it.

Valmont then consisted of buildings of several periods encircling a court. It survived the Revolution virtually undamaged; the loss of the machicolated entrance gate, the towers and the enceinte, and the blocking up of the arches of the charming Renaissance wing are due to the activities of an early 19c. owner, Comte Hocquart, Charles X's secretary.

At the time of writing, plans were being made to open the château to the public. For current information, inquire either at the abbey (*see* below) or at the Syndicat d'Initiative at Fécamp.

Nicolas d'Estouteville, who founded the **abbey** in 1169 (visits daily, 10–12, 14–18, except Sundays during the season and Thursdays), did so as an act of expiation which deserved to have been invalidated by his brutal treatment of the workmen who built it. His daughter, who tried to soften their lot, has survived in legend as a Norman St Elizabeth of Hungary: when her father asked what she was carrying, the bread piled in her apron, which was intended for the half-starved masons, turned into roses.

The church was largely in ruins before the Revolution, by which time only five monks remained in the community. Today, part of the transepts and four bays of the Renaissance choir, with an arcaded triforium running above them, remain, roofless but singularly undecayed. The intact Lady Chapel is a small treasure house. There is mid-16c. glass in the apse windows and the stone group of the Annunciation over the altar has been attributed to the 16c. sculptor, Germain Pilon, the creator of the tombs of François I and Henri II at St Denis.

Return to Fécamp by the road which follows the little river Valmont.

The first part of the coast road to Dieppe switchbacks in and out of a series of valleys, each ending in a small resort. **Saint-Martin-aux-Buneaux** has a church with two panelled naves, respectively 13c. and 16c., **Veulettes** has one dating from the early 12c. topped by a lantern tower and peopled by 16c. stone statues.

Saint-Valéry-en-Caux, bigger, with a past as a commercial port of some consequence, has a harbour driving deep inland which is today largely given up to fishing and sailing craft. On the Falaise d'Amont, which dominates the harbour and the town from the east (stairs up from the landward side), a monument commemorates the gallant rearguard action of the 51st (Highland) Division during the Allied retreat to Dunkirk in 1940. A memorial to the French 2nd Cavalry Division is on the Falaise d'Aval on the opposite side of the harbour. The town, rebuilt after being virtually wiped out in 1940, retains a few old houses, among them the splendid timbered Maison Henri IV on the west side of the harbour. One feature of the rebuilding, the little church of Notre-Dame du Bon Port, near the harbour, which was consecrated in 1963, is a triumph without and within. For once, an architect has mastered rather than been dominated by the medium of concrete, using it in just proportion, with a great penthouse roof of slate, and windows in which the greys and blues and greens of the sea form abstract patterns.

Eight kilometres further on, **Veules-les-Roses**, another old port, with an exceptionally charming hinterland, which attracted many artists when it began its new life as a holiday resort, has a curious church in which a square 13c. tower rises above a 16c. building. There is an unusually large number of stone and wood statues of varying periods and quality. The **Chapelle du Val**, 1½ kilometres south-east, on the road to Saint-Pierre-le-Viger, was a lazar house founded during the second Crusade, where lepers were sheltered as late as 1650.

An inland detour here will take in **Bourg-Dun**, a small town whose first parish priest was Dudo de Saint-Quentin, author of the 11c. chronicles of Normandy. The great church, with its remarkable central tower crowned by an axe-headed spire, has known continual rebuilding during the intervening centuries, but the north aisle and transept and part of the north wall of the choir remain from the church whose benefice was given to Dudo by Richard I, Duke of Normandy. Later rebuildings have left a 12c. nave, a 13c. central tower and a south transept whose vault, with spectacular pendant bosses, is a masterpiece of Flamboyant. The interior is richly interesting; see particularly the vault of the Flamboyant south transept, with its pendants and delicate arches, and the Renaissance font.

Pick up the coast road again at **Saint-Aubin-sur-Mer** and follow it eastward through two more small resorts, **Quiberville** and **Sainte-Marguerite-sur-Mer**. All three have ancient churches; in the last, the modern windows by Max Ingrand illuminate a 12c. apse and high altar. A left turn here will take you to the modern lighthouse on the Pointe d'Ailly, a noted look-out.

Varengeville-sur-Mer, its houses scattered over the wooded plateau up on the right, is a place in which to linger, or, indeed, to stay – it has a couple of small hotels. A left turn from the central cross-roads leads to the **Parc des Moustiers** (visits daily, from Easter to All Saints, 10–12, 14–19) where, over three-quarters of a century, a worthy setting has been created for an admirable house by Sir Edwin Lutyens (1869–1944), the English architect whose work ranged from country houses in Surrey to the Viceroy's House in New Delhi. Its garden merges into a wooded park filling the whole of a valley sloping down to the sea, with grassy paths marked out among the masses of flowering shrubs, which are at their best during May and June.

The road continues to the little cliff top church of **Saint-Valéry**, dating from the 12c., though with later additions, whose supremely beautiful site is poignantly at risk. A crumbling of rock here would carry away much of the little graveyard. The composer, Albert Roussel (1869–1937) is buried in it, as is Georges Braque (1882–1963), one of the first Cubists, whose last work in stained glass was the Stem of Jesse window in the church. It has other modern works, also a curious, twisted column with marine carvings.

Half a kilometre along the main road, on the Dieppe side, turn right for the **Manoir d'Ango** (visits, 1 April – 10 November, daily, 14–18.30), the country house which the great shipowner built in 1532–4, and in which he entertained on a princely scale. The devotion of a private owner, Madame Hugo-Gratry, has now restored to its original understated splendour a building distinguished by its quiet perfection. There is no hint of ostentation in these steep-roofed buildings set round a huge court, with a four-arched loggia opening on to it. The patterning of brick which decorates the walls reaches its apogee in the mosaic of brick and flint of the great dovecot.

On the way out of Varengeville, we pass on the right the chapel of **Saint-Dominique**, converted from an old barn, where there are more windows by Braque. The road continues to Dieppe by way of **Pourville,** a small resort which, in the earlier years of the century, attracted numbers of writers and actors, as well as painters.

ITINERARY TWO

Le Havre, Graville, Montivilliers, Harfleur,
Pont de Tancarville, Pont Audemer, Valley of the Risle,
Bec-Hellouin, Brionne, Château Harcourt, Le Neubourg,
Champs-de-Bataille, Beaumont-le-Roger, Louviers, Évreux,
Nonancourt, Tillières, Verneuil-sur-Avre, Conches-en-Ouche,
Bernay, L'Aigle, Mortagne, Alençon, Sées, Argentan,
Haras de Pin, Vimoutiers, Livarot, Orbec, Lisieux,
Saint-Pierre-sur-Dives, Falaise, Caen, landing beaches, Ouistreham,
Bénouville, Abbaye d'Ardenne, Thaon, Fontaine-Henry,
Douvres-la-Délivrande, Dives, Cabourg, Côte Fleurie,
Pont-l'Évèque, St-Hymer, Val de Touques,
Deauville-Trouville, Honfleur, Marais-Vernier,
Quillebeuf

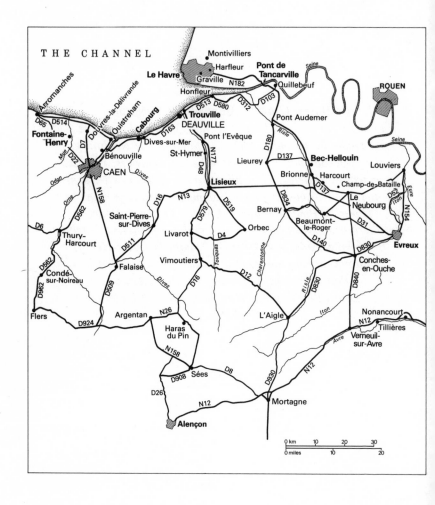

CHAPTER EIGHT

Le Havre – Graville – Montivilliers – Harfleur – Pont de Tancarville – Pont Audemer

CASIMIR Delavigne, the 19c. poet and dramatist, held that, after Constantinople, nothing was more beautiful than Le Havre. True, he was born there; true also, he was not writing about the new town. Even so, it is a judgment which would be found eccentric by the thousands of British visitors who disembark at Le Havre every year, only to get out of it with all speed. They do wrong. Site apart, few unbiased judges would call it beautiful, but a place which has a great modern port, a distinguished Museum of Modern Art and a Romanesque abbey church, and which, additionally, offers a morbidly fascinating example of disastrous urban design cannot fail to be interesting.

The **Le Havre** of today is the second new town to be built on the spot. In 1517, François I decided to construct a fortified port here to supplement those of Harfleur and Honfleur, which were already silting up. The first warship sailed into what is now the Bassin du Roi in 1518, and the new town took the king's name – Franciscopolis – and the arms of a silver salamander on a red field.

There followed a series of catastrophes which might have been seen as a punishment for hubris. In 1525 a freak tide destroyed much of the town, drowned a number of its citizens and landed twenty-eight fishing craft in its streets. The 2000-ton vessel, *Grande Nef Françoise*, which the king had ordered to be built, was destroyed on the stocks by a tempest; a few years later, in 1545, another warship, the *Philippe*, of 1200 tons, caught fire during a review and was burned out in the presence of François I. Worst of all, the site was a salt marsh, and it proved virtually impossible to consolidate the harbour walls. The tide entered the houses of the new town fairly regularly, and priests saying mass at the church of Notre-Dame got used to having to stand on a chair.

The metaphorical tide turned about 1540 with the advent of Girolamo Bellarmato, an Italian engineer in political exile in France, who had experience of working in the unstable soil of

Venice. He constructed the first docks and laid out two districts of the new town, Notre-Dame and Saint-François, which remain examples of admirable neighbourhood planning. Within a hundred years Le Havre had become one of the three chief naval bases in west France. By the first half of the 19c., it was second only to Marseille as a commercial port and its population of thirty to thirty-five thousand included representatives of all the trading nations of Europe, including Russia, as well as a small English colony.

The Place de l'Hôtel de Ville is the point of departure for visiting both the port and the new town. Before setting out, call at the Syndicat d'Initiative, which is just off the *place*, at the corner of the Rue du Général Leclerc and the Avenue René Coty, to pick up a street map and details of transport routes and parking regulations. The itineraries in the town centre described below were in fact covered on foot – I have a tendency to do things the hard way – but a great deal of Le Havre is best traversed on wheels, whether those of your own car or of a corporation bus. This fact indicates one of the cardinal faults of the new town, which is that much of it is simply not on the human scale.

During the season, starting at Easter, the Syndicat d'Initiative organizes boat trips round the **port**, with a commentary. Those seriously interested in ships and shipping may enjoy a drive round it. Start at the immense administrative building of the Port Autonome, between the inner harbour and the Bassin de la Citadelle. Its hall is open to visitors and there are hostesses to give information about the movements of liners, though no longer those of the magnificent *France*, pride of the nation, which was sold to a Saudi Arabian company in 1977.

Follow the Avenue Lucien-Corbeaux to the left, past the *gares maritimes* respectively of the Port Autonome and of the Compagnie Générale Transatlantique. From the Quai Johannes Couvert, on the seaward side of the latter, one can watch the 250,000-ton tankers which use the petrol port (not open to the public) across the Bassin Théophile Ducrocq. The complex of buildings beyond the end of the avenue is an electric power station.

Follow the Rue Général Cavaignac to the left, then turn right along the Quai de la Garonne. For a sight of the tide-gate whose span of 67 metres – a world record: most things in Le Havre are on the largest scale – allows vessels of a quarter of a million tons to reach the industrial zone to the east, turn right along the end of the quay and take the Avenue du 16me Port on the left. Otherwise cross

114

the Pont V and turn left along the north side of the Bassin Vétillart and the Bassin Fluvial to regain the town centre by the Rue Amiral Courbet and the Rue Marceau.

The battle for its liberation, in September 1944, left Le Havre with the most severely damaged port in Europe – it was two years before it could be used – and the better half of its centre flattened. The reconstruction was entrusted to the architect, Auguste Perret, a pioneer in the use of reinforced concrete, who had designed buildings as diverse as the church of Notre-Dame du Raincy, a suburb of Paris, and the Théâtre des Champs-Élysées. Perret was seventy when the war ended, but his imagination soared like the spire of Raincy. He envisaged a new town which, while keeping the principle of Bellarmato's chessboard, would achieve a perfect balance of space and volume, of horizontals and verticals, and incorporate monuments worthy of a town with a noble history. In Perret's original concept it would have been a vast pedestrian precinct, with all the traffic going underground. Cost apart – and it was the period of post-war penury – this would have taken more concrete than was to be found in the whole of France. That compromise made, Perret's plan was carried through, with the co-operation of his many pupils and disciples. The result has been described by a French writer as 'one of the most dismal urban landscapes to be found anywhere in France', where men scurry like mice in the shadow of gargantuan buildings, which are often undistinguished architecturally besides being constructed of a material which weathers so ungracefully that it is rotten before it is ripe.

The Place de l'Hôtel de Ville – this, again, is one of Europe's biggest – is an excellent spot at which to test one's reactions to Perret. The building itself, long, low and flat-roofed, with a rectangular tower, all curtain walling and raw concrete, rising at one end, fills one side of the square. It includes a theatre and exhibition hall. Round the remaining sides of the square's gardens are three-storey buildings punctuated by half a dozen tower blocks.

To the right, at No. 17 Rue Jules Lecesne, is the **municipal library**, which has a precious collection of MSS and incunabula inherited from the monastery of Saint-Wandrille. It inherited with them a tradition not common in France. When a German traveller, Frederic Shoberl, was here in 1840 he found that the municipal library, not, of course, housed in the present building, was open from 10 – 16 daily, except Sundays, and had a convenient reading room. Even today many French towns do not provide such a service. The library has a collection of Revolutionary literature and, as

115

might be expected, many rare books on seafaring and navigation.

From the *place* the Avenue Foch, conceived as Le Havre's Champs-Élysées, runs due west to the Porte Océane, which opens on to the Atlantic. The idea is heroic; the effect grandiose rather than grand. Before passing through the Atlantic Gate turn left into the Boulevard François I to visit the church of **St Joseph**. This, Perret's last and certainly his most extraordinary creation, is a memorial to the victims of the bombing of 1944 as well as a place of worship, and the architect saw its octagonal tower as the pivot of his town. The square church is no more than a base for the tower, which has been compared to a rocket on its launching pad. Inside, the brute concrete of the structure is exposed, but the walls of church and tower alike are a mosaic of light from myriads of narrow slabs of glass, their colours carefully graduated to marry the changing skies on the four sides of the church. Perret thought of his tower as a lighthouse, dominating land and sea but admitting, not diffusing, radiance.

Some people must like it. For myself, on two visits I have experienced the same intense relief upon escaping from the building and gaining the Boulevard Clemenceau and the yacht harbour via the Rue F. Lemaître. This is one of the few parts of Le Havre where it is preferable to walk, in order to enjoy the movement of shipping in the outer harbour beyond the rows of pleasure craft, with the long fingers of the north and south *digues* crooked round it.

At the end of the boulevard is one of the unquestioned successes of the new Le Havre, the **Musée des Beaux Arts**, whose spare lightness of glass and steel and aluminium is a welcome contrast to the inert mass of so many of the other buildings in the town. When the museum was opened in 1961 it was the most modern in Europe. The interior is planned on the principle of manipulating rather than enclosing space; screens and partitions can be adjusted to the needs of changing exhibitions. Light, too, is manipulated by means of a cellular aluminium shade and an arrangement of clear and opaque panels above the glass of the ceiling.

The collection is reasonably representative of the French, Flemish, Dutch and Italian schools, but the museum's fame rests on the works by Boudin and Dufy which have been bequeathed to it. Eugène-Louis Boudin (1824–98), a forerunner of Impressionism, was born at Honfleur, the son of a pilot, and spent most of his working life painting the seas and, even more strikingly, the shifting, luminous skies of the Normandy coast. Two hundred of the pictures here came from the artist's studio and were given to the museum by his brother, Louis Boudin. With another twenty-six paintings and seventy-six drawings and gouaches acquired from various sources, they trace his development from surprising, clumsy beginnings to the long years of mastery.

Raoul Dufy (1877–1953), who was a decorator as well as a painter, was born at Le Havre and started his artistic education at its École des Beaux Arts. In those early days he was influenced by the Impressionists. The elegance and gaiety which characterize his best-known works developed after he had gone to Paris and come in contact with the Fauves. He too found many of his subjects on the Normandy coast, but he was attracted less by the skies above it than by the movement of the people who frequented it. Most of his work here is made up of a gift from the artist in 1902 and another, much larger, made by his wife shortly before his death.

From the museum, continue along the Quai de Southampton, leaving on the right the jetty of Point Guynemer, with its radar and semaphore and congregation of tugs and pilot boats, and, just before the Viking Ferries, turn left into the Rue des Galions for the church of **Notre-Dame**, one of the relics of old Le Havre. It stands on the site of the original thatched, wooden chapel of Notre-Dame de Grâce. The present church, built between 1574 and 1638, is a mixture of Gothic and Renaissance. In the past its tower has served as both lighthouse and gun emplacement.

Walk along the north side of the church and cross the Pont Notre-Dame, which leads to the **'island' of St François**, bordered on three sides by the Bassin du Roi, Le Havre's oldest dock, the Bassin du Commerce and the Bassin de la Barre. This is what remains of Bellarmato's town. An aerial photograph – buy a postcard – will illustrate the contrast between the Wagnerian city behind and these modest houses of brick and slate, laid out in satisfyingly patterned squares, but there is hardly need for illustration. Crossing the bridge into the island is like slipping at last into a comfortable old coat made to fit.

At No. 1, Rue Jérôme Bellarmato, behind the church, a good 18c. house, well restored, has been converted into a **museum** of local history (entry free, opening times variable, check at the Syndicat d'Initiative). Besides maps and engravings relating to the early years of the port, and the usual maritime souvenirs, the museum houses the Cochet collection of Gallo-Roman and later antiquities found in Normandy and Brittany. The Abbé Cochet (1812–75), who was born at Sauvic, now a district of Le Havre, was a priest-archaeologist who did more than any other individual during the

19c., to preserve Normandy's historic and architectural patrimony at a time when it was seriously at risk from public ignorance and official philistinism. Shoberl, when he was here, collected many folk tales from the Abbé, who was then on the staff of St François. He described the Abbé as 'a very intelligent young man', while spelling his name 'Kochet'.

From the museum, continue along the Rue Jérôme Bellarmato to the Bassin du Commerce, and cross it by the bridge to the rather handsome Palais de la Bourse. Here the concrete is covered with thin slabs of grey-blue granite and the colonnaded façade is reflected in a piece of ornamental water. Turn left along the Quai George V for the Place Gambetta, which has a gigantic victory memorial, then right into the Rue de Paris to regain the Place de l'Hôtel de Ville.

The next two itineraries, taking in outlying areas, are obviously to be covered by car or bus – the latter routes are quite convenient. For the seaside suburb of Sainte-Adresse, leave the Place de l'Hôtel de Ville by the Avenue René Coty and bear slightly left into the Rue d'Ingouville, passing on the left the dismaying church of Saint-Michel, a cube of concrete with a detached belfry and a roof shaped like an open book. On the right of the Place Alphonse Martin is a far different church, **St-Michel**, the old parish church of the former hamlet of Ingouville, long become a pleasant and prosperous suburb of Le Havre. The present building, dating from 1480 and occupying the site of a Romanesque church, has suffered vicissitudes which included demotion to a chapel of ease. Since the war both status and fabric have been restored. There is an interesting use of dark flint with the white stone of the walls. The arms over the small *porte seigneuriale*, also carved in flint, are those of Jean Malet de Graville, who built the church.

The Rue d'Ingouville leads through the Place Alphonse Martin to the Rue des Gobelins, which follows a curving course to the Place Clemenceau, changing its name three times on the way. The *plage*, stretches in a shallow arc to the left. When Shoberl was here he noted that, probably because Le Havre was not a fashionable seaside resort, there was already mixed bathing, though the women wore 'bathing dresses of the most modest fashion, to which a ball dress is absolute nudity'.

In the *place* a statue of King Albert I of the Belgians recalls that, during World War I, this **quarter of Sainte-Adresse**, 'the Nice of Le Havre', whose southward-facing terraces climb the side of the Cap de la Hève, was the seat of the Belgian Government. Its name is sometimes said to be a corruption of St André. A more ingenious explanation is that, when a ship was heading for disaster on the rocks of the headland, and pilot and crew were kneeling to invoke every saint in the calendar, the master flogged them into action, crying that only *sainte adresse* (skill or dexterity) could save them. It did.

There is a grand view of the town and estuary from the summit of the headland, reached by the Rue du Roi Albert and the Boulevard Félix Faure. To extend it, climb to the platform of the **lighthouse** (visits from 8 in summer, 10 in winter, to one hour before sunset). Near by is the National Merchant Navy School. Return by the Route du Cap which leads to the sailors' chapel of **Notre-Dame-des-Flots**, 19c. Gothic and with many ex-votos. A little lower down, the brilliantly white cone of the Pain de Sucre is at once a daymark and a memorial to Général Lefebvre Desnouettes, a survivor of Waterloo, who was lost in a shipwreck off the Irish coast in 1832.

For a final view take the Rue C. Monet from the Place Clemenceau and turn left into the Rue Cochet, continuing uphill to the **Port of Saintes-Adresse**. A flight of steps leads to the viewing platform. To return to the Place de l'Hôtel de Ville, cross the Rue Cochet into the Rue Félix Faure. The way down to the Place Martin is obvious.

The last route takes us east and north-east to Graville and Montivilliers. The one now an industrial suburb of Le Havre, the other virtually a satellite, were once individual towns of some consequence, each of which grew up around a pre-Viking monastic foundation. Each has a Romanesque church as a witness to that past.

For the first, leave the Place de l'Hôtel de Ville by the Avenue René Coty, follow it round to the right and continue in a direct line to the Abbaye de Graville, by which time the Avenue René Coty has become the Avenue de Verdun.

It is believed that the first religious settlement here was established at Graville in the 8c. By the end of the 11c., it had developed into a priory. Its church was essentially that which we see today except for the choir, which is 13c., and the west front, which is 14c. The truncated north tower of the original west front survives; that on the south side was the victim, in 1360, of a 'scorched earth' policy adopted by the citizens, who feared it might be used as a gun emplacement by the English, who were threatening from Honfleur, which they then occupied. When you walk round the outside, notice the very Norman checkboard pattern in the gable of the north transept.

Since 1964, the church, which was badly damaged in 1944, has been closed for restoration. A visit to the excellent **museum** of archaeology and medieval sculpture housed in the monastic buildings adjoining, which are 13c., though they were modified during the 17c., and include a splendid crypt, is the more to be recommended (open daily, 10–12, 14–16, except Mondays and Tuesdays, All Saints' Day, 11 November, Christmas, New Year's Day and 1 May). It includes a series of photographs of the capitals of the north transept, for which the interior is famed. This is true grotesquerie, with fantasy running far ahead of technique.

There is a grand-stand view of the port from the terrace beyond the churchyard and a touch of wild surrealism within it, where the plastic carnations decorating a grave may be carefully placed in water. The huge statue of the Black Virgin near by was set up in thanksgiving for Graville's having escaped German invasion during the war of 1870–1.

If you are returning directly to Le Havre, take the former Rue de l'Abbaye, now the Rue Pablo Neruda, above the church. It leads, under various names, back to the Place Alphonse Martin. There are attractive glimpses of the estuary on the way and a memorable panorama from the Terrasse de l'Amiral Mouchez, in the Rue Georges Lafaurie, just short of the *place*. A detour by the Rue des Acacias, which turns off to the right just before the Cimetière Sainte-Marie, leads to the 250 hectares of the Forêt de Montgéon, which the municipality acquired in 1902, and laid out as a park which is part natural, part pleasure ground.

To extend the excursion to **Montivilliers**, follow the line of the Rue de Verdun as far as Harfleur and turn left into the N25. The town's name proclaims its origin; Montivilliers was originally Mostiervillier, the town of the monastery. St Philibert founded a convent in this valley sheltered by wooded hills in 683. Quenched by the Viking invasions, monastic life was restarted in the first quarter of the 11c., probably as a *cella* of Fécamp, probably, also, as a community of monks, not nuns. Its re-establishment as an autonomous nunnery in 1035 was due to Duke Robert the Magnificent, whose aunt Béatrice, daughter of Duke Richard I, was its first abbess. He endowed it so handsomely that, at the turn of the 11–12c., Montivilliers was able to carry through an ambitious building programme. Another period of prosperity three hundred years later was to be responsible for the curious appearance of the church today, its south side pure Romanesque, its north elaborately Flamboyant and out of proportion.

Montivilliers has a long history as a woollen town whose grey and scarlet cloth was in wide demand. By the 15c. wealth had brought so great an increase in the population that the nave of the abbey, which served as a parish church, divided by a screen from the nuns in the choir, was too small for its congregation. So the north side of the Romanesque nave was knocked down and replaced by the present one, extending well beyond the original north wall. Each half is admirable of its kind; the juxtaposition is disconcerting. Inside, the arch at the entrance to the apse of the south transept has a series of carvings in low relief, remarkable, some say unique, in Norman sculpture. Tentatively they have been dated at about 1100; they are certainly influenced by pre-Romanesque art.

Montivillier's cemetery still has the wooden gallery of its 16c. charnel house. To reach it, take the Rue Félix Faure from the church and continue along the Rue du Faubourg-Assiguet. The way to the cemetery is on the left opposite No. 7. There is a 15c. cross beside the charnel. To regain Le Havre, take the D32, which leaves the valley of the Lézarde by the smaller valley of the Rouelles, skirting the Forêt de Montgéon.

The 50-odd kilometres, give or take 3 or 4 for a detour, from Le Havre to Pont Audemer, provide an encapsulated version of Normandy at the start of a visit.

Harfleur, a town with a Gallo-Roman past, and, from the 9c. to the 16c., one of the most important ports of Normandy, is today to all intents and purposes an industrial suburb of Le Havre. The church of **St Martin**, whose Flamboyant tower is reflected in the surface of the Lézarde, and the château to the north of it, now the Hôtel de Ville, remain from more gracious days. There was a church on the site of St Martin in the 9c.; the present building is 15–16c. except for the fine but dilapidated west porch, which was added between 1630 and 1635. Inside there is a striking Renaissance organ case and a massive 17c. retable over the altar in the first bay of the north aisle. The château, with a pleasant public park behind it, remains a fine 16c. brick and stone house, despite zealous restoration in the 19c. It dates from 1653, and was built by Pierre Costé, whose father, a native of Le Havre, was raised from the bourgeoisie into the aristocracy by Henri IV.

Beyond Harfleur the N182 runs along the north side of the Canal de Tancarville, which enables Seine barges bound for Le Havre to avoid the sea passage at the mouth of the estuary. On the right the brindled cows graze against a frieze of chimneys; on the left the chalk cliffs rise steeply. Before the Pont de Hode, turn left for **St Jean-d'Abbetot**. The little 11c. church, high on the cliff above the river, is now closed, but the key can be obtained from the first house on the south side of the façade. In a sense it is a memorial to the Abbé Cochet. It was he who saved it when, in 1835, the local council wanted to sell it to raise the price of building a house for the schoolmaster. The church has a series of wall paintings, the most interesting of which are in the choir and crypt, ranging from the 12–13c. to the 16c.

Turn sharp right at the fork beyond the village to regain the N182 just before the approach to what is, technically and architecturally, Normandy's most distinguished post-war monument, the **Pont de Tancarville**. Its length of 1400 metres, with a single span of 608 metres, make it one of the biggest suspension bridges in Europe; its economic importance to the region is self-evident. Also it is perfectly beautiful in its precise, fine-spun tension between parallel and vertical and shallow curve. The construction took three-and-a-half years, from the end of 1955 to July 1959, and, a rarity in an industry whose accident rate is notorious, not a single life was lost.

The remaining 20 kilometres take us through picture-book Normandy, a country of thatch and half-timber, good brick houses and fine horses in green fields. **Pont-Audemer**, despite war damage, has kept many of its old houses and has the unfailing charm of a town which is threaded by a many-branched river, here the Risle. It is a pleasant place for an overnight stop. Its great church, dedicated to **St Ouen**, marries the simplicity of an 11–12c. choir and transept to a nave which was rebuilt at the end of the 15c. with the utmost magnificence. Roulland Le Roux, architect of the porch of Rouen cathedral, planned the work; only a master could have permitted himself such luxuriance of decoration without falling into vulgarity. The triforium, in particular, is exquisite in its airy elaboration. At this point, the money ran out; the clerestory is a mere apology and the roof could not be vaulted. There is a wonderful series of Renaissance windows: see particularly the vivid procession of the *confréries* (details under Les Andelys) in the second chapel of the north aisle, and the History of the People of God in the second chapel (from the east) of the north aisle. The baptistery at the west end of the north aisle has two delicate English alabasters of the late 14c., and, on the wall near by, a little Renaissance balcony so pretty that the skull grinning below it is a shock.

On leaving the church, turn right along the Rue de la République; there are attractive old houses in the Cour Canel which turns off on the right. Cross the road and come back on the other side for two more such survivals, the Rue Paul-Clémencin and the Rue Place de la Ville (not marked at this end, but the opening is between a fish shop and a café). The brick and timber houses here are being intelligently restored and the cobbled paving kept. Walk through to the Rue Notre-Dame-du-Pré. Near by, on the right, is the 17c. building of the Auberge des Vieux Puits. The interior, like the exterior, is picturesque to a fault, and the prices are *en suite*, but there is a dock leaf for this nettle in an adjoining *restaurant de routiers*.

Turn back along the Rue Notre-Dame-du-Pré and take the first left turn after the Rue Place de la Ville. It leads, by way of the Place Louis Gillain, where there is a good Louis XV brick and stone house, to the Place Victor Hugo, and so, left across a bridge over the Risle, back to St Ouen.

CHAPTER NINE

Valley of the Risle – Bec Hellouin – Brionne – Château Harcourt – Le Neubourg – Champs-de-Bataille – Beaumont-le-Roger – Louviers – Évreux

※

FROM Pont-Audemer, the green valley of the Risle runs south-west to Brionne, its 28 kilometres studded with tranquil villages and small towns. **Corneville-sur-Risle** is alternatively known as Corneville-les-Cloches, after the operetta by Robert Planquette (1848–1903). The carillon of twelve bells was cast in 1900, and destined for the church. Unhappily, the donor, the Marquis de la Roche Thulon, was unable to pay for them, and the carillon was sold privately, eventually to be acquired by a shrewd local hotelier. It can be heard on request – and on payment of a small fee – between Easter and September.

Appeville-Annebault got the second half of its name from Amiral Claude d'Annebault, a governor of Normandy, who rebuilt its 14c. church in the 16c., incorporating the original choir. Montfort-sur-Risle, with copper beech and willows beside the stream and the Forêt de Montfort coming up to its gates, is overlooked by the ruins of a castle whose origins go back to the era of John Lackland.

Nine kilometres further on, turn left into the valley of **Bec-Hellouin** for the Benedictine abbey whose links with England go back to the Conquest. Bec was one of the foci of that great flowering of European civilization which took place in the 10–11c., a centre of learning, art and government as well as of faith. Its founder was its first brother, the knight Herluin, or Hellouin, who, in 1034, changed his armour for the coarse habit of an anchorite. By 1041 thirty-one others had come to share his primitive poverty. The thirty-second, who presented himself in 1042, was the scholar-priest Lanfranc, who had left his native Italy to teach at Avranches and now longed to escape from his fame. After three years of prayerful obscurity he was persuaded to resume his teaching, and the community soon gained a reputation as a school for diplomats and royal officials as well as theologians; in an age when monarchs and nobles were commonly illiterate, it was the Church which provided most of a nation's civil servants. Lanfranc became the most valued counsellor of the young Duke William of Normandy, and was entrusted with the delicate mission to the Vatican which succeeded in obtaining the removal of the interdict imposed by the Pope for the breach of the laws of consanguinity which William had committed by marrying his cousin, Matilda of Flanders. It was natural that the Conqueror should appoint Lanfranc as the builder and first abbot of his new foundation at Caen, the Abbaye aux Hommes, which was part of the price of that removal (*see* under Caen). Long before its consecration Lanfranc had become Archbishop of Canterbury, an appointment in which Pope Alexander II as well as the Conqueror had a personal interest – he had been Lanfranc's pupil. Lanfranc's successor at Bec was St Anselm, also an Italian and one of the greatest minds of the time. He too was to become Archbishop of Canterbury.

The **abbey** at Bec is open daily for guided visits, 9.30–12, 14.30–18, except on Tuesdays and during times of services on Sundays and feast days. Today the most substantial relic of the medieval monastery whose church, modelled on Saint-Ouen at Rouen, was longer than Notre-Dame de Paris, is its detached belfry, the tower of St Nicolas. It dates from the 15c. rebuilding of the church, which was originally consecrated in 1077. The spire which once rose above the elegant pierced balcony of the tower has disappeared, but the saints whose statues crown each of its buttresses, Mary, Nicholas, John, Benedict, James, Andrew, Louis, Michael, survive. A plaque on one wall recalls that, during the 11–12c., Bec gave England three Archbishops of Canterbury, three Bishops of Rochester and seven abbots, those of Westminster, Chester, Battle, Ely, Colchester, St Augustine's, Canterbury and St Edmund's, Bury.

Of the church, only the bases of the pillars and a fragment of the blind arcade of the south transept remain to show its layout. It was deconsecrated after the Revolution and razed during the 19c. Bec's prosperity – it had large possessions in England as well as in France – and its exceptional renown had already ended. During the Hundred Years War it was virtually a fortress and its buildings were badly damaged. They were restored after 1450, but the glory had departed and decadence was rapid after the system of absentee commendatory abbots was instituted during the 16c.

The buildings beyond the church escaped deliberate destruction but were hideously dilapidated by years of use as a cavalry remount depot. They were constructed, or reconstructed, after the Maurist reform, which was introduced in 1627. Since 1948, when the abbey was classed as a historic monument and a congregation of Benedictines came back to their own, they have been lovingly restored. For the most part they are 18c., like the glorious Night Stairway, by which the monks descended from their dormitory to sing Matins in the small hours. The cloister, rebuilt in the mid-17c., keeps a single Gothic doorway, surmounted by a 13c. Virgin in Majesty. The carving in the other arches is the work of the remarkable Frère Guillaume de la Tremblaye, a gifted architect and sculptor.

The present church of the community has been converted from the majestic 18c. refectory of the Maurists. Blessed Herluin, the founder, lies in his stone coffin in the choir, beneath a striking modern wrought iron grille. The altar, of green Carrara marble, was a gift, in 1959, from the region of Aosta, St Anselm's native land; on the north wall a slab from Canterbury, inscribed 'Ut omnes unum sint', recalls Bec's ecumenical vocation as well as its English connection. The statues include a 13c. Virgin at the west end – the head is a modern replacement. Services are open to the public on weekdays (12 noon and 18.15) as well as Sundays: the Gregorian chant is a benison after the ineffable banality of the tunes which liturgical reform has brought to the average French parish church. The monastic buildings standing back on the (observer's) right of the church exemplify the good breeding of 18c. domestic architecture.

Beside the abbey is the entrance to a **museum** of vintage cars (open 15 March –30 September, daily except Thursdays, 9–13, 14–19.30; 1 October – 14 March, 10.30–13, 14–18). The village is rather consciously charming, with a renowned inn where damsels in 18c. dimity and muslin will wait on you at a price – four francs for a *demi-tasse* at my last visit – but the **parish church**, with a 14c. choir, should not be missed. It has a throng of 15–18c. statues which came from the abbey, and includes one of St Anselm, whose image is surprisingly rare in this, his own, region. There are two remarkable stone high reliefs of the 15c. in the choir: on the north side a Resurrection, on the south an extraordinary Trinity, with the crucified Christ supported by God the Father, almost as in a *Pietà*, and the Holy Dove perched on his left shoulder.

Brionne, 6 kilometres further down the valley, anciently an important junction of the Roman roads, has more accommodation and the appeal of not being too obviously geared to tourism. It is a thriving, rather sprawling market town, with a notably good *restaurant de routiers* in the central *place*. The 14–15c. stone and flint church, its squat tower capped with a sharp little steeple, has an elaborate late 17c. retable, the work of Guillaume de la Tremblaye, which came from Bec. The Syndicat d'Initiative, open only during the season, is in the *place* adjoining.

From the corner of the Place du Chevalier Herluin, the Rue des Canadiens and the footpath of the Vieux Château lead to the ruins of the 12c. **donjon** which dominates the town. It is worth the uphill slog even for those with no taste for medieval military architecture because of the wide views over the calm Valley of the Risle, especially good on a clear evening.

East of Brionne, the immense, fertile plain of Le Neubourg stretches as far as the Eure. It is not holiday country, a fact reflected both in the prices and in the character of some of the hotels, where you may sleep a little harder but will almost certainly eat a lot better than in some comparable establishments elsewhere, and reactions to it are likely to be entirely subjective. For some it is a sad steppe. Others, myself among them, are fascinated by its vast perspectives, with small, stout churches rising over the horizon like ships, and the atmosphere of the little towns speaking of a prosperity born of generations of good farming. **Le Neubourg**, 15 kilometres from Brionne by the D137, one of the most typical of them, is a good centre, and conveniently placed for the two most important châteaux of the region.

Harcourt, the first of them, 6½ kilometres on the road from Brionne, is open from 15 March to 15 November, daily except Wednesdays, 10–12, 14–18; otherwise Thursdays, Saturdays and Sundays, 14–17; it is closed during December and January. It was originally the seat of the family of the same name, was occupied by the English between 1418 and 1449, and later passed through various hands before becoming the property of the Académie d'Agriculture de France in 1828. During the intervening century and a half the Académie has greatly extended and improved the arboretum which owed its beginnings to a previous owner. It now covers 5 hectares, laid out with alleys, and includes magnificent specimens of Douglas pines, sequoias, thujas and cedars of Lebanon, among much else. With the signposted walks laid out in the adjoining park, the arboretum adds greatly to the pleasure of a visit.

The château, whose massive fortifications are being made good and, as far as possible, restored to their original appearance, dates from the late 14c. It was the third to be built on land given by Rollo to his companion-in-arms, Bernard le Danois, founder of the Harcourt family, in the first quarter of the 10c. Originally it is thought that sixteen towers guarded the walls of the enceinte, of flint and rubble banded with white stone. Eight, more or less dilapidated, remain. The severe 17–18c. inner façade of the donjon conceals an interior whose oldest parts date from the 14c. It houses a small local **museum**, including family relics, with a section devoted to the trees of the arboretum. On the left of the entrance is a 14c. well.

The village church lost its Renaissance porch in the course of road works in 1854, but has kept a 13c. apse whose seven bays have an exquisite purity and elegance. There is a nice little timbered market hall and, off the *place*, another memento of the Harcourt family in the Hôtel-Dieu built in 1695 by Françoise de Brancas, Princesse d'Harcourt, with material from walls which were demolished when she was modernizing the château. She is buried in the chapel of the hospital.

The extravagant size of **Le Neubourg**'s *places* testify to its past importance as a market centre, and the money still shows in the turn-of-the-century fantasy of some of the modern buildings. A 13c. window looking out on to the Place Aristide-Briand belongs to the remains of the 13–16c. castle, which was largely demolished in 1789. Here, in 1660, Alexandre de Sourdéac, Marquis de Neubourg, staged what is claimed to have been France's first opera, a performance of Pierre Corneille's *Toison d'Or*, by the Troupe Royale du Marais.

At the far end of the Place Dupont-de-l'Eure — he was the president of the provisional government of 1848, and his native town has set his statue here – the narrow east end of the church of **Saint-Paul** rises like the prow of a ship, with a clock for a figurehead. It was built during the 15–16c. on a scale to match the *place*, with a peculiarly Norman feature in a sharply pointed apse. The very beautiful lectern is 17c. and the statues, except for those on the high altar, which are 17c., are mostly 18c. Here too there is one of Saint Anselm, looking benign and bookish.

From Le Neubourg it is 4 kilometres north-west to the other château I mentioned, **Château du Champ-de-Bataille**, the present seat of the Harcourt family (visits 15 March – 30 June, Sundays, Mondays, Thursdays and public holidays; 1 July – 4 September, Thursday–Monday, inclusive, 10.30–12 and 14.30–18.30; 15 September – 14 March, Thursdays and public holidays only, 14–17). Forest surrounds the park of this great house (it was never a *château fort*) of the late 17c., built, says tradition, on the site of a battle between the armies of Riouf, Comte de Cotentin, and Guillaume Longue-Épée, the latter commanded by Bernard le Danois.

Graville Abbey,
Le Havre

The Pont de Tancarville.
1400 metres in length
with a single span of
608 metres

Aerial view of the Abbey of Bec-Hellouin, whose links with England
go back to the Conquest

The Château de l'Aigle dates from 1690 and is now the town hall

From its original proprietor the house passed by marriage to the Harcourts, to be lost after the Revolution. After suffering damages and indignities, which included being used as a prison at the Liberation, the house was restored to the family when the Duc d'Harcourt was allowed to transfer to Champ-de-Bataille the war damages due for the total destruction of the Château Harcourt at Thury-Harcourt. Since then he has carried out its restoration in co-operation with the *Monuments Historiques* organisation.

It is tempting to call the plan of the château unique. It consists of two near-identical wings of brick and stone with slate roofs, 80 metres long, facing each other across a grassy court. One is the house, the other, with *trompe -l'œil* windows, is the domestic wing, which now includes a *Salle des Fêtes*. They are linked on one side by a balustraded gallery with a central portico, on the other, which opens on to the park, by a low wall, topped by railings and punctuated by rectangular pillars, which has as its centre piece a monumental gateway. The classical figures which crown it represent Earth, Air, Fire and Water. Not the least remarkable feature of the remarkable whole is that its architect remains unknown.

The interior is rich in period furniture, tapestries and pictures, among the last a Fragonard of the Duc d'Harcourt, of the period, in the glowing yellow costume of a character from the Comédie Italienne. Equally interesting is a collection of relics which includes an autograph letter from Louis XIV to the first Duc d'Harcourt, then French Ambassador to Spain, and a record of the celebrations marking the millennium of a family whose service to France has covered virtually every department of the national life, culminating with the Resistance.

Those with a taste for this big, plain landscape may enjoy a day or so spent exploring its network of mostly quiet roads. **Boissey-le-Châtel**, 16 kilometres north-west of Le Neubourg by the D83, has a Renaissance château, with a ruined 12c. fortress beside it. There is a fine 15c. English alabaster altar piece in the little village church of **Écaquelon**, 5½ kilometres north-west of Boissey; that of **Bourg-théroulde**, 5 kilometres north-east of it, has a series of 16c. windows in the choir. Four kilometres south of Le Neubourg the **château of Omonville** offers an urbane 18c. façade overlooking a formal garden. In fact, only the central block and one wing was built by 1752, when the work was suspended. A century later, the château was completed according to the original plans of the architect, one Chartier, of Conches. The same care has been given to preserving or reproducing the 18c. interior, while the French formal gardens, which, under the French Second Empire, were laid out *à l'anglaise* have been restored. Unfortunately the château is not open for visits.

Beaumont-le-Roger, 13 kilometres to the south-west, on the edge of the Forêt de Beaumont, makes a pleasant half-day's excursion from Le Neubourg. In the 13c. there was a priory here, a dependency of Bec. Its dramatic ruins remain, built on a terrace pushed close against the chalk cliff into which caves, faced with stone arches, have been cut. The 'modern' church of St Nicolas, actually 14–16c., set high above the street, its south aisle acting as a buttress, has been restored after severe war damage. Regulus, the wooden figure of a Roman soldier at the summit of the tower, survived the bombing, and nods in time with the chiming clock, as he has done since 1826.

From Le Neubourg take the D133 north-west to **Louviers**, a town which has managed a smooth transition from the cloth-making, which was established here in the 12c., to the most modern light industry. Its church is soberly elegant within, gorgeously intricate without, with works of art which a cathedral might envy. The nave and choir were built in the first half of the 13c., the massive north-west tower, begun in 1414, remains unfinished. It was at the end of the 15c. that the exterior got its superb Flamboyant decoration, like an embroidered cloak thrown over the south side. For the full effect of the contrasted styles, walk round the church anti-clockwise, starting at the east end. The north side has a classical plainness, the bell tower is a fortress, the west door simple to modesty. Then one comes to the gables and pinnacles, pierced galleries and leaping buttresses of the south side, with the astonishing Porche Royal, an artefact which, in its time, has evoked all the clichés about lace, and carved ivory, and goldsmith's work, and continues to surpass them. The interior, with a gracefully lofty nave, its capitals carved with human masks, and low double aisles, calls for a leisured visit if one is to get the maximum pleasure from its wealth of statues and sculpture. Do not overlook such less conspicuous items as the 15c. *Mise au Tombeau* in a niche of the west wall, or the movingly primitive 14c. *Pietà* below the altar in the Chapelle de Challange near by, and do not fail to ask the sacristan if it is possible to see the 15c. Nottingham alabasters formerly in the church. They have been kept in safety since thieves were surprised in the act of removing them from the wall. Look, too, for the *Mangeur de Soupe* on the capital of the south-west corner of the crossing. The full-cheeked peasant clutching a bowl is a gibe at the citizens of Louviers, who, it is said, once allowed their town to be captured by an enemy because they were surprised at dinner. High up on the wall of the lantern there is a decorative little loggia from which, according to tradition, at Whitsun red rose petals were showered down on the priests. The south aisle has fine 16c. windows; the fresco of a gigantic St Christopher, with legs like tree trunks, on the wall of the baptistery is of the same period. Both windows and fresco have been restored.

From the west front of the church the Rue du Maréchal Foch, on the left, leads to the Syndicat d'Initiative, just off the Place Jean Jaurès, and the Rue de l'Hôtel de Ville, on the right, to a **Municipal Museum** which in both content and arrangement, is a good deal above what one might expect in a town of some sixteen thousand inhabitants. There is an absorbing display of the history of the local textile industry and an outstanding collection of ceramics. From the east end of the church the Rue de la Poste leads to the remains of a mid-17c. Franciscan convent, with the gallery of its cloister built round three sides of an arm of the Eure, where weeds comb the current and creepers hang over the water.

Though not obviously a tourist centre, Louviers is a very possible place at which to spend two or three nights while one explores this area. Those with a liking for smaller towns may prefer it to Évreux, 22 kilometres to the south. The road runs through wooded country following the valley of the Eure as far as **Acquigny**, which has a mid-16c. château. During the 18c. it was enlarged by the addition of two rectangular pavilions: the beauty of the whole is worthy of its setting beside the river. The church, also 16c. with 18c. additions, has sumptuous panelling and furniture. At Les Planches, beyond Acquigny, a right-hand turn offers an alternative route by the pretty valley of the Iton, no more than 7 kilometres longer than the main road.

Évreux's population, now around 50,000, has doubled since the end of the war. If, today, it is hard to recognize the 'pleasant little town, flanked by a forest, surrounded by hills and full of soldiers and clergymen' described by a traveller at the turn of the century, it is still pleasant.

The destruction of 1940, when the centre of Évreux burned for almost a week after German bombing, and of 1944, when Allied bombs flattened the area around the station, were only the latest episodes in the particularly stormy history of a town which has suffered because of its position near a provincial border. The first settlement here, the Mediolanum of the Gauls, at Le Vieil-Évreux, 6 kilometres south of the present town, was sacked by the Vandals in the 5c., and the walled town, established by the Romans on the present site, by the Vikings in the 9c. The centuries that followed were a catalogue of battle and fire and slaughter, its most horrible item the treacherous massacre by John Lackland of the entire French garrison, with the leading citizens. One can only marvel that elements of the 12c. church survive in the **cathedral**, whose restoration looks like being one of the triumphs of post-war reconstruction.

The building was Évreux's third cathedral, the first being the basilica of St Taurin, who founded the diocese in the 4c. The cathedral consecrated in 1076 was burned when Henry Beauclerc captured the city in 1119; fragments of its foundations were discovered in 1838. Reconstructed, it was burned again by Philippe Auguste in 1194. The present amalgam of virtually every phase of Gothic architecture, culminating with the Renaissance, is the result of building and rebuilding and restoration between the 12c. and 17c. The cathedral closes between 12 noon and 14.

From the wide Place du Général de Gaulle, an attractive turn-of-the-century layout, with Hôtel de Ville and Municipal Theatre looking out on lawns and flower beds and a limpid fountain, walk up the Rue de l'Horloge to the Place de la Cathédrale. Standing well back here, one gets the full effect of the north transept, which is the result of the restoration carried out by Bishops Ambroise and Gabriel Le Veneur, between 1511 and 1574. The Flamboyant reaches its full ripeness in the porch; indeed, this network of stone, this juxtaposition of fretted, narrow gable, and webbed rose and filigree parapets of galleries, is already a little overblown. The lantern rising behind it, which is octagonal, though the four turrets give the illusion that it is square, is earlier; it was added by Cardinal La Balue, Louis XI's chaplain and Secretary of State.

By contrast with this plenitude of ornament the balustrade and pinnacled flying buttresses of the 14c. choir seem restrained; the south side, where all the nave buttresses and all but one of the pinnacles are 19c. reconstructions, are simple by any standard. With the west front we are in the Renaissance, though its building was spread over half a century. The rather heavy south tower, with five storeys of colonnades, is a mid-16c. reworking of the tower of the 12c. church. On the north side the more interesting Gros-Pierre was added between 1612 and 1628. Both towers lost their upper parts in 1940, the one a short, octagonal slate tower, the other a cupola.

From the west end there is an impressive view up the nave, with the stout 12c. arches of its lower part blossoming into great Gothic windows above, to the choir, which is a globe of light.

The supreme distinction of Évreux's cathedral is its glass, which, happily, was removed for safety during the war, and the wonderful carved wooden screens of the ambulatory chapels. The grisaille windows on the north side of the nave date from 1400: that above the pulpit represents their donor, Bishop Guillaume de Cantiers, at his consecration. The pulpit itself, by Guillaume de la Tremblaye, came from Beç. A grille which shows the wrought ironwork of 18c. Normandy at its best closes the choir, vibrant with colour from its 14–15c. glass. The window of the 'three Maries' of 1452, in the slanting bay on the north side, commemorates both the end of the Great Schism of 1378–1429, during which there were rival popes at Avignon, and the entrance of Charles VII into Évreux after the expulsion of the English in 1441. King and rightful pope, Eugenius IV, appear among a troop of knights and churchmen in a glory of heraldry. Émile Mâle (1862–1954), the art historian and Académicien, called the three great golden east windows in honour of the Virgin the most beautiful of the 14c. The stalls were the gift of Charles le Mauvais, King of Navarre, in 1377. Behind the choir the Lady Chapel has windows dating from the latter half of the 15c., depicting the peers of France who were present at the sacring of Louis XI, who was a great benefactor of the cathedral. The king himself is portrayed in the second window from the centre on the south side, sheltering under the Virgin's mantle.

Panelled double doors of the 16c., elaborately carved, lead into the ambulatory from the transept. The glass of the south transept is 15c. In the east window Louis XI, this time in an ermine cloak powdered with fleurs-de-lis, is seen again, kneeling on a prie-dieu before the Virgin. The great rose, depicting the Coronation of the Virgin, surrounded by the whole host of heaven, is an orchestration of blue and crimson, gold and green.

In the ambulatory the chapels are closed by screens which are masterpieces of wood carving, mostly of the 16c., in which the Renaissance has not completely driven out the Gothic. The glass of the ambulatory chapels is glorious, and much of it 14c. The grisaille window in the fourth chapel is from the beginning of the century and there is more in the eighth and tenth, going down the north side, where there are silvery tints typical of the period. See the 15c. statue of the Virgin in the Lady Chapel and the *Pietà* of polychromatic wood, with its twisted, rigid Christ.

On the south side of the cathedral the Bishop's Palace of 1481, worthily restored, houses the excellent **Municipal Museum**, rich in a quantity of Gallo-Roman remains discovered in the district. There are two wonderful bronzes, Jupiter Stator and Apollo, and a 4c.

goblet of engraved glass. An odder Gallo-Roman relic is a hoard of 340 kilograms of silver and bronze coins of the 3c., found in 1890. Evidently it was military treasure, buried hastily at the expectation of a barbarian invasion, and never recovered. Now the whole has rusted into a mass that looks like nothing so much as a swarm of bees.

The upper floors of the museum are devoted to paintings of moderate interest – they include examples of Boudin, Jongkind, Harpignies – ceramics and furniture. The last is most attractively presented in a series of period rooms.

On leaving the museum, take the Rue de la Harpe, which leads from its south side, cross the Rue Victor Hugo and, a short distance further on, turn right into the Rue de Panette for the **Jardin Publique**. This is charmingly laid out on sloping ground, with fine trees and ornamental water. The bronze statues of Hercules, Apollo and Diana, cast by the Keller brothers who were responsible for most of the bronzes in the gardens of Versailles, were the gift of Louise de Bourbon-Penthièvre, Dowager Duchess of Orléans. The buildings of the neighbouring 17c. Capuchin convent, now used as a school, are at the bottom left-hand corner; its cloister, russet tiles contrasting with walls of pale ochre, are open daily during July and August, otherwise only on Thursdays, Sundays and public holidays.

Retrace your steps to the Bishop's Palace, then take the promenade along the bank of the Iton which follows the line of the old ramparts. Within living memory the river was an open drain; now it runs like crystal through a landscape of willows and swans and flowered banks. At the end of the promenade the Tour de l'Horloge, the belfry of 1490, rises 44 metres above the Place de Général de Gaulle. The bell in its elegantly pinnacled lantern is older than the belfry itself: it was founded at Mantes in 1406.

Saint-Taurin, the church which reputedly contains the tomb of the 4c. bishop, lies to the west. From the bottom of the Place du Général de Gaulle, turn left into the Rue du Docteur Oursel; this becomes the Rue Joséphine before reaching the church, which stands back from the road on the right.

The Benedictine abbey church, built at the end of the 11c., has known so much restoration and refashioning that it has even less unity than the cathedral. As it stands, it is mostly 14–15c., but the strictly classical west front dates from 1715.

Here too there is splendid glass; the 16c. windows of the choir illustrate the legend of St Taurin. The treasure of the church (if it is not on view, ask at the sacristy, or, failing that, the presbytery) is the

Châsse de St Taurin, a superb piece of 13c. goldsmith's work, made to contain the relics of the saint. In effect it is a miniature chapel of silver gilt, with bronze and enamel, with low reliefs illustrating incidents from the life of the saint. The rubies and emeralds and amethysts which stud it are artificial, replacements for the jewels which were lost probably during the upheaval of the Revolution, but the enamel is authentic.

The ancient tomb which is popularly believed to be that of St Taurin is in the tiny 11c. crypt beneath the choir. On your way out of the church note the odd holy-water stoup at the bottom of the south aisle; its base is a 14c. carving of a snail, with a human face.

CHAPTER TEN

Nonancourt – Tillières – Verneuil – Conches – Bernay – L'Aigle – Mortagne

✿

SOUTH of Évreux there is a plateau which, once one is through the edge of the forest on the outskirts of the town, reminds one of the plain of Le Neubourg, though with sheep to vary the arable farming. We are on the verge of the billiard table of the Beauce, 'the granary of France', whose character it shares; the amplitude and wealth of this country under ripening corn makes one realize the artificiality of many of our current concepts of riches. We are on the verge, also, of Normandy. **Nonancourt**, 29 kilometres from Évreux, was one of the towns which were fortified in the 11c. to hold the frontier, defined by the River Avre, against France. Richard Lionheart and Philippe Auguste signed their treaty of participation in the third Crusade in its château, of which only fragments remain. The huge church of **Saint-Martin**, dating from 1511, with an early 13c. tower, has splendid windows of the same period, and a couple of good statues, a Virgin and Child, which is possibly 14c., and a 15c. Saint-Anne. There is a fine 16c. organ case. The little town has kept some timbered houses; see particularly the Place Aristide-Briand, off the Grande Rue.

Tillières-sur-Avre, 11 kilometres to the west, was the first of these frontier towns to be fortified, in 1013. Now only one massive tower remains, level with the lowest of the three terraces on which the château was originally laid out. A fire in 1969 ravaged the interior of the church, whose nave is 12c. Thanks to the liberality of Cardinal Jean Le Veneur, Bishop of Lisieux and Grand Aumônier under François I, whose family owned the château, its decoration, particularly that of the south choir chapel, was an important example of Renaissance art. Restoration is in hand.

Beyond Tillières it is worth leaving the main Verneuil road for the D102, which branches off on the left to follow the valley of the Avre. Its green shade gives a foretaste of the landscape of the Pays d'Ouche, which we are approaching. Periodically the river vanishes underground, like so many of the streams of this region. **Montigny** has another 16c. church, dedicated to St Martin, with glass of the same period and, oddly for this inland area, graffiti of ships. Further on we come to the aqueduct which supplies the reservoirs of St-Cloud, near Paris. It begins at the confluence of the Avre and the Vigne, 3 kilometres or so further on.

Verneuil, the last of these frontier towns, sets one thinking of Rouen at the first glimpse of the splendid Flamboyant tower of the church of **La Madeleine**, which can stand as an equal before the Butter Tower. In fact Verneuil's tower, too, is said to have been at least partly financed from the proceeds of dispensations from Lenten abstinence. It was built between 1470 and 1520. The three storeys are crowned with the double diadem of a luxurious lantern and the buttresses are peopled by twenty-four statues.

Inside, the painted walls of nave and transept are put to shame by a series of 15c. and 16c. windows, with a particularly soft depth of colour in the Gothic choir. Pulpit and organ case, the former an elegant cage of wrought iron, are both 18c.; the many statues range from the 15c. to the 19c. The Lady Chapel has a striking painting of the Raising of Lazarus, blanched as his shroud and dazzled with life, by the 18c. painter Jean Baptiste Van Loo who, born in Provence of a Flemish family, worked for some time in England, with immense success. In the chapel to the south of it is the exquisite *Vierge à la Pomme*, of the 15c. or very early 16c. The marble tomb by David d'Angers in the south transept is a reminder of Normandy's part in the *chouannerie*, or Royalist rising against the Revolutionary Convention. It commemorates Comte Louis de Frotté, one of its leaders, born at Alençon, who was shot at Verneuil in 1800. Near by, a huge 16c. *Mise au Tombeau* has a classic restraint which is more affecting than David.

From the Madeleine, walk to the end of the *place* – the Syndicat d'Initiative is on the right – turn left into the Rue Thiers and follow it across the Place de Verdun to the Rue Notre-Dame, where turn diagonally left, and take the narrow street which opens opposite. The exterior of the church of **Notre-Dame** is pretty lamentable, the original 12c. building of *grison*, the ruddy pudding of the area, which was enlarged during the 15c. and 16c., having acquired a brick west front in the 18c., and, between 1872 and 1902, an apse and various other appendages in enthusiastic 19c. Romanesque. The interior is a museum of sculpture which rivals Écouis, most of it the work of local craftsmen. Some of the earliest and most remarkable of the statues are of wood, which does not invalidate the general truth that, though the Eure is Normandy's most thickly wooded region, the greater number of the statues which enrich even the most modest of its churches are of stone.

The font is older than the church; its base may be Carolingian. In the chapel east of it, the base of the altar has been made from a 15c. chest. The 16c. polychromatic wood statue of a man lying on a bed of straw, in a niche in the first pillar on the north side of the crossing, represents the 5c. St Alexis who, according to legend, spent the last seventeen years of his life working as a servant, unrecognized, in the house of his father, a Roman patrician. There is a good Renaissance *Pietà* in the north choir aisle. Beside it, the painting *Le Drapeau du Sacré-Coeur* by Georges Desvallières (1861–1950), a Parisian artist known chiefly for rather tortured religious subjects, is a 1914–18 war memorial.

There is a small alabaster Virgin of the 14c. on the north side of the apsidal chapel. Opposite, the quietly powerful statue of St Joseph, wearing the costume of the Corporation of Carpenters, is one of a series of stone statues produced at Verneuil during the late 15c. and early 16c., when the local workshop was employing sculptors from Rouen. The most outstanding piece of sculpture in the church is the elongated, exquisite wooden Virgin of the Calvary of the 12c. or 13c., on a pillar near the pulpit.

Walk back to the Rue Notre-Dame, and turn right for the Tour Grise, the massive drum tower of 1120, which was once the donjon of Henry Beauclerc's castle. The neighbouring 16c. church of St Laurent is now deconsecrated. There is a concentration of splendid old houses in the area between the Tower and the Madeleine. Cross the street diagonally left and walk down the Rue du Canon, where there are a number of timbered houses of the 15c. The masterpiece among them is that at the corner of the Rue de la Madeleine, with an angle turret and walls chequered in stone and flint. On the right-hand side, near the end of the street, a plaque marks the house of Artus Fillan, later to be Bishop of Senlis, who was largely responsible for building the tower of the Madeleine.

Walk back down the Rue du Canon and turn right into the Rue des Tanneries: No. 136 is a superb 16c. house with a Renaissance doorway and a façade adorned with four statuettes. At the end of the street, turn left into the little Rue du Pont-aux-Chèvres: the house at the corner of the Rue Notre-Dame is virtually its twin.

Retrace your steps and cross the end of the Place de Verdun into the Rue Thiers, which continues into the Rue Georges Clemenceau. There are more old houses here, also in the Rue de la Madeleine on the right and the Rue des Trois Maillets, on the left. In the latter a

16c. tower and a Flamboyant doorway are all that remains of the church of **St-Jean**. Time permitting, a visit should conclude with a round of the ramparts. Part of this promenade runs beside the Avre.

The stretch of country left of the line from Verneuil to Conches is largely taken up by the Forêt de Breteuil and the Forêt de Conches, the first private, the second domainal. If you do not plan to spend a day or two at Conches and make it a centre for exploring the area, it is worth taking a rather meandering route between the two points. Follow the main road north to **Breteuil-sur-Iton**, where the river has been tapped to form a lake between the town and the forest. The church of St-Sulpice has a handsome lantern tower which, like the earliest part of the nave, is 11c., and, inside, a 16c. balustrade to the organ gallery decorated with the figures of twelve angel musicians.

Turn left into the N830, which runs through the forest to **Rugles**, a small town typical of many in the Pays d'Ouche, in that it still engages in the iron industry which has been carried on in the area since Roman times. Today Rugles, like its neighbour, L'Aigle, specializes in making pins. Both its churches are remarkable. Notre-Dame-outre-l'eau keeps from its 10c. foundation the north walls of the nave and apse. St-Germain is huge, with a remarkable Flamboyant tower rising above its 13c. nave.

From Rugles, one has the option of following the N840 north along the Valley of the Risle as far as the twin villages of La Vieille Lyre and La Neuve-Lyre, where it turns right through the forest for Conches, or of branching off it at Aubenay into the main D61, which threads the forest diagonally, crossing the area sometimes known as The Desert.

Conches, set on a spur of rock rising out of the forest and bounded by a long loop of the river Rouloir, is a delightful town, with a ruined donjon, old houses, a wide main street and ample green space. But the town takes second place to the elegantly ornate 15–16c. church of **Ste-Foy**, with its series of windows which are among the finest existing examples of 16c. glass painting.

Town and church owe their modern origins – there were both Celtic and Roman settlements here – to Roger de Tosny, a descendant of Rollo, first Duke of Normandy and a forebear of that Raoul de Tosny who was the Conqueror's standard-bearer at Hastings. He returned from a pilgrimage to Conques-en-Rouergue, in Aquitaine, site of the cult of the child saint Foy (Faith), with relics, enlarged the existing church and changed its dedication from St Cyprien to Ste Foy, at the same time changing the name of the town from Chatillon to Conques, later modified to Conches.

Roger de Tosny's church was wholly rebuilt at the turn of the 15–16c. The apse and choir, the earliest part of the reconstruction, rise above the nave; the façade dates mainly from the early 16c., though the north tower, never completed, was added as late as 1620. The south tower, with its pierced and crocketed spire, slightly out of true, is a replacement for the original, which was wrecked in a hurricane in 1824.

Édouard Herriot (1872–1957), who was a writer as well as a politician whose career culminated in the Presidency of the French National Assembly from 1947 to 1954, said that, in the glass of Conches, Christian luxury had reached its extreme limit. If that is debatable, it is hard to counter his next sentence: 'The eye has no longer a glance to spare for the altar, it is all for the magic of the windows'. Those in the north aisle, devoted to the glory of the Virgin, begin with the sumptuous golden window of St Adrian and St Romain (leading his legendary monster captive) on either side of Our Lady, which is an outstanding work by Arnoult de Nimègue. The fifth window, of the Annunciation, is a copy of the original, which was destroyed by a fire in the workshop where it had been taken for restoration.

The seven remarkable choir windows, slightly earlier in date, are by Romain Buron, the 'Master of Gisors', who worked at Beauvais. In the upper lights, devoted to the Passion, he was clearly inspired by Dürer. The lower lights depict the life and martyrdom of Ste Foy. There is German influence also in the glass of the south aisle, devoted to the Sacrament of the Eucharist. Among them is the most celebrated window in the church, the Mystical Wine Press (fourth from the west end), whose intensity of colour comes from a Paris workshop. The ringing gold of the Fall of the Manna, next to it, is thought to be from the royal workshops of Fontainebleau.

The best of Conches's many old houses are opposite the church; it is possible to visit the remarkable cellars beneath them. Formerly, underground passages connected these with the cellars of the 12c. donjon whose ruins stand in the gardens on the south side of the church (access to it by a wooden staircase which is lethally slippery in wet weather). To visit its dungeons, apply to the concierge at the Hôtel de Ville on the other side of the public park. There is a memorable view over the valley of the Rouloir from the terrace between the donjon and the church; the rather fine statue of a wild boar which has stood there since 1958 symbolizes the untamed character of the Pays d'Ouche.

Return to the church and turn right along the Rue Ste Foy (the

Syndicat d'Initiative is at No. 20) which is prolonged by the Rue du Val. On the right, perhaps 250 metres beyond the Place Sadi Carnot, the hospital occupies the site of the former Benedictine abbey of St Pierre. Today, all that remains of its church is a row of flying buttresses and some Romanesque arches.

West of the town, the valleys of the Rouloir and the Iton are pleasant for pottering, leisurely motoring. The lordly view of Conches on its height as one returns to it, is in itself sufficient justification for such an outing. At **Bonneville**, about half-way to Évreux (branch right off the main road at Glisolles) there are the ruins of the Cistercian abbey of Notre-Dame de la Noël, founded in 1227 by the Empress Matilda, daughter of Henry Beauclerc.

The Bernay road leaves Conches by the valley of the Rouloir; the river rises from the lake on the left, just outside the town, and runs through a land of woods and water, with timbered cottages and attractive village churches, often chequered in stone and flint. **La Ferrière-sur-Risle** 14 kilometres on the way, has kept its beautiful little 14c. market hall. Its church, with an early 13c. tower, has a surprisingly rich interior, including a splendid Louis XIV altar.

Seven kilometres further on the **Château de Beaumesnil**, the façade of brick banded with stone, richly decorated but never threatening heaviness, reflected in water and set in a classical French park, is the most civilized sight which the first half of the 17c. has left us in this part of Normandy. Beaumesnil's first owner, or first recorded owner, was Robert de Meulan, whose father had been Regent of Normandy while the Conqueror was invading England. In the mid–13c. the property passed to the Harcourt family; during the Hundred Years War Henry V gave it to Lord Willoughby, the English commander between 1431 and 1436.

Of the medieval fortress, the foundations of the donjon, now transformed into a labyrinth, are all that remain. The present château dates from 1633, when the Marquis de Nonant, who had acquired Beaumesnil some thirty years earlier, commissioned Jean Gaillard of Rouen to draw up the plans. It was completed around 1640. Jean de la Quintinie (1626–88), an agronomist and landscape gardener who worked with Le Nôtre, is credited with having laid out the gardens.

Since then Beaumesnil has passed through various hands, including, after World War I, those of the Grand Duke Dimitri of Russia. During World War II, when it was owned by M. Jean de Furstenberg, archives and MSS from the Bibliothèque Nationale were lodged here.

Visitors are not admitted to the château, but they are allowed in the park (10–17) except on Sundays and during August: apply to the concierge on the left of the entrance. The chance of closer study of the house which Jean de la Varende, the novelist of the Pays d'Ouche, has called 'a dream in stone' is not to be missed.

Bernay, another excellent centre which is highly interesting in itself, has a place in literary history as the birthplace of the 12c. *trouvère*, Alexandre de Bernay, who evolved the iambic line of twelve syllables known henceforth as the alexandrine. The town still centres around the abbey founded in the 11c. by Judith de Bretagne, wife of Duke Richard II of Normandy and grandmother of the Conqueror. The Hôtel de Ville, the Syndicat d'Initiative and other public offices are housed in the 17c. conventual buildings; the abbey church, the museum and the shady public gardens are grouped together south-east of the Rue Thiers, the central section of Bernay's long main street (turn off it into the Rue Robert Lindet).

The **abbey church**, deconsecrated at the Revolution, when it had only seven monks, suffered scandalous mutilation and neglect during the 19c. when, for a time, it served as a corn market. It is now undergoing the restoration which will reveal it as a rarely interesting example of Romanesque in Normandy, rare because, started early in the 11c., it preserves Carolingian and even Merovingian traditions which survived the Viking invasions. The exterior, lopped of two bays of the nave, is lamentable; the interior (apply to the concierge at the museum, which opens on to the public gardens) fascinating above all for the carvings of the capitals, which are almost the only relief in its austere height. Particularly interesting are those recently discovered in the south transept, where the figures of beasts and men are as flat as a line drawing, unrelated to the shape of the supporting pillar, and those in the north choir aisle, which include ornament in low relief inspired by pre-Romanesque decoration. One of the craftsmen has signed his work with a clear 'Izembardus'.

The refectory of the monks, a vaulted 17c. chamber, now the courtroom, may be seen if you apply to the conciergerie south of the church. Some of the treasures of the monastic library, with those from other religious houses in the town, also from Bec, are now in the Municipal Library, thanks largely to Thomas Lindet, *curé* of Sainte Croix at the time of the Revolution, who has some claim to be regarded as the founder of public libraries in France. As a deputy of the clergy in the États Généraux he was the author of a decree passed by the Assembly in 1781 which kept the monastic libraries for the benefit of all.

Bernay's **museum**, one of the first to be founded in Normandy, occupies the handsome 17c. house, chequered in brick and stone, which was once the abbot's lodging. It is now a worthy setting for an outstanding ceramic collection, with Rouen pieces predominating. The tiles bearing the monogram of the Connétable Anne de Montmorency were made there in 1542, and came from Montmorency's château of Écouen in the Seine-et-Oise; the chessboard is the only one ever made in Rouen. Unfortunately the pieces are elsewhere. There are some interesting plates and dishes with designs of the Revolution and the Convention, mostly from Nevers. Note the *épi de faîtage*, an ornament traditionally crowning the rooftree of a house like a secular weathercock, because we shall see one or two in the town; they used to be made at Verneuil.

Cross the Place de l'Hôtel de Ville – the local worthy whose statue dominates it deserves his pedestal more than many of his kind for he is the 18c. surgeon, Jacques Daviel, who pioneered the operation for cataract – retrace your steps to the Rue Thiers and turn right. The enormous church of **Sainte-Croix**, which took the better part of a century in building, starting in 1374 with the choir, ending with the ornate west tower and undergoing later restorations and additions, is rich in furniture from Bec. Two of the most important items meet you as you enter the church, the pair of tombstones of 15c. abbots upright against the pillars of the organ gallery. Before continuing up the church, turn to see the gilded wood low relief of the Bearing of the Cross above the doorway. There are more tombstones of Bec abbots in the south transept – that of Guillaume d'Auvilars is particularly fine – but the most spectacular of the monuments from the abbey church are the sixteen great statues of apostles and evangelists, dating from the late 14c. or early 15c., on the pillars of the nave and choir, and the work ascribed to the monk Guillaume de la Tremblaye, the terracotta statues of St Maur and St Benoît at the entrance to the choir and the massive red marble high altar of 1685. The tender Nativity above it, with the figure of St Joseph in wood, Our Lady in terracotta and the radiant Child in marble, has been attributed, doubtfully, to the 17c. Marseillais sculptor, Puget.

If you feel you have seen the Entombment in the north transept before, you probably have: it is a cast of the 15c. one in the church of La Madeleine, Verneuil.

Turn right along the north side of the church and right again into the Rue Alexandre, where the *trouvère* was born. There are a number of interesting old houses along it. Cross the Place de l'Hôtel de Ville into the Rue de la Victoire, turn right along the Boulevard Dubus, then left at the railway station (subway for pedestrians) into the Rue Bernard-Gombert for **Notre-Dame-de-la-Couture**.

The church occupies the site of a former pilgrimage chapel, where the object of veneration was a statue of the Virgin said to have been found in a field – 'couture' here is a corruption of 'culture', in the farming sense. It is 15–16c., with walls patterned in black and white and a north-west tower with pinnacles and an elegant spire. The interior, except for the ambulatory and its chapels, is vaulted with oak. There are admirable 15–16c. windows and, in the choir, sixty-four oak stalls intended for leading citizens as well as clergy and singers. Forty-six of them were made in the year 1625 by two local woodcutters, Robert and Michel du Moulin, who did the pulpit of Sainte-Croix. The naïve 17c. Virgin on an unsuitable modern altar in the north transept is the object of the pilgrimage which still takes place on Whit Monday, with the local *confréries* taking part.

From the church, turn left up the Rue-du-Repos, then right by the Rue Kléber Mercier and the Place de Verdun, to the **Rue du Général de Gaulle**, which, with its continuation, the **Rue Thiers**, has some of the best old houses in Bernay. The 18c. mansion at No. 4, built by Gabriel, was the house of the collector of the Gabelle, or salt tax; No. 8, in the Rue Thiers, a 16c. house with a richly carved timber façade, the town house of the Duc d'Alençon. Best of all is the 16c. house behind No. 31 (entry to the court through the shop, L'Éveil de Bernay), a glorious brick building with barley sugar pillars, ceramic *épis* on the finials and a TV aerial between them.

A couple of kilometres north-east of Bernay, in the valley of the Charentonne, the village of **Menneval** has the oldest *confrérie de charité* in the region. It claims to have been founded in 1066, though the registers go back only to 1528.

For L'Aigle, leave Bernay by the D33, which runs up the valley of the Charente. **Broglie**, locally pronounced 'Brog-ly', elsewhere 'Bro'y', a riverside village at the foot of a wooded slope, was originally known as Chambrais. It took its present name from the Piedmontese family of Broglio, later Broglie, one of whose members, François-Marie, served in the royal army and became a Marshal of France. Chambrais, later to be elevated to a dukedom, came to the family in 1716. The succession was to produce two more Marshals of France, a number of statesmen and diplomats and, in a later generation, two distinguished scientists, the Duc Maurice de Broglie and his brother, Prince Louis de Broglie, who was a Nobel Prize winner in 1929. Their laboratory was set up in the north wing

Woman selling local lace
at Lisieux

The Basilica at Lisieux
built in honour of
St Thérèse of the Child
Jesus and a centre of
pilgrimage today

The Abbaye aux
Hommes at Caen

The 'theatrically picturesque' port of Honfleur

of the château, an enormous, low building – its two storeys of flint and pudding extending over 240 metres – which replaced an old fortress at the end of the 17c. Sadly, since it is rich in history, the château is not open to the public.

The church of **St Martin**, built in the second half of the 11c., of the *grison* typical of the Pays d'Ouche, keeps from that period its striking west front, with a blind arcade of crossed arches over the door and a little turret over the gable. The picture of St Sebastian being ministered to by the Holy Women north of the choir is attributed to Georges de La Tour, the 17c. Lorraine painter, whose use of chiaroscuro derived, if indirectly, from Caravaggio.

At **Anceins**, 17 kilometres further on, the D52 leaves the valley on the left for La Ferté-Fresnel. Leave the village by the D31 for Saint-Evroult-Notre-Dame-du-Bois, near the source of the Charentonne and on the edge of the forest of Saint-Evroult. Today the entrance porch, the abbot's lodging and some arches of the 13c. church are all that remains of the **Abbey of Ouche**, whose intellectual influence during the 12c. was comparable to that of Bec. The first monastery grew up around the forest hermitage of the 6c. St Evroult; the second foundation, in the 11c., counted Lanfranc and the Empress Matilda among its benefactors. Ordericus Vitalis (1075–1142), the chronicler, was a monk here; there is a monument to him in the *place* though he had to wait until 1912 before it was set up. Restoration of the abbey buildings began in 1966. There is a small museum containing some of its *objets d'art*, including two 13c. reliquaries.

From Saint-Evroult, the D13 runs east, first through woods, then across the plateau separating the valley of the Charentonne from that of the Risle. **L'Aigle** is a centre for wire-drawing, as well as the making of pins and needles, but the two thousand years of metallurgy which this valley has known has left little mark on the town. The church of **St Martin** is the mish-mash of styles to be expected when one knows that its building went on sporadically from the 12c. to the 16c., with extensive post-war restoration, but unexpectedly attractive in its contrast of the 12c. south-west tower of russet *grison*, with a short, slate-hung needle-pointed spire, and the white stone tower with an axe-head roof in the north-west, which was built during 1494–99. The modern statues in the niches on the south wall of the nave include a Sainte-Geneviève and a Jeanne d'Arc by Paul Belmondo, father of the screen actor, Jean-Paul. Only two of the 16c. windows, one on the south side of the choir, the other at the east end of the north aisle, survived the bombing of 1944. There is a

17c. altar of almost Venetian splendour and remarkable pendants in the south aisle.

The elegant château of 1690 in the wide *place* south of the church, a brick and stone building by Hardouin-Mansart, is now the *mairie*. Beside it, the Musée Juin 1944 recreates the Battle of Normandy by means of maps, wax figures and the recorded voices of Churchill, Roosevelt, de Gaulle, Leclerc and Stalin.

South-west of L'Aigle we are in the Perche, a land of hills and forests and pasture, where horse-breeding is at least half as old as the ironworks in the neighbouring Pays d'Ouche. The Great Horse of medieval battles and tournaments was evolved in these parts, a cross of Arabs brought home by the Crusaders with the honest native breed, made strong and supple by the rich grassland and the unevenness of the country. That grand draught horse, the Percheron, is his descendant.

The pleasantest route for Mortagne-au-Perche, another desirable stopping place in this region, is also the most direct, the D830, which runs through the Forêt de la Trappe and the Forêt du Perche, more than 2000 hectares of oak and beech and pine, hilly and studded with lakes. Seventeen kilometres from L'Aigle, a road on the right leads to the abbey of **La Grande Trappe**, a kilometre distant (no visits, but at 16 each day slides dealing with the life of the monastery are shown). La Trappe originated from a votive chapel built here in 1122 by Rotrou, Comte du Perche, in memory of his wife, who was lost in the White Ship, but owes its fame to the strict reform of the Cistercian Order instituted in the 17c. by the Abbé de Rancé. James II of England was among the great who made retreats here at that period. The Revolution brought the only break in the religious life which the abbey was to know in more than eight centuries. Even then a group of monks reorganized the community in Switzerland, until they returned to their home in 1812.

Mortagne, set on a hill, with mellow grey walls and russet roofs, and the sense of ease and space that often graces a provincial capital, has some justification for its claim to be the most beautiful town in France. During the 17c. there must have been much poverty along with the aristocracy which built its comely houses, for, in 1627, when Richelieu founded the Compagnie de la Nouvelle France, 150 families from the Perche emigrated to Canada. The emigration is commemorated in a modern window (third on the north side) of the church of **Notre-Dame**, whose south-west tower, first raised in the 17c., but the victim of successive calamity and restoration extending into the 19c., dominates the central *place*.

The church itself, built between 1494 and 1533 to replace the chapel of the old château, known as the Fort Toussaint, is remarkable for the carving of the nave roof, with garlands and pendants, and for the 18c. woodwork of the east end, which came from the charterhouse of Val-Dieu.

Leave the church by the north door, which has lost the upper part of its delicately carved Flamboyant gable, and turn right. Behind the east end the Porte Saint-Denis, a 15c. arch given two upper storeys in the 16c., which is all that remains of Mortagne's fortifications, houses a small **folk museum** (seasonal opening only). The 17c. building beside it was once the town house of the Comtes du Perche; beyond it the Palais de Justice, at the bottom of the Rue du Portail-Saint-Denis, is the old collegiate church of Toussaint, with a 16c. house on the left of it.

Turn right into the Rue des Quinze Fusillés, then left along it to the junction of the Rue de Longny: the hospice, once the old Franciscan convent, has an attractive 15c. **cloister** (apply to the concierge for entry).

Retrace your steps to the Place du Général de Gaulle and turn left past the arcaded market hall (the turreted house to the right of it is 16c.) for the Hôtel de Ville. The **public garden** behind it is a look-out over the landscape of the Perche.

There is agreeable motoring in the adjoining forests, where avenues originally pierced for hunting are now roads, though minor ones. Church-crawlers may be interested in **Loisé**, on the D8, which has a 15–16c. church, with more woodwork from Val-Dieu; **Autheuil**, with one of the few well-preserved Romanesque churches in the Perche, and **Tourouvre**, where there is a 15c. painting of the Adoration of the Magi.

From Mortagne to Alençon, the N12 runs for 35 uneventful kilometres, mostly through open country, crossing the Sarthe at Le Mêle and skirting the little Forêt de Bourse during the latter half of the route.

CHAPTER ELEVEN

Alençon – Sées – Argentan – Haras du Pin – Vimoutiers – Livarot – Orbec – Lisieux – Saint-Pierre-sur-Dives – Falaise

❧

ALENÇON's size and style, unexpected in a town whose population is well below thirty-five thousand, are due to a past as the seat of a ducal court, and its continuing prosperity to its position as a market and commercial centre for an area of fat farming country. It makes lace for prestige and Moulinex kitchen appliances for profit; the latter factory employs three thousand people.

Entering the town by the Rue Saint Blaise, you pass on the right the handsome brick and stone **Prefecture**, where Elisabeth d' Orleáns, Duchesse de Guise, spent the last twenty years of her life (1676–96). Opposite is the birthplace of Sainte Thérèse de l'Enfant Jésus, (*see* under Lisieux), with a communicating chapel.

Continue to the Place Lamagdeleine, the heart of the town, with the Syndicat d'Initiative at No. 60, Grande Rue, at the far side of it. The remarkable west porch of **Notre-Dame** was added to the church, whose building began in 1444, between 1500 and 1516. Its three gables, with their elaborately carved balustrades, which have more than a hint of Saint-Maclou, represent the summit of the Flamboyant. On the central gable is a group of the Transfiguration (the Christ is a replacement of 1966), famous for the fact that St John has his back to the street. The pinnacles and flying buttresses of the nave continue the mood: the east end, which was rebuilt in a ponderous classical style after a fire in 1744, is best ignored.

Inside, the nave gains height from the elongated arches of the triforium. Carvings of men and monsters and foliage decorate the vault, but the most memorable feature of the church is its 16c. glass. The windows on the north side are devoted to the Old Testament, those on the south to the New, with a marvellous Stem of Jesse in the west window, where living green mingles with a blaze of crimson.

North-east of the church the 15c. Maison d'Ozé contains part of

148

the local museum (open daily except Mondays, 10–12, 14–18; closes at 16 from 30 September to 15 March).

To see Alençon lace made, walk down the Rue du Pont-Neuf south-west of the church. The **École Dentellière** (open 15 May – 30 September, 10–12, 14–18; Sundays and Mondays, 15–18 only; 1 October – 14 May, 10–11.30, 14–17; closed Sundays and Monday mornings), is on the left, just before the bridge over the Sarthe, here a sluggish stream.

The origins of *point d'Alençon* are said to go back to the 15c. Its immense popularity began in 1665, when Colbert set up a royal lace factory in the town, so that French francs should not be spent on the newly introduced *point de Venise*. Today the factory, with its fifteen or twenty lacemakers, including apprentices, is a state prestige industry, like the factories of Sèvres and Gobelin. Seventy-five per cent of the work on view is destined to be the kind of gift exchanged by heads of state on courtesy visits. A piece of lace scarcely bigger than a postage stamp sells for 300f. and represents 25–30 hours' work.

Walk over the bridge and down the Rue-du-Mans to the Place de la 2me DB – the 2me Division Blindée, or 2nd Armoured Division, was Leclerc's unit – where a statue of Général Leclerc commemorates the fact that Alençon was the first French town to be liberated by his unit. Leave the *place* by the Rue de Sarthe, which crosses the river again. The church of **St Léonard**, on the left, Quaker plain without, has a graceful Flamboyant nave. The Rue Balzac – the novelist set two of his books, *La Vieille Fille* and *Le Cabinet des Antiques*, in Alençon – and the Rue Porte-de-la-Barre lead to the wide and breezy **Place Foch**.

On the left a pair of lowering, machicolated gate towers of the 15c., with a taller 14c. tower behind them, remain from the château which Jean, the first Duc d'Alençon, built on a site which had been fortified since the 10c. Beyond it, separated by the Palais de Justice, the late 18c. Hôtel de Ville, its façade crowned by a campanile, describes a taut arc. The **art gallery** and part of Alençon's superb collection of lace is housed here (opening times as for the Maison d'Ozé), unfortunately inadequately through lack of space. The collection is interesting, with peaks as varied as a Ribera of *Christ Bearing the Cross*, Philippe de Champaigne's *Assumption*, the livid, naked figure of Géricault's *Naufragé* and a *Mariage de la Vierge* by the Rouen painter, Jean Jouvenet (1644–1717).

Leave the *place* by the Rue du Collège, diagonally opposite. The **Municipal Library** on the left, once the chapel of the Jesuit College,

founded in 1620, stacks its books in carved cupboards of 18c. oak –
more spoils from Val-Dieu – and has 17c. low reliefs, of the four
Evangelists, from the Capuchin convent. There is more 17c. carving
on the door panels.

Opposite the library the Rue Langlois, and the Rues des Petites et
Grandes Poteries pass through a district of comely and substantial
18c. houses to regain the Place Lamagdeleine.

Alençon, with the forests of Écouves and Perseigne respectively
north-west and south-east of it, and the grandiosely named but
attractive Alpes Mancelles due west, is an excellent touring centre.
It is the eastern gateway to the recently constituted national park of
Normandy-Maine. The Syndicat d'Initiative can normally supply
details of routes through its 135,000 hectares and information
about possibilities for riding and fishing, but the centre for complete
documentation on the park is the Ferme du Chapitre, at **Carrouges**,
26 kilometres west of Alençon, a 15c. building which was once a
maison des chanoines.

The D26 leads to Sées by way of the Forêt d'Ecouves, which is
populated by red and roe deer and wild boar. The Signal d'Écouves,
rising a kilometre west of the right-hand turn for Sées, is one of the
two highest points in western France, the other being the Signal des
Avaloirs in the Alpes Mancelles. Both spring from the final upthrust
of the Breton granite.

Sées is a city-village with an exquisite cathedral. Convents and
colleges, seminaries and bishop's palace, keeping their atmosphere
even when they have lost their function, drowse around its spires in
a calm which makes it difficult to envisage the provincial metropolis
of Gallo-Roman Sées. The 13–14c. cathedral of **Notre-Dame**, originally dedicated to SS. Gervais and Protais, is at least the fourth to be
built on the site. Its immediate predecessor was destroyed by fire in
the frontier wars of 1174. The building it replaced had itself been
involuntarily set alight in 1048 by its own bishop, Yves de Bellême,
in an attempt to smoke out two of his enemies who had taken refuge
inside. The present building has suffered from the instability of its
foundations. The massive buttresses which mar the façade were
added in the 16c. to prevent the collapse of the towers; the spire was
reconstructed during the 19c. By contrast, the nave, which delights
alike by the harmony of its proportions and the refined richness of
its decoration, has not been restored since it was completed towards
the end of the 13c. At the crossing a sheaf of slender engaged
columns at each angle prepare the eye for the ethereal grace of the
choir. There is outstanding tracery in the rose windows of the

transepts, 14c. glass in the ambulatory chapels and 13c. in the high windows of the choir. On the capital of the pillar at the south-east end of the choir there is a gallery of thirty or so human heads, mostly comic. The 18c. marble bust of Christ in the south transept has been attributed to J.-J. Caffieri (1725–92); near by is the ravishing Notre-Dame de Sées, a late 13c. marble figure touched, or retouched with gold in our own day.

North of the church the 13c. chapter house, effectively restored, is now a **folk museum** (for opening hours, apply at the Hôtel de Ville). South-east are the 18c. Bishop's Palace in the Rue d'Argentré and the equally majestic Abbaye Saint-Martin, reached by a footpath opening opposite the palace. The one is now a school, the other a children's home.

From the abbey an avenue of limes leads to the Rue St Martin, with, on the left, the church of **Notre-Dame de la Place**, which has a dozen 16c. low reliefs of the life of Christ. Walk back along the Rue Saint Martin as far as the Rue de la République; to the right the 17c. chapel of the **Hôtel-Dieu** has some panels painted at the age of fourteen by Nicolas-Jacques Conté, the 18c. chemist and engineer. Conté, who was born at Saint-Géneri, near Sées, was one of the founders of the Paris Conservatoire des Arts et Métiers.

Departures from the flat and uneventful 25 kilometres of the road to Argentan will let one see three strikingly contrasted châteaux.

O, the most famous of them, which is a kilometre down the Médavy road (turn right just before Mortrée), was until recently used as a children's holiday home, which meant a ban on visits between 1 July and 10 September. This may no longer apply: ask about current hours at the Syndicat d'Initiative at Alençon. Access is to the park only, but is well worth while for the closer views it affords of a building whose chequered walls and mitred roofs, surrounded by a moat so wide that the house seems to rise from a lake, are strikingly beautiful.

Its three pavilions, late Gothic, early Renaissance and 18c. respectively, are built round a courtyard whose fourth side is closed by a balustrade. The oldest part was built for Jean I d'O, whose family was already distinguished at the time of the Crusades, and who was himself Chamberlain to King Charles VIII. Charles d'O continued the work, but the château owed most of its magnificence to Charles' grandson, François d'O, who was Finance Minister and Master of the Wardrobe to Henri III, and a leading member of that monarch's retinue of favourites.

Vastly rich in his own right, he further enriched himself from state funds, but his competence in exacting taxes from the citizens of France seems to have outweighed his dishonesty. Only if this was so can one account for his having kept his post under Henri IV. Certainly it was not due to the King's unawareness, for, when he pronounced François d'O's panegyric, Henri de Navarre is recorded as saying: 'S'il faut que chacun rende ses comptes là-haut, ce pauvre O se trouvera bien empêché à fournir de bons acquits pour les siens' ('If we all have to present our accounts in heaven, poor O will be hard put to it to produce valid receipts for his').

'Poor O' died bankrupt and the château was sold to pay his debts, passing through several hands before, some years ago, it was acquired by the Association for the Development of Naval Social Work.

Three kilometres further on, two tremendous cylindrical towers, which acquired slate domes and lanterns in the 17c., mark the entrance to the château of **Médavy** (visits on application in advance). They are all that remain of the medieval fortress, the four corners of whose ramparts were marked by towers. The present château, a gracious 18c. building, whose central block occupies the site of the old donjon, was started by Maréchal de Médavy, the victor of the battle of Castiglione, whose exploits are recorded in a painting which hangs in the hall of the château. After his death in 1724 it was completed by his brother, the Marquis de Grancey, at so ruinous a cost as to leave his successors no option but to dispose of the property. Today it is once more occupied by the Médavy-Grancey family.

Sassy, the third of this group of châteaux (to reach it, follow the D219 back to the main road, cross it and turn right), is open daily from 15 to 18 at Easter and Whitsun and during June, July and August. The exterior, of soft pink brick, with stone, looking over three descending terraces to the satisfying pattern of a formal garden, is ravishing; nothing in this perfect 18c. building betrays that the work, begun in 1760, was interrupted by the Revolution and completed only under the Restoration.

Its owner is a descendant of Étienne Pasquier (1529–1615), the great jurist whose monumental *Recherches de la France* occupied him for over forty years. He found time, nevertheless, to conduct a vigorous polemic against the Jesuits, whose claim to the right to teach in the University of Paris he opposed in 1565, and even to write some minor verse. A later member of the family, Étienne-Denis Pasquier (1767–1862), whose father was guillotined during the Revolution while he himself was arrested as a Royalist, became Chancellor of France when that office was revived in 1837. The outstanding treasure of his library, which, with his portrait and other souvenirs, is to be seen at the château, is a copy of his *Catéchisme des Jesuites*, with notes in the author's own hand.

St Christopher-le-Jajolet, a kilometre further on, has become a centre of pilgrimage for motorists; you may wish to avoid it on the saint's day, 25 July, and the Sunday after, when they come in droves to salute a large statue of the saint and have their cars blessed. Bear right to regain the main road.

Argentan, a major road and rail junction, was massacred in August 1944, when the pincer movement of the Allied armies enclosed the last pocket of German resistance. By the 21st of the month, when the Battle of Normandy ended with the capitulation of the German Seventh Army, more than three-quarters of the town had been laid waste.

The 12–13c. **donjon** of the château on the north-east side of the central Place Mahé is a good viewpoint for seeing the extent of the new building. Across the *place* the 14c. triple-towered château of the dukes of Alençon is now the courthouse. The neighbouring chapel of Saint Nicolas, also 14c., which once served it, now houses the Syndicat d'Initiative, also a fine 18c. altar piece. If, after Alençon, you are still interested in lace making, get directions here for visiting the Benedictine abbey of **Notre-Dame**, where it is still made by the nuns.

Cross the *place* diagonally for the church of **Saint Germain**, whose restoration has been a heroic task. Its building extended over three centuries, culminating in 1642, when the west tower got its lantern dome. There is a splendid Flamboyant north porch, with a 16c. statue of the Virgin between St Joseph and St John.

The interior, unusual in having a four-sided apse and transepts also ending in apses, has a particularly graceful triforium and a double choir ambulatory, with elaborate pendant bosses in the outer gallery. There is a 16c. stone *Pietà* on the south-east pillar of the nave and a panel painting of the Adoration of the Magi, dating from 1602, in the south transept. The carving of a saddle-pack mule half-way up a pillar on the south side of the crossing is more likely to be a relic of a large-scale medieval Crib than a likeness of the beast who carried the materials for the building of the church, as legend says. More fancifully, it is sometimes said to commemorate the ass which died from the effort of carrying Saint Germain to Ravenna and was restored to life by its owner.

From the north side of the church, the Rue de la Vicomté leads to the 15c. **Tour Marguerite**, the last relic of the fortifications. The Hôtel-Dieu further along on the right, was an 11c. foundation which, in the 12c., benefited from the munificence with which Henry II tried to atone for Becket's murder. This part of the town has an air of faded splendour shared by the Gothic-Renaissance church of **Saint-Martin** in the street of the same name, despite the elegance of its octagonal tower.

In the rather sad little *place* beyond the church two slate-domed towers mark the 18c. Hôtel Raveton which sheltered Charles X on his way to exile in Britain in 1830. The Sous-Préfecture at No. 11, Rue Pierre Ozenne, off the Rue Saint Martin, was the town house of Jules le Corday, cousin of Charlotte (*see* under Caen). At No. 17 James II stayed in 1692 after the failure of his attempt to land in England and reclaim his throne.

There is pretty country west of Argentan. At **Écouché**, 9 kilometres along the Flers road, where a tank marks the spot at which Leclerc's 2nd Armoured Division cut the Paris–Granville road on 12 August 1944, there is a vast but unfinished 15–16c. church. It stopped at choir and transept because the means of the little town could not match its vision. Behind are the ruins of the 13c. nave.

Beyond Putanges the main D909 passes the twin pepperpot towers of the château of **Crèvecoeur**. **Rânes**, 11 kilometres further on, has a formidable donjon. In the church opposite there is a 15c. painting of the Virgin of Pity. The N816 leads back to the Flers–Argentan road.

East of Argentan the imperative excursion is that to the Haras du Pin, the **National Stud**, known as the 'Versailles of the horse'. By the main road it is 15 kilometres distant: the detours suggested are equally practicable if you are taking in the Haras on the way to Vimoutiers. Leave the town by the D113 which climbs through the Forêt de Gouffern before dropping down to **Chambois**. Here, on 19 August 1944, the northern and south-western Allied armies made their junction to encircle the German Seventh Army in the 'Falaise pocket'. The great 12c. donjon witnesses to the strategic importance of the spot. The church of **Saint Martin**, of the same period, has on one of its beams the date 2 November 1473 and the name of the carpenter, Jean Yon. Take the D16 to **Le-Bourg-Saint-Léonard**. Its 18c. château, with tapestries and period furniture, is now the property of the commune, which intends to open it to the public. The English-style park is already open from 8 to 18.

The *haras*, founded by Colbert, is 4½ kilometres further along the road to **Nonant-le-Pin** (visits at half-hourly intervals, 9–12, 14–18). Mansart planned the director's château, its terrace commanding sweeping views over pasture and woodland: from the *cour d'honneur* there are vistas along three grand forest drives which converge on it. There are more than one hundred stallions at stud (numbers depleted between 1 March and 15 July): English Thoroughbreds, Anglo-Arabs, French hacks and hackneys, the cobs and Percherons of Normandy. Their daily parade, saddled or in harness, is worthy of the setting.

Exmes, built on a plateau 4½ kilometres north of the *haras*, with extensive views, was the old capital of the Pays d'Argentan. Its 11–12c. church replaced a far older building, possibly 5c., which is believed to have been the seat of a bishop. Beyond, the D26 runs north to Vimoutiers. The town is at the south-west end of the Pays d'Auge, which is the opulent heart of Normandy, a land of fine horses and blossoming orchards, green as Gauguin and flowing with cream and cider. The natural centre for exploring it is Lisieux, and, before 1944, when it had perhaps the finest assembly of timbered houses in Normandy, one would have recommended it without hesitation. Modern Lisieux, in spite of its multitude of hotels of every category, would not be my choice for more than an overnight stop; others, too, may find one of the smaller towns within 20 or so kilometres of it, Orbec, Livarot, St Pierre-sur-Dives to the south, Pont l'Évêque to the north, a more congenial base.

Vimoutiers, rebuilt in a reasonably comely fashion since 1944, is a centre for Calvados and cheese. 'Calva', the apple brandy whose documented origin goes back to the mid-16c. is, in fact, made all over north-west France, but the *appellation controlée* article comes from the Pays d'Auge. The Chevaliers du Trou Normand, which is the glass of Calvados taken half-way through a vast meal to enable you to continue to the end, meet at Vimoutiers. At the village of **Camembert**, 8 kilometres south-west of the town, a wayside stele commemorates the farmer's wife, Marie Harel – her farm, Beaumoncel, is on the slope of the valley, above the church – who, at the end of the 18c., evolved the method of making cheese which has brought fame to the village. Local legend says that she got the recipe from a priest whom she hid during the Revolution. The statue of her which, in 1928, was set up near the east end of Vimoutiers' nasty 19c. Gothic church, whose blue-grey and cheese-coloured stone and aggressively vivid windows inevitably survived 1944 unscathed, looks authentic: Madame Harel is depicted broad in the beam, with a pitcher on her hip and a firm stance in her sabots. It was decapitated in the bombing: the replacement, beside the new market hall, which was the gift, in 1956, of 400 men and women who worked in a cheese factory in Ohio, is a pretty soubrette whose relation to the former statue typifies the difference between factory and farmhouse Camembert.

On the road to **Livarot** a short right-hand detour (D268) will take in the **farmhouse museum** devoted to the Cubist painter, Fernand Léger who was born at Argentan in 1881. One returns to the main road at Sainte-Foy-de-Montgommery, cradle of a family illustrious in both France and England. Livarot, strung out uphill, has given its name to a more esoteric and more remarkable cheese, pungent, unctuous, incomparable, which existed in the 13c. and is mentioned in the Roman de la Rose, though by the improbable name of 'Angelot'. If you are tempted to complain of its price, remember that it takes five litres of milk to make six hundred grammes of Livarot and that the process, from cow to counter, takes a hundred days.

Turn right out of the town. The D4 passes through the Forêt de Livarot and crosses the upper valley of the Touques on its way to Orbec. It is an area rich in manor houses so harmoniously placed in their setting as to look almost like natural features.

Orbec is a typical Norman town, unspoiled and unselfconscious. The busy Rue-Grande threads through the heart of it, with old houses both on the main street and in the side streets. Its most striking landmark is the glowing apricot brick façade of the 15c. hospice chapel, topped by a little belfry. In the Rue des Osiers, the next turning on the same side going uphill, there are a number of 15c. houses. Another particularly fine one is the Hôtel de l'Equerre, No. 19 on the Rue-Grande – but the 'tiles' used to form a decorated pattern on the façade are *trompe-l'œil* painted plaster. At No. 7, the 17c. Hôtel de Croissy, a plaque recalls that here Debussy wrote 'Jardins sous la Pluie'.

The whole is dominated by the massive tower of **Notre-Dame**. Its base, in English style, is 15c., the upper part late 16c. The church, also substantially 15c., has a good 14c. tombstone in the north aisle. There are four 16c. windows, one in the north aisle over the 1914–18 War memorial, three in the south, with – outstanding among them – a Stem of Jesse, bleak as a bone, with prophets and patriarchs nesting in the bare branches against a sky of Perugino blue.

The Lisieux road runs through the valley of the Orbiquet, passing

156

on the opposite side of the river at Les Cesnes-Rocray, 9 kilometres on the way, the beautiful early 17c. château of **Mesnil-Guillaume**, its brick and stone corner watch-towers crowned with lantern domes, a moat surrounding it on three sides.

Lisieux, the capital of the Lexiovii tribe under the Roman Empire, is a provincial capital today but, besides being a thriving industrial and market town, it is, as the scene of the short life of Thérèse Martin, who became the Carmelite saint and mystic, Thérèse de l'Enfant Jésus, an important centre of pilgrimage. The centre of the modern town remains the old market, the Place Thiers, three sides largely surrounded by new buildings of seemly brick and stone, the fourth framing the towers of the oldest Gothic church in Normandy and one of the finest in France. Until the end of the 18c. **St-Pierre**, whose building, begun around 1170, was completed about half-way through the 13c., was a cathedral. The purity and sobriety of its style is particularly impressive in the nave, whose narrow height is set off by the massive cylindrical pillars. The Lady Chapel, triumphantly rebuilt during the 15c., is one of the few good works which may be placed to the account of Pierre Cauchon, who was consecrated Bishop of Lisieux shortly after he had condemned Joan of Arc to the stake. His tomb was discovered in a vault on the left of the altar in 1931: a badly damaged effigy in the south transept may be of him, but may equally well be that of another Bishop of Lisieux, the Franciscan Jean II de Samois.

On the (observer's) left of the church the old episcopal palace, now the Palais de Justice, keeps the sumptuous reception hall of the bishops, the *Chambre Dorée* (open daily, 9–12, 14–18, apply at the conciergerie under the arch). The painted ceiling and the walls lined with gilded Cordoba leather are extremely handsome, but do not take too seriously the attributions you may be given for some of the pictures.

The **Musée du Vieux Lisieux** (open daily except Tuesdays, 14–18), reached by the Rue du Docteur-Degrenne from the bottom of the Place Thiers and a bridge over the Touques, is interesting for its illustrations of pre-war Lisieux's many timbered houses. It is set up in one of the few to have survived. South of the Place Thiers, in the Place de la République, reached by the Rue Henri Chéron and the Rue Mathurin, there is a fragment of a Gallo-Roman road, of the 1c. or 2c. A.D., its paving grooved by chariot wheels, which was found during the public works carried out after 1944. A 3c. Gallo-Roman column stands beside it.

Leave the *place* by the Rue Pont Mortain and cross the Boulevard

Sainte Anne. Facing you is the Syndicat d'Initiative, with, on the left, the **Carmel** where Sainte Thérèse was admitted at the unprecedentedly early age of fifteen years and three months, after she had made a direct request to the Pope during a pilgrimage to Rome. She died there three months before her twenty-fifth birthday. The relics shown (visits daily, 7–12, 14–17) include the child's cascade of toffee-coloured hair which was cut off when she took her final vows and the school exercise books in which, during the last weeks of her life, she wrote the story of her spiritual pilgraimage: *L'Histoire d'une âme*.

The pilgrimage continues with a visit to the ornate and gargantuan **basilica**, modelled on the Sacré-Cœur in Paris, with a freestanding campanile rising beside it. Speak as you find, as they say. I find it horrible, and worse than horrible when floodlit. On the way from the Basilica to Les Buissonnets, Sainte Thérèse's childhood home, by way of the Boulevard Jeanne d'Arc, and the Boulevard Duchesne, there is a welcome antidote in the elegant Flamboyant church of Saint Jacques. Restored since 1944, it is to become a museum of religious art.

The rather over-upholstered atmosphere of **Les Buissonnets** goes far to explain those aspects of the saint which contemporary tastes may find alienating. Even sanctity usually conforms to the social background against which it is manifested. The fact that the language of 19c. provincial piety jars today should not be allowed to diminish the stature of a heroic soul.

Two interesting châteaux are within easy reach of Lisieux. **Saint-Germain-de-Livet**, 7 kilometres to the south, off the main road for Livarot (guided visits daily, 10–12, 14–18; closed 15 December – 15 January, and on Thursdays during the winter) is a remarkably beautiful 16c. house, with a moat reflecting the many-shaded tiles of its roof, and the walls patterned in white stone and rose and greenish brick. The *salle des gardes* retains traces of its 17c. frescos and one room contains furniture owned by Delacroix, most eminent of the 19c. Romantic painters, whose mother was connected by marriage with the Rieseners, a family of cabinet makers and painters who were the last private owners of the château.

Le Val Richer, 3½ kilometres north-east of La Boissière on the main Caen road (visits only by advance request) was adapted from the 17c. abbot's lodging of a 12c. Cistercian monastery, now vanished. It was the home of François Guizot, statesman, historian and Anglophile, whose rigid attitude is generally held to have precipitated the Revolution of 1848. Le Val Richer is the 'Blanc Mesnil' of

Gide's *Si le grain ni' meurt*: the novelist was mayor of the neighbouring commune of La Roque Baignard from 1896 to 1899.

St-Pierre-sur-Dives, 20 kilometres distant by the N11, is within
striking distance of Caen (27 kilometres) for those who dislike
spending holiday nights in large towns, and is well worth staying in
for its own sake. It is a zestful country town which makes boxes for
most of the cheese produced in Normandy. The great 12–13c. **abbey
church** succeeded a Romanesque building which was largely destroyed by fire in 1106, during the fighting between the Conqueror's
sons. Fragments of that church survive in the lower part of the walls
of the transepts: the splendid lantern tower is late 13c. or early 14c.
On the floor of the nave, beginning about a third of the way up,
there is a *gnomon*, or sundial rod, with signs of the zodiac to the
right of it, which extends diagonally into the south aisle. In the
chapter house, south of the church, and contemporary with it, the
13c. enamelled tiles produced at the famous workshops of the Pré
d'Auge, which once adorned the sanctuary, have been laid out in a
rosette, three metres across. For entry apply at the house next to the
church, No. 6; failing that, No. 2 round the corner; failing that, try
the *mairie*.

Across the Rue de Falaise, in the Place du Marché, bordered with
chestnuts and as wide as a prairie, are the vast *halles* built by the
monks of the abbey in the 13c., with honey-coloured stone and
russet tiles (key at the Café du Marché).

Beyond Orbec the N811 rises out of the valley of the Dives to
cross the modest wooded heights of the Monts d'Eraines to **Falaise**,
wonderfully sited above the narrow valley of the Ante, and still a
most appealing town, though it has been two-thirds rebuilt since the
fighting of August 1944, which was the climax of the Battle of
Normandy.

The immense **castle** crowning the rocky spur at the south-east end
of the town incorporates fragments of the 10c. donjon where William the Conqueror was born to the future Duke Robert the Magnificent, then aged seventeen, and 'la belle Arlette', daughter of a
local tanner, whom, says tradition, he had seen washing the
household linen in a spring below the ramparts, which is still a public
washplace.

The castle we see (16 May – 15 September, open daily, 8–12,
14–19; 16 September – 15 May, 9–12, 14–18, closed on Tuesdays
and Fridays and from 10 January to 25 January) is largely that of
Henry Beauclerc, who rebuilt the donjon and surrounded it with a
twelve-towered enceinte. It was the scene of the assassination of

Arthur of Britanny, imprisoned in the castle by his uncle, King John.

The entry to the enceinte, with the Syndicat d'Initiative near by, is from the Place Guillaume le Conquérant where William rides his bronze horse eternally to the victory of Hastings. The 18c. Hôtel de Ville on the left has half a dozen of the nine Bronze Age helmets found in the Monts d'Eraines in 1831.

In the thickness of the wall of the 12c. keep there is a tiny chapel with a plaque (modern) listing the names of the knights who followed William to Hastings. A curtain wall links the donjon with the five-storey Tour Talbot, built during the 13c., which was a German observation post during 1944. Lighter stones in its walls mark the repairs carried out after the advancing Canadians had bombed it from Mont Mirat across the valley.

On leaving the enceinte, turn right and follow the line of the walls downhill to the Fontaine d'Arlette: from here there is a wonderful view of the buttresses supporting the donjon. The road, in parts a footpath, continues to the 13c. Porte des Cordeliers, which leads to the Place Saint-Gervais. The **church** has a splendid 12c. lantern tower and a richly Flamboyant apse. The interior, where the right-handed cant of the choir is very noticeable, offers a striking contrast between the Romanesque south side and the 13c. north.

From the north side of the church the Rue de Brébisson leads to the ruined Porte Lecomte. Beyond it, old houses on either side of the road spill downhill to the battered little Romanesque church of **Saint-Laurent** on its spur of rock. Return to the Place Guillaume le Conquérant. **La Trinité**, on its north-eastern side, is another composite church, with elements dating from the 13c. to the 16c., and an unhappy little spike of a spire which replaced the original lantern in 1821.

Continuing to the north-east, the Rue Paul Doumer and its continuation lead to the suburb of Guibray, whose fairs were once the most important in France. The church of **Notre-Dame** has kept most of its 12c. character, despite an 18c. restoration of the interior which has defaced choir and crossing with a dreadful plaster roof. It is hard, though, to regret the stucco group of the Assumption of the same period at the east end. Anachronistic it may be, but the upward surge of the figures is irresistible.

Three kilometres along the rather dull main road to Caen the 16c. château of Aubigny (no visits) is a perfect set piece, with the tall, narrow mansards and steep slate roof of the house filling the end of a broad avenue. It was built at the end of the 16c. for the family of

Morell d'Aubigny, in whose ownership it has remained, reflecting in the austere simplicity of the exterior and the tiled floors and raftered ceilings of the interior something of the character of a race which has produced generations of distinguished soldiers. Nine of those generations are buried in the church, which has a remarkable memorial showing six of them, covering the period 1625–1786, kneeling in chronological order.

CHAPTER TWELVE

Caen

❧

NINE hundred years on, Caen, razed and rebuilt, modern industrial centre and seat of an ancient university, is still the Conqueror's city. Before he made it his preferred base, the small river port at the confluence of the Orne and the Odon, overlooked by a spur of rock which made it a natural defensive point, seems to have had no history. Since, it has been involved in most of the major events in the record of northern France, but its axis remains that east–west line running from the abbey which William's Queen, Matilda, built under the battlements of his castle, to his own Abbaye aux Hommes.

Ironically in view of what was to come, one of William's first recorded acts there was to call the council which promulgated 'the truce of God', in 1061. By this, in the ecclesiastical province of Rouen, there was to be no war between Wednesday evening and Monday morning. Whoever broke the peace was to be punished by banishment, excommunication or the refusal of burial. Its most recent breach was the Battle of Normandy, during which Caen suffered a month's continuous bombardment, which left it three-quarters destroyed. The rebuilding, in the creamy 'Caen stone', is the one unquestionable success of Normandy's post-war reconstruction.

The new town, like the old, centres on the **Place St Pierre** below the castle, and a plan for a systematic visit still divides naturally into sections corresponding to the five enceintes, separated by open spaces, which made up the medieval city. Start with a visit to the Syndicat d'Initiative in the 16c. **Hôtel d'Escoville** on the west side of the *place* (there is also a tourist information office near the railway station). The full Renaissance splendour of the house is seen in the inner court, whose central block, with a vast, perfectly proportioned dormer window, has, in the angle, a graceful loggia with a spiral staircase crowned by two cupolas. On the right-hand wall are carvings of David and Goliath, and of Judith holding up the head of Holofernes.

Nicolas Le Valois d'Escoville, who built it, was the richest man in Normandy at the time, and in the centre of the *place* is a rich man's church. **St-Pierre** was begun, on the site of an earlier church, in the 13c., when Caen's prosperity rivalled that of Paris, and embellished by the town's wealthy burgesses over the next three hundred years. Its spire, the gift of one citizen, which has been rebuilt after a naval shell shattered it in 1944, had not a single interior support, but its octagonal sides withstood a bombardment by Amiral Coligny's troops during the 17c. Wars of Religion. There is a fine rose window above the 'west' porch – actually the church is oriented almost due north and south – and the nave has a profusion of pinnacles and balustrades and delicate flying buttresses, but the prodigy of the exterior is the Renaissance apse, surmounted by pinnacles like candelabra and standing free of the choir. A branch of the Orne, which once ran beneath it, was paved over in 1862.

The interior overwhelms with the richness of the decoration, whose luxuriance increases as one moves east. The capitals of the second and third pillars on the north side of the nave are carved respectively with rabbits in a cabbage field and with highly secular human subjects, which include Lancelot and Gawain, and Aristotle, bridled and enslaved by his mistress. Each of the five arches of the 16c. choir vault has an intricately worked pendentive; that nearest the high altar, a post-war replacement, is a life-size figure of St Pierre. Only the extreme delicacy of the ornate frieze in the sanctuary saves it from vulgarity; the roofs of the five apsidal chapels are similarly lush. Do not miss the door of the sacristy on the north side. The panels, carved with scenes from the lives of St Norbert and St Augustine, are framed between pillars which are Gothic on the right, Flamboyant on the left, with a joyfully pagan tympanum of Pan and cupids.

The **castle**, rescued from its former dilapidation, is now surrounded by green lawns which have transformed this part of the city. A round of the ramparts, which, as they stand, date from various periods between the 12c. and the 15c., is memorable for stunning views over the town, and provides in the Porte des Champs, on the east side, a remarkable example of 14c. military architecture. Within the walls, the 12c. chapel of St George, once the garrison church, is a memorial to the Normans who, through the centuries, have died for their country. An unknown civilian victim of 1944 is buried in the south transept (open 10–12, 14–15.30).

The massive square building second on the left of the entrance, with a doorway framed in sawtooth carving, is the miscalled Salle de l'Échiquier de Normandie, a rare example of 12c. domestic architecture. Adjoining it, excavation has revealed the foundations of the square donjon built, like the Échiquier, by Henry Beauclerc.

Between the Échiquier and the castle entrance the 17–18c. Logis du Gouverneur now houses the **Musée de Normandie** (open daily except Tuesdays, 10–12, 14–18, or 14–17 in winter; tickets admit also to the Musée des Beaux Arts) whose collections have far more than the human interest common to folk museums. Items like the best of the rustic pottery, or the carved wardrobes which were in effect bride chests, deserve to be judged by aesthetic standards.

The **Beaux Arts Museum** (hours as for the Musée de Normandie), whose discreet and admirably functional modern building is on the right of the entrance, is a comprehensive collection particularly strong in works of the 16c. and 17c.

Caen was one of the fifteen French towns to benefit from the artistic spoils of Europe brought home by Napoleon's armies, but the most important picture in the gallery, a Virgin and Child by Roger van der Weyden, came from the bequest of the 19c. scholar and collector, Pierre-Bernard Mancel, friend of Barbey d'Aurevilly (*see* under Saint-Sauveur-le-Vicomte). It included ceramics, MSS. and rare books, but its outstanding item was a remarkable collection of engravings, including examples by Dürer, Rembrandt and Jacques Callot (1592/3–1635). The last-named, one of the greatest etchers of all time, who was born at Nancy and returned there after a sojourn in Italy, left in his 'Grandes Misères de la Guerre' (1633) a document of the horrors of the Thirty Years War.

To reach the new university buildings north of the château, take the footpath starting from the right of the donjon, or, if driving, follow the Avenue de la Geôle, the Rue du Vaugueux and the Rue Léon Lecornu anti-clockwise round the ramparts. Caen's **university** was a by-product of Agincourt. Founded in 1432 by the Duke of Bedford, then Regent of France, it was refounded ten years later by Charles VII, who refused to recognize even the good works of the former occupying power. The university did much to establish Caen's reputation as the 'ville de sapience' and the 'Athens of the north': during the 17c. the merchant princes who had built their magnificent *hôtels particuliers* here were ceding the leadership of local society to lawyers and academics. The town's Académie des Sciences, Arts et Belles Lettres was founded in 1652 and interrupted only briefly by the Revolution; the Société d'Agriculture et de Commerce, founded in 1761, was dissolved at the Revolution but revived in 1801. The new buildings, which are among the most modern in France, are enviably sited on high ground and have great dignity and amplitude. On view in the **library** is the bull of Pope Nicholas concerning the second founding: the renascence of the university since the war is symbolized by a bronze phoenix, by Louis Leygue, on the terrace.

On leaving the university, turn right for the small **Protestant cemetery** at whose south end, facing the university car park, is the grave of Beau Brummell, who fled to France in 1816 to escape his creditors. He was British Consul at Caen from September 1830 to March 1832: the loss of that post and the accompanying salary put him into a debtors' prison for two months of 1835. The sometime favourite of the Prince Regent and arbiter of London society died, lonely and deluded, in the convent hospital of Le Bon Sauveur in 1840, at the age of sixty-one (not sixty-two, as the tombstone set up by his brother and sister states). His grave, which is said to have been 'soon lost in weeds and ivy' is today well kept; at the time of seeing it even had a wreath of bay and dried flowers.

Further along the Rue du Gaillon a right-hand turn leads to the Rue des Carrières and the 1954 church of **Saint Julien**. This vast, domed ellipse of ferro-concrete, with an interior lit by four and a half thousand coloured glass tiles, is the most rebarbative religious building I know, by a crematorium chapel out of a super cinema of the 'thirties. Visitors who are similarly affected may like to spend a restorative few minutes in the pleasant **Jardin des Plantes** across the Place Blot before continuing down to the Rue de la Geôle to regain the Place St Pierre. No. 31 in the Rue de Geôle, the 14c. Maison des Quatrans, rebuilt in the 16c. and ravaged in 1944, has been successfully restored and now houses the *Monuments Historiques*.

The next section of the visit takes one east of the Place St-Pierre. The stout **Tour Guillaume le Roy** is all that remains of the advanced defences of the château. It looks across the Place Courtonne to the oldest part of the port, the Bassin Saint-Pierre. Caen was already a thriving port when it shipped its stone across the Channel to build English cathedrals, but its great expansion came in the mid-19c., when the town was linked to the sea by a maritime canal beside the Orne. Today the port handles some two million tons of cargo a year, importing chiefly coal and oil products, exporting steel from the great works at Mondeville, in the south-eastern suburbs and agricultural products from the hinterland.

Turn left up the steep Rue Le Roy. There is suddenly a provincial air about this part of the town, extending to the shady Place de la Reine Mathilde, which is dominated by the façade of **the Abbaye de**

la Trinité, or Aux Dames. With St-Étienne, or the Abbaye aux Hommes, it represents what must be the most magnificent atonement for sin ever offered by erring human creatures. The sin was the marriage, in or about 1050, within the bounds of consanguinity and without papal dispensation, of Duke William and his cousin, Matilda of Flanders. When, in 1059, Lanfranc prevailed upon Pope Nicholas II to raise the order of excommunication against the couple, each engaged to found an abbey at Caen, so that William's new town should follow older models in being enclosed between religious houses.

Both were Benedictine foundations. Matilda's Abbaye aux Dames was dedicated on 18 June, 1066, when her husband seems likely to have taken advantage of such a gathering of the barons as well as the bishops of Normandy to complete his plans for the conquest of England, which he accomplished on 14 October. He also established the aristocratic vocation of the new foundation by placing his daughter, Cécile, in it: she was to become the second abbess of La Trinité.

Building seems to have gone on sporadically until 1130, but the church is still largely 11c. and, except for a 13c. chapel in the south transept, wholly Romanesque in style, however often the fabric may have been renewed. The façade, between the towers, was entirely rebuilt in the mid-19c., when the church, which had been deconsecrated for decades, threatened to collapse. The gratuitous tympanum over the centre door was an aberration of the restorer. Originally the towers were crowned with spires to accord with those of the Abbaye aux Hommes, which are the centre of the westward view. They were destroyed during the Hundred Years War: the existing rather lumbering tops, with balustrades and bull's-eye windows, were added in the early 18c.

The interior, less lofty than that of St Étienne, is richer in ornament, with crenellated borders to the nave arches and much variety in the carving of the capitals. The unusually wide transept has interestingly contrasted chapels. That in the south arm, used as a chapter house, dates from the second half of the 13c. – see the women's heads carved on the supports of the arches. In the north arm the original twin apsidal chapels have been reconstructed; their ground plan was uncovered during excavations in the 19c.

At the entrance to the choir, the bones of Queen Matilda lie beneath the same slab of black marble – extolling her royal lineage and her piety and generosity – which was posed in 1083. The east end culminates in a radiant *cul-de-four* apse, with two tiers of windows and a *trompe-l'œil* ambulatory, in fact a colonnade. Its capitals, like many in Normandy but none elsewhere in Caen, were inspired by a medieval bestiary, and include what is perhaps best described as a hearsay elephant, with mahout. Beneath the choir – access by a low-roofed staircase in the south transept chapel – is a perfectly preserved crypt which is one of the most ancient parts of the church.

The early 18c. monastic buildings which now serve as the Hôtel-Dieu – the Order which staffs the hospital uses the choir and transept of the abbey as its chapel, so they are not accessible during services – are the work of Guillaume de la Tremblaye, who planned also those of the Abbaye aux Hommes.

Across the Place de la Reine Mathilde, the ruined façade and south aisle, set in a little garden, are all that remains of the 12c. church of **Saint-Gilles**, built as the parish church for the population which grew up round the abbey. From the Place St Gilles take the Rue des Cordes left, past the deconsecrated church of **St-Sépulcre**, where a Romanesque doorway survives in an otherwise 18c. building. Follow the Avenue de la Libération and the Rue Montoir back to the Place St Pierre.

For the Abbaye aux Hommes, turn left from the *place* into the bustling Rue St Pierre. Nos. 52 and 54, their timbered fronts carved with statuettes, are two of Caen's finest surviving 16c. houses. Further along is the graceful octagonal spire of the church of **Saint-Sauveur**, originally Notre-Dame de Froide-Rue, with houses crowding close about it. Effectively it is two churches, a Renaissance nave having been added in the 15c. on the ecclesiastical south side – here is another church oriented north-south – of an existing Gothic one. The south flank, facing on the narrow Rue Froide, has at the junction of choir and nave a charming little exterior spiral staircase, blossoming into a vault, whose original purpose remains conjectural.

At No. 126 in the **Rue St Pierre**, just before the steep-pitched red roofs of the Place Malherbe, a plaque on the leprous façade records that it was the birthplace, in 1555, of François de Malherbe, poet and arbiter of poesy. The Rue-Écuyere leads on to the Place Fontette, with the pale gold façade of the late 18c. Palais de Justice on the right and, ahead, a pair of pretty 18c. houses framing the opening of the Rue Guillaume le Conquérant like twin lodges. Before following it, turn left into the huge **Place Louis Guillouard**, so that your first impression of the Conqueror's foundation will be one of the great views of Europe, the east end of St Étienne, a counterpoint of arc and pyramid, vertical and curve, with, on the left, the harmonious façade of the 18c. conventual buildings, a French formal garden laid out before them. The choir and apse, with their superimposed roofs, are 13c. but preserve the unity of the building.

On the far side of the *place* the red tiles of a 15c. lantern tower rise above the ruined church of **Vieux-Saint-Étienne**, where time had begun the work of destruction before the bombs fell. The 13c. choir survives and some intelligent consolidation has kept the whole as an integral part of the *place*. Look for a battered equestrian statue on the north side of the church; it is a 12c. representation of the Emperor Constantine. Across the Rue Arcisse-de-Caumont a saw-toothed *arc brisé* doorway from the 12c. Hôtel-Dieu has been mounted in the façade of the old Collège du Mont, itself 14–17c.

When you have looked long enough to add the prospect to the permanent capital of your visual memory, go back to the Rue Guillaume le Conquérant, and, at the end of it, turn left past the tall grey obelisk commemorating the Duc de Berry to confront another, more austere, which you may come to rate above it. The west front of **St Étienne** rises before you, stern and naked as a cliff, supported by four massive buttresses that might be the outcrops of a cliff and pierced by two rows each of five totally undecorated windows. The formula, a rectangle with flanking towers and three doors, is the classic Norman one which was to spread all over Western Europe, but those who know the great churches of Northern Italy will sense the cousinship: understandably, since the Italian Lanfranc, William's chief adviser, whom he appointed as the first abbot of his new abbey, is thought to have had a hand in the planning of the work, which was started about 1063. With the towers, built at the same time as the façade, austerity is left behind, or below, since the detail grows richer as they rise. The spires, twins but not identical, were added in the 13c. Until 1566 a third spire crowned the lantern tower. In that year it collapsed, bringing part of the choir down with it. The present squat, octagonal spire, built on the surviving base, has been described as a dressing on a gaping wound.

The interior is monumental in its breadth and purity; the effect depends not on detail but on rhythm and the arrangement of space, and, once more, on its unity. Money helped with the last. While St Étienne was building, the spoils of conquered England were pouring into Normandy, so that there were no delays imposed by lack of means. The church which was dedicated in 1077, the same year as Canterbury Cathedral, was substantially complete. Later, two pieces of good fortune were to preserve that unity. The roof of the nave was vaulted in the first half of the 12c. without any modification of the pillars. At the beginning of the 13c., developments in the liturgy led the monks to replace the Romanesque choir with a larger one, having an ambulatory with radiating chapels. The result might have meant splitting the church into two stylistic halves, but the 'maître Guillaume qui excellait dans l'art des pierres', ('Master William who excelled in the stonemason's art', as his memorial slab on the exterior of the apse describes him), to whom the task was entrusted, was told to respect Lanfranc's building. He followed his instructions so faithfully that the transition from Romanesque to Gothic is almost imperceptible. All might have been lost at the beginning of the 17c., when the choir was largely rebuilt after the collapse of the lantern, but the Prior of the period, Dom Jean de Baillehache, abjured the temptation of contemporary architecture and recreated Maître Guillaume's work. There is a fine 18c. organ case in the tribune of the south transept; the instrument itself is one of the largest in France.

On the wall of the ambulatory on this side a tablet commemorates the period from 6 June to 9 July 1944, when the abbey was a shelter for many hundreds of townspeople while Caen underwent an intensive bombardment. An old Norman tradition affirms that, as long as the kings of England are on the throne, no harm will befall the church of St Étienne. On 8 June two members of the Resistance helped to uphold its credibility when they made contact with General Montgomery to tell him of the number of refugees, sick and wounded, who were housed in the abbey and in the great convent-hospital of Le Bon Sauveur near by. They were told to mark the area with red crosses, and the buildings did indeed escape destruction, if not damage. There are vivid contemporary accounts of the scenes at St Étienne, the floor covered with straw in which families marked out their territory with chairs, the air sharp with the smell of disinfectant, each day ending with mass, a sermon and prayers for those in danger of death.

In the choir a marble slab before the high altar recalls an earlier and more sombre spectacle, the dreadful burial of the Conqueror in September 1087. When he died at Rouen, sons, relatives and courtiers alike forsook him in the scramble to divide the spoils. His corpse, stripped by his servants, was left untended for days before being brought to Caen. The funeral procession was disrupted by an outbreak of fire; in the abbey the ceremony was halted when a burgher named Asselin claimed that his father's house had once stood on the spot at the crossing of the transept where the grave had been dug. William, he said, had driven his father out of it illegally, and Asselin would not allow the king to be buried there without restitution. On the spot the bishops and nobles had to find sixty sous, with the promise of more, before the service could go on. Finally, as it was being lowered into the grave, the bloated corpse burst, releasing such a stench that the congregation hurried from the church, leaving the monks to complete the burial with all speed.

Originally the spot was marked by a tomb of German goldsmiths' work, long vanished. The grave was profaned by the Huguenots in 1562 and such of the scattered bones as were recovered were again dispersed during the Revolution. There may be a femur beneath the present stone, which dates from 1802.

The one hundred and eight choir stalls, with interesting misericords, are early 17c. and the work of local craftsmen. The adoring angels flanking the Louis XVI high altar have been attributed to Antoine Coysevox (1640–1720), chief sculptor of Louis XIV. The wrought iron railings are modern; a panel in the south ambulatory records that two sections were given by the town of Hastings to mark the ninth centenary of the birth of the Conqueror.

A visit to the **abbey buildings** (open daily, except Tuesdays, for conducted tours, 9–12, 14–19; closed during one winter month) is strongly recommended, both for its intrinsic interest and for the views of the south side of the church. From 1804 to 1960 they housed the Lycée Malherbe, originally a Royal *lycée*, since then they have given Caen an enviable Hôtel de Ville. There is superb carved woodwork in the parlour, the *salle de fêtes* and the old monks' refectory, a noble, vaulted chamber which is now a reception hall. At one end of the last there is a splendidly preposterous painting of the Conqueror's arrival in England. The *salle de mariage*, once the chapel of the *lycée*, before that the chapter house, with equally beautiful woodwork, keeps the remarkable prior's chair of solid oak. There are three impressive wrought-iron staircases, that in the Vestibule d'Honneur in particular straining the laws of balance to their limits with the daring of their ramps.

The *salle des garde* of the Gothic abbey, purged of the more unfortunate effects of a 19c. restoration and with two of the original beams in its chestnut roof, now provides a stately meeting place for the municipal council. In the cloister, the third to be built on the spot, which gives a memorable view of the towers of the church, the Tuscan-style architecture of Guillaume de la Tremblaye is so perfect a complement to the Romanesque fabric above it that one is

almost tempted to rejoice at the destruction of its Gothic predecessor by Mazarin after it had been damaged during the Wars of
Religion. In one corner, beneath a pretty 18c. clock, recently re-
gilded, one sees still the board on which the daily duties of the
monks were posted.

North of St Étienne (continue towards the Bayeux road, then
turn right up the Venelle Saint Nicolas) is the purest example of
Romanesque in Caen. **St-Nicolas**, built by the monks of St Étienne
in 1083, to serve as the parish church of the neighbourhood, has
known no radical alteration since, the 15c. west tower being merely
an addition. Now that the restoration is complete, it is to become a
museum of ecclesiastical art – it is to be hoped that the overgrown
churchyard which is part of its charm will not be too determinedly
spruced up.

Return along the Rue Guillaume le Conquérant as far as the
Place-Fontette, then bear left into the **Place Saint Sauveur**, with a
statue of Malherbe in bays and buskins punctuating it. The best
collection of 18c. houses in Caen is to be seen here. Also the *quartier*
is one of the most promising in the town for finding small family
restaurants where you can get an authentic and relatively inexpensive meal, in contrast with the centre, which tends to divide between
elegant restaurants and sad snackeries. The church, **Vieux Saint-
Sauveur**, or Saint-Sauveur du Marché, one of the earliest in Caen,
with the crossing and the lower part of the lantern dating from the
12c., has fared worse than St-Nicolas since it was deconsecrated. It
is built round with houses and the nave serves as a market. From the
east end of the church (north side) the Rue-Pasteur crosses the Rue
aux Naups, with, on the left, the gracious ruin of the church of the
Cordeliers, clothed with crimson creeper, into the Rue des Cordeliers. The Hôtel de Colomby, at No. 6, is an imposing, turreted
house of the first half of the 17c. Turn right, then left into the Rue
Calibourg for the château and the Place St Pierre.

Leave the Place St Pierre by the Boulevard du Maréchal Leclerc: the **Hotel Than**, at No. 77, with the salamander of François I
on the *fronton*, is one of Caen's four surviving Renaissance houses.
Turn right into the Rue du Moulin, then left into the Rue de
Strasbourg for the Place de la République. Behind the Préfecture at
the far end of it is a church startlingly different from the typical
Romanesque and Gothic of Caen. The calm classical façade and
lantern dome of **Notre-Dame de la Gloriette** proclaim a perfect
example of the so-called Jesuit style. It was consecrated in 1689 as
Sainte-Catherine-les-Arts and came to deserve the name during the

Revolution when, as a 'constitutional' church, it escaped pillage and, having an enlightened *curé*, acquired some superb furnishings from other churches in the town. The splendid high altar, with a gilded *crèche* inspired by that of Val de Grâce, had been commissioned in 1707 for the Abbaye aux Dames, but is better placed where it is. The pulpit and grille of 18c. wrought iron are from the same source.

Behind the post office the Rue Sadi Carnot, with the modern Municipal Theatre on the left, leads to the huge green space of the **Prairie**, the bright tan of its race track frequently enlivened by trotters at exercise. Over on the right, facing it, are the new buildings of the Lycée Malherbe. South of the Prairie (turn right at the bottom of the Cours Général de Gaulle) there is a shady, almost rural walk beside the Orne, with rapt anglers along its banks and gardens sloping down to the water on the far side.

Cross the river by the Pont Bir Hakeim and continue along the Rue Saint-Michel, under the railway bridge and uphill to the right for the church of **Saint-Michel-de-Vaucelles**, which was started in the 12c. and underwent successive enlargements to keep pace with the growth of this south bank district. The result is a little 12c. tower on the south side – the squat spire was added probably in the 14c. – a 15–16c. choir and a late 18c. 'Jesuit' façade, with a domed tower, approached by a rather fine staircase.

Return to the Orne by the Rue de Vaucelles and cross the bridge to the Promenade de Sévigné. The Marquise, whose series of letters to her daughter are a valuable source of information on the manners and customs of the 17c. as well as a model of French prose, approved of Caen, which, she said, had 'les plus beaux bâtiments' and 'les plus belles églises', besides being 'la source de tous nos plus beaux esprits.' The Rue Saint Jean leads north through an area where, during the early 19c., most of Caen's considerable English colony was concentrated.

Like Saint-Pierre, the Flamboyant **Saint-Jean** was a parish church of the rich bourgeoisie. Indeed, its 14c. west tower was modelled on that of Saint-Pierre, but was never given a spire because the foundations were soon discovered to be dangerously unstable. Today the tower tilts noticeably out of true. The rest of the church was effectively rebuilt in the 15c., after being destroyed during the siege of 1417, when the English took Caen for the second time. It has been successfully restored since 1944. The present choir stalls and the retable came from the church of the Carmelite convent and the painted wooden statues of Saint Norbert and Saint Benoît from the

172

Abbaye d'Ardenne (*see* below).

From the house opposite the west front of Saint-Jean (No. 148), which was then the home of her elderly relative, Madame de Bretteville, Charlotte Corday set out for Paris in July 1793, to assassinate Marat. Seldom have both protagonists in a tragedy been so traduced by popular history as the leader of the 'Mountain', the violently extremist group in the Convention, and his assassin – the one represented as blood-sodden, deranged, and a quack doctor into the bargain, the other as, at best, a hysteric, at worst, a virago and/or harlot. In fact Marat, whose medical diploma was awarded by the University of St Andrews in 1775, expressed his passion for justice in the service of the poor and the incurable sick as well as in political extremism. Charlotte Corday, the intelligent, well-educated daughter of a noble though impoverished family, was an impassioned, but also an informed supporter of the moderate Girondin party in the National Assembly, several of whose members had taken refuge in Caen, hoping to recruit Normandy to their cause. By killing Marat she hoped, as she said at her trial, 'to give peace to[my] country'. The 'harlot and hysteric' went to the guillotine with calm dignity, condemned to wear the red smock of a murderess, but wearing with it the white gloves of a well-bred young woman of the *ancien régime*.

Walk past the east end of Saint-Jean into the Place de la Résistance – the gilded statue of Joan of Arc was brought from Oran in 1964 – and turn up the Avenue du 6 juin for the Place Saint Pierre. Ahead of you is the most exhilarating sight of the Conqueror's city, the ramparts of the castle rising like a white cliff from the surrounding green, and, above them, the leopard standards of Normandy, gold on crimson, licking the sky in calm airs, hard as so many sails in a wind.

CHAPTER THIRTEEN

**Landing beaches and the coast to Ouistreham –
Bénouville – Abbaye d'Ardenne – Thaon –
Fontaine-Henry – Douvres-la-Délivrande –
the coast east to Dives – Cabourg**

CAEN is a convenient base from which to visit the scenes of the
Allied landings of June 1944. Another day might well be devoted to
the places of interest in the band of rich farmland between the town
and the coast. They include, in Fontaine-Henry, the finest Renaissance château in Normandy.

The Allies decided in the spring of 1943 that the invasion should
be launched on the coast of Calvados, and, during the following
winter, mounted camouflage operations in south-east England to
foster the German belief that it would be aimed at the Pas-de-
Calais. Consequently, that section of the Atlantic Wall was strengthened, and by June 1944 there were twenty-five German divisions
north of the Seine and only seventeen in the triangle formed by the
Seine and the Loire. As the gravestones in Normandy's German
cemeteries testify, the Wall was manned largely by those who, in
military terms, were elderly, with 60,000 troops of non-German
nationality, prisoners from the Russian front who had 'volunteered'
for service in France. Of the five landing areas, the two westernmost, Utah and Omaha beaches, (*see* under Cotentin section) were
assigned to the Americans. British and Canadian units landed at
Gold, Juno and Sword, betwen Arromanches-les-Bains and the
mouth of the Orne.

From Caen, take the direct route to **Arromanches**. The sandy
beach, sheltered by cliffs to the east and west, was designated as the
site of one of the two artificial harbours which the Allies built for the
landing of reinforcements and supplies before any of the Norman
ports were liberated. The massive prefabricated elements were
towed across the Channel and the work of assembling them began
on D-Day plus one. Mulberry Harbour A, at Vierville, 21 kilometres to the west, was destroyed in an unseasonable storm on 19

174

June, but, during the first hundred days of the campaign, two-and-a-half million men and half-a-million vehicles were landed at Arromanches's Mulberry B, known to the French as Port Winston.

Its 12 kilometres of deep roadstead, created in eight days by the sinking of 60 blockships and 146 caissons, was an instant Cherbourg, whose traffic, at its peak, was heavier than that port's. Some débris of the epoch remains, so many items of military archaeology: rusted guns outside the Musée de Débarquement; stranded on the shore, among the delving, shrimping children, the hulk of one of the landing craft which, on D-Day, put ashore 14,000 British assault troops. The **museum** (open daily, 9–12, 14–19, winter 14–18) contains, along with plans, photographs and relief maps, models of the component parts of the harbour which are faithful to the point of reproducing the movement of the tides under the pontoons of the floating jetty. An Admiralty film, made at the time, records the events of the landing and a diorama recreates them.

Out to sea, there is a reminder of an earlier projected invasion which was unsuccessful. On a spring tide, low water reveals a group of reefs 2 kilometres offshore to the north-east. They are known as the Calvados, which gave their name to the department, and Calvados, it is suggested, is a corruption of Salvador, the name of a vessel which was wrecked on them in 1588, after the Invincible Armada had been scattered by the great storm which completed the victory of the British Navy.

Arromanches was the western limit of the British and Canadian landings. Turning east, we pass fragments of the Atlantic Wall still standing along the sands of **Ver-sur-Mer**. The little town, standing a couple of kilometres back from the sea, has a four-storey church tower of the 11c. On the beach of **Graye**, on the outskirts of Courseulles-sur-Mer, Churchill and King George VI landed respectively on 12 June and 16 June, to spend a few hours with the troops.

It was at **Courseulles**, a small resort and fishing village, previously known chiefly for the quality of its oysters – there is still a diorama devoted to them, open daily, Easter to 30 September, 10–12, 14.30–18.30 – that, on D-Day, the Allies created a temporary artificial harbour by sinking twelve blockships. The small port itself, which penetrates deep inland, was of great value before the completion of Mulberry Harbour. Today, with a yacht harbour to supplement the continuing attraction of its oysters, Courseulles is enjoying a popularity which has encouraged a good deal of new building. On the **Place 6 Juin**, near the beach, a granite monument

175

commemorates the landing of General de Gaulle on 14 June 1944, when he came to instal the first provisional government of the 4th Republic. Another memorial on the *place*, a Sherman tank of the Sixth Canadian Armoured Division, spent twenty-seven years under the sea before being fished up in 1971. Courseulles's **château**, whose entrance is at the inland end of the Rue de la Mer, is an elaborately decorated Henri IV building, restored since 1944.

East of Courseulles, the small towns along the coast, all of which have their place in the records of the landings, make this part of Calvados virtually one seaside resort of the type which the French call 'familial'. All have wide, sandy beaches, from which the tide recedes to reveal rocks yielding rich harvests of shrimps, crabs and mussels, and banks of seaweed which enable the tonic effects of iodized air to be among the publicized attractions. The distinctions between them tend to be inland, where the 12c. and 13c. churches are a reminder of how greatly ecclesiastical building in this part of Normandy benefitted from English money after the Conquest.

Bernières, from whose beach the first reports of the landings were written, has a church whose size relates to the town's past as a considerable fishing port, rather than to its more modest present. The 13c. tower, three storeys, with corner turrets, and, above them, an octagonal spire rising to almost 70 metres, is of cathedral style and proportions.

Saint-Aubin, Langrune – the second syllable derives from the Scandinavian root which gave us 'grön-' in 'Grönland' the Danish name for Greenland – and **Luc** are virtually a single resort, occupying some 4 kilometres of the sea front. Luc adds to the usual seaside attractions an open-air theatre in its public park. The church here is a modern Romanesque mock-up, but the tower of the 12c. church, with a parapet added in the 14c., still stands in the cemetery. Langrune's 13c. church has another notable tower, crowned by a soaring pierced spire. At Saint-Aubin, the monument to the British and Canadian soldiers who landed here is mounted on a German blockhouse which still has its gun.

Lion is a twin village, Bas and (relatively) Haut. The church, with a Romanesque tower, is down by the sea. Up on the small hill of Haut-Lion is a château of the later 16c., with the typically high roof of the Renaissance, a stairtower and two overhanging watchtowers. The cannon near the gate bears the arms of Philip II of Spain, to support the claim that it came from one of the ships of the Invincible Armada. Hermanville-la-Brèche has a memorial to the Allied soldiers who landed here set up in the Place Cuirassé-

Courbet, itself named after the old French cruiser which was sunk offshore as one of the blockships sheltering Sword Beach. Colleville Plage, the next seaside village, is now known as Colleville-Montgomery Plage, in recognition of the Commander-in-Chief of the Twenty-First Army Group, whose ancestors are said to have come from the neighbourhood.

Riva Bella, a more ambitious resort, was the eastern limit of the landings, and the point at which the only French Commando to take part in the D-Day operations came ashore. With **Ouistreham**, we are in a different atmosphere. Anciently it was the port of Caen, and so the traditional landing place for the English during their expeditions against the city. Now that it is little more than a halt for vessels going up the Orne canal to Caen it has found a new rôle as an international yachting centre, so that daily in the season there is the exultant sight of sails crowding out of the harbour mouth with the tide.

From the port the Avenue Michel Cabieu leads up to the town. A tablet near its end tells us that Cabieu was a sergeant who, on the night of 12 July 1762 repulsed single-handed an attack by the English. The occasion was a raid by a party put ashore by Admiral Rodney, with orders to burn the little town. They had taken two forts when Cabieu set out with musket and drum, firing the one, beating the other and shouting orders to a non-existent force to such good effect that the English fled. Well might the sergeant be promoted to general in one bound, and lauded successively by Louis XV, the Convention and the Emperor Napoleon I. He got a pension, too.

The 12–13c. church of **Saint-Samson** has a superb west front, with three tiers of mostly blind arches above a richly carved doorway, the whole amply justifying Edouard Herriot's description of it as a marvel, though one might question whether it is an 'adorable petite' marvel. While not heavy, it is as rugged as a fortress. The model for the upper part of the nave was probably the Abbaye aux Dames, for whose nuns the church was built.

The main road back to Caen leads through **Bénouville**, where a plaque and a memorial mark the entrance to Pegasus Bridge, spanning the canal and the River Orne, which was named for the emblem of the British Sixth Airborne Division, who captured it on the night of 5–6 June 1944. On the far side of the bridge, at **Ranville**, 2,566 graves in the British military cemetery testify to the cost of taking it, destroying the bridges over the Dives and its tributaries, and reducing the German strongpoint of Merville, at the mouth of the Orne, all of which objectives were attained on D-Day.

Just beyond Bénouville, also on the left of the road, is one of the most improbable maternity homes in France, which Claude Nicolas Ledoux, architect to Louis XVI and also to that most discerning patron, Madame du Barry, built for the Marquis de Livry. The marquis was thinking in terms of a *petit château* in the modish neo-classical style, but Ledoux, a brilliantly original architect, then at the outset of his distinguished career, had a larger vision. Between 1768 and 1777 he caused to be built a vast mansion with a central porch whose style and scale suggest a fragment of the Parthenon. The interior decoration, carried out by a Caen architect, J.F.E. Gillet, was appropriately sumptuous. By the time the Marquis de Livry died, in 1789, the bills, mostly outstanding, totalled two million livres. Having little prospect of being able to clear them, his widow sold the property, in 1792, to a purchaser who was guillotined in the following year. The château was sequestrated, but later restored to the marquis's family, who kept it until 1927, when they were succeeded by the mothers and babies of the Department of Calvados.

Back in Caen, in the approach to the Rue Basse, look out on the right for the crenellated wall, flanked by two towers, of the **Manoir des Gens d'Armes**, whose name comes from the pair of stone statues which guard the larger tower. The house was built in about 1540 and partly rebuilt during the following century: the wall we see is all that remains of the enceinte which once enclosed it.

For Fontaine-Henry, leave Caen by the Bayeux road. Opposite the village of Carpiquet, on the outskirts of the town, a left-hand turn leads to the **Abbaye d'Ardenne**, a Premonstratensian foundation of the 12c., which shares its site with two farms, though the small white houses of suburban Caen are advancing, it seems, inexorably. The buildings were in ruins during the 19c.; now, after grave damage in 1944, they are being restored. There is a beautiful 13c. entrance gate, and, in the first farm on the left, a tithe barn of the same period, like a cathedral, with majestic roof timbers. The red-tiled church on the second farm (likely to be closed during restoration) is an admirable example of 13c. Norman Gothic. In the low building opposite are the old mill and older press of the monastery.

Return to the main road and, at **Rots**, whose 12c. church owes its size to the fact that it was a dependency of Saint-Ouen, turn right onto the D170 to **Lasson**. Its Renaissance château has been attributed to the Caen architect, Hector Sohier, because of the kinship of its striking decor with that of his church of Saint-Pierre. The church tower is a 13c. pastiche done in the 18c.

Continue through Cairon. At the village of **Thaon**, 2½ kilometres further on, a lane on the right, just beyond the modern parish church – this is best walked – leads down to a 12c. church, lost in a green valley, with a stream at its foot and trees almost obscuring the pyramid roof of the central tower. It has been deconsecrated since 1840 – looking about, you wonder when, or how, it could ever have assembled a congregation – but the key can be obtained at the neighbouring house. Inside, there is a floor of beaten earth underfoot and a noble timbered roof overhead. The carving of the capitals and arches is more than commonly interesting. The whole is a small masterpiece and an inexplicable one. Nobody knows how, or why the church was built.

Return to the D170: the village of **Fontaine-Henry**, set beside the Mue, is 2 kilometres further on. The château (open Thursdays, Saturdays and Sundays, 14.30–18.30), standing in a park which was laid out *à l'anglaise* under the Restoration, is a supreme example of Renaissance magnificence. It was built during the late 15c. and the first half of the 16c. by the Harcourt family, its then owners, on the site of the 12–13c. fortress of Henri de Tilly. This *château fort* seems to have been largely destroyed during the Hundred Years War. Its successor, with a great mitred roof, deeper than its supporting walls, framed between a pepperpot tower and the exquisitely decorated façade of the main building, introduced another age.

Two cellars of the old building remain, also the 13c. chapel. The raftered entrance hall was once the kitchen, and retains its vast chimney, with three fireplaces. There is a fine spiral staircase decorated with a high relief of Judith and Holofernes. The pictures include a Mignard of the child Louis XIV as the god of battles; over the chimney-piece in the *grand salon* are paintings by Rigaud, Philippe de Champaigne, Poussin and Watteau.

Continue along the D170, which follows the pleasant valley of the Mue, to Reviers, and turn right for **Douvres-la-Délivrande**. This is the oldest centre of pilgrimage in Normandy. Indeed, a pagan goddess is said to have been worshipped at the Celtic settlement of *la delle Yv-rande* before her image was replaced in the 4c. by a statue of the Virgin. The first sanctuary was destroyed by the Norse raiders in the 9c.; the present handsome, if rather grandiose church was built during the second half of the 19c. A marble niche in the north side of the choir, with discarded crutches among the votive offerings, houses the Black Virgin which is the object of the pilgrim-

179

ages, the most important of which takes place on the Thursday after the Feast of the Assumption (15 August). The present figure is believed to date from the 16c. The main road back to Caen passes through the village of **Epron**, whose rebuilding after the devastation of 1944 was paid for by a national collection organized by the French Radio. Lots were drawn to decide which of the shattered villages of Calvados should benefit, and Epron's name came out of the hat.

East of the Orne, the seaside resorts are a good deal more elegant, also, usually, more expensive than those along the Côte de Nacre. Around the turn of the century a French writer said that these 'villa villages' were like American cities in their mushroom growth, describing the whole area as 'un Far West de fantaisie, de luxe et de high-life', so providing evidence that 'franglais' was adulterating the French language earlier than is generally supposed. The fantasy was evident in the confident and often engaging nonsense of a good deal of the architecture, nowhere more so than in that of the first resort of any size, which is also in many ways the most typical.

Cabourg, at the mouth of the Dives, the principal model for the Balbec of Proust's *À l'ombre des jeunes filles en fleur*, was planned in 1860, to meet the new fashion for seaside holidays, and the coherence of its lay-out remains impressive. A peacock's tail of avenues fans out from the casino and the Grand Hotel at the centre of the long sea front, which is now named the Promenade Marcel Proust. The sands are magnificent, even by Norman standards, but this resort, as is testified by many admonitory notices about eating, and exercising dogs, and riding bicycles, is not 'familial'. Cabourg's clientele has changed with changing tastes, which include the relatively recent enthusiasm of the French for foreign travel. The rich who a century ago were building villas in Normandy, are today buying up plots in Sardinia; Paris's 'café society' spends its Friday-to-Mondays rather at Deauville; the modern equivalent of Proust's fellow guests at the Grand Hotel are likely to be in the Caribbean or the East Indies, and the hotel itself is delighted to receive conferences. But the resort is determined to remain 'select' even if it is no longer aristocratic, and the perfume of the 'nineties still lingers on the landward side of the Grand Hotel, where the great spread of lawn and flower beds is ringed with pleasantly – well, most of them are pleasant – preposterous villas.

There are worse places in which to spend a few days on the coast, particularly as, over the river and virtually one with Cabourg, is the old town of **Dives-sur-Mer**. The river mouth having silted up, Dives is today about 2 kilometres from the sea, a small industrial town, devoted chiefly to metallurgy and the manufacture of plastics. In the 11c. it was a major port, and it was here that the Conqueror assembled his army and fleet for the invasion of England. William's victory at Hastings, even if he had not had the advantages of cavalry superiority and infantry armed with long-range missiles, would still have been less remarkable than the diplomatic offensive which preceded it. The Conqueror obtained the papal blessing and banner for his enterprise, both vitally important to its success, and instigated a diversionary attack by Harald Haardraade against the north-east of England which drew off the English forces. He succeeded in keeping his own army together, and in good heart, when contrary winds held it up at Dives for a month. Estimates which put the size of that army at about 50,000 men-at-arms, with 20,000 other ranks are now known to have been wildly exaggerated. It is unlikely to have numbered more than 7,000 all told, and maintaining the discipline of a force even of that size during the waiting period was a sufficient achievement. True, two-thirds of it consisted of troops from Brittany, Maine, Aquitaine, Flanders and France, who would probably not have decided to pack up and go home as lightly as the Normans.

A list of William's companions-in-arms – the names are not too easy to decipher – was set up at the west end of the church of **Notre-Dame** (turn down the Rue-de-Manneville from the central cross-roads) in 1861 by the Caen Archaeological Society. Notre-Dame was Proust's 'church of Balbec'. The present building, 14–15c., with the surrounding graveyard transformed into an attractive garden, retains the 11c. church served by Benedictines from the priory of Troarn, the four massive arches supporting the lantern tower. Its size, vast for a small town, is only partly explained by the former importance of Dives as a port. From the 11c. until the Wars of Religion this was a pilgrimage church whose object of veneration was a figure of Christ which was dredged up by fishermen between Cabourg and Dives. After a lawsuit – is this the first recorded instance of the Norman passion for litigation? – possession was granted to Dives, but, says the legend, it proved impossible to make a cross to fit the figure until, three years later, a perfect one was found on the shore. This crucifix was destroyed by the Calvinists, and a replica, saved during the Revolution, is now in the north transept, below a window illustrating the legend. Formerly the miraculous Christ was exposed in a tribune, the *haute chapelle*, distinct from the rood loft which spanned the width of the crossing. Above the north porch a chimney recalls the time when the monks' cells were in this part of the church.

Only slightly later in date than the church is the market hall in the **Place de la République**, with a huge, rippling roof of russet tiles and silvery rafters. The narrow building in the *place*, with an overhanging tower, and, at the back, four rows of windows above the ground floor, is the old *gendarmerie* of the 16c.

Back at the cross-roads the Hostellerie de Guillaume-le-Conquérant, a former posting inn and once the residence of the seigneurs de Dives, whose oldest parts are 16c., now houses a **craft centre** in its courtyard. One might perhaps dispense with some of the accompanying tarting up, but the total effect of geraniums and white fantail pigeons against a background offering every variety of surface interest in the brick and tile and timber of roofs and façades is immensely beguiling. Henri IV is reputed to have spent a day here, recovering from the effects of a surfeit of oysters. Madame de Sévigné was certainly a guest in her time: her chair is on view.

CHAPTER FOURTEEN

Côte Fleurie – Pont-l'Évêque – St-Hymer –
Val de Touques – Deauville-Trouville – Honfleur –
Marais-Vernier – Quillebeuf

CABOURG marks the beginning of the Côte Fleurie, that strip of coast which, as Percy Dearmer noted at the beginning of this century, owes its distinction to the fact that its first colonizers were careful to plant trees before they built their villas. The luxuriant greenery in which they are framed constitutes much of the charm of these mostly small resorts. The beaches are splendid, the coast, once the marshes at the mouth of the Dives have been left behind, is undulating, rising here and there to impressive cliffs, and the country inland is attractive.

From Dives, the D45 gives a sweeping view of the coast during the 2 kilometres to **Houlgate**. The château which crowns the Butte Caumont, at the entry to the town, is 19c., so, nearer at hand, is the pillar in the Rue de Caumont, commemorating the departure of William and his barons for the conquest of England. It was put up in 1861 by the Caen archaeologist, Arcisse de Caumont. Houlgate's sands and promenade rival those of Cabourg. It, too, offers the standard holiday amenities, from casino to marina, but has only a miniature golf course against Cabourg's eighteen-holer. Where Houlgate scores is with its setting in the valley of the Drochon, which runs through the town, and the striking cliffs of the Vaches Noires, which rise east of the promenade, beyond the casino and the Syndicat d'Initiative. It is possible from here to walk along the foot of the cliffs to Villers – but take care to start on an ebbing tide. The corniche, continuing the Rue des Bains and the Rue Baumier, curves round the Butte d'Houlgate to run inland through Auberville before dropping to Villers-sur-Mer, another version of the same model, with a broad sweep of sands before it and a half-circle of wooded hills behind. Two-and-a-half kilometres south-east of **Villers** there is an imposing Louis XIII château which, during the 18c., was owned by the Marquis de Branoy, an eccentric in the grand style. On the death of his father he hung not only the château but also the surrounding trees with crêpe and caused ink to flow from the fountains.

Blonville and **Bénerville**, pretty villages, the one on the slopes, the other at the foot of Mont Canisy – on its summit a traditional Norman village has been constructed with stone and timber from decaying old houses in different parts of the province – make up a single resort. Simpler and smaller than the three through which we have passed, it might be a pleasant base for those who want to dip no more than a toe in the sophistication of Deauville–Trouville, 4 kilometres further on.

Properly one should speak of Trouville–Deauville, for, of the two resorts which face each other across the mouth of the Touques and share a railway station, it is the former which is the older; it was the first resort to be established on the Côte Fleurie. The vogue for sea-bathing was already established at Dieppe when, at the beginning of the 1830s, the landscape and marine artists, Eugène-Gabriel Isabey (1803–86) and Charles Mozin, a pupil of Leprince, came to work at what was then a small fishing village consisting of a few thatched cottages. Mozin showed pictures of Trouville at the Salon of 1834. Alexandre Dumas *père* made the village known among writers, saying that a bathe on these sands equalled ten years of health.

By 1858 **Trouville** was advertising the attractions of its 'small, clean houses, besides two hotels, bathing machines which can be wheeled down to the water and bathing costumes which can be hired'. Already it had its first casino, consisting of 'a lobby, a cloakroom, a saloon forty feet by twenty feet, offering shelter against the ardour of the sun, one piano, four journals, a library of five hundred volumes [they included Scott and Fenimore Cooper as well as Paul de Kock and Eugène Sue], also tables for playing and comfortable chairs'.

Those early simplicities were soon forgotten. Development was in the air, and a *notaire* who had thought of buying the whole beach for 10,000f lived to see its value rise to five or six million. Trouville became the favoured resort of the court of Napoleon III. Boudin painted the Empress Eugénie and her ladies, in their crinolines, scudding across its sands before a breeze. It was from here that, in 1870, the Empress escaped from France in the yacht of an English friend, Sir John Burgoyne.

In spite of royal patronage, it seems to have been less expensive than Dieppe. Alphonse Karr, the novelist who popularized Étretat, speaks of its being 'encombré à la saison des bains par des gens qui trouvent la vie trop chère à Dieppe', and a visitor of the period recorded that while women at Dieppe and Boulogne needed four or five *toilettes* a day, three sufficed at Trouville. Bathing was not mixed; if men were in sight they were required to keep 200 metres offshore, which was less hazardous than it may sound as the beach slopes very gradually.

As the great hotels went up along the sea front, the villas climbed the slopes. The town has two waterfronts, the quay facing west over the Touques and the port where there are still fishing boats as well as pleasure craft, and the promenade and sands forming a right angle with them, the vast casino marking the transition. The quays provide the commercial and Coney Island element, with the morning chaffering at the *poissonnerie*, which was done up with timber and red tiles in 1936, and the line of amusement stalls. Half-way along the Boulevard-Fernand-Mourcaux, which runs beside them, a plaque over the *Pharmacie du Port* recalls that Flaubert spent the summer of 1853 in the house. He had first visited Trouville as a youth with his parents in 1836. It seems probable that the inscription on the plinth of his statue near the Casino, which claims that the novelist's 'émotions sentimentales et esthétiques les plus vives furent trouvillaise' is a delicate reference to that visit. During the course of it, Flaubert met Madame Schlésinger, eleven years his senior and the wife of a music publisher, with whom he fell violently and enduringly in love, though he did not declare his passion until thirty-five years later, when the lady was widowed.

Today the casino, a Louis XVI building with the Syndicat d'Initiative in a wing, offers every conceivable distraction to those who enjoy having their idleness organized, with a cinema, dancing, and a restaurant to supplement the roulette, baccarat, black-jack, boules, *banque ouverte* and *chemin de fer* which go on from 15–03 every day of the year. Thermalism, the marine 'cure' so popular in France, is among the activities introduced more recently. There is an Olympic swimming pool on the seaward side and the resort provides for the whole range of sports, including sand-yachting. In the Rue Général Leclerc, which runs parallel with the last section of the Promenade des Planches, the Villa Montebello has been transformed into a museum (open daily, 18 June – 18 September; week-ends only from 2 April – 11 June) where one can compare the lavish present with Trouville's beginnings. Further along you reach the corniche, with grandstand views along the coast.

Deauville, Trouville's aristocratic neighbour on the west bank of the Touques, was the result of a deliberate act of creation rather than an organic growth, and looks like it, with its strictly rectangular lay-out. The sands are more extensive than those of Trouville, the totally flat site less appealing. Deauville was the brain-child of the Duc de Morny, Napoleon III's illegitimate half-brother, who was gifted as a businessman as well as a statesman – he is reputed to have made a fortune from speculation and the manufacture of beet-sugar – who, with a consortium whose members included Dr Oliffe, physician to the British Embassy in Paris, drained the marshes on the left bank and laid out a race course. Another crop of villas sprang up, two hundred and fifty of them within three years. There were palatial hotels also, as the Revd Charles Merk noted in the book on the Normandy coast which he published in 1911. He added: 'The true life is not, as in Trouville, in the hotels and on the sands, but within its stately residences, and finds expression in balls and concerts, in dances and frivolities, which last but a summer month'.

Allowances being made for the tastes of another age, that remains true today. The equipment of the resort is unparalleled, whether one thinks of the two race courses, the lawns and flowers of the Terrasse which lies behind the six hundred metres of the prom-enade with, at its centre, the casino, which is a 1912 version of the Trianon, and the Babylonian splendours of the Pompeian baths, or the newest project, the building of the Port Deauville. This is in effect a seaside village at the east end of the promenade where boat owners can tie up their craft outside the door. Essentially it is all geared to 'le high-life'. 'Glittering' would be the word of choice for the season, when the rich and very rich frequent Deauville, but it is a short season, starting in July and culminating with the Grand Prix which is run on the fourth Sunday in August.

There is some continuation into September and the world-famous yearling sales take place in November as well as August. From September to March the Casino d'Hiver operates daily, there are numerous conferences and, at week-ends, a pretty regular flow of Parisians getting a quick breath of air, hence the effort of Deauville to present itself as the 'twenty-first *arrondissement* of Paris'. Stars and aspiring stars of stage, screen and disc, in partic-ular, feel it is helpful to be seen and, if possible, photographed strolling along the *planches* or taking an aperitif at the Bar Soleil. At mid-week, by contrast, there is an ineffable desolation about these vast, unpeopled areas of meticulously ordered space. It is like being on an empty stage with the curtain up.

If you are staying at some point between Cabourg and Trouville, an easy day's motoring will let you see something of the hinterland as well as the whole coastal strip. From Trouville turn up the valley for **Touques**, 1½ kilometres from the mouth of the river. Like Dives, this is an old port of consequence which has been lost in the sands, until the Revolution it had its own Governors. Thomas Becket laid the foundation stone of its parish church, dedicated to St Thomas, which has since added a Flamboyant choir and an early 17c. doorway to the Romanesque nave. Sadly, the 11c. St-Pierre, which is among the most important Romanesque churches of the region, with a fine 12c. lantern tower, is now dilapidated as well as deconsecrated.

The ruin above **Bonneville-sur-Touques**, 1½ kilometres to the south-east, is all that remains of the Conqueror's castle of Bonneville, now reduced to the enceinte, five towers and the donjon (guided visits, Sundays and public holidays, 14–18; 14–17 in winter). Three-and-a-half kilometres beyond Touques, on the left, is the 15c. manor of **Canapville**, once the country residence of the bishops of Lisieux, and a particularly good specimen of the local style, with a stone stairtower and a timbered façade.

Pont l'Évêque today has two more bridges over the Touques to reinforce the one, built by a bishop of Lisieux, from which the town takes its name. Its cheese has been known for more than seven hundred years; in 1230 Guillaume de Lorris spoke of it in the *Roman de la Rose*. The small town, strung out along the main road from Caen, keeps a surprising amount of its appeal, bearing in mind the number of its timbered houses which were lost in 1944, when it was first bombed by the Allies, then fired by the retreating Germans. The Flamboyant church of St-Michel, with a massive tower and Renaissance pendants in the choir aisles, has been successfully restored, though the ancient glass has gone. Level with the church, but on the other side of the main road, is another worthwhile restoration, the Hôtel Montpensier, a Louis XIII house with splendid diapered effects of brick and stone.

Near the second bridge, in the direction of Caen, the lurching black and white building with an overhanging balcony in the Place du Tribunal is the old convent of the Dames Dominicaines de l'Isle. Opposite, the Hôtel Brilly, an 18c. brick and stone house which was the birthplace of the playwright Robert de Flers (1872–1927) has been converted into a singularly handsome Hôtel de Ville. Further along, at the third bridge, this one crossing the Eau d'Yvie, what look like the oldest surviving houses seem to be dissolving gently into the stream which they overhang.

Pont l'Évêque is a very possible place at which to stay if you want to visit but not spend a night at Lisieux, or to explore in detail this outstandingly green and fertile corner of Normandy. Avoid, though, a room facing on to the main road; the traffic is heavy and passes early and late. Eight or 9 kilometres to the east, the hamlet of **St André-d'Hébertot** (turn right at St Benoît) has an idyllically set château, whose early 18c. façade is framed between an early 17c. tower, reflected in a broad moat, and a small *pavillon* added in the mid-19c. In the churchyard behind it, dominated by the 11c. tower of five tiers, with a slate spire, is buried the chemist, Nicolas-Louis Vauquelin (1763–1829).

South of Pont l'Évêque, **Manneville-le-Pipart**, 4 kilometres along the main road for Lisieux, has a panelled 17c. church in which even the columns of the nave are of timber. At **Le-Breuil-en-Auge**, 5 kilometres further on, the manufacturing centre for Pont l'Évêque cheese, there is a timbered château dating from the first half of the 16c.

For a more comprehensive tour of the area, leave Pont l'Évêque by the secondary road for Lisieux (D48) and take the right-hand fork for **Pierrefitte-en-Auge**. The church here, 13c. in its oldest part, has a wonderful 17c. Calvary on the rood beam and a number of statues dating from the 15–17c., but its outstanding features are the wall and roof paintings of the 17c.

The D280, on the right, leads to the lost village of **St-Hymer,** whose priory church was one of the last active centres of Jansenism, that austere doctrine of predestination and rigorous piety, which gained considerable ground in the French church during the 17–18c. St-Hymer's first religious house, a monastery founded in 1067, was refounded a few years later as a priory dependent on the Benedictines of Le Bec-Hellouin, under whose guidance it flourished greatly. From 1717, eight years after Louis XIV had expunged Jansenism from its original homes, the abbeys of Port-Royal in Paris, and of Port-Royal-des-Champs in the Val de Chevreuse, St-Hymer, under its prior, the Abbé Raymond de Roquettes d'Amade, became the 'Port Royal de Normandie', building up a remarkable library and conducting a school.

Today the priory buildings, which date mainly from the 17c., with a little work surviving from the 16c., and were restored during the 18c., serve as a hospice, their early severity lost in a profusion of roses and fuchsia and wisteria. Until recently an exhibition devoted to the beginnings of Jansenism could be seen at the presbytery opposite. At the time of writing its future is uncertain, but it may find a home at Pont l'Évêque – ask at the *mairie*.

The church is 14c., with an earlier chapel, entered by an admirable Romanesque arch, on the south side of the choir. The windows are outstanding 14–15c. work; the north chapel of the crossing has notably beautiful carved altar fronts of the 16–17c. Among the pictures are a sketch for the Last Supper, by Philippe de Champaigne, and a St Martin and a St Hymer at prayer by the Rouen painter, Jean Restout (1692–1768). The setting for the whole comes out of the twenty-third psalm, which makes the ceramic flowers and ghastly monuments of black, white and red marble in the churchyard the more dismaying.

The D280 brings you back to the main road for Caen. Turn off it to the right at La Haie Tondue for the small hill-top town of **Beaumont-en-Auge**. There was a priory here too, but its monks, rather than embracing Jansenism, started a military school whose most illustrious pupil was the Marquis de Laplace (1749–1827), the astronomer and physicist. His statue stands in the central *place* and a plaque marks his birthplace. The priory church, now serving the parish, is 11–14c. Five kilometres further along the D118, turn left for the isolated church of **Saint-Pierre-Azif** (if locked, ask for the key at the grocer's in the village), whose 12c. choir has a remarkable collection of Flemish paintings. The D118 regains the coast road at Villers-sur-Mer. If your starting point was one of the resorts further west, by following the D281 south-west to the Caen road and turning seaward off it a short way past Dozulé, you can get a glimpse of the 16c. château of **Cricqueville**, with walls of the same chequered brick and stone as the houses of the village.

From Trouville to Honfleur is 15 kilometres by an almost extravagantly scenic corniche which, in the high summer, is commonly so busy that drivers can give its beauties only very secondary attention. East of Hennequeville, now virtually one with Trouville, the road rises to one of its highest points over the cliffs of Les Greniers, which are rich in fossils. Beyond them **Villerville**, a lively small resort, rises in terraces above a sheltered beach, the only one on this section of coast. The town is mentioned in a charter of 1195 and has a partly Romanesque church, but it was not 'discovered' until members of the 19c. artists' colony at Trouville prospected east. Fashion followed and the first villas were built in 1870, but Villerville seems to have realized early the perils of rampant development. It founded a society to preserve the natural charm of the countryside whose first members included the actress Réjane

(1856–1920), Alexandre Millerand (1859–1943), later to be President of the Republic, and a member of the chocolate manufacturing Menier family.

Cricqueboeuf has a picture-postcard 12c. church, muffled in ivy, **Pennedepie** a part-Romanesque, part-Gothic one, with a number of ancient statues. From **Vasouy**, perched on a modest height, with another 12c. church, the road skirts the hill of the Côte de Grâce to run into the most remarkable seaport town in Normandy.

It is undoubtedly the absence of a bathing beach which has enabled **Honfleur** to keep its character. The inner harbour, surrounded by slate-hung houses, the old fortress of the Lieutenance and the timber church of Sainte-Catherine are theatrically picturesque, with the gleaming petrol tanks over the estuary to point the drama, but this is life, not theatricals. Honfleur is a working port, with the appropriate supporting industries, including ship-repairing, timber and metalwork.

It has been a place of importance since the 13c., when it was a walled town. Edward III took it in 1346, and for the next hundred years it was to pass back and forth between French and English as, in the Wars of Religion, between Catholic and Protestant. Honfleur was the last of the Norman towns to accept Henri IV. The great period was the 16–17c. Honfleur's seamen rivalled those of Dieppe as explorers, navigators, corsairs – the distinction between them was commonly blurred. They are credited with having reached Brazil, Labrador, and the Cape of Good Hope. Le Paulmier de Gonneville is even believed to have touched Australia during 1503–5. Just over a hundred years later Samuel de Champlain, who was commissioned to colonize Canada, which France had neglected since, in 1535, Jacques Cartier of St-Malo had taken possession of it in the name of François I, sailed from Honfleur to found Quebec in 1608. He was not a Norman, having been born at Brouage, in the Charente-Maritime, but there were Honfleurais among the four thousand Normans and Percherons who later populated the colony, with the co-operation of shiploads of young women, the so-called 'filles du roy', who were dispatched after them. These came from all parts of France, and Queen Marie-Thérèse herself – we are by now in the 1660s – is said to have been personally concerned in seeing that they were reasonably prepossessing ('sans rien de rebutant a l'extérieur') as well as 'saines et fortes pour le travail de la campagne'. Soon the Normans were fishing for cod off Newfoundland.

The heart of the town remains the inner harbour, or Vieux Bassin, built by Duquesne (*see* under Dieppe) at the bidding of

Louis XIV between 1668 and 1684. Enlarged between 1720 and 1725, it remained Honfleur's main harbour until the 19c. saw the beginnings of the commercial docks to the east. Today the Vieux Bassin is chiefly a yacht harbour, though there is a certain amount of interchange with the fishing vessels which tie up in the Avant Port. Its unique character comes from the tall façades of the houses which surround it, many of them slate-hung as well as slate-roofed. Near its mouth is the 16c. **Lieutenance**, once the home of the Governor of Honfleur, and all that now remains of the fortifications, which were razed between 1684 and 1690, by order of Louis XIV, not by the enemy. The tiles of its roof strike a note of warm colour in the surrounding greys and blues. The Porte de Caen, a relic of the old town wall, has been incorporated into the building, and a black marble slab on the façade commemorates Champlain's sailing for Canada.

On the west side of the basin a needle spire rising above the roof-tops of the Quai Sainte-Catherine marks Honfleur's timber church – walk up the Rue des Logettes from the Place Hamelin before the Lieutenance. **Sainte-Catherine** is unique, not in being built of timber – there were other timber churches in Normandy, though very few survive – but in the manner of its construction. It dates from the last years of the 15c., when the end of the English occupation had left Honfleur largely in ruins. Money was scarce, the stone-masons of Normandy were already over-burdened with repairing the ravages of the Hundred Years War, and time pressed. Honfleur decided that its church should be built of the material nearest to hand, the timber of the forest of Touques, and by its own craftsmen, the shipwrights of the port. It seems to have been projected as a temporary expedient, and in 1468 consisted only of the present north nave. By 1496, when the increasing population was overflowing its new church, the town evidently decided that it was good enough to be permanent and a twin nave was built to the south of it. Look up into the roofs of both and you will see the hull of a ship, built tight and trim to withstand time and weather.

During the Restoration somebody had the misbegotten idea of covering with plaster the roof beams and the supporting posts that marched down the aisles like an avenue of trees, and sticking a large neo-classical porch on to the façade. All has now been made good and you see once more the traces of the axe on the timber, with, here and there, the natural fork of a tree squared off to act as a support.

In contrast with that rugged simplicity, the organ gallery has exquisitely carved panels, with angel musicians playing seventeen of

191

the instruments in use during the 16c. The organ itself is by the 18c. organ builder, Nicolas Lefèvre of Rouen. There are numerous statues and a 15c. bronze lectern with a memorably imperious eagle.

The free-standing belfry across the *place*, equally of wood, but slate-hung, is stayed at the angles, like a mast. There are old timbered houses in the Rue des Lingots, which opens behind it, and more in the Rue de la Bavole, the continuation of the Rue Brûlée, south-east of the church.

For the **Musée Eugène-Boudin**, leave the Place Sainte-Catherine by the Rue du Puits, where an inscription on No. 29 records that the Dutch landscape and marine painter, Jongkind (1819-91) stayed there when he was working at Honfleur, and turn right into the Rue des Capucins. At No. 13 the composer, Grétry (1741–1813) lived while he composed two of his light operas and, for variety, played the organ at Sainte-Catherine. The museum, recently rebuilt and enlarged, is in the Rue Albert Ier, on the right. Boudin (1824–98), the son of a Honfleur pilot, who, at the age of ten, was already making the trip up the Seine from Honfleur to Rouen as a cabin boy, ranks as the precursor of Impressionism, though the British can claim that Bonington and Turner had preceded him in rendering the shifting light of sea and sky off the coast of Normandy. He had no early art training; it was the chance of being apprenticed to a stationer at Le Havre, and later himself working as a stationer and picture framer there, which enabled him to meet painters like Isabey and Millet, whose advice and encouragement were invaluable to him. Finally a scholarship from the municipality of Le Havre took the self-taught young man to Paris, where he studied for three years. He came back to Normandy in time to deflect towards landscape painting a fifteen-year-old boy from Le Havre, who was then more interested in caricature. The lad's name was Claude Monet. Jongkind was working at Honfleur. It was from the friendship of these three, and their stays, with other painters, at the farm of 'la mère Toutain', at Saint-Siméon, to the west of Honfleur, that the Impressionist school grew. The farm is now a well-known restaurant on the Trouville road, just outside the town; pilgrims should not look for the simplicity, still less the prices of those early days. Boudin himself had to wait until nearly the end of his life for public success, though his work, particularly his handling of the skies which fill so large a part of his canvases, was from the first admired by his fellow painters.

Despite its title, the museum is not outstandingly rich in works by

Boudin, but it has a very comprehensive collection of the artists who made up the 'School of Honfleur', also of the many later painters who have worked in and around the town.

The Rue Albert Ier opens into the Rue Homme de Bois (the head of the wooden man is carved on the front of No. 25): turn left along it for the Place Jean de Vienne, with the 18c. building of the hospital which was founded in the 11c. Baudelaire's mother had a house here, now vanished, where her son wrote 'L'Invitation au Voyage'. Parallel with the Rue Homme de Bois, on the seaward side, the Rue Haute leads back to the Vieux Bassin. Its handsome houses, dating from the 16c., 17c. and 18c., were mostly those of shipbuilders: No. 15 was the birthplace of the composer, Erik Satie (1866–1925). East of the Bassin, the 14c. church of St-Étienne is now an **ethnographic and folk museum** (guided visits, 10–12, 14–18 daily in summer; closed on Fridays from October to April, and for the month 15 January – 15 February). It includes some statues originally in the church and an important display of the regalia of the *confréries* (*see* under Lyons-la-Forêt), but pre-eminently this is the place to study the past of the port. The material ranges from paintings and ship models to the only known register of samples of the cottons of Rouen, which the slave traders used as currency. Behind the Hôtel de Ville, at the seaward end of the quay, are two 17c. salt stores. In the event the fish-curing industry did not develop in proportion to their size.

From the landward end the Rue Montpensier and the Place de la Porte de Rouen, with the Syndicat d'Initiative on the left, lead up to the church of **St Léonard**, which, the first church on the site having been destroyed during the Hundred Years War, has emerged from many vicissitudes and much rebuilding with a most beautiful 16c. façade and an octagonal tower of 1760. The lectern, also late 18c., is the work of the brothers Béatrix, two of the best-known of the coppersmiths working at Villedieu-les-Poêles at the time.

Nobody should leave Honfleur without visiting the Calvary and chapel of the Côte de Grâce, the plateau above the town. From the Place du Puits a footpath leads up to it by way of Mont-Joli; passing the château where, during their somewhat hectic escape from France in 1848, Louis Philippe and his queen found shelter from 26 to 28 February. By car, if you must (the distance is only a kilometre or so), follow the road that strikes up to the left from the Rue Lucie Delarue-Mardrus, the continuation of the Rue des Capucins. The **Côte de Grâce**, which commands a panorama of the whole Seine estuary, has been a place of pilgrimage for centuries; ships' companies who had had a narrow escape at sea came to give thanks to Our Lady. Nowadays the most important pilgrimage is at Whitsun. The present church, architecturally heteroclite, but of great charm, with its domed porch and turret and overhanging trees, replaced a chapel founded by Richard III, Duke of Normandy, which was lost in a landslide in the 16c. It was built between 1600 and 1615, on land given by Madame de Montpensier. The walls are covered with ex-voto tablets and naïvely-spirited paintings of vessels, often in sore straits.

Honfleur is an ideal base for a leisurely exploration of a particularly appealing corner of Normandy, with the Forêt de St Gatien to the south-west and some interesting churches in the more open country directly south. Eleven kilometres east, by the coast road, are the ruins of the 11c. Benedictine abbey of **Grestain**, now a farm. An inscription and a mosaic mark the spot where 'la belle Arlette', the Conqueror's mother, is buried beside her lawful husband, Herluin de Conteville, and their son, Robert de Mortain.

Follow the coast road to Foulbec where, instead of turning left into the main N815, cross it and bear right for St Samson, then left for St Samson de la Roque. From here the D103 cuts across the Low Countries of the *marais-vernier*, once a bay in the Seine estuary, which, since Henri IV called in Dutch engineers in 1607, has been gradually transformed into polder, seamed by canals, with good grazing land, fertile market gardens, a model farm and in the south-east a fair-sized lake, teeming with fish and water fowl. The road crosses the N810 on the far side of the *marais* and runs down through St-Aubin into **Quillebeuf**.

Though in lesser fashion, the old port has the same kind of appeal as Honfleur, and at least as long a history. An MS of 1025, mentions it among the lands restored to the Abbey of Jumièges by Guillaume Longue-Épée, and the details make clear that it was already a place of some importance. It was the old capital of the Roumois and a haunt of the Viking pirates. Until the 13c. Quillebeuf was the home port of the Seine whalers and all its history has been dominated by its key position at the mouth of the estuary. For centuries it has been a pilot station. Henri IV gave the pilots of Quillebeuf a special status in gratitude for the loyalty of the town, which had been the first in Normandy to acknowledge him. He even tried to change its name to Henricarville, but this proved no more durable than the Franciscopolis of Le Havre.

The little town keeps its dignity, though nowadays the harbour is so quiet that you are aware of the slurping of the water against the jetty which is a twice daily reminder that it is here that the *mascaret* begins to build up. Only the arrival of the ferry for Port Jérôme, whose giant petrol installations are, in spirit, a thousand miles distant, breaks the tranquillity at regular intervals. In its crossings it passes over the wreck of the *Télémaque*, lost here in 1790, with, said rumour, the jewels of the French royal family aboard.

There are good grey stone houses in the Rue-Grande, notably the 16c. Maison Henri IV, where the king is said to have stayed, but the marvel of this staunchly Huguenot town is its early 12c. church. The choir was rebuilt in the 16c., but the central tower, with its double tier of arches and *colonettes*, and the elaborately decorated west porch are masterpieces. The 16c. windows include, on the south side, a procession of *confréries de charité* in the reign of Henri IV.

ITINERARY THREE

Cherbourg, Tourlaville, Nacqueville,
Presqu'île de la Hague, Barfleur, Gatteville,
Saint-Vaast-La-Hougue,
Val de Saire, Flamanville, Barneville-Carteret,
Bricquebec, Saint-Sauveur-le-Vicomte, Lessay, Coutances,
Coutainville, Hambey, Villedieu-les-Poêles, Granville,
Îles de Chausey, La Lucerne, Granville to Avranches,
Mont Saint-Michel, Val de Sées, Sélune, Mortain,
Abbaye Blanche, Domfront, Lonlay, Bagnoles,
Couterne, Carrouges, Flers, Condé-sur-Noireau,
Pontécoulant, Vire, Saint-Michel-de-Montjoie,
L'Angotière, Torigni, St-Lô, Cerisy, Bayeux, Balleroy,
Mondaye, Creullet, Creully, Brécy, Saint-Gabriel,
Longues-sur-Mer, Port-en-Bessin, Colleville-sur-Mer,
Formigny, Vierville-sur-Mer, Isigny, Carentan,
Sainte-Mère-Église, Valognes

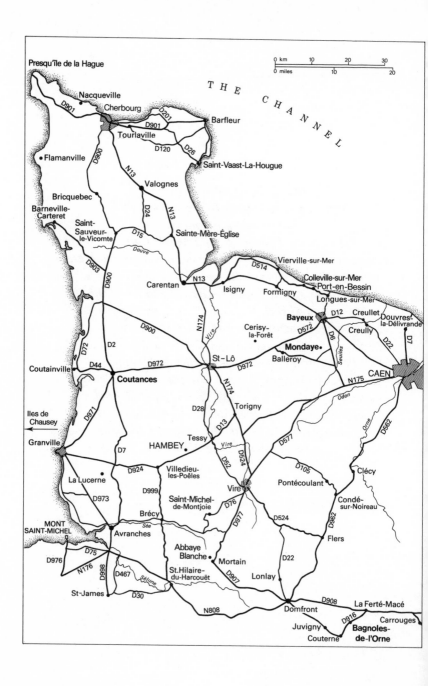

CHAPTER FIFTEEN

Cherbourg – Tourlaville – Nacqueville – Presqu'île de la Hague – Barfleur – Gatteville – Saint-Vaast-La-Hougue – Val de Saire

'TOMORROW's Channel inn' – it was Vauban, the engineer who fortified the borders of France in the 17c., who so called **Cherbourg**. Its site, where the Channel meets the Atlantic, was indeed strategically ideal for a great port, commercial as well as military; its conformation, a crescent-shaped bay, with little depth of water inshore and no shelter from the pounding of the north-west gales, was all against it. Approaching Cherbourg by sea today, one still wonders at the scale of the sheltering breakwaters which converted so unpromising a shore into a man-made harbour. The first of them, a massive *digue* several kilometres out to sea, with moles driving out from the shore towards its eastern and western extremities, has three forts to guard its length of 3,300 metres. Work on it started in 1776, almost three-quarters of a century after the death of Vauban, who had done no more than give Cherbourg the defensive works appropriate to a naval base. Louis XVI came to watch the laying of one of the ninety enormous cones, their frameworks stuffed with rubble and mortar, which were sunk to form a foundation, but king and several generations of workmen were in their graves, and the ninety cones multiplied almost past reckoning, before the movement of the tides shaped the accumulated material into an island which is the base of the breakwater which was completed in 1853. The Channel ferry passes between its eastern end and the tip of the eastern mole to enter the Grande Rade, or outer roads, then between two more stone jetties sheltering the Petite Rade, before it ties up at the Gare Maritime.

Sadly, when so much labour and ingenuity have gone into its construction, the 'Channel inn', through much of its history, has failed to attract a full company of guests. Its function as a trans-Atlantic port, which began in 1869 and developed after 1933, when the dredging of a deep water channel enabled the biggest liners to berth instead of anchoring in the roads and landing their passengers by tender, died with the ocean passenger trade. The trans-Atlantic terminal west of that used by the Normandy ferries is now out of commission. The commercial port suffers from its remoteness from Paris. There was a brief period during 1944–45 when, as an Anglo-American base, Cherbourg's traffic was twice that of New York in 1939. Today its trade is less important than that of Dieppe or La Rochelle, and the most impressive activity is that of the naval dockyard, which builds France's atomic submarines.

The town behind the port is worth more than the bed-and-breakfast stop which tends to be the norm for travellers. Within its borders it can offer an art gallery, notable for a section devoted to Millet, who was born near by, a museum of the Liberation, a botanical garden rich in tropical specimens; in the immediate neighbourhood are two châteaux with attractive parks, a 10–11c. manor house and the oldest church in the Cotentin. Also, Cherbourg is a convenient base from which to explore the eastern and western extremities of the peninsula, both of which are relatively little known, and each of which deserves a full day.

Start your itinerary with a call at the Syndicat d'Initiative, at No. 2 Quai Alexandre III, to collect local maps and check on the current opening times of museums, châteaux and the like. It is reached from the terminal by following the Valognes road due south and turning right across the Pont Tournant.

Here, with the bustle of the waterfront to entertain the patrons of the café terraces facing it, is the true heart of Cherbourg. To explore the geographical centre take the Rue Maréchal Foch into the **Place du Général de Gaulle**, where busts of Molière, Corneille and Boîeldieu along the front of the theatre look down on the lively market.

From the *place* continue along the Rue Maréchal Foch into the Rue Gambetta, then turn right into the Rue Emmanuel Liais, which leads to the **park** of the same name. Liais, a former mayor of Cherbourg, who was naturalist, botanist and sometime Assistant Director of the Paris Observatoire, left to the town his house and the park surrounding it. This is planted with the semi-tropical trees and shrubs which thrive in the soft climate of the tip of the Cotentin Peninsula. Their variety, supplemented by extensive greenhouses, makes the park of serious interest to botanists, as the cool, green lawns, misted by fountains, make it a pleasant place in which to spend an hour on a hot summer day. The house contains a **museum** of natural history and ethnography, whose opening times you will already have ascertained.

For the musuem, cross the Rond Point Leclerc and walk down the Rue Grande Vallée, which opens out towards the sea. The Hôtel de Ville, on the left, was at the time of writing still housing, inadequately, the **museum and art gallery** founded in 1835 by Thomas Henry, who gave the town of his birth the collection of pictures which he had built up during his career as an art expert attached to the national museums. A few years later the collection was augmented by a gift from the family of Jean François Millet, whose wife came from Cherbourg. The painter was born in 1814 at the neighbouring hamlet of Gruchy, the son of a peasant, and himself worked on the land before starting his formal art training at Cherbourg. He later worked in Paris, under the fashionable historic painter, Paul Delaroche, to whose influence was probably due the fact that his earliest successes were with period pastels. Surprisingly, in view of the sombre palette and uncompromising realism of the later works which were to make his reputation, many of these had a distinctly sensual character. By 1848, when 'The Winnower' was shown at the Salon, Millet had found his true source of inspiration, the gruelling life of the peasantry among whom he had grown up. During the following year he settled in Barbizon, where, as a leader of the unsentimental landscape painters who had settled there, he worked for the remaining twenty-five years of his life, often in extreme poverty and occasionally suffering accusations of fomenting socialism.

The **Millet Room** in the museum contains documents and photographs as well as paintings and drawings. The paintings include an early self-portrait showing the painter of peasants looking the reverse of rustic in a velvet-collared black coat with a snowy shirt frill. By the time this book is in print the opening of the projected new art gallery should have allowed the proper display of a collection which, hitherto, it has never been possible to hang in its entirety. It is particularly strong in its Dutch and Flemish as well as its French section, and has a surpassing treasure in the Virgin and Child by the Master of the Legend of St Ursula, a superb example of medieval painting.

Of the two monuments in the *place*, that to the *Résistants* of the Cotentin – 101 men and 7 women from the department of La Manche were executed during the Occupation – incorporates a stone from Struthof, the only concentration camp on French soil. The obelisk, with its fountain and flower beds, commemorates the visit to Cherbourg in 1814 of the Duc de Berry, second son of the future Charles X, the last Bourbon king of France. The Duc was assassinated in 1820, as he left the Paris Opéra, by a saddler named Louvel, who hoped, by his stroke, to extinguish the dynasty. It was to prove a vain hope. The Duc had a posthumous son, the Comte de Chambord, and the Bourbon line ended only with his death in 1883.

The Place de la République opens on to the broad Place Napoléon, laid out with gardens which separate it from a small bathing beach, man-made like the harbour. At its centre the Emperor rides his bronze horse on a pedestal whose legend recalls the words with which, in 1803, he decreed the construction of the naval base: 'J'avais résolu de renouveler à Cherbourg les merveilles de l'Égypte'. The statue, by Le Véel, is a posthumous gesture. It was erected in 1857, a year before the work on the base was completed, a tribute to the cult of Napoleon I, which was foreshadowed by Louis Philippe's ordering a new statue of the Emperor to be placed on top of the Austerlitz column in Paris, the original having been hauled down by the Royalists in 1814. Cherbourg had a particular place in the cult, for it was here that, in 1840, the frigate *La Belle Poule*, commanded by the Prince de Joinville, Louis Philippe's third son, brought the Emperor's ashes, to be transferred to the S.S. *Normandie* for the next stage of their journey from St Helena to the Invalides.

Turn right for the church of the **Sainte Trinité**, which occupies the site of a church founded by the Conqueror. The present building, which was started in 1423, and completed in 1504, is Flamboyant with accretions, of which the least happy is the lumbering tower added in 1825. The south porch is decorative, with delicate tracery and a huge pendant keystone. Inside, on the eastern face of the two pillars of the crossing, are the remains of the 14c. English alabaster altar piece whose carving, mutilated as it is, is instinct with life. The pulpit and the group of the Baptism of Christ over the high altar are by the 18c. Cherbourg sculptors, Armand and Pierre Fréret. From the church follow the curve of the waterfront back to the Pont Tournant.

The **Fort du Roule**, crowning the hill of the same name, which rises to the south of the town, is best visited in the late afternoon, since the view from the terrace is most impressive towards sunset – but remember that the **museum** which occupies part of the fort closes at 18 from 1 April to 30 September, inclusive; at 17.50 for the rest of the year. The fort is accessible by car, but the walk up the easy zig-zag lets one enjoy the prospect over the port and the town broadening out as one mounts. To reach it from the Pont Tournant, continue along the Quai Alexandre III to the Place Jean Jaurès, turn left into the Avenue François Millet, then right, past the **Jardin Publique**, with its sloping, informal lay-out, luxuriant flower beds and 14c. entrance gateway, brought here from the ruined Abbaye du Vœu. Just beyond it, turn left uphill.

The fort, which was built in 1854, was modernized by the Germans in 1943–44; its entrance hall has frescoes on the heroic scale which some may find disconcerting. Beyond, in the room devoted to old Cherbourg, the history of the port since the Middle Ages is evoked with the aid of paintings, engravings, seals and models. Its more recent history, when, on the personal orders of Hitler, the vanquished Germans reduced the harbour to 'a field of ruins' rather than leave so valuable an asset to the Allies, is introduced by the *salle des cartes*, in which the progress of the Allied armies after the Normandy landings is lucidly set out on large-scale relief maps. The succeeding rooms contain memorabilia ranging from a tricolor made from the silk of three parachutes dropped on the peninsula on 6 June 1944, to a bottle of champagne (Moët et Chandon) taken from the underground shelter where Admiral Hennecke and General von Schlieben surrendered on 26 June, which keep their poignant actuality. In the basement there is a display devoted to the French Resistance.

A visit to the Gare Maritime is a pleasant pendant to the survey from the Fort du Roule. From the tip of the Quai de France, particularly when a fresh breeze whips up the sea, one can enjoy the illusion of being on shipboard. The backward view includes the two basins of the naval dockyard, well to the west. Only French nationals may visit it, which is a minor deprivation since the workshops where France's atomic submarines are built are closed to all visitors.

Each of the two neighbouring châteaux makes a pleasant afternoon's outing. At **Tourlaville**, which is now owned by the town of Cherbourg, the house is not open to the public, but the well-timbered park, of which they have the freedom daily from 14 to 18, or 17 in winter, is well worth a visit. Leave the town by the N801, turn right into the D63 and right again at the cross-roads, a bare kilometre further on. At the next junction, where three roads meet, walk down to the right.

Théophile Gautier found the first sight of Tourlaville, which, at that time, was picturesquely dilapidated, like a stage set for the opera. The grey Renaissance house, roofed with slate in the same shade, framed in trees and looking across a sheet of water, still justifies that impression. But if this is the perfect backdrop for a lyric opera, the story for which Tourlaville actually was the setting is a subject for Webster. The brother and sister, Marguerite and Julien de Ravalet, who grew up in the enclosed world of the château during the second half of the 16c., grew also into an incestuous love which survived the marriage with a loutish husband thirty years her senior arranged for Marguerite by her parents. The brother and sister fled, to be traced and arrested in Paris in September 1603. A few days later Marguerite gave birth to a son. On 2 December she and Julien, found guilty of incest and adultery, were executed together. She was twenty-one, he seventeen years old.

Nacqueville, 8 or 9 kilometres west of Cherbourg, makes a pleasant afternoon's excursion. The guided visits (14, 15, 16, 17 daily, Tuesdays and Fridays excepted, from Easter to All Saints) include admission to a specimen ground-floor room and an extended tour of the outstandingly attractive park laid out *à l'anglaise*. Leave Cherbourg by the Rue de l'Abbaye passing on the right the sad ruins of the 12c. **Abbaye du Vœu**, which was founded by the Empress Matilda, daughter of Henry I of England. They were ravaged by fire in 1944 and restoration has been slow. Five kilometres out of the town turn right along the coast road, N3. At Querqueville, 2 kilometres along it, a signpost points steeply uphill to the tiny chapel of **Saint-Germain**, which is the most ancient church building in the Cotentin, and possibly in western France. It is built of narrow slabs of schist in a herring-bone pattern. The nave and east end, with its rare plan of three equal apsidal chapels, each ending in a *cul-de-four*, are from the 10c. or early 11c.; the overweening central tower was slapped on top after the turn of the 17–18c. Continuing archaeological research, which means that the chapel is liable to be closed to visitors, is expected to establish its origins more precisely.

Nacqueville is down a road leading to the left from the hamlet of La Rivière, 1½ kilometres along the N135. The house, niched in trees, was built at the end of the 16c. and the beginning of the 18c., of the local granite, with faintly rose tiles on the gabled roof and the round tower. Twin pepperpot towers flank the ivy-covered gatehouse, of the late 16c., which has been admirably restored. The arms over the entrance are those of Hippolyte de Tocqueville, brother of the historian and political scientist, Alexis, who owned the château during the 19c.

On either side of Cherbourg there are dramatically contrasted stretches of country and coastline, each of which deserves a full day. Either is worth a longer stay, but while, to the east, there are quiet, pleasant resorts, with the normal hotel provision, those who are attracted by the vast solitudes of the **Presqu'île de la Hague**, to the west, will find only limited and simple accommodation. This is Normandy at its most Breton, at the time of equinoctial gales suffused with the beauty and terror of great winds and raving water, in spring and early summer verdant and blossoming. The wild flowers, enormous, velvety primroses and banks sheeted with violets echoing the colour of the sea that is seldom out of sight, are voluptuously beautiful. There is an incandescence of gorse, with goldfinches flashing a more vivid yellow above it.

For a day's excursion, continue along the coast road from La Rivière. At **Urville-Nacqueville**, a small bathing resort 2 kilometres beyond it, an English raiding party landed in August 1758, to sack the town of Cherbourg and badly damaged the port. On the left is the fortified manor house of the Dur-Édcu, a rugged 10–11c. building remarkable for having three superimposed mills. The Syndicat d'Initiative at Cherbourg will have told you if it is open to visitors; at the time of writing it was not.

Landemer, another bathing resort at the mouth of a wooded valley, marks the beginning of a more spectacular coastline. **Gréville-Hague**, 3 kilometres on, has a 12c. church, with tower and choir chapels added in the 16c., which Millet painted. His statue, by Marcel Jacques, stands near by. The hamlet of **Gruchy**, where Millet was born, is a kilometre to the north-east. The road continues for another half-kilometre to reach the sea at cliffs 50–60 metres high, cut by deep watercourses. The curious spine of granite thrusting out into the water here is the Rocher du Castel-Vendon.

Between Gréville and Omonville, the road cuts across the remains of the Hague-Dicke, an ancient fortification which once ran across the peninsula, ending at Herqueville. Until 1953 it was believed to have been a defence against the Viking pirates: excavations in that year established that it was in fact part of the defensive works built by the Vikings. Beyond it the road rises over the 120-metre Mont Pali, then drops down to Omonville between buttresses of hydrangea to run beside the sea through **Port Racine**, reputedly the smallest harbour in France, and Saint-Germain-des-Vaux before swinging inland to **Auderville**. The church here has a chastely elegant 13c. choir and the churchyard a new manifestation of folk art, if folk art is defined as something that people do for themselves instead of copying out of a book. On a number of graves the rectangle which, when not grassed, is usually filled with gravel or chippings is covered with fragments of bottle glass. The idea may seem repulsive, the result, a lucent mosaic of amber, green and crystal, is oddly attractive and greatly to be preferred to the plastic and ceramic fancies which proliferate elsewhere.

It is possible to take a car down the hill to the low, sandy point of the Cap de la Hague, the north-west tip of Normandy, but far better to walk the kilometre or two through what, for most of the year, remains a radiant wilderness. Ahead, a lighthouse marks the Gros du Raz, the biggest rock in the outwork of reefs, with, beyond them, the tide rip of the Raz Blanchard, which separates the mainland from Alderney. The granite cross away to the right commemorates the French submarine *Vendémaire* which was rammed by the cruiser *Saint Louis* during manoeuvres off this coast in 1912. The lifeboat station in the minute harbour of **Goury**, the only shelter on this section of the coast, has two slip-ways, allowing launching at any state of the tide. Its record testifies to the perils of this shore off which there is an 8-knot current. Between 1870 and 1971 the lifeboat went to the rescue of 170 ships and saved 350 lives.

Returning to Auderville, turn right for the spectacular *route en corniche*, which winds through heather and bracken above the sandy crescent of the Baie d'Ecalgrain. At Dannery the D202 turns off on the right for the Nez de Jobourg. There is a walk of about a quarter of an hour from the end of the road to the other aspect of this land's end of the Hague, the thundering drop of 128 metres from the savage rocks of the headland into the savagely reef-strewn seas. The tiny inlet of the Anse de Sennival divides the Nez de Jobourg from the Nez de Voidries, to the north, which has magnificent viewpoints over the whole west coast of the peninsula as well as a series of caves in the headlands, picturesquely named – *la Grande et la Petite Église, le Trou aux Fées, la Grotte du Lion* – and mostly inaccessible.

The D401 joins the N801 for Beaumont at **Jobourg**, which epitomizes the past and future of the Hague. The isolated village to the left has a 12c. church whose massive, saddle-back tower and low roof, giving the impression that the building has been battened down against a gale, are typical of the region. On the right, towards Cherbourg, a fenced-off area of 220 hectares encloses an atomic centre, producing principally plutonium. The enormous quantity of fresh water which it uses comes from a dam with a capacity of 400,000 cubic metres: after treatment, which reduces but does not eliminate its radioactivity, the water is discharged into the Raz Blanchard, 5 kilometres from the coast. France's plans greatly to enlarge the centre has caused anxiety in the Channel Islands as well as in Normandy.

From Jobourg, the N801 leads directly back to Cherbourg: alternatively there are two rewarding coastwise loops. The shorter, by the D403, passes through Herqueville and Herquemoulin to plunge down to the sea, then climb back to Beaumont. For the second detour, leave Beaumont by the D318, which passes through Vauville and Biville, with immense prospects which, in clear weather, extend as far as the cliffs of Flamanville to the south. **Vauville**, a hamlet set beside a lagoon and sheltered by dunes which continue for 8 kilometres south of it, has a 17c. château, with an older donjon, and, beside it, a rustic church with a Romanesque nave and a Gothic choir. **Biville**, up on the plateau, is famous for its gliding ground. It is the centre of a pilgrimage to the tomb of the Blessed Thomas Hélie who, according to tradition (unauthenticated) was Saint Louis's chaplain. An enamel chalice and a brocade vestment woven with the arms of France and Castile, which are said to have belonged to him, are shown. The white marble tomb dates only from 1910, when it replaced an older one; the choir of the church is authentically 13c., though much restored. We rejoin the N801 a short distance beyond Sainte-Croix-Hague.

The north-east of the peninsula, where the granite slides gently into the water around the point of Gatteville, is another, softer country. Leave Cherbourg by the D16, a low corniche with small pebble or shingle beaches, frilled with foam, on the one hand, rising slopes of gorse and bracken on the other. At Bretteville the D320 goes off diagonally to the right. A couple of kilometres down it is an ancient burial site, the *allée couverte*, where neolithic tombs have been discovered. The passage, 16 metres long, formed by a double line of stones, with a logan-stone, is what remains of a collective tomb.

At Fermanville a road to the left leads to the wild Cap Lévy, with one of the most modern lighthouses in France – it is open to visitors. Past Fermanville the D10 takes us to **Saint-Pierre-Église**, from which the family of the Abbé de Saint-Pierre, author of what may be the earliest peace plan, the 17c. *Projet de Paix Perpétuelle*, takes its name. The present château, an outstandingly pure example of mid-18c. architecture, replaced that in which the Abbé was born. A modern statue of him stands in the *place*, overlooked by a 17c. church which incorporates part of the original 12c. building in the north aisle and the apse. The elaborate tower is also 12c., but was later heightened and given overhanging turrets at each corner, with a balustrade running between them.

Five kilometres along the main road for Barfleur is the imposing château of **Tocqueville**, whose origins go back to the 12c., though the oldest part of the present building is 15c. and the main body of the house 17–18c. Alexis de Tocqueville (1805–1859), political scientist, historian and politician, whose *La Démocratie en Amérique* foresaw the dangers of state paternalism and examined the influence of social equality, inherited the property in 1856. He wrote some of his books here, besides constructing the ornamental water which reflects the turrets and mansards of the château. Surprisingly, the bust of Tocqueville on the left of the road was not set up until 1936.

The way continues through the placid green of the Val de Saire to the small town of **Barfleur**, an admirable place for a quiet holiday, which has survived the transition from important fishing port to sailing centre and bathing resort without losing its virtue or its dignity. Here, according to tradition, was built the *Mora*, the vessel which carried William Duke of Normandy to the conquest of England. A bronze seal on a rock near the lifeboat slip-way marks the ninth anniversary of his setting forth. From Barfleur, in 1120, sailed the *White Ship*, carrying the son and heir of King Henry I of England, with his sister and half the court, to go down on the reef of Quillebeuf, with only one survivor, the butcher Bérold, to carry the ill tidings. In the Middle Ages Barfleur was a favourite cross-Channel port for Anglo-Norman royalty, heaven knows why, since the currents as well as the reefs off this coast are formidable. Today, good granite houses stand round the wide harbour, overlooked by a 17c. church set on a little rocky height. The relics of Marie-Madeleine Postel, foundress of the Sœurs de la Miséricorde at Saint-Sauveur-le-Vicomte, who was born at the hamlet of La Bretonne, now part of Barfleur, and canonized in 1925, are in the north transept. A tablet on the house at the corner of the street leading down from the church records that the neo-Impressionist painter, Paul Signac, lived in it from 1932–35.

The standard excursion is to the lighthouse of **Gatteville**, on the Pointe de Barfleur, 4 kilometres to the north by road. By taking the footpath along the shore, which turns off the D116 after it has crossed the stream of Pont-au-Ferre, you will save a kilometre while reducing by one the throng of cars which, at week-ends and on public holidays, destroy the character of this, like other wild, bright places. The lighthouse, 71 metres of granite, with a range of 56 kilometres, was built between 1829 and 1835, when the 18c. tower which it replaced was converted into a semaphore. It is worth climbing the 365 steps to the lantern for the piquancy of the view, with the torn rock and glistering weed of the shore in front and lush pasture behind. Gatteville village, a kilometre inland, is a surprise. Where, so near the coast, you expect a group of fishermen's cottages, there is a big, flower-bordered *place*, with, at one end, the sailors' chapel of Notre-Dame-de-Bon-Secours, which has an 11c. apse. The church opposite was largely rebuilt in the 18–19c. but retains its 12c. saddle-backed tower, built veritably of the pebbles of the seashore, gilded with lichen and roofed with silvery slate.

Saint-Vaast-La-Hougue (pronounced Saint-Va) is 11 kilometres to the south; the coast road passes several of the fortified manors which are typical of this part of Normandy. From Réville, with a 12–15c. church, set on a rocky buttress, a road turns off on the left to pass through the hamlet of Jouville, with a sheltered bathing beach, to the Pointe de Saire, from which there are wide views up and down the coast. The D1 runs on between tamarisks to the softer country beside the Bay of Réville. **Saint-Vaast**, with almost 2,400 inhabitants to Barfleur's less than 900, one broad main street leading down to the harbour, fortifications out of yesterday's wars and noted oyster beds, is perilously picturesque, but too massive and spacious to risk degenerating into a tourist trap. The fishing survives along with the sailing and the holiday beaches. The town owes the fortifications which give it its character to a French naval disaster of 1692, when a fleet under Amiral de Tourville sailed to take part in a projected landing on the English coast which was to reinstate James II. It was annihilated by a superior Anglo-Dutch force, supported by the weather. Vauban's great defences were designed to prevent a repetition. Today's ramparts and the tower of the Île de Tatihou look out over the oyster beds of the bay, which is as quiet as a pond in anything but an east wind. At low tide during the equinoxes the bay dries out so that it is possible to walk over to Tatihou.

To reach the Fort de la Hougue, which guards the south-west approach to the bay, leave on the left the jetty with its lighthouse, and the sailors' chapel whose white painted apse serves as a daymark, and walk along the kilometre of the embankment skirting the Grande Plage, off which one can swin in deep, quiet water. Today sheep safely graze round Vauban's donjon. There is no admittance to the enceinte but a footpath follows the line of its walls.

In summer there are boat trips from Saint-Vaast to the **Îles Saint-Marcouf**, 13 kilometres to the south-east. Two of these, the Île du Large and the Île de Terre, are fortified, which did not prevent the English from investing them in 1795 and using them as a base for harrying shipping between Cherbourg and Le Havre. They stayed until 1802, when the Treaty of Amiens brought a short-lived peace between Britain, France, Spain and Holland.

The road back to Cherbourg runs through the full luxuriance of the Val de Saire. From Quettehou the D26 rises through apple orchards to **Le Vast**, a picture village with a 15c. church set on the banks of the Saire which here has modest falls. The D120 continues westward through rich parkland to join the N801 6 kilometres from Cherbourg.

CHAPTER SIXTEEN

Flamanville – Barneville-Carteret – Bricquebec – Saint-Sauveur-le-Vicomte – Lessay – Coutances – Coutainville

✣

FROM Cherbourg to Coutances is 100 kilometres by the coast road, 70 by the more direct inland one, the two routes converging at La Haye-du-Puits.

South of Vauville, the west side of the Cotentin is a long holiday beach, its bleached infinities of sand broken by the granite cliffs of Flamanville and the headland of Carteret and punctuated by resorts with plentiful hotel accommodation. The D64 from Cherbourg reaches the sea at Siouville-Hague, a resort with a fair range of the standard holiday attractions. Diélette, where iron was worked as recently as 1962, the galleries running under the sea, has the curiosity of two harbours, one within the other, protected by granite jetties. The sandy beach extends on either side of the south jetty. From here, a coastguard path along the cliffs leads to the Cap de Flamanville in 6 rough kilometres. The town of **Flamanville**, standing 1½ kilometres back from the sea, has a 17c. château incorporating two towers which survive from an older manor. Only the park is open to the public; among its palms and hydrangeas is the *pavillon* which the Marquis de Flamanville built for Jean-Jacques Rousseau in 1778 – but the philosopher preferred Ermenonville.

From Flamanville the D517 is a corniche above the wide bay of Sciotot. After that it is sand all the way, except for the rocky outcrop of the Pointe de Rozel. The dunes hereabouts, which alternate with grassy hollows known locally as 'mielles', are the highest on the Normandy coast.

Carteret, strictly Barneville-Carteret, as the towns lying respectively east and west of the Gerfleur estuary are a single commune, has three sandy beaches. The Cap de Carteret, which protects the town from the north and west winds, divides the small, sheltered Plage de Carteret from the 11 idyllically uncluttered kilometres of the Plage de la Vieille Église to the west. For the energetic there is a coastguard path round the headland; motorists should take the Avenue des Deux Plages on the landward side. About half-way along it is crossed by the Avenue de Phare, leading on the left to a lighthouse which may be visited, on the right to the highest point of the headland, the Roche Biard, which has an orientation table. From both Jersey is visible in clear weather. The ruined church above the shore, from which the beach takes its name, was abandoned in 1686. It is thought that the first village of Carteret was built here, rather than beside the estuary. Returning towards the harbour, we pass on the right the Gare Maritime. In the season there are daily excursions to Jersey: the crossing takes an hour.

At low tide it is possible to walk across to Barneville Plage on the east side of the estuary, whose liveliness makes it a complement to the Vieille Église, though paradoxically, the sand with its careened boats seems more divisive than the brimming tide peopled by the butterfly sails of pleasure craft. **Barneville's** 11c. church, much rebuilt and restored – the machicolated tower was added in the 15c. – retains its carved capitals. The most remarkable church in this area is Notre-Dame de Portbail, 8 kilometres south-east. Leaving Barneville by the road for La Haye-du-Puits, we pass the monument commemorating the US army's cutting across the Cotentin Peninsula on 18 June 1944. For **Portbail**, turn right at the cross-roads of La Picauderie. This small seaside resort was a bustling port before the Norse invasions, and its Christian past is as least as old. In 1956 a chance discovery revealed the remains of a hexagonal baptistery of the 6c., the only one of its type known to exist north of the Loire. The harbour-side church of Notre-Dame, not to be confused with the parish church of St Martin, in the centre of the town, is late 11c. or early 12c. The capitals are remarkable for their vigour and vitality, particularly those at the entrance to the apse, whose carvings include three standing figures, the central one of which is said, on no very firm grounds, to be an abbot of Lessay – the abbey had a priory here. (For admission to both church and baptistery, apply to the Syndicat d'Initiative at the *mairie*.) The main road goes on to La Haye-du-Puits; the tower we see as we enter the town is the donjon of the château which was built in the 11c. by Richard Turstin Haldup, founder of Lessay.

For the inland route, leave Cherbourg by the D900, which climbs out of the heather and bracken of the valley of the Divette to run south through green, unemphatic country. This is *echt* Normandy, more preoccupied with dairy and beef cattle than with tourists, and **Bricquebec**, fortress and market in a setting of wooded hills, epitomizes it. Monday here, when the great, sloping market place that opens out before the castle gate is seething with activity, evokes

Flaubert's Normandy more vividly than anything else I know. The sandwiches sold at the barbecue stall consist of a fair-sized steak clapped between about half a *baguette*; there is the eternal callousness of the peasant in the summary fashion in which the bewildered piebald calves are bundled in and out of lorries; the lines of a face gazing out blankly over the chest-high wall of a *pissotière* are duplicated in the carvings of many a church.

Bricquebec's **castle** (visits, 9–12, 13.30–19 in season, otherwise 10–12, 14–17; Sundays and public holidays 10–12, 14–17) was one of the major strongholds of the dukes of Normandy. After Agincourt, Henry V gave it to William de la Pole, Earl of Suffolk, who, in 1429, handed it back to the French as part of the price of his ransom. The enceinte, with its flanking towers and splendid polygonal donjon of the 14c., has survived intact: the *corps de logis* is now a hotel in whose storehouse and garage the vaults of the *salle des chevaliers* are still to be seen. There is a small **museum** of local history and ethnography in the Tour de l'Horloge.

North-west of the market place is a noble promenade with two double rows of oak, chestnut and plane. Turn right out of it and follow the line of the *place* for a sight of the graceful 17c. façade of the Château des Galeries, set in an overgrown park. The 11c. doorway let into a wall on the right-hand side of the Rue de la République, leading downhill from the castle, is the last relic of the old parish church, which was demolished in 1906. One of Normandy's two Trappist monasteries, **Notre-Dame-de-Grâce**, is $2\frac{1}{2}$ kilometres north of the town by the D121. It is open for visits (men only) at 15 on weekdays: women may attend services at the abbey church where the office is sung, in French, at 8.15 and 18.20 on weekdays, at 11, 15.30 and 20 on Sundays and feast days.

The two monuments of **Saint-Sauveur-le-Vicomte**, 14 kilometres to the south-west, the massive 14c. keep of its château, and the church, with some 13c. work, happily survived the bombing of 1944. This was the town of Barbey d'Aurevilly (1808–89), critic, dandy modelled on Beau Brummell, not quite an aristocrat, who is the novelist of the Cotentin as Jean de la Varende is the novelist of the Pays d'Ouche.

An old people's hospice now occupies the château which Edward III gave to Sir John Chandos: visitors may enter the partly ruined enceinte, with Rodin's bust of Barbey, looking supercilious, at the entrance. There is a **museum** devoted to the writer in the postern (open 9–12, 14–19 in season; out of season ask at the hospice). Barbey is buried beside his brother, Léon d'Aurevilly, in a small cemetery outside the château wall: walk round to the left from the entrance. A plaque marks the comely 17c. house in the Place Ernest-Legrand, off the main street leading away from the château, where he was born.

The church, on the left of the same street, has a striking *Ecce Homo* of 1532 on the north pillar of the chancel arch, also a 14–15c. St Jacques de Compostelle. The memorial to Catherine de Longpré, who was baptized here and died in the odour of sanctity in 1668 at Quebec, which she had helped to found, recalls the link between Normandy and French Canada.

Nineteen kilometres due south of St-Sauveur there is another Bénédictine abbey which is a marvel alike for the integrity and simplicity of the original plan and the triumphant result of the decision to rebuild it, stone by stone, after it had been wrecked by German mining and Allied bombardment. **Lessay** was founded in 1056 by Turstin Haldup, seigneur of La-Haye-du-Puits. Twenty-four years later the foundation was confirmed by the Conqueror, who was a kinsman of Turstin, his wife, Matilda, and their three sons: St Anselm, who was then Abbot of Bec, and the Archbishops of Canterbury and York. The abbey's wealth was soon to include important possessions in England.

Completed by the end of the 11c., the church was badly damaged during the Hundred Years War, but the restoration was an exact reconstruction.

At the beginning of World War II, Lessay was the only monastery in the old diocese of Coutances whose buildings had survived virtually intact from the *ancien régime*. At the end it was an abomination of desolation, the tower down, the roof wrecked, the walls shards. Audacity, inspired lunacy almost, decided on a scrupulous reconstruction, reclaiming every scrap of the remaining stone and taking infinite pains to find material as nearly as possible identical with which to supplement it. Craftsmen worked with tools like those used by their medieval predecessors and, by leaving out the later accretions, restored the original purity of the building. The work took thirteen years, at a cost to the *Monuments Historiques*, whose architect-in-chief, Monsieur Y.M. Froidevaux, has here ensured his lasting reputation, which no doubt entailed the deferment of work on other ancient buildings.

We approach the church from the east, so that the first impression is of the gable of the choir rising above the cone of the apse, with the squat tower crowning the whole in a disposition of masses which has the inevitability of perfection. The rough tiles of the Hague have been used for the roof and the local schist for the main walls; only the tower, apse, façade and upper windows are of the limestone quarried near Valognes. The interior takes you at a stroke. 'Order is heaven's first law'. There is matter for endless study in Lessay, but the essence is here, in the advance of the seven wide bays of the nave through the choir to the climax of the *cul-de-four* apse, with its two tiers of windows. The ogival arches are now believed to be older than those of Durham, which was previously thought to have been the first great church to apply a discovery which was ultimately to make possible the luminous walls of Gothic cathedrals. Moving down the church from the apse one can trace its development. The choir and the two westernmost bays of the nave were completed by the end of the 11c.; the remaining five bays were added early in the 12c. Clearly, the master builder responsible for the first phase knew something of the new technique of crossed diagonal arches supported by pillars: equally clearly he had no practical experience of its use. His arches stayed up, but, in the fashion in which they fell on the cornice as often as on the capitals, there is a hint of those early artists who painted elephants and camels from hearsay. From the third bay of the nave – this second phase of the work was probably carried out by another master builder – the arches fall square on the capitals.

The high altar, a monolithic slab set on two blocks of stone, is worthy of its setting, as is Lambert-Rucki's wooden crucifix which hangs above it. In the north choir aisle the old altar has been reconstructed; for the south an ancient altar slab which had been used as a paving stone was rescued, repaired and set on a column. There is an exquisite baptistery in a 15c. chapel in the south transept, its floor a mosaic of tide-worn pebbles, the font scooped from a block of stone in a shape that follows the smooth curve of a shell, the outer wall left unfinished. The engraved bronze cover of the water reserve is the single artefact in a place where all else seems shaped by waves and wind.

The baptistery is the one part of the church which is radiant with daylight. Elsewhere there is a luminosity that is subtly not white, but rather ivory, with hints of green and gold. It is achieved by windows executed by Madame Flandrin-Latron in abstract designs inspired by the interlacing patterns of Celtic ornament in tones of grey, ochre and palest yellow, with an occasional note of deep green, purple or dull blue.

The road for Coutances runs due south across the *lande de Lessay*, 5,000 hectares of pancake-flat plain. Here, in the 13c., the

217

Bénédictines established the *foire de Sainte-Croix*, which added substantially to the income of the monastery. It flourishes still as one of the most important fairs in Normandy, notably for horses. Each year, for three or four days at the end of the first fortnight in September, there is brisk dealing in the leggy colts and the pied cattle of Normandy. On either side of the main road the tents of the accompanying fun fair are set up, with the enormous eating and drinking, sausages spitting over charcoal and gigots on spits, inseparable from a popular gathering hereabouts.

A detour by the D72, towards Créances, will take in the ruins of the oldest fortified castle in Normandy. **Pirou**, dating from the 11–12c., is dominated by a 13-metre watch-tower which contrasts with the bland classical façade of the existing château (visits 2.30–6.30, 15 July – 31 August).

Coutances signals from afar, a city set on a hill with the pale spires of the cathedral driving up from its summit. Coutances, or Constantia, is first mentioned as a see in 571, when it had a basilica, probably on the site of the present church of St Pierre. In 836 the clergy, bearing the relics of St Lô, fled from the Viking invaders, the bishop finally establishing himself at Rouen, and in 900 the Norsemen occupied the city and completely destroyed the cathedral. The church which succeeded it in the 11c. was built 'with money from Italian spoils', as Henry Gally (knight and M.P.), who made an architectural tour of Normandy in the 1830s, tells us rather primly. The first of the spoilers were the successors of those Norman knights who, on their way back from a pilgrimage to the Holy Land in 1016, helped the southern Italians in their struggle against the Saracens. Under the leadership of Guillaume Bras de Fer, Robert Guiscard and Roger, sons of Tancrède de Hauteville-la-Guichard, half-way between Coutances and St-Lô, they returned to conquer the whole of southern Italy. In the 11c., Apulia and Calabria which, today, are regions of emigration, were receiving immigrants from Normandy. In the ten years 1062–72, Robert Guiscard conquered Sicily, which his family ruled until 1265. Norman tenacity and sense of order triumphing over the local mores, they made of it one of the two most efficiently organized states in Europe. The other was England, also under Norman rule.

The cathedral whose building had been started at Coutances in 1030 had made little progress when Geoffroi de Montbray, a soldier-priest who went to Hastings with the Conqueror, was appointed to the see. To raise the funds needed to continue the church he journeyed to Calabria to appeal to Robert Guiscard, the results being so spectacular that, by 1056, the cathedral and the bishop's palace were virtually completed. The rate of progress may have involved an element of jerry-building for, though the lightning that caused the collapse of the central tower in 1091 could be classed as an act of God, the rebuilding involved extensive restoration of the apse, transept, chapels and west towers.

Early in the 13c., after the town had been ravaged by fire in 1218, a Gothic **cathedral** was built, not in place of the existing one, but largely above and around it. From the interior, the structure of the Romanesque west towers, which served as scaffolding for the Gothic, can be clearly seen. From the outside it is hard to believe in the existence of that solid core, so airily slim are the twin, though not identical, towers crowned by octagonal spires. Their height is enhanced by the slender turrets pierced with narrow bays: it is a similar insistence on verticals that gives an effect of lightness to the massive central tower. The façade is a rare blend of richness and grace. Quatrefoils pierce the balcony that crosses the porch below the west window; the balcony above it, like the gables over the rose windows, is a prodigy of delicate openwork. The sculptured reliefs of the Virgin which decorated the tympanum were destroyed at the Revolution when the cathedral was transformed into a Temple of Reason. So were the statues in the niches. Gally tells us that these included likenesses of Tancrède and six of his sons – he had twelve, also three daughters.

The small door on the left, known as the 'door of St Lô', commemorates the miracle credited to the 6c. bishop who, when he first entered his cathedral, gave back her sight to a blind woman. To this day the Bishops of Coutances use it for their first and last entrances, when they take possession of their cathedral and when they are brought to it for burial, though no longer in the first instance do they approach barefoot and kneel on the threshold.

From the west door the first impression of the interior is the total purity of its lines: everything is subservient to the upward impulse of the clustered columns of nave and choir. The lantern, which suffuses the crossing with light, is said to have been admired by Vauban.

Look longer and you will realize that, though the first impression is of austere perfection, the detail of the interior is ravishing. Roses and foliage luxuriate over the blind triforium; the balustrades are varied in their design; partitions of lacy stonework divide the nave chapels. There are traces of a 15c. fresco over the altar of the second chapel of the south aisle: in the last, the Chapel of St Francis, a 17c. wooden high relief of the Kiss of Judas makes a curiously affecting contrast with a mutilated, infinitely worn carving of the Crucifixion.

A double ambulatory runs round the choir. The outer aisle is lower than the inner, its arches combining with those of the shallow radiating chapels. The apsidal chapel has, along with an assortment of modern tombs of bishops, an outstandingly beautiful 14c. statue of the Virgin, which is recognized to be one of the finest of its kind in Normandy. During the Revolution it was taken to the neighbouring church of St Nicolas, to be restored to its rightful place after World War II.

Fifteen of Coutances's windows are 13c.; the three oldest, depicting St Thomas of Canterbury, St Blaise and St George, are in the north transept. There is more 13c. glass in the high windows of the north aisle of the choir and in the apsidal chapel, though the latter has been several times restored. The Louis XV marble high altar, impressive in itself, is more than a little disconcerting in this setting. In the south transept there is a sombrely glowing Last Judgement window which dates from the 14–15c.

Formerly it was possible to climb to the triforium gallery and the lantern tower on application to the sacristan. Now, because, according to the authorities, the upper parts of the cathedral are not properly protected, visitors must have a permit signed by the Conservateur Régional des Bâtiments de France, at Caen. If you are seriously interested in medieval building techniques it is worth taking the trouble of obtaining one. Apart from the fresh perspectives of the cathedral which one gets from the heights, there are points where one can study the fashion in which the fabric of the Gothic cathedral has been mounted on the Romanesque scaffolding.

The view from the top of the lantern tower which, in clear weather, extends as far as Jersey, is interesting also for the detail of the town, which has been largely rebuilt since 1944. The Allied bombardment which flattened much of the centre, though sparing the cathedral, was only the most recent episode in the stormy history of a place which, today, impresses chiefly by its cloistral calm. It changed hands several times during the fighting between Richard I of England and his brother Robert Courte-Heuse and again during the Hundred Years War. During the Wars of Religion it was sacked by the Huguenots, and it suffered also in 1639 during the revolt of the *Nu-Pieds*, the peasant rising against the introduction of the salt tax, which originated at Avranches.

The post-war plan of the town is particularly successful in its treatment of the Place du Parvis, the wide square before the cathedral where the Monday markets are held. From the west front turn left into the Rue Geoffroi de Montbray, for the church of **St Pierre**, whose Flamboyant Gothic is a complement to the spring-time immaculacy of the cathedral. It was built during the 15c. and early 16c. to replace a 13c. church which had been wrecked during the Hundred Years War. Only the central lantern, built between 1550 and 1580, is Renaissance; its corbels and pinnacles and trun-cated crocketed spire, as rich as a wedding cake (very good wedding cake) are the answer of its age to the great 'Plomb' of the cathedral. The church has been closed for restoration, which is likely to be a long job, so visitors may have to take on trust the interior, which is restrained in decoration – the pillars have no capitals – except for the charming Flamboyant balustrade of the gallery which runs unbroken round nave, transepts and choir.

From St-Pierre take the Rue Herbert opposite and continue across the Rue Quesnel Morinière to reach the **Jardin Publique**, which was originally the garden of the Hôtel de la Morinière. This is laid out in terraces on the slope overlooking the valley of the Bulsard, and though there are flowers, notably roses, to enhance the pleasures of order and perspective, the garden's chief glory is its trees. They include rarities like the gingko, the *arbre aux quarante écus*, and the Virginian tulip tree. An obelisk in the centre of the garden commemorates the donor, Jean-Jacques Quesnel Morinière. The statues include a bust of Remy de Gourmont (1858–1915), the writer and critic who lived at Coutances, and, in the bottom left-hand corner, the unhappy Amiral de Tourville (1642–1701), commander of the French Fleet at the débâcle of La Hougue, who was born at the manor of La Vallée, near Agon-Coutainville. From the garden wall near by one can glimpse the three remaining arches of the town's aqueduct, a medieval construc-tion which was badly mauled during the Wars of Religion and has been much rebuilt and repaired. There is a small museum in the house, with tapestries, 18c. drawings and a bronze head of the Emperor Hadrian.

Return to the Place du Parvis and take the Rue Tancrède on the left. The church of **Saint Nicolas** has a 13c. doorway which is all that remains of a chapel which formerly occupied the site. The existing church has undergone a sequence of building, rebuilding and resto-ration extending over six centuries.

Behind the church, the Square Le Brun, with its statue, com-memorates not Charles the 17c. painter but Charles François, Duc de Plaisance and Third Consul after the Eighteenth Brumaire. The bronze is by Antoine Étex (1808–88), one of the sculptors who contributed to the Arc de Triomphe at the Étoile.

Coutances has what is virtually a seaside annexe in **Coutainville**, a well-equipped resort with a particularly safe sandy beach, which is 14 kilometres distant by the D44. South of it, the long, sandy Pointe d'Agon shelters the mouth of the Sienne. The tide here goes out 5 or 6 kilometres, so that one looks across a wide stretch of *tangue*, like that of the Bay of Mont St-Michel, to the much smaller and less sophisticated resort and fishing port of **Regnéville-sur-Mer** across the estuary, which has a 13–14c. church and the remains of a 13c. château.

For the return to Coutances take the northward detour by **Blainville-sur-Mer**, another pretty seaside village, and **Saint-Malo-de-la-Lande**, the first with a part-Romanesque, the second with a 14c. church. At **Gratot**, 4 kilometres from Coutances, one can visit the remarkable 14c. and 18c. manor of Argouges (1 July – 1 September, 10–12, 14.30–18.30, otherwise Sunday afternoons only). Part of the moat and ramparts survive. The most picturesque view of the farmhouse is the Renaissance façade, gabled and turreted, which faces the inner courtyard. For good measure the house is associated with one of the classic legends, that of the fairy who marries a mortal. Always the union is idyllically happy; always there is a prohibition attached, in the form of a word which must not be spoken, an act which must not be committed; always the husband transgresses. Here it was the word 'death' which must not be spoken. The lord of Argouges uttered it, and his wife vanished, leaving her footprint on a window ledge. The village church has a graceful 13–14c. tower. At the entrance to Coutances we pass at close quarters the aqueduct seen at a distance from the Jardin Publique.

CHAPTER SEVENTEEN

Hambey – Villedieu-les-Poêles – Granville – Îles de Chausey – La Lucerne

THE direct route from Coutances to Granville is well neglected for an inland detour which will let the traveller see the gracious ruin of the abbey of Hambey and, in Villedieu-les-Poêles, one of the most characterful small towns in the region, besides travelling through a gently undulating landscape which is a refreshment after the small steppe of the Lande.

Leave Coutances by the D7 for Villedieu, then turn left into the D27 and the D58 for **Hambey**. The **abbey** (visits daily, 10–12, 14–19; 17 in winter), 3 kilometres beyond the small town in the soft valley of the Sienne, was founded during the first half of the 12c. by Guillaume Paynel, head of one of the greatest families in the west of France. It seems to have been completed by 1248, for, in that year, the general chapter of the Bénédictines was held at Hambey. There was another period of building during the first quarter of the 14c., when the church was enlarged by three bays.

The abbey's period of peaceful growth ended with the English occupation after Agincourt, and decline set in after it was handed over to commendatory abbots in 1559. Cardinal de Richelieu was one of these absentee landlords. When, at the Revolution, the abbey buildings were confiscated by the state, the community had already ceased to exist. The church was still in good condition. Its destruction began only in 1810, when it was sold, to become, effectively, a quarry. Two of the pillars of the choir vanished; those of the cloister were carted off to support a shed on a local farm; the west front was demolished during the Restoration. That there was anything considerable to preserve when the Société des amis d'Hambey was founded before World War II is due largely to two successive 19c. bishops of Coutances, Mgr Daniel and Mgr Bravard. By shoring up the choir in 1860 the latter probably prevented its total collapse. Since 1965 the abbey has been the property of the Department of La Manche: the walls have been consolidated and the maintenance work continues.

The Paynel arms are still distinguishable above the Romanesque main gateway. Beyond it, the skeleton of the great church, green and gilded with leaves and lichen, recalls that other magnificent ruin, Jumièges, though here it is the choir that remains standing, open to the sky. Its pillars, and those of the sanctuary, have the lofty elegance of those of Coutances. They are from the first half of the 13c., building having started at the end of the 12c. with the apse and its five radiating chapels and the ambulatory.

Excavations in the church during 1933 revealed the tombs of Louis d'Estouteville, the gallant defender of Mont St-Michel in the 15c., and his wife, Jeanne Paynel. A year later, to mark the fifth centenary of that action, two slabs were placed over their resting place in the centre of the choir.

The monastic buildings grouped round the vanished cloister are private property whose owners, M. and Mme Beck, earned the award of the *Chefs-d'œuvre en péril* for the long and patient programme of restoration which they have carried out. Its triumph is the regenerated 13c. chapter house, which is divided into twin naves by a line of six granite columns. In the *parloir*, or *Salle des morts*, adjoining, a central pillar supports late 12c. groined arches. The paintings of cinquefoil and fleur-de-lis in the vault are 13c. The library, where specimens found during excavations are displayed, separates the *parloir* from the *chauffoir*. This was used also as a writing room, a merciful dispensation when one thinks of monastic scriptoriums where the ink froze in winter. During the 17c. it became a kitchen: the old wall oven is below the window. Most of the ancient buildings of the west wing were pulled down in the 17c., to be replaced by the abbot's lodging, but the kitchen, with its vast hearth, remains. The wooden Christ is believed to be 14c.

Villedieu, due south after one has turned out of the D258, long known for its coppersmiths and bellfounders, is a small town with an air of importance greater than its population, a mere four and a half thousand, would seem to warrant. It has the attractive combination of a long history and a lively industrial present, with tourism as only one factor in its visible prosperity. Set at the crossing of two major routes, that from Paris to Granville and that from Normandy into Brittany, it has long had important monthly fairs; its hotels, accordingly, are of a number and standard which make it a good overnight stop. These days the coppersmiths turn out their quota of souvenir gewgaws, but they continue to produce the fine kitchen utensils which earned them their reputation.

Street scene in the old quarter of Caen

The interior of the Cathedral at Coutances

Up to the 12c. Villedieu, then no more than a village beside the river Sienne, was known as Seinnêtre. Henry I of England established there one of his earliest *commanderies* of the Knights Hospitaller of St John of Jerusalem, later known as the Knights of Malta. They followed the tradition of their order in naming the new house Villedieu – actually Villa Dei de Salta Caprioli, or, in the vernacular, Villedieu de Sault-Chevreuil. Since 1655 the founding of the *commanderie* has been commemorated every fourth year by a procession, the *Grand Sacre*, on the third Sunday after Whitsun. The next is due in 1983.

The first coppersmiths seem to have been established in the town not long after the Hospitallers; according to one tradition it was the Knights who introduced the craft of working in copper. According to another, very doubtful one, they arrived from the neighbouring village of La Lande d'Airou after it had been irreparably damaged by a cyclone in 1158.

The craftsmen began by making church ornaments, going on to produce milk-cans lined with tin, then ewers and secular ornaments. By the 17c., Villedieu's leaping goat had given way to the frying pans, the 'Poêles' of the town's present name. Today the workshops turn out virtually everything that can be made of copper. The glow of the articles stacked and hung outside the granite shopfronts which line the Place de la République is so heartening as almost to make one pardon the proportion of godwottery.

The church of **Notre-Dame**, granite like the houses, though it is substantially 15c. retains elements, like the four buttresses of the façade, of the original Notre-Dame-de-l'Ospital which the Knights of Malta built about the turn of the 12–13c. The nave, whose sobriety contrasts sharply with the ornately Flamboyant tower and apse, dates from the end of the 17c., a fire in 1692 having destroyed half the church and part of the town.

The interior has a 16c. stone Virgin of Pity which is immensely eloquent in the stiffness and awkwardness of its proportions. Note the skull grinning from the stool on which the Virgin is seated. The painted wooden statues of the 17–18c. set out in the choir aisles were taken from baroque altars dismantled in 1898. There are good 18c. stalls and pulpit.

The town is rich in old houses, some with inner courts where, in a simpler age, each coppersmith worked on his own doorstep. The way to the bell foundry and the copper museum passes the best of them. From the west end of the church cross into the Rue du Pont Chignon, which runs diagonally to the right. The **foundry** on the left (visits 8.30–12, 13.30–17, except on Sundays and Mondays) is on the site occupied by the *commanderie* of the Knights of Malta. The little group of men who practise their art at the end of a straggling garden, sweet with roses and lilac and syringa, are the successors of the itinerant bellfounders who, 800 years ago, halted beneath the church tower and constructed their moulds and furnaces on the spot. In recent years bells from this small, comfortably cluttered workshop have gone to cathedrals from Quimper to Quebec, churches from Seoul, Korea, to St Mary, Gate of Heaven, New York.

One or other of the blue-overalled men will pause in his work to explain the technique which is as old as the craft itself. A dummy bell of clay, with ornaments and inscriptions in wax, is placed on a core of loam and covered by the cope box, or outer section of the mould, which takes the imprint of the wax. The dummy bell, hardened by firing, is then broken and the cope box replaced on the mould, ready for the delicate operation of casting, or pouring molten metal into the space between them. The casting of a new bell is a ceremony. Local parishioners are invited to watch it and the priest, wearing his stole, comes to consecrate the molten metal. The alloy used here is 78 per cent copper, 22 per cent tin: it speaks deep and sonorous even from a grounded bell struck with a piece of metal. If you are lucky one of the craftsmen will assemble an octave for an impromptu recital, which, if he finds the English visitors *sympathiques*, will include 'God Save the Queen'. And if you want a souvenir of Villedieu a handbell that chimes as sweet and true as the giants in the tower might be a better buy than a miniature copper warming-pan.

For the **Musée de la Poeslerie** (open from 15 June to 15 September) retrace your steps towards the church and turn left into the Rue du Docteur Havard.

Several of the entries between the houses give on to cobbled, flowering courts with names from the Middle Ages – Cour-Bataille, Cour de l'Enfer, Cour de la Luzerne. Continue up the hill into the Rue Général Huard for the Cour aux Moines at No. 17, and the copper museum which has been installed in the Cour du Foyer at No. 27. Here, with a collection of ancient copperwork, there is a reconstruction of a workshop in the exact surroundings in which the craft was first practised.

Granville, 28 kilometres west of Villedieu, is a fortress port looking over the exultant Atlantic wastes, with a past of piracy and deep-sea fishing, and a present in which commercial shipping underpins tourism.

It was the English, seeking a base from which to attack Mont Saint-Michel, who in 1439 made a Gibraltar of the fishing village grouped about a chapel on the rock. Three years later they were expelled from it by Louis d'Estouteville, the Governor of the Mont. The early fortifications were demolished in 1689 by the Marquis de Louvois, Louis XIV's Under Secretary of State for War, and the man who gave bayonets to the French infantry, who realized that the resources necessary to defend them were not available. Six years later the English bombed the town heavily from the sea as a reprisal for the exploits of the corsairs who were the right arm of the French navy during the wars of the 17c. and 18c. Another English bombardment in 1803 was trivial by comparison with the Allied aerial attacks of World War II.

The approach from Villedieu is through green pastures. Seven-and-a-half kilometres on the way is the zoo of **Champrépus** (visits daily 8–12, 14–20), where a collection of animals and birds live in a gelded kind of freedom.

We enter Granville by its main street, the Rue Général Leclerc, which runs downhill towards the narrow isthmus linking the new town with the 'Roc' on which the old town was built. It was a natural defensive point, which was further strengthened by the cutting across the isthmus of a ditch known as the 'Tranchée aux Anglais'.

From the centre of modern Granville, reached by the Rue Couraye, the continuation of the Rue Général-Leclerc, take the Rue Dr-Paul-Poirier on the right and turn left up the Rue des Juifs. At the end of it, the drawbridge before the Grande Porte takes you into the 18c., whose spirit lingers between the composed granite façades of the old town. The gateway is early 16c., though much patched and rebuilt: over the arch a tablet commemorates the heroic and successful defence of the garrison against the Marquis de La Rochejaquelin's Vendéens in 1793.

A visit to the **museum** of Old Granville, at the top of the steps immediately to the right of the Grande Porte (open daily, 10–12, 13–17 during the Easter holidays and from 1 June to 14 September; Thursdays and Sundays only during the rest of the year) makes an excellent prelude to a walk round the walled town and the harbour. The old Logis du Roi, which houses it, once formed part of the defences of the Grande Porte. Here are the relics of the seafaring past of Granville, whose fishermen were catching cod on the Newfoundland Grand Banks in the 16c. By the end of the 18c. there were 110 ships with 4000 men fishing there. In winter there was oyster fishing in the bay of Mont Saint-Michel. The deep-sea fishing dwindled through the 19c. and is now extinct. The oysters lasted longer: they were carefully conserved. By 1816 there were rules requiring that the catch should be sorted on the spot and the small ones put back into the sea. It was disease which wiped them out almost entirely in 1923–4.

The museum illustrates that history with documents, charts and log books, and a splendid range of ship models and pictures. Among the records is that of the most recent occupation of Granville, which took place on 9 March 1945, after the town had been liberated by the American Army. It lasted an hour and a half. The invaders were a German Commando unit still holding out in Jersey, who were badly in need of provisions. During their raid on the town they took prisoner a number of incredulous American officers, as well as replenishing supplies. Even more appealing are the witnesses to the domestic prosperity which was built up on more than three centuries of seafaring, fine furniture and fine clothes and fine faces in portraits and photographs. There is also an attractive collection of the *coiffes* which were formerly worn regularly in Basse Normandie, the *bavolette* of Granville, the *grande volante* of Coutances, which looks like a balloon about to take off, Avranches's exquisite *papillon*, their net and lace and cambric handled with an art that makes intricacy look simple and the skill of a modern milliner elementary by comparison.

There are good houses in both the long, parallel streets which are the heart of the old town. From the museum turn right up the steps and, at the opening of the Rue Lecarpentier take the first turning on the left into the **Rue Notre-Dame**. Nos. 15, 54 and 76 are 18c. houses; the three buildings at the corner of the Rue Cambernon are 17c. The Rue St. Jean, to the north, has another 17c. house at No. 15, and a particularly attractive mansarded one from the 18c. at No. 61.

Continue along the Rue St Jean, walking away from the church, until it opens into the **Place de l'Isthme**, a plateau forming so commanding a look-out that it is hard to believe that the Roc is nowhere more than 40 metres above sea level. In clear weather the view from the direction table extends northwards to Carteret, north-west to the Îles de Chausey and, exceptionally, Jersey, and southwards to the last rocky outcrop on the west coast of the Cotentin, the Pointe de Carolles.

Steps lead down from the platform to the casino and the beach. To make the round of the ramparts, turn left into the Rue du Nord. This, effectively, is a cliff walk, which, like seascapes on any rocky

coast, is most exhilarating in heavy weather, when the sea is
unleashed below.

The church of **Notre-Dame**, crowning the ridge of the Roc, marks
the start of the round. It is 16–17c., but traces of the church which
the occupying English built during the Hundred Years War to
replace the original chapel on the Roc are thought to remain at the
east end. The modern windows are attractive. There is an interesting holy water stoup from the 15c., but the main interest is not the
furniture but the folklore. According to tradition the ancient statue
of the Virgin in the Lady Chapel was found on the shore off Cap
Lihou, the old name for the tip of the Roc. Each year, on the last
Sunday in July, the statue is carried in procession among the banners that defile during the Grand Pardon des Corporations et de la
Mer. One window of the chapel depicts the procession returning to
Granville, bearing the figure.

The sailors' chapel in the south aisle, with a good collection of
ex-votos, is dedicated to St Clement, otherwise Pope Clement I,
third in succession to St Peter in the Holy See. For the clue, see the
gilt anchors hanging here and there among the ship models. There is
historical evidence that Pope Clement I was a wise administrator:
he was also the subject of exuberant legend. It has variations, but all
have the saint ending in the sea off the Crimea. According to the
local version he asked to be thrown in with an anchor round his neck
so that the faithful should never find his grave. A few days later the
sea withdrew more than a league, revealing 'a simple chapel where
the body of the saint lay with the anchor behind him'. After smiling
indulgently at the former beliefs of simple Continental seamen,
British visitors may like to reflect that the correct title of what we
know as Trinity House is 'The Guild of the Holy Trinity and St
Clement'.

From the church, continue along the Boulevard Vaufleury, which
is bordered on the right by the modern barracks. About 400 metres
on, the **Aquarium** (open daily in season, 9–12, 14–19) has a display
of both indigenous and exotic fish and shellfish. Recently there has
also been a pool of dolphins. The road roughens, but there is a path
of sorts to the very end of the Roc. Mournful relics of the Atlantic
wall survive here. Better go up into the lantern of the **lighthouse**
which was built on the point in 1827 (apply to the keeper) for a yet
more lordly panorama stretching as far as the coast of Brittany.
Below the lighthouse a footpath follows the rim of the point, with
plunging views and a close involvement with the sea. It leads to
the north rampart and the vast terrace of the Boulevard des

Terreneuviers overlooking the harbour, a most agreeable spot for idling. A gateway of 1715 behind the customs house, known as the Porte des Morts, gives on to the Noires Vaches steps which lead down to the port. Look up and back for the sight of a quaintly pleasing building, turreted and slate-hung, below the church. Below, the row of houses backing on to the Roc includes the former inn (No. 25–25b) where, in 1830, the Prince de Polignac, Charles X's Foreign Minister, was arrested after signing the ordinance which led to the July Revolution. A sailing centre, with a sheltered basin, has now been installed east of the wet dock, and there is a splendid walk to the end of the west jetty, with seas crashing against the granite mole and the ships coming home with the tide rocking in the swell at the harbour mouth.

The harbour is the departure point for the **Chausey Islands**, a group of rocks and reefs and islets 12 kilometres offshore, from which was quarried the granite which built much of Granville and all of Mont Saint-Michel. This is the classic excursion from Granville, fifty-five minutes each way in normal weather. Unlike the Channel Islands, the Chausey archipelago is French territory. Legend says it is the remains of the Forêt de Scissy, which was drowned in A.D. 709 – the lost land of Lyonesse has as many forms as it has locations. It is said that 52 islets are permanently above sea level and 365 are uncovered at low tide, which is the kind of neat figure that few people would be persevering enough to check. Only La Grande Île, 2 kilometres long and 700 metres across at its widest point, is inhabited today. The community of about a hundred lives chiefly by lobster fishing; there are a chapel, a schoolhouse and a couple of small hotels on the island. The fort south of the spot at which visitors come ashore was built between 1860 and 1866 as a defence against the English. Happily they never came in anger and it has not heard a shot fired. It is worth climbing to the lantern of the **lighthouse** (apply to the keeper) on the point beyond it for the sight of the whole archipelago, above and below the surface of the water, spread out at one's feet.

From the lighthouse a footpath follows the west coast of the island to **Port Homard** round the headland. The beach here is dominated by another fort, this one built in 1558, which has been converted into a house by Louis Renault, founder of the motor firm. Near by are the remains of a convent of the Cordeliers, who maintained a community here for two hundred years from 1343.

For the beach at Granville, turn your back on the harbour and walk to the right along the Rue Lecampion, or, if you have wandered as far as the sailing centre, diagonally left into the Rue Saint-Sauveur. Both lead to the Rue Docteur-Paul-Poirier and so to the Casino overlooking the sea. The Syndicat d'Initiative, at No. 15, Rue Georges Clemenceau, is close by. There is a short but pleasant promenade and a beach which is the paradisaic seashore of childhood. Granville has enormous tides: at the spring equinox there is 14 metres difference in depth between high and low. Even between the equinoxes the sea which has been lapping or leaping about the promenade retreats a good kilometre, to reveal an expanse of weed and rock-pools, rich in shrimps and prawns and the tiny, quicksilver fish which the French call 'équilles', or 'lancons'. Beyond are the firm sands over which you can walk the 2 kilometres to the neighbouring small resort of Donville-les-Bains. At high tide a footpath along the low cliffs will take you there in little more than a quarter of an hour. It is reached by a flight of steps at the east end of the promenade which lead to the Christian Dior Gardens. These were once the property of the designer's family. The unexpectedness of this calm, green enclosure, fragrant with wallflowers or roses according to season, among so much sand and salt and granite, is no small part of its attraction.

Granville is a convenient starting point for visiting the Premonstratensian Abbey of La Lucerne, the relatively little-known and most gracious ruin 12 kilometres to the south-east. Turn left off the main Avranches road at Cran, 16 kilometres out of Granville. **La Lucerne**, set in the valley of the Thar, is 3 kilometres further on (visits daily 9–12.30, 14–19). The church, whose foundation stone was laid by Achard, Bishop of Avranches and former Abbot of St. Victor, Paris, was completed in 1178, except for the tower, which was added between 1180 and 1200. La Lucerne founded four daughter houses, Ardenne, near Caen, Beauport, in the Côtes-du-Nord, Mondaye, near Bayeux, and Belle-Étoile, in the Orne, and, during the 18c., was the only religious house in the region which never had a commendatory abbot.

The long period of decay which followed the Revolution ended only in 1959, when the Association of the Friends of the Abbey of La Lucerne, with the help and support of the *Monuments Historiques* and the departmental authorities, began a programme of consolidation and restoration. Half the pleasure of a visit today comes from seeing the rebirth of the building in their hands.

Entering by the gatehouse – the *Salle de Justice* above the porch is occasionally used for exhibitions – you see on the left, beyond the old tithe barn, a dovecot with 1500 pigeon holes. The west front of the church faces you, much as it looked when the first stage of the building was completed, except for the central window, which was not pierced until the turn of the 14–15c. To be here alone, with no anachronistic sight and no sound to be heard except the tap of chisel on stone to tell that the work of reconstruction is going on, is to be transported in time.

The nave is roofless. Its south side still has the complete series of seven arches with small, splayed windows above. Only one remains on the north side. By contrast, the square central tower, its height accentuated by the three lancet windows on each face, is intact. Once the lancets were blocked, so that the tower could be used as an overflow for the dovecot. They have now been repierced and fitted with louvres. The original five bells, the oldest, Notre-Dame, dating from 1317, which were founded at Villedieu, were melted down for cannon to save 'la patrie en danger' during the Revolution: in 1969 five new ones, also founded at Villedieu, were hung in the tower.

The outstanding triumph of the restoration is the choir, whose reconstructed roof, completed in 1967, enables one to visualize the 12c. church; austere in the tradition of the order, which went in for sumptuous services in the most severe surroundings, and not 'modern' even when it was built. Since 1970, after the reconstruction of the east window and the addition of an altar designed by the admirable M. Froidevaux of the *Monuments Historiques*, the choir and transept have once more been used for services.

Of the cloister, which was rebuilt between 1700 and 1712, only the north-west corner remains; enough to serve as a model for reconstruction if a large enough number of the original pillars can be salvaged from the farm buildings round about. The four little Roman arches in the south-west corner once sheltered the lavatorium.

The 18c. abbot's lodging can be seen from the south-east of the cloister; the ruined, ivy-covered aqueduct on the left once carried water for the spinning factory which occupied the buildings after the Revolution.

From the west end of the cloister, walk round to the right to see the massive south door of the abbey, which was rebuilt after the Wars of Religion, and the remains of the refectory, with the 12c. cellars beneath it. Alongside, the former guest house, with massy roof beams, stands entire. Next to it, at the west end of the south aisle of the church, the owners of the spinning factory installed a forge. Today the narrow space has been transformed into a chapel of the Blessed Sacrament.

From the abbey take the D105 to Sartilly and turn left into the D109 for **La Haye-Pesnel**, where there are remains of an 11c. château. Beside the church, which has a number of 15c. statues, there is an oddity in the shape of a 'republican bell', cast at a time when most bells were being melted down for cannon, which is inscribed (spelling reproduced):

Liberté—Egalité — Vive la République
Vive les Patriote — Périsse le tirans
leurs satellites et tous les aristocrate
May 1793 – l'an 2eme de la République.

CHAPTER EIGHTEEN

Granville to Avranches

THE 33 kilometres of coast road from Granville to Avranches is one of the most memorable drives in the Cotentin. **St Pair**, 3½ kilometres on the way, is a pleasant family resort with a promenade overlooking miles of firm sand. There was a church here in the 6c., founded by the saints Pair and Scubilion, who came from Poitou to evangelize the Cotentin. Nothing remains of that primitive oratory, but the present church, whose nave and transept are in the Gothic of 1877, has a good Romanesque tower and spire and a 14c. choir where the burial place of the two missionary saints is marked by tombs of the same period.

After St Pair there is a string of seaside villages. **Jullouville**, with villas scattered among pine trees, **Bouillon**, **Carolles-Plage**, where the attractively wooded Vallée des Peintres opens to the south-east and **Carolles-Bourg**, whose church has a 12c. tower. Then the road runs uphill, the pyramid of Mont Saint-Michel rises magically out of the corn, and, as one climbs to the highest point of the corniche, the immensity of the bay opens out, on a clear day bounded by the Breton coast, on a misty one illimitable, dissolving in shifting distances.

St Jean-le-Thomas is a picture village, lit with mimosa or dripping with wisteria according to season, but the long road which runs down to it is unnecessarily disfigured by hotel signs. The square-towered church in the Rue Yve-Dubosq is an amalgam of the 12c, the 15c. and the 16c. The sands begin here; there is good bathing. Five hundred metres beyond **Dragey** a signpost marks the right-hand turn for the Manoir de Brion, one of the oldest continuously inhabited houses in Normandy (visits daily, 1 April – 31 October, 14–18). The southern half was built in 1066, as one of the first daughter priories of Mont Saint-Michel. It was dedicated to St Lawrence, part of whose arm was kept in the chapel, and the monks grew wheat and grapes to provide the Mont with bread and wine. The northern half was built in 1526; the second floor windows with their classical medallions are an early example of Norman Renaissance work. Visitors are shown the ground floor rooms, with fine granite fireplaces, the 11c. cellar and the room where Jacques Cartier slept when he was received at Brion by François I and given his commission to organize the voyage, in 1535, that resulted in the discovery of Canada. One of the islands in the St Lawrence was named by him Brion Island, in memory of his stay here.

From **Genêts**, with a 14c. church, the very minor D35E leads in less than 2 kilometres to the dunes of Bec d'Andaine, where, at high tide, it is possible to bathe off a bank of firm sand. The sea goes out 14 kilometres, leaving a waste of sand and mud across which, with a guide (inquire in the Place des Halles in Genêts village), it is possible to walk the 6 kilometres or so to Mont Saint-Michel. To try this expedition without one is purely lunatic; the surface of the sands is uncertain and the sea runs in over the flats and, worse, through the channels that seam them, with terrifying speed. On the far side of Genêts the N811 swings left for Avranches, which looks out from its hill-top over the bay and the estuary and valley of the Sée.

Avranches is a cathedral town without a cathedral; the see, which dated from A.D. 511, ceased to exist in 1790. Four years later the 11c. cathedral dedicated to St Andrew, which stood on high ground on the north-west side of the city, collapsed, apparently from natural causes, though the building may have been weakened by the damage it suffered during the Wars of Religion, when Avranches was known as 'l'Allumette de la Ligue'. The west towers, which survived the collapse, were blown up in 1812.

The town centres on the wide Place Littré, with the Hôtel de Ville at one end and the Syndicat d'Initiative at the other. Walk past the left side of the former to see the tower of the Porte Beaudange which was the fortified entrance on the south side of the town before turning left under the splendid lime trees of the Allée des Juges. This, one rejoices to see, is being replanted systematically. The alley borders the green of the Jardin de l'Évêché. Général Valhubert, whose statue stands in it, was a son of Avranches who was killed at Austerlitz.

On the right, at the end of the alley, is the **museum and library** (open daily except Tuesday, 9–12, 14–18 from Easter to the end of September), housed in what were the outbuildings of the Bishop's Palace. The palace itself, built in the 15c., incorporated part of an earlier building whose massive walls survived the fire which largely destroyed the rest of the structure in 1899. In the 19c. the outbuildings were used as a prison; today the low, vaulted rooms are an ideal setting for the treasures of the monastic library of Mont Saint-Michel. Its contents span eight hundred years, from the 8c. to the 16c. and the claim 'unique in France' is justified. Here are the oldest copy known of Cicero's *De Oratore*, a 9c. MS on ivory vellum, with ruled margins; a history of the abbey written in the 10c. and the later chronicle of its 12c. abbot, Robert de Torigni. The red capitals in the *Sic et Non* of Abelard are as fresh as though the page had been newly turned; a 12c. cartulary of Mont Saint-Michel, which was the gift of Richard II, Duke of Normandy, has a vivid full-page line drawing. The list could be extended – a 13c. bible, a copy of Boethius' *Treatise on Music* from the second half of the 12c., a number of 11–12c. MSS illustrated with miniatures in the Anglo-Saxon style. There are many incunabula and later printed books and a collection of magnificent bindings from the 16c., 17c. and 18c.

In the same rooms there are some interesting 14c. alabasters and stone carvings; elsewhere in the building regional exhibitions are staged periodically.

Diagonally left as you leave the museum is what remains of the Bishop's Palace, which is today the *gendarmerie* and courtroom. The *salle des pas perdus*, once the chapel of the palace, has a fine spiral staircase in the central turret.

Continue through the Place Daniel Huet, past the Sous-Préfecture to the open space known as the *plate-forme*, whose central green is currently being subjected to what looks like being a long-term archaeological operation. Here, until that collapsed in 1794, stood the cathedral of Avranches. The single remaining relic of it does not strike the eye immediately. Towards the right of the *plate-forme* is a broken pillar and a hexagon of unclipped grass surrounded by posts and chains. Among the scatter of waste paper and dog dirt you will find a slab of pinkish granite. On this stone, at the door of the cathedral of Avranches, runs the inscription: 'After the murder of Thomas Becket, Archbishop of Canterbury, Henry II, King of England and Duke of Normandy, received on his knees from the Papal legates the apostolic absolution, 21 May, MCLXXII '. The inscription does not tell us that Henry came barefoot, in the white robe of a penitent. The ceremony took place at Avranches because, after his excommunication, it was Robert de Torigni, Abbot of Mont Saint-Michel, which was in the diocese of Avranches, who had used his influence to have a council held there. The view from the terrace commands a fine sweep of the valley of the Sée as well as the bay.

Turn back from it and note the name of the farthest left of the several parallel roads leading back to the town centre, the Boulevard des Abrincates. The Abrincanti were the Gaulish tribe whose capital city this was: Avranches is a corruption of their name. In the Rue de l'Auditoire, another of the parallel streets, the long house with white shutters and stepped end gables, standing well back from the road on the left, is the old deanery of Avranches (not open to visitors). The original 13c. house was rebuilt in 1764 and, by a too rare natural justice, is occupied today by a passionately erudite antiquarian and local historian. At the end of the street it is worth strolling down the steep little **Rue Engibault**, on the left, which is a narrow, cobbled lane straight out of the Middle Ages, before turning right for the Place d'Estouteville. This is dominated by the remains of Avranches's fortifications, a donjon which is now a private house and the Saint Louis tower behind the *mairie*, where lived, a tablet tells us, Hugues Goz (Le Loup), Vicomte d'Avranches, (c. 1070–1101), Vicomte Palatine of Chester, (1070–1101), Governor of the Château of St James, Counsellor of the Conqueror and friend of Anselm, an ascending list of distinctions. The ruined ramparts, sprouting broom and harebells, date variously from the 10c. to the 14c. but have been many times rebuilt. Beneath these walls, in 1639, the *Nu-pieds* of Normandy, the peasants who rebelled against the imposition of the salt tax, set up their stronghold. The revolt, which broke out spontaneously, was taken in hand by Jean Quetil, known as Jean Nu-Pieds, who organized the rebels into armed bands. He himself remained as elusive and invisible as the Scarlet Pimpernel, transmitting his orders through lieutenants. One of them, Captain de Mondrins in his other persona, was a priest named Morel who lived in a suburb of Avranches. The 'Armée des Souffrances', as the peasant bands were called, terrorized and pillaged a wide area, even marching on Rouen. Finally the revolt was brutally crushed by Jean de Gassion, Maréchal of France, who exterminated the last redoubt at Avranches.

From the Place d'Estouteville the Rue d'Orléans leads to the church of **St Gervais**, whose 19c. tower has a peal of twenty-three bells. There are some good examples of medieval carving and goldsmith's work in the treasury, and, in its far different fashion equally rare, a tin chalice used during the Revolution. In a 19c. reliquary is the skull of St Aubert, the 8c. Bishop of Avranches, who founded the Abbey of Mont Saint-Michel. He did so, says legend, on the express instructions of the Archangel himself, who appeared in a dream to the Bishop while he was making a retreat on the mount, then known as Mont Tombe, and told him to build a chapel on the rock. When he woke Aubert doubted the authenticity of his vision and took no action, whereupon St Michael appeared again, repeating his command. Still the bishop hesitated. On the Archangel's third appearance he drove home the message by giving the bishop a tap on the head so peremptory that it left a thumb-print. The skull has an appropriately shaped dent.

The Rue St-Gervais leads left from the church to the Place Angot, where it joins the Rue de la Constitution. Turn left here for the **Patton Memorial**, which is set on a roundabout where the Stars and Stripes flies above an island of American territory – the soil on which the monument stands, like the trees with which it is planted, was brought here from different states of the Union.

On this spot General Patton had his HQ when the Third U.S. Army entered Avranches on 30 June 1944, during the break-through which was to carry the U.S. forces west into Brittany and east to Laval and Le Mans. The monument's base is a six-pointed star, each of its rays indicating the route taken by one unit. Pointing due east is that of the Second Armoured Division of the Free French. Their march had started at Chad, in Francophone Africa, when, after the fall of France in 1940, General Leclerc raised the French flag and vowed that it would not be furled until it flew from the spire of Strasbourg cathedral. The record here, Falaise, Paris, Baccaret, Strasbourg, Berchtesgaden, is a reminder that the vow was more than accomplished. Those interested in comparative national psychology may enjoy setting the legend on the Patton Memorial, which reads: *Réalisant la percée d'Avranches dans le vacarme de ses blindés en marchant vers la victoire et la libération de la France, la glorieuse armée Americaine de Général Patton a franchi ce carrefour* ('Making the Avranches break-through in the roar of its tanks, while marching towards victory and the liberation of France, General Patton's glorious American Army passed over this cross-roads') beside the lapidary inscription on the British and Commonwealth memorial on the outskirts of Bayeux: *Nos a Gulielmo Victi, Victoris Patriam Liberavimus* ('We whom William conquered have freed the country of the Conqueror').

From the monument, take the Boulevard Maréchal Foch to the Place Carnot, passing on the left the late 18c. buildings of the Lycée Littré. Now a state *lycée*, this claims to have been founded in the 11c. by Lanfranc. The *place* is wide and void and windy, one end of it filled by the church of Notre-Dame-les-Champs, 19c. Gothic in granite. St-Saturnin, in the Rue du Docteur Gilbert, behind it, is thought to stand on the spot where Avranches's first bishop built his church.

At the other end the Place Carnot opens on to the **Jardin des Plantes**. Originally this was the garden of a Capuchin convent founded in 1618. The building was later occupied by sisters of the Ursuline order; the gardens had long belonged to the municipality, which has since cherished them as the chief ornament of a town with a reputation for the growing of flowers. They slope down the sheltered side of the spur on which Avranches stands, benefitting from the notably mild climate. There are noble trees, including a fine cedar of Lebanon; a small, domesticated waterfall makes a cool splashing; an 11c. doorway from the chapel of Saint Georges de Bouillé has been rebuilt on a mound above the terrace.

The terrace looks out from a height of a hundred metres over a view that is intoxicating for its vastness as it is inexhaustible in its variety. According to time and weather and season, the water, the wilderness of sand, the silhouette of Mont Saint-Michel set in the midst of it, can change in texture and substance, as well as mere colour, from a harsh rock rising out of harbour mud to an airy tower above a blue and scalloped bay, and from that to a wraith clothed in drifting veils of mist.

Aesthetically, a tour of Avranches should end here, for perfection, in the glittering unreality of a night of full moon. But for English visitors there remains a pilgrimage which, when they leave the gardens, will lead them left along the Corniche Saint-Michel. The road passes the 17–18c. buildings of the former Bénédictine Abbey of Sainte-Anne des Moutons. Continue downhill along the Rue du Général de Gaulle. The cemetery lies to the right, across the **Rue de la Liberté**. Here Avranches's English colony had that most irrefutable symbol of possession and permanence, its own burial plot, granted by a municipality which recognized that the colonists gave tone to the town as well as bringing it hard cash. It lies at the far end of the enclosure after you turn left from the main gate.

Avranches's British colony was established at about the same time as that of Dieppe; when Ruskin noted its existence during his tour of Normandy in 1848 some of its members had been there for a quarter of a century. It was the restoration of the monarchy in 1815 which had re-opened France to those of the British who lived abroad from choice, though they did not arrive in any number until 1830. The French were convinced that they were fleeing their native fogs, and some, no doubt, were seeking a milder or brighter climate. Many went to France as a later generation was to go to

Spain or Portugal, mainly because, the cost of living on the Continent being lower than that in Britain, they could adopt a life-style to which they could hardly have aspired at home, or continue one which they had enjoyed at various outposts of Empire. Those who went to Avranches did so because, besides being an attractive town, it was relatively accessible at a time when transport was still rudimentary, and because few of the seaside places which might have rivalled it were as yet developed for visitors.

Did some choose Avranches rather than Dieppe because of the character of its English colony or was it that, like attracting like as friends and relatives joined the earliest settlers, the character developed naturally? Certainly, to read of life in the respective colonies is to be struck by the difference in atmosphere. Dieppe was fashionable and very faintly raffish, attracting celebrities, taking its tone, perhaps, from the nearness of Paris, which, by the later 19c., was leaving its imprint on a good deal of the Normandy coast. Avranches was sober and well-bred. Its English wrote and botanized and painted in watercolours, as was to be expected in a society drawn mainly from the upper middle classes, with a fair leaven of clergy and what a French chronicler called 'honourables Misses sur le retour' – single gentlewomen of a certain age – whose members seldom got their names into the newspapers. Another local historian, writing in 1844, said there were normally two or three hundred English in Avranches. They congregated chiefly on the west side of the town, usually buying rather than renting houses, warning each other of the advisability of bringing carpets from England, because of the excessive price of French ones, usually agreeably surprised by the relatively low cost of domestic service. On the last it seems unlikely that many of his compatriots were as perceptive as Dr James Hairby who, in *Avranches and its vicinity*, wrote that there was no country where masters and servants were more closely united by a reciprocal and moving feeling of protection and appreciation than they were in France. For that reason the best French domestics were found only in French households, where they were treated more like humble friends than like dependent servants. Dr Hairby, with three titles to his name, was only one, though the most considerable, of a number of English authors whose works, poetry, pedagogy, travel, were published in Avranches.

Travel books figured largely in the English library, whose catalogue for 1880 included *Around the Kremlin, Across Africa, Arctic Exploration, Bokhara*, and, a little poignantly, *England and*

The isolated splendour
of Mont Saint-Michel

An aerial view of the
Abbey of Mont Saint-
Michel at low tide

The interior of the
Cathedral at Bayeux

The crypt of the
Cathedral at Bayeux
which dates back to
the 11c.

the English. There was a juvenile section and the periodicals numbered *Aunt Judy's Magazine* along with *Blackwood's, The Cornhill Magazine* and the *Edinburgh Review*. Some of the children of the colony went to local schools, but 'an English gentleman' – this may have been the Rev. Thomson, author of a book entitled *The English Gentleman* – ran a private school for junior boys. For young ladies there was an establishment directed by Madame Philbert, 'who has lived in England for many years'.

Like the colony at Dieppe, the Anglo-Avranchins had their own church, which worshipped in a building lent by the municipality, and, also like the Dieppe colony, they indulged so enthusiastically in the classical Anglican pastime of quarrelling with the rector that, at one period, there were rival congregations, each with its own priest.

Where the two communities differed markedly was in the extent to which that of Avranches contributed to local life. Social contacts between English and French seldom went further than occasional formal entertaining, but the Société d'Archéologie had English members, French and English botanists collaborated, and in 1886 the colony gave what was described as 'a memorable theatrical production' in aid of the church which they hoped to build (they never did).

As sportsmen they conformed to the French stereotype of their nation. Stendhal, in his *Mémoires d'un Touriste*, published in 1837, wrote that the 'crowd of English' who frequented Avranches were such skilful anglers, charming the trout and salmon of the Sienne on to their hooks by using artificial flies, that they aroused the jealousy of the Normans to the point where they broke off social relations and even contemplated suing the incomers. It sounds improbable, even for a people so inclined to litigation as the Normans. What is established is that it was the English who introduced horse-racing to Avranches. The first steeplechase was run in the 1840s; appropriately, if sadly, when the founder, Mr John Moggridge, died in 1854, it was while Avranches was enjoying 'des fêtes hippiques particulièrement belles'. The colony founded an archery club and celebrated the marriage of the Prince of Wales with a cricket match.

They were given, also, to enlightened good works. In 1871, during the Franco-Prussian War, the local newspaper, *l'Avranchin*, paid a vibrant tribute to the generosity of the Société Anglaise de Secours pour les Malades et les Blessés de la Guerre. What the best of them did as individuals is conveyed in the valediction of the Archaeological Society's *Revue* to the family of Arthur Ropes, of King's College, Cambridge, which left Avranches in 1896. They were, said the *Revue*, 'a family of apostles, men and women rivalling each other in charity, not that charity which consists in opening one's purse and emptying it into the hand of the poor, but that personal well-doing which visits the destitute, consoles the afflicted and brings the light of human understanding to the gloomy dwelling of the unfortunate'.

By that time the English colony had dwindled to what the *Revue* describes as a few families who were scarcely remarked, 'secluded as they are in the cottages of the neighbourhood'. What had so diminished it was the vogue for the seaside, and the consequent growth of towns like Dinard, and Paramé, near St Malo, for, with rare exceptions, its members did not leave Avranches for England, but in order to live somewhere on the French coast.

Recently the municipality, concerned by the neglected state of the English cemetery, particularly glaring in a country which sets much store by funerary pomps, tidied up the worst of jungle, but could do little to make it less forlorn. Headstones tilt and topple, kerbs crumble, epitaphs are illegible. It is not tragic, only a meet subject for a Betjeman-esque elegy. Traveller, drop a tear or a chrysanthemum, rub a little moss off a tablet or say a prayer, according to your kind. The naturalists and racing men, the clerics and retired civil servants, the half-pay colonels and the honourable Misses deserved better than this.

Avranches is quite a practicable base from which to visit Mont Saint-Michel. If you prefer to avoid a drive of 22 kilometres each way, **Pontorson**, the last Norman town before the Breton border, is well provided with hotels, though it has suffered inevitably from the commercialization which is inescapable for a town which, for more than a thousand years, has been a halt, first for pilgrims, later for tourists bound for the abbey. Once there was a château here, built to protect the passage over the River Couesnon, which divides Normandy from Brittany. There is still an interesting church, dedicated to Notre-Dame, which is said to have been founded by the Conqueror in thanksgiving for his escape from the shifting sands of the river during his campaign against Conan of Brittany. The legend is illustrated in detail in one of the choir windows but in fact the oldest parts of the church, which are the choir and the south arm of the transept, date only from the second quarter of the 12c.

Beyond Pontorson, the 9 kilometres of straight road leading to Mont Saint-Michel cross territory dotted with parishes which once formed part of the abbey's vast possessions. Huisnes, for example, is believed to have belonged to it as early as the 8c.

CHAPTER NINETEEN

Mont Saint-Michel

MONT Saint-Michel, which, every year, receives more visitors than any other monument in France except Versailles and the main tourist attractions of Paris, is a conical granite islet, on whose lower slopes houses cling as close as scales. From its summit there grows a church, its spire topped by a statue of Saint Michael, whose sword flashes 160 metres above the sea. It is a wonder to which one never becomes accustomed: in a sense every sight of it is a first sight.

The **Gothic abbey** is open 9–11.30, 13.30–18 from 15 May to 30 September, and from 9–11.30, 13.30–16 from 1 October to 14 May. During the height of the season, tours set off every quarter of an hour, with commentaries in English and the major European languages as well as French. During the fortnight 15–30 July the *Monuments Historiques* arrange four lecture tours daily: these are considerably more detailed and extended.

During the Gallo-Roman period the island is believed to have been a centre for the cult of Mithras the sun god. His shrines were often in high places: one of the most famous was on Mount Gargano, in Apulia. After the spread of Christianity it was converted into a shrine dedicated to the Archangel Michael, also connected with high places, who was said to have manifested himself there. M. René Herval has found a plausible basis for the legend of Bishop Aubert and the Archangel. He suggests that, before 708, Aubert had made a pilgrimage to Gargano, and, on his return, had been inspired to build a church on the rock which he saw daily from Avranches. Certainly, it was to Gargano that he dispatched a party of monks to bring relics of the saint for the new church.

Aubert's church was an oratory built below the peak of the rock, where he installed a college of twelve canons. From the first the sanctuary attracted pilgrims: according to a medieval MS, Charlemagne came to pray there before an expedition against the Bretons. In the 10c., when legend and tradition give place to history, the oratory was replaced by a church which survives beneath the Gothic one. A town was already growing round it. Aubert's canons had by now so departed from their early, prayerful austerities that their way of life was a scandal. Richard I, Duke of Normandy, replaced them by fifty Bénédictines brought from the Abbey of Saint-Wandrille, and work started on a programme of building which was to continue for 500 years.

It was the fourth abbot, Hildebert, who conceived the idea of enlarging the summit of the mount by constructing massive foundations in the form of a series of crypts, 'a hollow rock, built by the hands of man upon the solid rock', as one writer has called them, against its flanks, and so providing a level platform on which the Romanesque abbey was built. It was a period when architects were often learning on the job, as the collapse of so many Norman towers testifies, and, one night in 1103, the north aisle of the church fell down, bringing much of the dormitory with it. The damage was made good and, before the end of the 12c., the church had been given a new west front, with twin towers, and the new abbey had been completed with domestic buildings set against the new crossing of the church.

Its life was to be short. In 1203 the Bretons, fighting for Philippe Auguste, King of France, against John Lackland, King of England, (whom the mount, at this time, supported), fired the town, and the flames destroyed a large part of the abbey buildings on the north side. The 'Marvel', the Gothic building which succeeded them, was financed partly from the reparations paid to the abbey by Philippe Auguste. Little less marvellous than its architecture was the speed of its building: the *Salle des Hôtes* and the Refectory, the *Salle des Chevaliers* and the exquisite cloister were all completed within twenty-five years.

The building which went on during the next three centuries was partly dictated by the fact that the mount became increasingly a military abbey. A garrison, paid for in part by the king of France, was stationed there, and increasing attention had to be given to the fortifications. An English garrison based on Mont Tombelaine, the neighbouring island, was a constant threat during the Hundred Years War, but it never stopped the flow of pilgrims, who were able to buy safe-conducts.

The atmosphere of a religious house which was half fortress – after the short peace which succeeded the Hundred Years War the mount fought off several attacks by the Huguenots during the Wars of Religion – was not conducive to holy living. Decadence was hastened by the institution of the commendatory system in 1525; one of the absentee abbots, who were not required to be priests, was

Henri de Lorraine, who was appointed as a child of five. By 1622 the laxity of the monks was such that the reforming Maurists came to live up to their reputation for piety and learning, coupled with the grossest aesthetic vandalism.

After the Revolution, by which time there was scarcely a community to destroy, though there were vast riches to plunder, the abbey became a prison, whose first inmates were three hundred priests who had refused to accept the civil constitution of the clergy. Elsewhere in the building there were weaving sheds; in the abbey church, divided into two storeys, prisoners made straw hats. Surprisingly, during the whole of this period, the choir was regarded as a sacred place and reserved for services.

An imperial decree of 1863 ended the misuse of the abbey, which was declared a historic monument in 1874, so assuring its restoration. The work of maintenance is perennial, with the constant possibility of new archaeological discoveries. After being leased by the Bishop of Avranches in 1865, then once more deconsecrated in 1886, the church was finally restored for worship in 1922. Pilgrimages once more take place, the most important being on the first Sunday in May and the nearest Sunday to the Feast of St Michael, 29 September. During September and October 1966, to mark the millenary of its founding, Mont Saint-Michel was occupied temporarily by a group of monks from Bec and Saint-Wandrille, and since 1969, a monk from Bec has been detailed permanently to the abbey, where he says mass daily at 12.15. The public is admitted.

Ideally a first visit – it is not serious to think in terms of a single visit to a monument which it would take a lifetime to come to know intimately – should begin with a circuit of the rock. Only so can one grasp the logic of a building whose scale and intricacy are such that, until one knows it well, it is difficult during even the best of conducted tours to be sure how the section one is seeing fits into the whole. On days of high tides it is possible to make the trip by boat; at low tide – but check the times of the tide before starting – one can walk dry-shod round the west and north of the mount. On the east you may have to paddle. As you turn left, or west, from the entrance gate at the south of the mount, the buildings rising overhead like a cliff, with the spire of the church showing above them, are the Abbot's Lodging and the Governor's House, neither of which is shown to the public. West of them an incline runs up to the platform known as the Saut-Gauthier, named after a one-time prisoner who leapt from it. Supplies for the monastery were winched up the incline.

The block at sea level is the barracks built in 1928 for the *gendarmes* who were posted here at the time. Beyond it the 16c. Tour Gabriel, topped by a little turret intended to serve as a windmill, is all that remains of the old ramparts on this side of the mount. Continuing along the foot of the steep rocks, with, above, the Plateforme de l'Ouest before the façade of the church, you come to the tiny chapel of St Aubert, which is 13c. or 14c. Near by is a spring, said to have been discovered by the saint, which, until the 15c., was the community's only source of fresh water. It was fortified during the 15c., to serve as an advance post as well as to safeguard the vital supply.

We are now on the north side of the mount, where the rocks give way to a tree-clad slope usually described as an oak wood, though during several wanderings along its paths I have yet to find a single oak among the ash and sycamore. From here one can grasp the plan of the Marvel, where the monks, poised between sea and sky, were as isolated as though they had been in the desert. It consists of two immense, buttressed buildings, the base of their walls merging into the rock. The western building, which is slightly the lower, is topped by the cloister, with the *Salle des Chevaliers* and the *Cellier* in the two storeys below. The top storey of the building to the east, with its row of slender windows, is the refectory. Below it is the *Salle des Hôtes*, below that the Almonry.

After that introduction, return to the single entrance to the town, the **Porte de l'Avancée**. The defences here are a three-dimensional lesson in medieval warfare and the tactics of a siege. In the Cour de l'Avancée, on which the sea encroaches at high tides, invaders would be penned in a small triangular space. The *corps de garde des Bourgeois*, on the left, was built in 1530. On the right, the pair of cannon, with a little cluster of the stone balls which they fired, are a relic of the single occasion on which the defences were passed. In 1434, before the Cour de l'Avancée had been built, the English who occupied Mont Tombelaine – a posting which must have surpassed in frightfulness even that of the Roman legions to Hadrian's wall – mounted an attack which breached what is now the second gate, the **Porte du Boulevard**, and penetrated the barbican. They had been aided in doing so by Abbot Robert Jolivet, who, after completing the fortifications of the mount, unaccountably went over to the enemy, taking with him the knowledge of the weakest point in the defences. The attackers were vanquished before they could scale the town wall by the garrison under Louis d'Estouteville, who had held it steadfastly while the English overran the mainland, with

the citizens, and even the monks turning out in support. They re-
treated in such disarray that they left behind the cannon known as
the Michelettes. The traitor Jolivet was later to become doubly
infamous by acquiescing in the condemnation of Jeanne d'Arc.

Today, the grimness of the barbican, which one enters by the *Port
du Boulevard*, is relieved by the famous *hôtel de la Mère Poulard*,
with a crowd gathered perpetually before its windows to watch the
concoction of the famous fluffy omelettes in a long-handled copper
pan which is shaken over an open fire. If your budget is decently
modest leave it at looking. No reproach to the good mère, but, here
as at other of the mount's eating places, you must expect to pay for
ambiance, so best to put a cream cracker in your hip pocket and hold
out until you get back to Pontorson.

The third gate, protecting the entrance to the town, which still
keeps part of its portcullis, is the *Porte ou* **Logis du Roi**, where a
token royal garrison was lodged as a reminder of the monarch's
rights in the mount. Originally it was defended by a moat and
drawbridge. If today's visitors are dismayed by the roaring bazaar
they find in the **Grande Rue**, the main street of the mount, on the
other side of it, let them remember that hucksters have lived off
pilgrims since the Middle Ages, when they sold holy medals, and
bulbs of lead filled with the sands of the bay. They were certainly
here when Dr James Hairby, of Avranches, came in 1840: he spoke
of 'shopkeepers who deal in medals and scarves for the pilgrims'. He
found the townspeople to have a great resemblance to the *lazzaroni*
of Naples. At that time their chief source of a livelihood was the
cockles of the bay. Both sexes commonly had two or three cockle
belts round their waists; the women tucked up their petticoats to
reveal legs which – through overmuch paddling? – were 'as thick at
the ankle as the knee'. Dr Hairby adds that they suffered from
'phthisis, asthma and inflammatory complaints in general, also
dysentery and gastric ailments', as a natural consequence of their
mode of life, which included a diet of mutton and cockles, virtually
unrelieved. He describes their houses as 'hovels', so perhaps we
should salute progress, though it means that few of the 15c. and 16c.
houses lining the steep and narrow Grande Rue have kept their
timber façades. One of the best of those that remain is that of the
maison de l'Arcade, with an overhanging upper storey and a watch-
tower built into the ramparts, which is on the right as one passes
through the *Porte du Roi*. Near it is the **Musée Historical** (open
daily, 8–18.30, 1 March to 30 November), not to be confused with
the **Musée Historique**, opposite the entrance to the abbey, which has

waxworks and dioramas, though the same ticket gives access to both.

The parish church of **St Pierre**, opposite the museum, is more interesting for its furniture than its architecture, which is 15c. and 16c., with the lower part of the pillars surviving from the original building of the 11c. It is paved with funerary slabs, many of former officers of the mount. Among them is that to Jean de Surtainville, who has an epitaph in sonnet form. There is a memorial also to Vincent Rogierie, the mason who built the tower of the abbey church which, in 1897, was replaced by the existing tower and spire. The high altar dates from 1660; the silver altar of St Michael in the south aisle, crowned by a statue of the saint represented as a rather Tennysonian knight, has an array of ex-votos including the sword of the 19c. Général Lamoricière, who won fame in Algiers, then, after exile, ended his career as commander of the pontifical forces. The statues are from the 15c. to the 18c.; see particularly a big, plain St Anne with the Virgin, on the left of the entrance, which is late 15c., and a 16c. Virgin and Child in the Lady Chapel. Against the south wall there is a tomb whose 15c. effigy was badly mutilated during the Revolution. The 13c. font is carved from a single block of stone. In the treasury (apply to the sacristan) there is a head of Christ of the 15c. or 16c. which came from a *Pietà* once in the abbey church.

Rather than follow the cobbled Grande Rue, where, in season, the crowds are so thick on the ground that one walks in procession, turn into the covered alleyway which runs beneath the apse of St Pierre. The path passes through the little churchyard behind it, where there is a fifteenth century cross. Beyond, it climbs a flight of steps and turns left for the *terrasse de la Gire* on the south slope of the mount. On the way there are glimpses into the small gardens of the houses stacked up the slope, where there are occasional, unexpected trees, a syringa, a copper beech, a bay. From the *terrasse* a short flight of steps leads to the *chemin de ronde*. Turn right along it, with the south side of the abbey overhead and a vast view of the bay on the right. We pass the **Musée Historique** (visits 8–19). Just beyond it is the long, arcaded front of the *Maison de la Truie qui file*, where once pilgrims bought their cockle shells and ampoules of blessed sand and today's tourists buy their souvenirs.

We are now at the top of the great stone staircase of the Grande Degré, the culmination of the Grande Rue, restored from an impassable ruin during the early years of this century. Before us is the outer defence of the abbey, the 14c. **Châtelet**, with crenellated towers banded in grey and rose-coloured granite on either side of the portcullis. Any assailants who passed it would be confined in the aptly named *Escalier du Gouffre*, a steep, vaulted stairway. It leads to the 13c. *salle des gardes*, where the slope of the rock has imposed a floor on two levels. Across a small court is the *Aumônerie*, built in the late 11c., which is divided into two naves, with groined vaults, by a row of pillars. Here visitors take tickets and await their guides for a tour which lasts forty-five minutes to an hour.

For practical reasons the tours deal with one level of the abbey at a time, rather than one period, hence the value of a preliminary round of the rock. At peak periods the normal order of the route may be slightly modified and the visit a little shortened. The *Cellier* is not usually shown in the summer and, outside the lecture tours, only small, out-of-season parties are likely to have the luck to climb by the *escalier de dentelle* to the upper balcony, or to see the tiny, pre-Carolingian church, Notre-Dame-Sous-Terre.

The following assumes the most complete visit in the usual order. It begins with the ninety steps of the *Grand Degré Intérieur*, which, since the 13c., has divided the abbey from the world. On the left are the administrative buildings, the *Baillerie* and abbot's lodging, where distinguished guests were received, on the left the church of Saint Martin, which, strictly, is a crypt chapel. Near the top are the recently restored Gothic arches of an early 16c. cistern. Two bridges span the stairs; the fortified stone one was built in the 15c.

The *Grande Degré Intérieur* ends at the *plate-forme du Saut-Gauthier*, from which one gains the *parvis* of the church. Here enormous prospects open on to the Breton coast as far as Mont Dol, with the random scribble of the course of the Couesnon across the sand flats suddenly becoming as strict as a canal as the eye follows it to the land. Before 1780 most of what is now the *parvis* was taken up by the first three bays of the church – the seventy metres of the present nave is little more than half of the original length. At that time the façade was flanked by two square towers. On the classical west front which replaced it, it is kinder not to dwell.

The first impression of the interior of the church is of the unity between nave and choir, though the one is Romanesque, the other Flamboyant Gothic. It is due to the relative lightness of the construction of the nave, notably on the south side, which is a remarkable achievement for the latter part of the 11c. – perhaps understandably, the builders who restored the north side after it collapsed in 1103 were less daring – and the lack of ornament in the choir, which was built between 1450 and 1521, to replace a circular

Romanesque one. The obdurate granite has imposed its own reserve: elegance here depends on line and proportion. The whole is drenched with light from the great windows of the clerestory and the narrow bays of the exquisite triforium.

For carving, one must go to the diadem of apsidal chapels. The first on the south side has a low relief of the four Evangelists, the first on the north side of Adam and Eve being turned out of Paradise and another of the Harrowing of Hell. All three date from the 16c., as do the five low reliefs of English alabaster which form a retable in the second chapel on the north side. In the crossing there is a 13c. polychromatic stone Virgin, ample and serene. This is all that remains of the splendour of sculpture, woodcarving and stained glass which adorned the church before the Revolution.

The intricacies of the choir are all exterior. A modern spiral staircase leads from the second chapel on the south side out on to the lower gallery of the apse, among the profusion of pinnacles and flying buttresses which make the choir, seen from the distance, look like an elaborate reliquary set above the monumental walls and buttresses of the Marvel. At close quarters you realize the balance and tension, thrust and counter-thrust, which give strength to so apparently fragile a construction, which is lightened still further by such devices as piercing the abutments which support the flying buttresses.

Up one of the flying buttresses another stairway, the famous *Escalier de Dentelle*, so-called because of its open balustrade, leads to the upper balcony. From here the modern spire, narrow as a needle in the distant view, seems enormous. The figure of the saint is by Emmanuel Frémiet (1824–1910), who did the equestrian statue of Joan of Arc in the Place des Pyramides in Paris. The bay is boundless: to be up here at the moment when the rising tide comes licking over the sands at a speed which at the equinox can reach 30 k.p.h. is to grasp the reason for the old title of the abbey, St-Michel-au-Péril-de-la-Mer.

From the north side of the church, passing the façade of the monks' dormitory, whose windows were remodelled in the 13c., we go on to the **cloister** which forms the top storey of the western section of the Marvel. It was built between 1225 and 1228 to replace the sombre and chilly cloister where the monks formerly took their recreation. Here they would be already half-way to heaven in their airborne court which is goldsmiths' work in the delicacy of its execution and a superb feat of engineering in its steely strength. The four galleries are supported by 227 slim shafts, in which granite mingles with granite agglomerate and Purbeck marble. Those on the outer side are disposed in a staggered, double arcade, with a narrow, groined vault between the rows. This is Anglo-Norman Gothic, the English influence being evident particularly in the profusion of flowers and foliage in the carving above the arches and in the spandrels. In the western walk, near the crucifix which faces the door of the refectory, there is a badly worn figure of St Francis giving the date of his canonization (1228) which is the earliest known representation of the saint. The four heads in the carved frieze of the west gallery are thought possibly to be those of artist craftsmen who worked on the cloister. In this gallery, a door which now opens on to the void was to have been the entrance to a chapter house which was planned by Abbot Richard Turstin but never built. The garden in the centre of the cloister has been reconstituted according to a description in an ancient manuscript, though what is a delight to the eye may prove an anxiety if damp penetrates to the roof of the Knights' Hall below. On the south side is the lavatorium, where, each Thursday, took place the ceremony of foot-washing, a symbol of humility commemorating Christ's washing the feet of his disciples on Maundy Thursday.

The **Refectory**, east of the cloister, now mercifully restored to its original state after the indignities it suffered at the hands of the Maurists, who filled it with two storeys of dormitory cells, is arguably the most perfect 13c. interior in Europe. The immense hall, which was completed in 1217, has a barrel roof of oak. It is lit by rows of tall lancet windows, set so deep in their sharply-angled embrasures that they are invisible from the door, where one sees only their shapely arcades. On the right side a pulpit for the lector, whose duty it was to read aloud when the monks were at meals, has been fitted into the width of two bays. Also on the right is a door which once led to the kitchens, where a hoist brought provisions up the thirty metres from ground level, and took down the broken meats to the almonry for distribution to the poor.

From the Marvel we go on to the **Romanesque abbey** which underlies the Gothic. The chapel of Notre-Dame des Trente Cierges, in the crypt below the north transept of the church, which was begun early in the 11c., was modified early in the 13c., largely to support the new building of which it was the foundation. Traces of 12c. and 13c. wall paintings were found here.

The *Promenoir des Moines*, the **cloister** below the dormitory, whose heavy gloom is the antithesis of its successor, is also from the early 11c. In 1136 the arches were replaced by the present ogives, supported by squat pillars with square, simply decorated capitals, which are among the earliest examples of Gothic work in Normandy. The *Salle d'Aquilon* below it, with two naves of groined vaults, was the original almonry.

The pre-11c. dungeons,pits where the monks confined robbers and the 19c. kept political prisoners, are on to the west. Near by is the entrance to the pre-Carolingian church, Notre-Dame-Sous-Terre, which is below the western terrace.

Loving and scrupulous labour has recreated, or rather, revealed the chapel which saw the marriage of Duke Richard II. It is small and holy – eight metres by nine – divided lengthways by two broad arches supported by a central pillar. Above the altar at the east end of each nave is a platform where the relics were deposited. The walls here are 1 metre 80 centimetres thick; the arches keep the original flat red bricks which may be a heritage from the Romans. It is now thought that the stonework behind the altar in the south nave may come from Aubert's oratory.

We cross beneath the nave of the church to the crypt of the Saut-Gauthier, where, during the 19c., prisoners worked a treadmill to bring goods up the stone incline. The load on the sled fitted with rollers might be as much as two tons. The wheel shown was made from the wood of two or three treadmills which were used.

Beneath the south transept of the church is the 11c. chapel of Saint Martin, with a *cul-de-four* east end and remarkably broad arches. Then comes the architectural *tour de force* of the Crypte des Gros Piliers, each of whose drum pillars, five metres in circumference, supports one of the Gothic shafts of the choir of the church overhead. It was built between 1446 and 1450, of Chausey granite.

The tour ends in the middle storey of the Marvel, with the majestic Gothic halls of the *Salle des Hôtes* and the *Salle des Chevaliers*. The former was the chief guest chamber of the abbey, where Saint Louis, Louis XI and François Premier were received. The 35-metre length of the hall is divided into twin naves by columns whose capitals are carved with foliage treated with the utmost refinement. There are two hearths: in one of the window bays latrines have been constructed in the lower part of the outer wall. Even in its present stripped simplicity the hall has an incomparable elegance. Originally the windows were filled with stained glass, the walls were hung with tapestries, the floor glowed with glazed terracotta tiles.

The adjoining *Salle des Chevaliers*, so-called because, after 1468, it was used for the early chapters of the Order of St Michael – the tradition that Louis XI founded the order here is dubious – is more robust in concept. Its slightly irregular shape is divided into four ogival naves by pillars whose carved capitals have an immense variety. This was the monks' scriptorium, with light flooding in from the great west window as well as the north-facing bays and, as in the *Salle des Hôtes*, latrines arranged between the outer buttresses. It was purpose-built for that copying which was so large an element in the preservation and dissemination of learning in Europe. The monasteries themselves held it in such importance that a 9c. capitulary laid down that only earnest and mature men should be employed to copy the Gospels, the Psalms or the Missal, since errors in the words might introduce errors into the faith. In this great room, where the two hearths at which the copyists warmed their numbed fingers and sometimes thawed their ink could never completely overcome the effect of the north winds, there is the echo of another voice from the Middle Ages. It is that of one of the nameless scribes who smoothed their parchment with razor and pumice, and slaved and shivered and squinted in so many monastic writing rooms. It comes from a medieval MS: 'Vous ne savez pas de que c'est que d'écrire, elle vous courbe le dos, vous obscurit les yeux, vous brise l'estomac et les côtes. Prie donc, ô mon frère, toi qui lis ce livre, prie pour le pauvre Raoul, serviteur de Dieu, qui l'a transcrit tout entier de sa main dans le cloître de Saint-Aignan'. Let us indeed spare a thought for poor Raoul as we leave the abbey at the point at which we entered it, the almonry.

The visit should end with a circuit of the ramparts, but spare a little time first for the **abbey gardens**, entered by an archway on the left as one emerges from the *Escalier du Gouffre*. They are laid out in terraces, with opportunities alternately to see the Marvel from unexpected viewpoints and to rinse one's eyes with distances. The line of the ramparts, built between the 13c. and 15c., with some later modifications, can be seen clearly from the top of the Grande Degré. A short flight of steps on the left leads to the Tour Claudine at the foot of the Marvel, a strongpoint which dominates the last section of the stairway so as to make it virtually impassable for assailants. The path drops to the little pepperpot of the Échauguette du Nord and turns right for the crenellated Tour du Nord, a lookout over the whole of the bay. One of the houses on the right during the next stretch has a gargoyle-like a winged mastiff. The 15c. Tour Boucle offers a superb view of the choir of the abbey church. In the wall near the little Tour Cholet there is a low relief of a seated lion supporting the arms of Abbot Robert Jolivet, who was largely responsible for the outer defences of the mount. The Tour Basse, the Tour de la Liberté and the Tour de l'Arcade lead back to the Porte du Roi.

CHAPTER TWENTY

Val de Sée and Sélune reservoirs – Mortain –
Abbaye Blanche – Domfront – Lonlay – Bagnoles –
Couterne – Carrouges

꘠

THE Bocage, east of Avranches, an undulating country, in which
small fields, netted with hedges, alternate with rocky outcrops, saw
some of the fiercest fighting of the Battle of Normandy. The broken
ground, ideal for defensive action, was ill-suited to tank warfare; the
Americans, in particular, to whom it was a wholly unfamiliar ter-
rain, had to revise their tactics in the field. Since the *guerre des Haies*
a new chapter has been written into military manuals in the U.S.A.
It is an area of thriving small towns, which are equally agreeable as
overnight stops or as a base for two or three days' leisurely exploration.

From Avranches to Mortain, around 30 kilometres as the crow
flies, there is an attractive route which follows the valley of the Sée,
where the N811 is a winding scenic way. Brécy, a favourite spot for
trout and salmon fishing, has a 17c. château of brick and stone. At
Sourdeval, perched high above the confluence of the little
Fyeurseul and the Sée, which has been completely rebuilt since
1944, turn right for Mortain.

A roundabout southern route will take in the small departmental
capital of Saint-James and the impressive reservoirs of the Sélune
Valley, and also give a glimpse of several châteaux. Leave Avranches
by the N176 for Pontaubault, another village rebuilt since 1944,
whose only relic of its past is the doorway of the Romanesque
church set up in the cemetery. From here the N789 runs due south
for **Saint-James**, set above the River Beuvron, which has the
remains of a castle built by the Conqueror before he invaded
England. Its history before its destruction during the 17–18c. is
typical for a strongpoint in what was for long border country,
disputed by the Dukes of Normandy and the Bretons and attacked
by the English in the 15c. One-and-a-half kilometres to the east
is the château of **La Paluelle**, with an open gallery and terraces

254

framed by balustrades. The main body of the house is in the style of Louis XIII but one wing goes back to Louis XI. The memorial and cemetery of the American Third Army, with the graves of 4,410 soldiers who fell in the region, is 2 kilometres south-south-east of the town.

From Saint-James, head north again for Ducey by the D467 and turn right into the D85, which leads down into the valley of the Sélune. There is no access to the small dam of La Roche-qui-Boit, built between 1915 and 1919, which was a prototype of its kind, but the D582 on the left and a narrow road turning right off it lead to the **Barrage de Vezins**, thirty-six metres high, which was completed in 1931. The artificial lake winds for 16–17 kilometres between hills, craggy or wooded. Boats can be hired. At the Auberge du Lac, turn right to get back to the D85, which crosses the Ponts des Biards, with views along the lateral valley of the Ivrande, to join the D30 at **St-Hilaire-du-Harcouët**. This active market town is one of Normandy's post-war rebuildings. The big, 13c. style church is in fact 19c., though the tower is a survival from an older building.

Mortain was the starting point for the counter-attack which the Germans launched towards Avranches on the night of 6–7 August 1944, in the hope of cutting off Patton's Third Army from its bases. The Allied bombardment which helped to destroy it destroyed also more than three-quarters of the town. If today Mortain, strung out along the hillside above the steep gorge of the river Cance, does not look rawly new, it is because, as someone has said, the granite gives to new things some of the dignity of age as it gives to old things the freshness of youth.

The collegiate church of **Saint-Evroult** escaped the ruin. It was founded in 1082 by Count Robert de Mortain, half-brother of the Conqueror, and his wife, Matilda, as a college of sixteen canons. All that remains of their church is a doorway which has been preserved in the south wall. The present building, started probably in 1216 and completed without any interruption to disturb the unity of its style, is Gothic, but a pure, primal Gothic which is a total negation of the arrowy arches and lacy stonework which the non-specialist tends to associate with the period. The loftiness of a west front which is severe but not grim, with three tall lancets set above a doorway framed by pairs of blind arcades, is accentuated by its position above street level, and by the steep pitch of the plain gable. The tower at the south-east corner of the choir is a triumph of strict elegance, with two narrow windows on each face rising from a few metres above the ground to the saddle-back roof.

The interior does not disappoint. There are no transepts, nothing interrupts the solemn march of the massive cylindrical columns from nave to apse, with, above them, the line of a blind arcade. Only the apse and the aisles retain their stone ogival vaults. Those of the chancel were replaced around the end of the Middle Ages by a timber barrel ceiling, which, in about 1860, was obscured by the present plaster vault. When funds are available it is hoped that the plaster will be removed.

Twenty-four of the choir stalls, with carved misericords, are 15c., as is the font. The 18c. high altar comes from the abbey of Savigny-le-Vieux, midway between Mortain and Fougères, which was founded in 1114 by the hermit saint, Vitalis. His order, which united with the Cistercians in 1147, had an English house at Furness Abbey.

Mortain's rarest treasure is the remarkable *chrismale*, a small *coffret* of gilded copper, perhaps Anglo-Irish work, dating from the 7c., which was used either as a reliquary or as a portable pyx. Its sides are embossed with figures of Christ blessing, SS. Michael and Gabriel, and the Trinity. A Saxon inscription has been translated as: 'God bless Eada who made this chrismal'. It is thought that the Conqueror may have taken the *coffret* from an English church and given it to that which his half-brother had founded. The *chrismale* is kept under lock and key, but may be shown on request at the presbytery to visitors with a serious interest. 'Serious interest' means just that. It is discourteous to disturb a busy parish priest merely to gratify curiosity.

Opposite the church the ground slopes down to the picture-postcard scenery beside the river, which is the delight of brochure writers. The bosky paths beside the Cance are Corot, later period, who did in fact paint here, and I do not care for Corot. Those who do can obtain from the Syndicat d'Initiative at the *mairie* a guide to the footpaths which lead to the Petite Cascade and the Grande Cascade, which latter was painted by Courbet, not Corot. To get to the starting point for these wanderings, take the Rue Bassin, opposite the church, to the Place du Château (only vestiges of the castle remain), then turn left beside the Caisse d'Épargne and right at the corner (signposted). Those who persevere as far as the Grande Cascade will be rewarded by a 12c. church at Neufbourg, at the opposite side of the valley from Mortain, which is on the route.

A far better walk is that up La Montjoie, the hill behind Saint-Evroult. From the church follow the signposts for the Petite Chapelle, and, at the top of the hill, turn right along a grassy track bordered with pine trees. It leads to the chapel of **Saint-Michel**, set on a rock at the end of the ridge, with a belvedere beside it commanding a sweep of country that extends as far as the coast of Brittany. In the near distance the road for Saint-Hilaire cuts straight as a ruler through a tide of green; in the far distance, in clear weather, the outline of Mont Saint-Michel is painted on the sky. It was from this point that medieval pilgrims got their first sight of it as they neared the end of their long and often painful journey, hence the name of the hill, Mont Gaudi, or Mont de la Joie.

In a nearer past it was known as 'Hill 314', the height on which the Second Battalion of the 120th Regiment of U.S. infantry, the 'lost Battalion', was surrounded during the German counter-attack of August 1944. They held out from 6 August to 13 August, when they were relieved. The little neo-Gothic chapel (opening times, particularly out of season, are rather fitful: ask at the Syndicat d'Initiative at Mortain) has been transformed into a memorial to the U.S. soldiers who fell in the action.

At the exit from Mortain, on the road to Sourdeval and Vire, is another of Vitalis's foundations, the former **Abbaye Blanche**, a convent established about 1120 (open daily; guided visits 10–12, and 14–18 in summer, and may be arranged for groups at other times). After the Revolution the abbey became successively the *petit séminaire* for Coutances and the *grand séminaire* for the missionary congregation of the Pères du Saint-Esprit. Since 1970 it has been a centre for spiritual activities. The 19c. additions to the building loom inescapably, but there survives from the original abbey part of the only Romanesque cloister in Normandy and the 12c. church, as well as a number of 12c. rooms, one of which was the chapter house. During the 19c. the fragments of the cloister were assembled in a single gallery along the side of the church, but the arrangement of a block of masonry between each group of two or three columns is the original one of the last quarter of the 12c. The carved capitals, though simple, are surprisingly varied. The church, consecrated in 1206, is a pure example of Cistercian art, governed by its three imperatives: beauty, simplicity and logic.

Domfront, 25 kilometres to the south-east, if less good than Mortain for walks that start at the door of your hotel, is an excellent centre for exploring a particularly attractive part of the Bocage. It is also a dramatic evocation of feudal Normandy: the first sight as one approaches of the minatory finger of the castle and the ramparts of the medieval town crowning the rocky outcrop that rises 70 metres above the plain makes an indelible impression. The fortress claims to be the oldest and was certainly one of the strongest in Normandy. According to rather misty tradition there was a village on the hill-top in the 6c., clustering round a chapel which was built by the hermit Saint Front (hence Domfront), but it was 1011 before Guillaume de Bellême, known as Talvas, a Norman noble whose father, Yves de Creil, had been a military engineer at the court of King Louis IV, built a castle on the height and the village grew into a town which became the capital of the Passais. The lords of Bellême lost their castle to William the Conqueror before the century was much more than half-way through; towards 1123 Henry Beauclerc began to gird the rock with the ramparts which we see today. It was here that Henry II, who spent more time in his dukedom than in his kingdom, received the papal nuncio sent to reconcile him with Becket. Of the many sieges which the fortress endured, the bloodiest was that of 1559, when Montgomery, who had accidentally killed Henri II during a tourney, newly converted to Calvinism, defended it against overwhelmingly superior Royalist forces. He surrendered only when the garisson of 150 men had been reduced to fifteen, most of them wounded. There were few chivalrous honours of war in the reception of his surrender by the Royalist general, Matignon. Montgomery was stripped of his honours and possessions before being executed in Paris.

On the way up to the old town by the Rue de la Gare, we pass the little granite church of **Notre-Dame sur l'Eau**, which was built by the monks of Lonlay as a priory between 1050 and 1100. Originally it was a perfect example of the Romanesque style, a Latin cross with a central tower almost as broad as it was high, an apsidal east end and a nave of six bays. In 1836, despite the pleas of the novelist, Prosper Merimée, four of the bays were lopped in order to build the road from Domfront to Mortain and Mont Saint-Michel. The old doorway has been built into the new façade.

Walk round the church to see the particularly satisfying east end before entering it to admire the double row of arcades in the choir, framed by a wide chancel arch. The altar, a noble slab of granite dating from the 11c., is the oldest in Normandy. 12c. wall paintings, apparently restored during the 15c., have been uncovered in the south transept and there is a polychromatic Virgin and Child of the 14c. Of the same period is the tomb with the effigy of a knight which is reputed to be that of Guillaume de Bellême but which is in fact that of Pierre Ier Ledin de la Chalerie. Do not miss the inscription on the tomb of the Marquise Ledin, wife of Brice Coppel, who died in 1613, aged twenty-three.

Passant ce marbre ne regarde,
Ma cendre n'est sous ce tombeau.
Car mon cher mari me la garde
Et son cœur en est le vaisseau.

Until the 18c. the church was the burial place of many of the leading families of the Passais. The thirty-seven granite slabs commemorating them have now been moved into the churchyard.

The walled town is entered from the Grand Carrefour at its south-east end. Once twenty-four towers defended the walls. Those that remain are domesticated, wedged between dwelling houses or themselves used as such, with geraniums at the windows and terraced vegetable plots sloping down from them. There is room for only two parallel main streets along the crest of the ridge. From the Grande Rue turn right into the Place de la Liberté, which is dominated by the modern church of **St Julien**, which almost reconciles one to buildings with more ferro-concrete than stone and slate in their composition. It has the confidence of its period (1925): there is a bold spaciousness about the plan of four great intersecting arches with an octagonal dome. In the apse there is a vast fresco-cum-mosaic of the saint presenting the church to Christ, with more mosaic in the Way of the Cross round the walls of the nave.

A short street going off diagonally right from the façade of the church leads to the Place du Panorama, with views north along the valley of the Varenne. Beyond it to the left are the old prison and the Hôtel de Ville, which has a collection of pictures by Charles Léandre (1862–1934), who was born at Montsecret, some 20 kilometres north of Domfront. A footbridge above a road which was once the moat leads to the **castle gardens**. The building remains impressive though it is no more than a shard, with only two walls standing of Guillaume Talvas's square donjon, which was blown up in 1610, on the orders of Henri IV. There are fragments of towers, one of which, the *Tour de Presle*, is a belvedere with the most dramatic of outlooks. Below there is a straight drop to the limpid river, running here through the narrow gorge known as the Val des Rochers. The crag rearing up at the other side of it is the Tertre Sainte Anne, where Matignon's forces set up the cannon which breached the ramparts during the last siege of the castle. South and west, the forest rolls away in tides of green-blue like the Atlantic, with such occasional landmarks as the rocks of Mortain and, southward, the distant cone of Mont Margantin.

An easy day's motoring based on Domfront will take in the 11c.

church of Lonlay l'Abbaye and a number of the charming country houses, manors rather than châteaux – the French word for them, *gentilhommière*, is explicit – which are numerous in this part of Normandy. The first of them is 3½ kilometres along the road to Tinchebray. **La Chalerie** (exterior visits only) is distinguished by an unusual carved roof over the porch. It was built in the 16c. by the Ledins de la Chalerie, the family which governed Domfront, of whom the Marquise whose epitaph we read in Notre-Dame-sur-l'Eau was a member.

Notre-Dame-le-Lonlay, 9 kilometres from Domfront, in the kind of riverside setting which the builders of medieval religious houses chose so unerringly, was founded a little before 1020 by Guillaume de Bellême, which makes him the founder also, if at one remove, of Notre-Dame-sur-l'Eau. All that remains of the conventual buildings is the Gothic doorway to the chapter house. By contrast, the abbey church, with a square lantern tower rising over the crossing between the Gothic choir and a Romanesque transept, which has been restored since 1944, looks new-minted. There is no nave, but it is not true, as is sometimes stated, that none was built. It survived until the end of the 16c. A collection of fragments of pottery and tiles found during recent excavations is shown in the chapter house.

From Lonlay a narrow but navigable road leads south-west to join the D134. Upon reaching it, turn left for the scenic set piece of the Fosse Arthour. Here the river Cance comes down in a series of falls between steep granite walls. A local legend, disregarding Malory, says that Arthur and Guinevere ended their days peaceably here. The D134 joins the N807 at St-Georges-de-Rouellay; turn left for Domfront. At Roullé, a right-hand turn about 600 metres before the bridge over the Egrenne leads to what remains of the manor of La Saucerie, a gatehouse flanked by 15–16c. towers.

East of Domfront the D908 runs through the Forêt d'Andaine, nearly 1400 hectares of oak and beech and birch and pine which extend as far as Bagnoles-de-l'Orne and continue beyond it in the Forêt de la Motte. The whole of this tract of woodland, from two to three hundred metres above sea level, broken by the kind of 'picturesque' rocky outcrops much beloved of French sightseers – the taste was perhaps implanted by the Barbizon school of painters – is included in the Regional National Park of Normandie-Maine, whose 135,000 hectares straddle the regions of Basse Normandie and the Pays de Loire. There is a project for setting up in the Forêt d'Andaine a game park which would preserve all the species native to the region.

Follow the D908 as far as the Étoile d'Andaine, the centre of the forest, then turn right for Juvigny, passing on the left as one comes out of the trees the little chapel of St Génevi6eve. Beyond it you will see from afar one of the oddest buildings in Normandy, the **Phare de Bonvouloir**, an inland lighthouse indeed. For a nearer view, take the farm road which turns off to the left, about 700 metres on foot. The *phare* is a frail column, 26½ metres tall, affixed to a more solid tower. With the adjoining *colombier* and well, and part of the farm buildings, they are all that remain of a 15c. château. At Juvigny turn right into the N807 for Domfront.

Geographically, **Bagnoles** is a slightly better centre than Domfront from which to explore this area, but spas are an individual taste. For the benefit of addicts like myself who may make it a base I will assume it as a starting point for excursions in the eastern part of the area. For those who prefer to remain at Domfront the extra driving entailed is not excessive. The small town, whose population, with that of the adjoining commune of Tessé-la-Madeleine, is only about 1500, is an odd outpost of worldliness – well, relative worldliness – among so much granite and greenery. As a spa it has a respectable antiquity, even if one discounts the legend of Hugues, lord of Tessé, date unspecified, whose horse, Rapide, being near knackered, wandered off into the Forêt d'Andaine and a month later came frisking home, having left half his years and all his ills in a warm fountain in a gorge of the Vée. Serious history begins in the 16c. when, the land having been appropriated for the crown, the spa began to be known beyond the immediate neighbourhood. By the 18c. it was attracting large numbers of sufferers from circulatory ailments, who were dunked communally in one of three baths, through which the waters passed successively. The first was for men, the second for women, the third for the poor, apparently irrespective of sex. Not until 1840 did the amenities of a fashionable health resort begin to grow up about the spring.

The site is enchanting. The Vée here forms a lake, now prettied up round the edges and reflecting the pale façade of the casino. The bath-house is set in a wooded park, which is the more attractive for being laid out on broken ground, with footpaths leading to viewpoints like the 'Saut du Capucin' – he was a monk who vowed that, if the waters cured him, he would leap the four metres separating two points of rock. An added pleasure in strolling these pine-scented paths is that you may see a red squirrel. Everywhere you can study the French in pursuit of that earnest enjoyment of fragile health which amounts to a national pastime. I know of nowhere else where adults embark in *pédalos* while warmly wrapped against possibly cool breezes.

For the **Château de Couterne**, some 5 kilometres south of Bagnoles, continue along the Rue des Bains, with the bath-house on your left. The neo-Remaissance château dominating a pleasant municipal park on the right is now the Hôtel de Ville of Tessé. The D335 for Couterne is on the left.

The château was built by Jean de Frotté, minor poet and *grand commis*, who was in some sense Burghley to the Elizabeth of Queen Marguerite of Navarre, sister of François Ier, one of the most enlightened of royal patrons of the arts. Originally the house, built between 1542 and 1549, consisted of a single storey, with two round towers. It was not until the late 18c. that it was given upper storeys, wings were added and the rear gained its present 18c. decorum. Since the château is not open to the public one can do no more than admire its rosy brick and granite reflected in the lake. The loss is the greater because Couterne is one of the relatively few châteaux which have remained in the occupation of the same family since its building and have kept relics of a history which includes the stormy period of the Wars of Religion, when members of the family who had turned Calvinist suffered persecution, exile and imprisonment, remaining staunchly Royalist the while. In a later generation, Louis de Frotté, a member of another branch of the family, was General-in-Chief of the Chouans in Normandy, and stayed a night at Couterne during his campaign. He was shot in 1800 on the orders of Napoleon, who was then First Consul.

East of Bagnoles, the **Château de Carrouges** (open daily except Tuesdays, 9–12, 14–18 in summer; 10–12, 13.30–16 in winter) is within easy reach. Take the N816 to **La Ferté Macé**, a bustling little industrial town with a lively Thursday market and a gastronomic reputation for tripe served *en brochette*. An 11c. or 12c. tower, now used as a sacristy, is all that remains of the original church here.

Carrouges, on its hill-top, is about 15 kilometres to the south-east. For eight centuries the estate was owned by two of the great families of Normandy, for the first three after 1150 by the Comtes de Carrouges. One of them, Robert, who was among the 119 who defended Mont Saint-Michel under Louis d'Estouteville, had his lands confiscated by Henry VI, whom he had first supported and later deserted during the Hundred Years War.

In 1450 the property passed by marriage to the family of Le Veneur de Tillières, who held it until it was acquired by the state in 1936.

The 16c. gatehouse of diapered red and black brick, with twin pepperpot towers on either side of the high mitred roof, was built by Cardinal Jean Le Veneur, abbot successively of Bec and of Mont Saint-Michel and friend of Rabelais, who mentions him in *Pantagruel* (his great-nephew, Gabriel, whose friends included Catherine de Médicis, did even better by receiving a dedication from Machiavelli). In the 17c., Comte Tanneguy II, as French Ambassador in London, negotiated the marriage of Charles I and Henrietta Maria. Later he fell out of favour with Richelieu and the family knew a period of decline. Tanneguy's grandson, François, with an estate cumbered by debt and with six daughters for whom he had no hope of finding marriage portions, drove the lot to the convent of the Visitation of Alençon, where they entered the order.

The château, red brick clasped with granite, is built in a huge, irregular quadrilateral round an inner court and surrounded by a broad moat. The oldest part is the square, machicolated donjon on the left of the entrance, probably built in the 14c. and remodelled during the 15c. The south and east wings are respectively Henri IV and Louis XIII. To the right of the château a grille whose luxuriant grace is remarkable even in Normandy, a region of splendid wrought iron work, leads to a terrace overlooking the River Udon. The grille is perhaps the most notable of the additions which Jacques Le Veneur made to the château during the 17c. The balustrades bordering the moat were refashioned during the 18c.; so was the entrance porch.

When the château was taken over by the state in 1936 it was both dilapidated and denuded of much of its furniture and many of its pictures. Since then, the *Monuments Historiques* has carried out an admirable restoration. The conducted tour, lasting forty-five minutes or an hour according to the pressure of numbers, includes the room where Louis XI stayed in 1473. The woodwork is 200 years later in date. The most outstanding of the remaining six rooms which are shown are the *salon des portraits* and the *antichamber d'honneur*. In the former one can trace the same face appearing in different centuries, above a cuirass, or under a powdered wig, or framed in ringlets. The room has a magnificent fireplace with a painted canopy and 17c. furniture. In the *antichambre d'honneur* there is an incomparable harmony of colour, made up of the warm red flooring tiles and the paler tones of the brick walls, with the Renaissance chairs upholstered in a dim rose red that links them. The raftered ceiling has a great cross beam which, during the mid-17c., was ornamented with gilded cartouches. The climax is the late 16c. *escalier d'honneur*, this also of brick, which climbs round the rampant arches of a square cage.

CHAPTER TWENTY–ONE

Flers – Condé-sur-Noireau – Pontécoulant – Vire – Saint-Michel-de-Montjoie – L'Angotière – Torigni – St-Lô – Cerisy

✣

NORTH and north-west of Domfront and Bagnoles stretches the so-called 'little Switzerland', a region of orchard and pasture, crags and wooded hills, cut by the valleys of the Orne and the Vire and threaded by many lesser streams. It is admirable country for walking or gentle motoring, with centres to suit most tastes. Vire, to the west of the area, is an interesting town, as well as a commercial centre. Clécy, in the Orne valley, amply provided with hotels, is particularly good as the starting point for a variety of short excursions. Those who prefer to avoid tourist centres, however modest, might be happier at **Pont d'Ouilly**, where the Vire joins the Orne.

Flers, 20 kilometres north of Domfront, if it would not be most people's choice for an extended stay, is a useful overnight stop if you want to spend a day in the Orne valley. The town, largely rebuilt since 1944, is thriving, with modern light industries added to its century-old cotton and the still older iron. Its château, now the *mairie*, stands in a large, well-wooded park on the west of the town – take the Rue Jules Cevelot from the central Place Duhalde and turn left into the Rue J. Salles. Strolling beside the lake here it is difficult to realize that, technically, one is still in a busy industrial town. The **château**, surrounded by a moat, is pleasing, with sleek, bell-shaped domes crowning the late 16c. towers on either side of the classical central building. Besides the municipal offices it houses a **museum** and **art gallery** whose pictures include a number by Charles Léandre (*see* under Domfront).

Both Flers's churches are mediocre 20c., but it is worth following the Rue du Champ de Foire, which runs south-east from the Place du Perron, to see the *petite chapelle*, properly the chapel of the Immaculate Conception, in the grounds of what was the *petit séminaire*. It is built of reinforced concrete, pierced and improbably charming for that medium, particularly inside, where the roof is sky blue and white and most of the available surfaces are decorated with frescoes and mosaic.

A day's excursion from Flers can comfortably take in the Château de Pontécoulant, while giving a fair impression of the landscape of rock and river north-east of it. Take the N162 to **Condé-sur-Noireau**, another little cotton town largely rebuilt since 1944. There is a 12–15c. choir in the church of St Martin, on the way in from Flers. Jules Dumont d'Urville (1790–1842), who discovered *Terre Adélie*, 2500 kilometres south of Tasmania, was born at Condé: his statue is in the Place de l'Hôtel de Ville, with three stones from that territory at its feet. You may see a kingfisher streaking up and down the river hereabouts: they can be surprisingly urban birds. The church up the hill, Saint-Sauveur, is a rather successful example of restoration, with the old exterior preserved and a glowing chestnut vault looking down on the reconstructed interior.

Pontécoulant is 8 kilometres to the north-west by the D105, which follows the valley of the Durance, and the D298. The château (guided visits, 9–12, 14–18, 14–15 in winter; closed on Tuesdays and during October) a couple of kilometres beyond the village, whose oldest parts are late 16c., is as far removed from classical French formality as is its splendid park, which was laid out *à l'anglaise* in the late 18c.

From the 14c. to the 20c. the property belonged to the family of Le Doulcet, which originated in the Savoie, and which was to provide France with distinguished soldiers from the reign of Henri IV onwards. Its most remarkable member was the Comte Louis Gustave, born in 1764, who, as a schoolboy at Versailles, met Louis XV. He supported the Revolution and became the representative of Calvados in the Convention, but opposed the September massacres and voted against the execution of Louis XVI. Soon afterwards he was obliged to emigrate to Switzerland, where, while earning his living as a joiner, he met the future King Louis Philippe, who was supporting himself by teaching mathematics. Later, back in France, Louis Gustave was created a count of the empire by Bonaparte, rallied to Louis XVIII in 1814 and was made a peer of France, and, after 1830, went on to serve his old companion in exile, Louis Philippe. He died in 1853.

The last representative of the family, the count's grand-daughter, Madame Barrère, left the château to the Department of Calvados. It is now a museum which preserves rather successfully the atmosphere of a private house. Along with the family portraits and souvenirs there is fine furniture, including a number of pieces from

Indo-China. The dining room has a porcelain stove from which rises an extraordinary garlanded pipe.

Return to Condé-sur-Noireau, and continue along the N162 to **Clécy**. The little town, set on a hill in a curve of the Orne, is picturesque almost to a fault and offers all the pleasures of a rural holiday – fishing, boating, riding. There is even a 'miniature Switzerland' in the Parc des Loisirs. The 16c. *manoir de Placy* has a small museum of Norman craft and folk art (open daily, 9–18 from 15 June to 1 October, otherwise Sundays only) and the Syndicat d'Initiative at the *mairie* will supply a guide to walks in the neighbourhood.

If you feel like spending two or three nights in this region and find Clécy's very real charm a little too self-conscious, then continue north for about 10 kilometres to **Thury-Harcourt**, which is less a resort but still a pleasant centre, and adequately provided with hotels. The town has been rebuilt, solid and honest and grey, since 1944, but the church preserves its 13c. façade. Little remains of the 18c. château of the Ducs d'Harcourt which, with the important collections it contained, was burned by the retreating Germans.

For those staying here, the village of **Aunay-sur-Odon**, 14 kilometres to the north-west by the highly scenic D6, is something of a show piece of post-war reconstruction in Normandy, and could be the object of a pleasant afternoon's drive. Virtually obliterated during three days in June 1944, it was rebuilt in native stone between November 1947 and August 1950. The church took longer; started in 1949, it was not completed until 1958, but its scale makes it an impressive gesture of faith in a predominantly secular age.

The return from Clécy to Flers can be made by way of Pont d'Ouilly and the N811, which follows the valley of the Noireau till it meets the Vère at Pont Erambourg. The latter is a swifter and more dramatic river, with a good deal of old established industry along its steep-sided valley. Nowadays the former cotton mills are mostly converted to electronics or the manufacture of asbestos.

From Flers to **Vire**, take the road for Tinchebraye, which winds between the small lake of Landisacq and Mont Crespin. The little town specializes in the manufacture of gardening tools, which makes it an unexpected birthplace for the writer André Breton (1896–1966), one of the leaders of the Surrealist movement. Around Tinchebraye, in 1106, took place the battle which ended the rivalry for the throne of England between the Conqueror's sons, when Robert Courte-Heuse, Duke of Normandy, was defeated by his youngest brother, Henry Beauclerc, and spent the remaining twenty-eight years of his life in captivity. The small, stout church of **St-Remy**, dating in part from the same century, was fortified during the Hundred Years War, hence the machicolated angle tower. Notre-Dame-des Montiers, near the cemetery, though negligible architecturally, has a good example of the *perques*, or *poutres de gloire*, which are typical of the churches of Basse Normandie. These slender curving beams, often decorated with foliage, bearing a rood, were during the 17c. and 18c. placed in many of the chancel arches left vacant when liturgical changes caused the removal of the *jubé*. They often fitted most happily into a position designed for a far different artichectural feature, which makes one regret the more the disappearance of many of them during 19c. restorations.

Vire, built on a promontory which is skirted on the south and west by the river of the same name, is a strongpoint which has been fortified possibly since the 8c. It is the natural capital of an opulant region, a place of enormous eating, whose *andouilles*, or rough-cut sausages, made according to a traditional recipe, as well as its butter, are renowned throughout France. Its citizens include a recent World Champion in the preparation of *tripes à la mode de Caen*. The main gate of the town is the Porte-Horloge. The machicolation over the narrow entrance and below the parapets of the flanking towers testifies to its function in the 13c., when Vire was wholly contained within ramparts of which few traces now remain. The square tower was added in 1480. For the Syndicat d'Initiative, turn right into the Rue du Calvados.

Beyond the town, the church of **Notre-Dame**, built in the same warm-toned granite, predates it in its oldest parts. There are fragments of 12c. work in the lower part of the nave. The church of today, the heavy pillars of the nave contrasting with the airy choir, whose roof is decorated with lavishly carved and painted bosses, is 13–16c.

Further on, the lime-bordered Place du Château opens on the left. All that now remains of the **castle** which Henry Beauclerc built at the beginning of the 12c. are two walls of the donjon. West of it there is a miniature inland corniche walk round the granite spur, with superb views of the surrounding country. Walk up the Rue Notre-Dame, beside the church and turn left into the Rue des Cordeliers. Beside the Sous-Préfecture the short Rue des Rames leads by way of a road tunnel and a well-trodden footpath to the classic viewpoint of the **Rocher des Rames**, dominating the valleys at the confluence of the Vire and the Varenne. These are the Vaux de

Vire, which added a word to the French language. Olivier Basselin, a popular poet who lived here in the 15c., wrote drinking songs which, in the early 17c., were edited and published by a more academic poet, Jean Le Houx, under the title of Vaux-de-Vire, from which evolved *vaudeville*. The valley where Basselin earned his living as a fulling miller has acquired a number of modern factories during post-war rebuilding, but has not entirely lost its character of an industrial village in which small workshops alternate with vegetable patches or a tethered goat. For a closer view, take the path leading downhill from the Rochers des Rames, turn left into the Rue Jean Le Houx, then left again, following the course of the river back to Vire.

The lower town has gardens laid out on the slope below the castle and a small lake formed by damming the Vire. Across the river the old Hôtel-Dieu has been converted into a **museum** which is worth a visit if only for the fine Norman farmhouse which has been reconstructed in its grounds.

An unusual and extremely rewarding excursion from Vire is that to the granite museum at **Saint Michel-de-Montjoie**, 15 kilometres to the south – leave the town by the D76 and, at Gathemo, turn right into the D39 for Saint-Michel. The **museum**, set out in a hill-top park at the heart of this granite country, is the best kind of regional display, in which the rock from which was hewn so many of the buildings which we have seen during our journey can be studied in all its varieties. An excellent documentation traces the history of its working through the centuries, and the uses to which it has been put, from the megaliths of Carnac, in Brittany, to the slab covering the grave of the Unknown Soldier under the Arc de Triomphe, in Paris, which is of the local blue granite. The tools shown take us from crude mallets and chisels to modern quarrying machinery, the specimens range from the boulders in their raw state to slabs polished as smooth as satin. A protest that polishing is a betrayal of the nature of a natural substance whose essence is its obdurate grittiness is met by the information that the polished slabs are used as benches for laboratory work of the utmost precision. On this rugged height, where the objects you see seem to have grown from the soil rather than to have been assembled, where the distant view may give you a glimpse of that triumph of granite, Mont Saint-Michel, while in the valley at your feet the mist has still not cleared, you feel you are touching the bones of the landscape.

To vary the return journey, at Gathemo, turn right for Perriers-en-Beauficel. The road winds downhill to Chérence-le-Roussel, where the D911 leads left through the narrow, twisting valley of the Sée, 8 or 9 kilometres of continually changing river scenery. We pick up the main road back to Vire at Sourdeval.

St-Lô is 30 kilometres north of Vire by the main N174. The alternative, by Pontfarcy and Tessy-sur-Vire, is more interesting and lengthens the route by only some 15 kilometres, even allowing for detours and side turnings.

Leave Vire by the D52. After Beaumesnil the road follows the valley of the Dromme to Pontfarcy, then enters an attractive stretch beside the River Vire as far as Tessy. Here turn right over the river, then left into the D359 for **Troisgots-la-Chapelle-sur-Vire**, a hamlet with a population of less than fifty, which has been a place of pilgrimage since the 12c. The church has a 15c. statue of Notre-Dame-de-Vire on the left of the entrance.

From La Chapelle, turn right for Cretteville, then right again into the D551. The first right-hand turn off it leads to the **Château de l'Angotière** (visits, Easter to All Saints, 14.30–18.30, daily except Tuesdays), a Renaissance manor which, both in its character and in its site, a natural platform overlooking the valleys of the Vire and the Jacre, is of the essence of this part of Normandy. The interior, which has splendid granite hearths, the earliest dated 1717, 17c. and 18c. furniture and some fine Chinese porcelain, keeps the atmosphere of a house which has remained in private hands. The wooded park is open to visitors and walks through it are indicated.

Return to the D551 and turn left for Condé-sur-Vire. The road runs between the river and the escarpment of the Rochers de Ham; about a kilometre along it there is a footpath to the top (signposted). From Condé the D86 brings you back to the main Vire–St-Lô road a short distance south-west of Torigni.

Some may prefer **Torigni** to St-Lô as an overnight stop on the way to Bayeux. In spite of being on a main road the little town, with its pink and white château and glorious avenues of lime and chestnut, has periods when it is suspended in a calm so profound that the plop of a trout jumping in one of the two lakes is an event. It is an unlikely place to be linked with Monaco, but this was once the home of the Grimaldis, rulers of that principality.

Torigni had a fortified castle in the 11c.: of this nothing remains. In 1450 the domain passed by marriage to a Breton nobleman, Jean Gouyou de Matignon, and, towards the end of the next century, the transformation of the donjon into a modern **château** began. The building in the new Italian style which François Gabriel, ancestor of Jacques Gabriel, who designed the Petit Trianon at Versailles, planned for Jacques de Matignon, Maréchal of France, reflected the magnificence of a family of princely power and influence. It was vast; what remains today is only the central block. Three buildings were set in a V-shape round a *cour d'honneur* open to the north. It has been said that the Maréchal, in building, 'voyait grand' and that his grandson, who was largely responsible for the sumptuousness of the interior, 'voyait surtout riche'. Claude Vignon (1593–1670) spent three years decorating the walls of the *grande galerie* with immense panels depicting the family history of the Matignons. The park to the north-west was laid out by Le Nôtre.

In 1715 Jacques-François Léonor de Matignon married Louise-Hippolyte, heiress of the Grimaldis, who were Genoese by origin, and assumed the family name, with the titles of Prince of Monaco and Duke of Valentinois. The twelve-metre wall north of the Promenade du Bel Air which skirts the larger lake was built by him to protect his Mediterranean bride from the winds of Normandy. Throughout the 18c. the château was in effect a court, like that of the German princes. The building survived the Revolution, as did the family, which was popular locally, though a large part of the priceless contents were sold by auction. Piecemeal demolition began later, and was systematized by the *Ponts-et-Chaussées* when, in 1813, they were building a road from Saint-Lô to Vire. They knocked down the wings of the house and drove a road through the park to carry away the building material. One architectural feature lost at that time, the elegant balustrade bordering the Promenade du Château, has since been restored.

The central block, with its surviving contents, which included a number of portraits and tapestries, was saved by the municipality, who bought it for use as an Hôtel de Ville. That it is worth visiting today is due to an equal enlightenment on the part of their successors. With the co-operation of the *Monuments Historiques*, the château, which was gutted during 1944, has been successfully restored and, more remarkably, worthily furnished with pieces from the 17–18c., and Aubusson tapestries (visits daily, 1 April – 30 September, 10–12, 14–17; apply to the concierge).

What was once the great gate of the château, built of the same red pudding, with bands of white stone, and topped by the Matignon arms, survives in the Rue Robert du Mont (turn left from the château, then down to the left). The church of Saint-Laurent, near by, served as the chapel of the château during the 18c. Its many family monuments were destroyed in 1792, but post-war windows commemorate two members, Robert de Torigni, who, during his abbacy, which lasted from 1154 to 1186, made Mont Saint-Michel a centre of learning, and Léonor I de Matignon, who, during the 17c., was Bishop first of Coutances, later of Lisieux.

Around the turn of the century, Joseph Pennell, the topographical artist, went to Saint Lô, the old Briovera, or bridge over the Vire, and made some attractive drawings of the twin spires of the cathedral and the luxuriantly carved façades of the timbered houses which crowded about it. Today his art would be exercised on two mutilated towers and the severe, though not unsympathetic, logic of the new civic centre and Préfecture. **Saint-Lô** paid the penalty of being a strategic road junction by being 80 per cent devastated during the period 3–25 July 1944, when the Americans were struggling to break through to the south. At least the rebuilding has cleared the ramparts of the old town of the houses which clung to them, so that the walls springing from the crag rise with a massive dignity above the River Vire. And if one may deplore one or two of the ferro-concrete follies, there is reassurance in the way in which the lusty, gusty life of a French market town has reestablished itself in the outwardly inhospitable surroundings of the new centre, the Place du Général de Gaulle. One of the follies is here, a free-standing 32-metre tower. The Syndicat d'Initiative is in the bottom left-hand corner: the Hôtel de Ville opposite houses the **municipal museum** (open daily, 14.30 – 17, except Monday and Friday). Its outstanding item is a series of seven late 16c. tapestries. The paintings include Matignon portraits. The single feature of the *place* which is not post-war is the doorway of the old prison, which has been converted into a memorial to the *résistants* of the department. Behind it, forty-two of them died during the Allied bombardments of July 1944.

Before going on to the church of Notre-Dame, west of the *place*, take a stroll along the **Promenade des Ramparts** (signposted). It is laid out with gardens where hawthorn and cubes of clipped box in shaded greens accentuate the mass of the bastions which are welded into the rock. St Lô was first fortified in the 12c., when its rulers, temporal as well as spiritual, were the Bishops of Coutances. By the 13c., it was one of the major strongpoints of the province. During the Wars of Religion it was first held by the Protestants, then taken by the Royalists under the Maréchal de Matignon, who was later to be a stout shield to the Huguenot citizens against Catholic persecution.

Notre-Dame was virtually the only building in the old town to escape total destruction in 1944, though all that was left standing

271

were the walls and the south tower without its spire. The 14–15c. collegiate church has been rebuilt, but there has been no attempt to replace the north tower and the spire, or to reconstruct the original west front. Instead, the south tower and the remaining fragments of the north have been consolidated, and a plain wall of greeny schist built behind them, the whole looking a great deal better than it sounds. By a small miracle the exterior pulpit on the north side of the church, a perfect example of Gothic grace, with a miniature spire rising from its canopy, escaped damage. This was its second deliverance: during the 19c. there was a misbegotten plan to remove it, which was foiled through the intervention of Victor Hugo. There are only three or four such pulpits in France; the others, all dating from the second half of the 15c., are in Brittany. St John Eudes, (1601–80) founder of the congregation of Eudists, preached here in 1675.

Inside, one is more conscious of the asymmetrical plan of the church, which broadens from west to east. Over the centuries more land became available for building, so that it was possible to give the Flamboyant choir a double ambulatory, with chapels. The windows include one in the south aisle which is said to have been given to the church by Louis XI in 1470. (This survival is no miracle: the glass was removed during the war.) West of the church is the Place de la Préfecture, which is one of the better examples of post-war civic building.

From the east end of the Place du Général de Gaulle, the Rue du Neufbourg leads to the big church of **Sainte-Croix**. Only the 12c. west door remains of the original abbey church, but the façade in 1860 Romanesque pastiche fills the end of the *place* rather well. Doubtless the Meccano bell-tower set up beside it in 1954 gives pleasure to some.

A plaque at the cross-roads just beyond the church commemorates Major Thomas D. Howie, C.O. of the 2nd Battalion of the 116th Regiment of US Infantry, who, when the Americans were advancing on the town, vowed to be among the first to enter it. He was killed at the head of his men on the day before Saint-Lô fell: in a gesture which the French would perhaps appreciate more vividly than the English, the first column to enter the town carried with it Major Howie's body and placed it on the ruins of the tower of Sainte-Croix.

From the cross-roads the Bayeux road leads to the celebrated **National Stud** created by an imperial decree of 1806 (visits daily, 10–11.30, 14.30–17). From mid-February to mid-July most of the

272

stallions are on circuit: during the rest of the year there are 210 thoroughbreds to be seen. Even those who do not care deeply about horses are likely to find the driving displays at 10 on Saturdays, from the end of July until mid-September, and still more the galas of Ascensiontide, attractive simply as spectacle. Those who do care will enjoy a visit even during the off-season. To see a local farmer bringing a cob or Percheron to be served is to realize why the quality of farm horses in Normandy is generally high.

Eight kilometres south-west of Saint-Lô there is another château by François Gabriel, the architect of Torigni. He built Canisy for Hervé de Carbonnel, who had married a daughter of the Maréchal de Matignon. Leave the town by the Villedieu road: on the left, a couple of kilometres along it, is the Hôpital-Mémorial France–États-Unis, built with American co-operation, which, when it was opened in 1956, was among the most modern in Europe. A mosaic by Fernand Léger decorates the façade.

The D38 for **Canisy** turns off on the right. The present château succeeded an early fortress of which all that remains is a 12c. round tower, with a conical roof, much restored and remodelled. Like Torigni, it is polychromatic, though here the local stone which is relieved with white is a greyish purple rather than rose-red. There is a particularly fine gatehouse, with tall, steep-pitched slate roofs. Only the attractive park is open to visitors.

Another excursion from Saint-Lô is of major interest: the abbey of **Cerisy-la-Forêt** is one of the great buildings of Normandy. Leave the town by the Bayeux road. Just off it on the right, 3½ kilometres on the way, **la Barre-de-Semilly** has a small, perfect Romanesque church whose walls of herring-bone schist suggest an earlier date than the 12c., when it was in fact built. There has been a good deal of restoration during the intervening centuries, the most recent that of the panelled roof of the nave after 1944, but the remarkable sanctuary is original. The N172 continues through the Forêt de Cerisy, mostly oak and beech, where there are both roe and red deer. From the cross-roads of L'Embranchement, the D13 on the left leads directly to the abbey, which is to the east of the small town of Cerisy.

Vigor, Bishop of Bayeux, founded a religious community here early in the 6c. It disappeared during the Viking invasions, to be refounded in 1032 by Robert the Magnificent, and dedicated to St Vigor. What, in Normandy, was equivalent to royal patronage gave it an auspicious start, and its power and prosperity grew under the Conqueror, who continued to show it favour. No trace remains of these first buildings: the present nave dates from a rebuilding towards the end of the 12c. The choir and sanctuary followed about 1100, and, during the 13c., a Gothic façade was added.

Today's west front is a blank wall, the result of what M. Lucien Musset, an authority on the Romanesque churches of Normandy, has justly called 'une des plus sottes mutilations que l'on puisse rêver'. Originally the nave had eight bays; in relatively recent times the monks allowed the five westernmost to be used as a parish church, building a screening wall to divide it from their own choir in 1747. During the Revolution, when the monks left, the parishioners moved into the abbey church, and, in 1811, the commune lopped off the redundant five bays, leaving the truncated church with the old dividing wall as its west front. Even the fact that the money thus saved was used to restore the central tower, which had been struck by lightning, does not extenuate the folly.

Inside, the shortened nave is all height and light: the radiance makes one see the case for clear as against tinted glass, persuasive as is the argument of the restorers of Lessay. The elevation is in three levels, the arcades growing taller and slimmer as they rise, with twin arches in the gallery, three in the clerestory, where the mass of the wall is lightened by a pierced passage. The roof of the nave, a superimposed vault of wood and plaster, was added in 1872. Early in the 18c. the north transept underwent a rather clumsy restoration.

M. Musset calls the choir the most beautiful Romanesque one in Normandy, adding that the only comparable example is at Peterborough Cathedral. It has kept the soberly beautiful stalls which the woodcutters of Cerisy made from the oaks of the surrounding forest around 1400. The remains of the 13c. monastic buildings beside the church (visits, 1 July – 15 September, weekdays, 10–12, 14.30–17, Easter to 11 November; Sundays and public holidays, 14.30–19) include the 13–14c. *Chapelle de l'abbé*, a miniature version of the Sainte-Chapelle in Paris.

CHAPTER TWENTY–TWO

Bayeux – Balleroy – Mondaye – Creullet – Creully – Brécy – Saint-Gabriel

BAYEUX is an atmosphere as well as a town possessing a magnificent cathedral and, in its tapestry, a unique historical document. I can think of nowhere else in Normandy where the hurried visitor misses so much. It is a place to be stayed in, and, ideally, one should stay over a Sunday, when life is governed by the cathedral bells and formidable old ladies, hatted and gloved, march to mass, oblivious of the crowds of sketchily dressed tourists; for the virtue of Bayeux lies not only in the fact that it escaped damage during the Battle of Normandy – it was the first town to be liberated – but that it has escaped also many of the changes of an industrialized society. Balzac, if he returned to this bourgeois stronghold, where his married sister lived, and where he set two of his novels, would recognize aspects of the provincial France he knew. It seems fitting that a recent implantation here should be, not a modern industry, but the HQ of a national bank.

There was a town of some importance here in Gallo-Roman times, Baiocassium Augustodurum. Saint Éxupère founded a bishopric in the second half of the 4c., but did not build a cathedral. Early in the 10c., Rollo the Dane, having accepted baptism, married Popa, daughter of Count Béranger, Governor of Bayeux, and the town became in some sense a Viking capital. The Scandinavian language persisted here well after the Norsemen who had settled further east were speaking French – an early instance, possibly, of Bayeux's resistance to change.

About half-way through the 11c., Bishop Hugues began the building of a **cathedral** virtually the size of the present one, which was dedicated by his successor, Bishop Odo, in the presence of his half-brother, the Conqueror. Less than thirty years later, during the dispute between the Conqueror's sons for the Duchy of Normandy, Bayeux was captured by Henry Beauclerc's soldiers and most of the upper part of the cathedral was destroyed by fire. Only the crypt and the two west towers survived. The nave was rebuilt in the mid-12c.

275

by Philippe d'Harcourt; during the 13c. it was adapted to the Gothic style, to accord with the new choir. Finally, in 1477, under the episcopacy of Louis d'Harcourt, the central tower was added.

Standing before the west front one can see even more clearly than at Coutances how the Romanesque work underpins the Gothic. At both cathedrals shortage of funds meant that as much as possible of the old building had to be incorporated into the new. The two upper storeys of the towers rise in their original elegance out of the massive buttresses of the 13c. Above them, the Gothic takes over in the exquisite octagonal spires with their slender corner turrets.

The opposite pavement of the Rue La Forestier gives the best view of the south side of the cathedral. The small door surmounted by a gallery half-way along it is 12c. Further along, the richly decorated porch, framed with pierced bell turrets, sets out in detail the story of St Thomas of Canterbury, with its sequel, the expiation of King Henry II. A rather shaky tradition avers that it was near Bayeux that the king set the tragedy in motion by exclaiming: 'Who will rid me of this turbulent priest?'

The east end is memorable for the steely delicacy of the flying buttresses supporting the narrow height of the choir. Its lower storey is of perfect simplicity, with lancet windows above a pointed arcade which encloses the apse. Neither simplicity nor perfection are words which can properly be applied to the central tower, the walls of whose 13c. base rise foursquare just above the roofs of choir and transept. The ornate octagonal structure above it was added late in the 15c. Its original lead roof was destroyed by fire in 1676 and replaced early in the following century by a classical cupola, the work of a local architect, which, judging from contemporary illustrations, was relatively inoffensive. The alarming developments came half-way through the 19c., when, as the foundations of the cathedral were found to be sinking beneath the weight of the cupola, it was seriously suggested that the remedy was to pull down the whole tower, and probably the greater part of the transept with it. Happily the townspeople vetoed the idea, and, through the ingenuity of an architect, undeservedly named Crétin, and an engineer of the Chemins de Fer de l'Ouest, it was found possible to raise the tower slightly while the pillars of the crossing were strengthened. Unfortunately, the restorers went on to add a second octagonal storey to Bishop Louis d'Harcourt's tower, and to top the lot with a copper dome and spire in Louis Philippe Gothic. According to Herriot, 'in this unfortunate addition glitters all the bad taste of the Second Empire', and it really is rather nasty. Perhaps the fact that the stability of the tower is once more causing anxiety – it seems likely to be encased in scaffolding for years – may be seen as what old people used to call 'a judgment'. By contrast, the interior, to which, because the cathedral is built on sloping ground, one descends by a flight of steps, represents a triumphant marriage of two periods. The carvings in the spandrels are a revelation of the number of influences which reached the craftsmen of medieval Normandy. Along with the bearded man, the monkey and the jester, and the two bishops – the suggestion that they represent Odo and Philippe d'Harcourt need not be taken too seriously – there are serpents and dragons and beasts of fable, and convoluted ornament inspired by sources as various as Eastern silks and ivory carvings, Scandinavian art and illuminated manuscripts from Ireland or England.

The west window, which was the gift of the guild of cooks, is the only one which has kept its 15c. glass. Unfortunately, it is largely obscured by the organ. There is a splendidly rhetorical 18c. pulpit.

The huge Romanesque piers of the crossing were 'Gothicized' in the 13c. and rebuilt during the 19c. There are a number of 15c. wall paintings in the south arm of the transept, an Annunciation over the first altar, a Crucifixion and the legend of St Nicolas over the second. The murder of Becket is modern.

The choir, raised above the level of the nave and ambulatory, is Norman Gothic in its utmost purity, with exquisite pierced *rosaces* between the arches of the glorious triforium. Round the roof are medallions executed in the 13c. and restored in the 19c., depicting the first twenty-one Bishops of Bayeux.

The 18c. marble high altar is partly modelled on that of Notre-Dame de Paris, with a gilded bronze cross and candlesticks by Philippe Caffieri, one of an Italian family of sculptors and metal founders, many of whom worked in Paris. There are forty-nine stalls from the late 16c.: the bishop's throne is a century later and was remodelled in the 19c.

Many chapels have kept their 18c. wrought iron grilles; that of the first chapel on the south side once formed part of the *jubé*. The third and fourth ambulatory chapels have frescos of the 15–16c., considerably restored, and that next to the apsidal chapel grisaille paintings of the 16c. of scenes from the life of Saint Pantaléon.

The best things in the north aisle are two altar pieces: that in the third chapel (moving westward), dedicated to St Martin, of early 17c. carved wood, portrays *la Bonne Mort*. The other, in the westernmost chapel, is a monument at once of folk art and popular piety, an elaborate plaster representation of the Virgin, with the symbols of her litanies, dating from the 18c. or possibly the late 17c.

To visit the crypt, the treasury and the chapter house, apply to the sacristan. All are more than optional extras. The crypt of Odo's cathedral is divided into three naves by two rows of pillars, most of which retain their 11c. capitals. Some suggest an even earlier origin, on the evidence of a pattern of laurel leaves which seems to have been copied from Gallo-Roman work. The tomb of a canon, in a recess on the left of the altar, and the wall painting above it, are 15c.

The treasury, housed in a 13c. building which still has two cupboards of the same period, contains an 11c. Arab chest of carved ivory, decorated with silver gilt and inscribed with a Muslim blessing.

The chapter house, which was built about 1200, is paved with 15c. terracotta tiles: the design in the centre is a labryinth, or 'road to Jerusalem'. A 14c. fresco of the Virgin, supported by the chapter of the cathedral, fills the apse. The ivory crucifix is said to have belonged to Madame de Lamballe, the faithful friend of Marie-Antoinette, who met a horrible death in the Paris massacres of September 1792. In the 15c. chapter library, now a *musée lapidaire* (shown on request) are a number of capitals which were taken from the supports of the central tower when it was rebuilt in 1851.

The 'tapisserie de la reine Mathilde' as the French call the **Bayeux tapestry**, is in the former Bishop's Palace on the south side of the cathedral (open daily, 9–12, 14–18.30 from Easter to October; 9.30–12, 14–17 for the rest of the year; ticket admits also to the Musée Baron Gérard). On the wall near the gateway of the palace a bronze memorial recalls the liberation of Bayeux by the 50th (Northumbrian) Division on 7 June 1944.

The tapestry, the most precious medieval document in existence, is shown under glass on the first floor of the museum. It is not tapestry, nor the work of Queen Matilda, but embroidery in coloured wools on linen. Experts agree that it dates from the late 11c., and that it was almost certainly commissioned by Bishop Odo to adorn his new cathedral. Whether the embroidresses were English or French is still disputed. It remained the property of the cathedral until the Revolution, though, until the beginning of the 18c., the world of art scholarship did not know of its existence. In 1804 Napoleon had it brought to Paris to help to convince public opinion that it was possible to invade England.

To the modern viewer, nothing is more astonishing than the pace and movement of what has been called 'a long film', whose fifty-eight scenes set out the history of the Conquest from Edward the Confessor's sending Harold on a mission to William, Duke of Normandy, to the Conqueror's coronation at Westminster. Colour is used to indicate perspective, and the liveliness and freshness of the whole are a delight. If you are at Bayeux in mid-season, when the crowds press, it is well worth getting to the Bishop's Palace promptly at 9 so as to be able to enjoy the tapestry in peace.

Until 1975 the town's lacemaking school was lodged in the same building. There were only a scant handful of pupils when it closed on the death of the last lacemaker. Bayeux's lace industry, killed by changing fashion and economics, was established at the end of the 17c. There are some beautiful examples of its products, particularly Second Empire shawls, in the **Musée Baron Gérard**, that occupies the original Bishop's Palace, a building north of the cathedral, which incorporates elements from the 13, 15 and 16c. It has also an excellent display of the china made here between 1812 and 1951. In the archaeological department on the ground floor there are two wonderful effigies of M. and Mme de Sainte-Croix, the lords of Rye. Beside the museum, in the little **Cour de Tribunaux**, tented over by the branches of an enormous *arbre de la liberté*, a plane tree planted in 1797, is the Palais de Justice which was once part of the Bishop's Palace. It is worth finding the concierge, whose *loge* is under the Norman archway, in order to see the court room and the council chamber of 1516, which was once the chapel of the palace. Both have strikingly beautiful ceilings, the first of oak and gilded bronze, the second decorated with paintings by Jean de Canossa.

The streets of Bayeux are rich in **old houses**. Starting from the west front of the cathedral – there is a pretty 16c. house, with carvings of Adam and Eve at No. 6 in the Rue Bienvenue facing it – walk down the Rue des Cuisiniere towards the main road which cuts through the town from south-east to north-west, taking four different names along its course. At the corner of the Rue des Cuisiniers it is the Rue Saint Martin, and the glorious timbered house of the 14c. which marks it is now the Syndicat d'Initiative. Walk up to the left and turn into the Rue Franche; No. 5, with a tower in the courtyard, is 15–16c. Beside it, at No. 7, a gravel drive between neat hedges leads to the 18c. Hôtel de la Crespellière. Return to the main street and continue up the Rue Saint Malo. The Hôtel du Fresne, otherwise known as La Madeleine, its front decorated with figures of saints, is 15–16c. There is a Renaissance house, the little *manoir d'Argouges-Gratot*, in the Cour Courquemaron, at No. 60. At the corner No. 82, marked by a plaque, is the house where Alain

Chartier, poet, diplomat and political writer, was born in 1385. After leaving the Sorbonne, Chartier became secretary and notary to Charles VI and the Dauphin, later Charles VII. He undertook diplomatic missions to Germany, Rome and Venice, and, in 1428, was sent to Scotland to negotiate the marriage of Queen Margaret with the future Louis XI. The taste for decoration is shown in many less ancient and distinguished houses, among them No. 73 in the Rue Saint Malo, which has ceramic portrait medallions and swags of fruit and foliage, and No. 77, which has a frieze taken from the Bayeux tapestry.

The Rue Alain Chartier leads to the vast **Place Saint Patrice** where, on Saturdays, the produce, and with it the life, of the fertile Bessin pours into the market. The 18c. building on the left as we enter it is the former convent of La Charité. On the far side, the graceful Renaissance tower of Saint-Patrice, three diminishing circular tiers above four rectangular, is all that remains unaltered of a church which, in the mid-16c., was built on the site of a Romanesque predecessor.

From the *place* one may continue as far as the Jardin Botanique and the monument to the Allied landings of 1944 at the north-west entrance to the town. For convenience the route will be described here, as will, in the appropriate places, others striking out beyond the centre of the town, but those who cannot face so much walking – in this instance about 2 kilometres – have the alternative of driving round the ring boulevard, stopping as needed.

Pedestrians, then, should leave the Place Saint Patrice by the Rue Docteur Moulin, and continue over the boulevard into the Port-en-Bessin road, which leads to the pleasant oasis of the **Jardin Botanique**. What looks like a canopy roofing a sanded *rond-point* in the garden is a prodigious weeping beech trained over a trellis. From the south end of the garden, a road leads past the sports ground to a monument, twenty-one slabs of ruddy granite commemorating both the battle of 6 June 1944 and General de Gaulle's visit to Bayeux. The Rue de Vaucelles, which soon becomes the Rue Saint Patrice, takes you back into the town, passing on the left the mid-17c. manor house, La Caillerie, and the 17–18c. buildings of the old Ursuline convent, now a college.

A short distance beyond the Place Saint Patrice the Rue Général de Dias on the right, leads to the **Place du Général de Gaulle**. There are a number of fine old houses here, including a Renaissance manor with elegant plastered windows at No. 13 and, at No. 20, a 16c. house with a roof so steeply pitched as to be almost vertical.

The *place* is girdled with splendid lime avenues, in one of which a monument commemorates de Gaulle's speech at Bayeux on 14 June 1944, on his return to French soil. Past it, the Rue Bourbesneur has the finest building of them all, the Maison du Gouverneur (No. 10), part 15c., part 16c., and distinguished by a hexagonal stair tower. Continue to the Rue des Chanoines, on the left, which leads back to the cathedral; No. 17 was the birthplace of Arcisse de Caumont, the 19c. archaeologist who is credited with establishing the science in France. The tall cylinder with a pierced conical cap which rises above a house at the corner of the street is often taken for a *lanterne des morts*, that is, a hollow stone pillar in which a light was placed to mark the site of a cemetery or tomb; actually it is a 13c. chimney, a rare survival.

The British – in fact, British and German – military cemetery is on this side of the town, on the Littry road: turn into the Rue de la Poterie and take the lane which leads south-west. There are 4661 British graves, and 1837 names on the memorial to those who have no known grave.

The Rue de Nesmond leads from the east end of the cathedral to the late 17c. building of the former seminary, whose chapel has a double apse. The Rue Saint Exupère continues to the church of the same name (turn right in the Rue Saint Jean), one of the few survivors of the fourteen parish churches which Bayeux possessed in the 17c. It is fairly banal 18c. rebuilding, but in the crypt there are a number of sarcophagi which are said to be those of the early bishops of Bayeux, and which are certainly Merovingian.

Saint-Vigor-le-Grand, the remaining church which repays a visit, is a kilometre along the Courseulles road. The saint founded a monastery here in the 6c.; in the 11c., probably about 1066, Odo established a Bénédictine monastery on the site. Its fine church was destroyed early in the 19c. All that remains today is a porter's lodge of the 13c. and a great barn of the same period, which did not gain architecturally when it was converted into a chapel for the nuns of Notre-Dame de la Charité more than a century ago. But the parish church, rebuilt in the 19c., keeps in the choir a red marble stool which is said to have belonged to the saint. To this day Bishops of Bayeux, upon their appointment, come to Saint Vigor to sit on it before taking possession of their episcopal chair.

There are a number of expeditions to be made from Bayeux, none involving more than an easy half-day's motoring through the fat, green land of the Bessin to the north-east or the more wooded country on the south-west. The imperative one is to the **Château of**

Balleroy (visits daily, except Thursdays, 9–12, 14–18), an early masterpiece by François Mansart. He was twenty-eight when he designed it for Jean I de Choisy, Chancellor to Gaston d'Orléans – the house was a decade in building – and he was to do nothing better in the forty years which remained to him.

Take the Saint-Lô road out of Bayeux. The tower 1½ kilometres along it is that of the 12–14c. church of Saint-Loup-Hors, built on the site of one of the town's early sanctuaries. **Noron-la-Poterie**, 7½ kilometres further on, is a centre for the manufacture of the local stoneware. Here bad money co-exists with good: there is a horrid line in garden gnomes and the like, but they have not driven out the traditional utensils for kitchen and dairy. At La Tuilerie, a kilometre out of Noron, turn left into the D73 for Balleroy. Mansart planned the village as well as the château; its stone houses line what is in effect an avenue leading to a forecourt laid out with embroidered flower beds, with low farm buildings on either side. The château, built of pinky-grey schist relieved with white stone, stands back behind its green moat, unostentatious and perfect in the symmetry of the central building, crowned by a small lantern, rising above the wings, the whole framed by two small pavilions at the corner of the *cour d'honneur*. The ground floor rooms have their original panelling. On the first floor, the sumptuously decorated *Grand Salon* has a ceiling painted by Mignard. The panelling here, painted to simulate marble, is set with royal and near-royal portraits, also by Mignard. Louis XIII, above the hearth, presides over an assembly which includes Louis XIV, his brother Philippe, Anne of Austria and Madame de Montespan, favourite of Louis XIV and mother of seven of his children.

We can return to Bayeux by way of the Premonstratensian Abbey of **Mondaye**, which has a notable classical church (church open daily; monastic buildings shown on request at the porter's lodge; guided visits, Sundays and public holidays, 14–18). From Balleroy, follow the main road for Tilly-sur-Seulles as far as la Senaudière, then turn left into the D33 and left again for Juaye. The dome and octagonal tower of Mondaye signal from a distance. The church is remarkable above all for its unity: it is the most successful classical composition in Normandy to have been planned, and largely executed, by one man.

Nothing now remains of the abbey which was founded here in 1200. The present buildings date from the resurgence of religious zeal which the Premonstratensian Order enjoyed during the 18c., when, by a happy chance, the community included a monk who was a painter as well as a gifted architect. Eustache Restout Pére belonged to a Norman family of artists whose best-known member is his nephew, Jean Restout, of Rouen. He gave thirty seven years of his life, from 1706 to 1743, to the rebuilding of Mondaye, creating for the interior a painted décor as harmonious as the perfect façade. Harmonious, be it noted, rather than inspiring or exultant. The mind approves of it all – that this church should, briefly, have been a Temple of Reason seems not altogether inappropriate – but when the heart leaps it is to the wonderful harping and trumpeting angels of the organ loft, by the Flemish sculptor, Melchior Verly, or the same artist's terracotta Assumption over the altar in the Lady Chapel, where the sense of movement is so strong that the spectator, also, has the illusion of being borne upwards. The church is a memorial chapel to the British and Canadian troops who fell during the Battle of Normandy. In the cloister of the abbey is the sole relic of the medieval monastery, a 14c. statue of the Madonna and Child.

Return to Bayeux by the road which passes through the village and crosses the Aure to join the D67. Just after the right turn into it, we pass the 18c. château of **Juaye-Mondaye**, preceded by a graceful flight of steps.

There are four more châteaux in the prosperous farmland east of the town. Leave Bayeux by the D12 and, 2 kilometres beyond Villiers-le-Sec, turn into the D22 for **Creullet**. The graceful building just outside the hamlet is a 17c. reworking of a château dating variously from the 14c., 15c. and 16c. In June 1944, General Montgomery set up his caravan HQ in the park surrounding it, and on 12 June he met George VI, Churchill and General Smuts in the *Salon Rouge* of the château.

Just beyond is the village of **Creully**, set above the River Seulles. The 12c. church here, mishandled during the 19c., was built by the lords of the adjoining château of Creully (visits daily, 9–11.30, 14–18). Originally it was a feudal fortress which Henry Beauclerc gave to his natural son, Robert of Kent. Later it was bought by Colbert, whose family owned it until 1750. Since 1946 it has been the property of the municipality, which uses it as a *mairie*. The enceinte of the medieval fortress remains, with two vaulted rooms of the 12c. The square donjon was added in 1358, the tall octagonal tower in the 15c. Below the main block of the building, a smiling 16c. country house, are 12c. cellars. The whole is both an archaeological document and a visual delight, as well as being the antithesis of Balleroy.

With **Lantheuil**, 2 kilometres south-east of Creully, we are back with the decorum of the 17c., the elegance of the façade comp-lemented by the urns and clipped yews of the approach. It was built by Jacques Turgot, *maître des requêtes* and *intendant* of Rouen, and a member of the family which produced Louis XVI's Finance Minis-ter, Anne-Robert-Jacques Turgot.

The last château in this cluster is **Brécy** (open daily, except Tuesdays) which is a couple of kilometres south of the village of Saint-Gabriel-Brécy, itself 2 kilometres west of Creully by the D35. Its owner, the novelist, Jacques de Lacretelle, has likened his château to a little Norman peasant girl with the finery of an Italian princess thrown round her shoulders. It is a happy description for this unassuming 17c. house, manor rather than château, before which extends a vast formal garden in the Italian style, rising in five terraces which are embellished with urns and balustrades and wrought iron gates. The garden is usually attributed to François Mansart, who, it is suggested, found designing it a relief from his more exigent task at Balleroy. The small church beside the house, no longer used for services, is mostly 13c.; the tower and the charming little porch were added in the 15c.

Saint-Gabriel has the remains of a priory founded in 1058 by the monks of Fécamp. The monastic buildings grouped round a central court date from the 13c. to the 15c. and are now occupied by a *Centre d'Apprentissage Horticole* – apply for permission to visit. Of the 12c. church which succeeded the first on the site, only the choir remains. It is renowned for its sculptures; some of them recall the exotic decoration of the nave of Bayeux Cathedral.

From Saint-Gabriel the D35 and the D126 lead back to Bayeux.

CHAPTER TWENTY-THREE

Longues-sur-Mer – Port-en-Bessin – Colleville-sur-Mer – Formigny – Vierville-sur-Mer – Isigny – Carentan – Sainte-Mere-Église – Valognes

THE first stage of the route from Bayeux to Cherbourg takes one along the coastal strip north-west of the town, whose sandy beaches are punctuated by low cliffs.

Leave Bayeux by the D104 for **Longues-sur-Mer**, which has the remains of the 12c. Bénédictine abbey of Sainte-Marie on its outskirts (visits Thursdays only, 14–18). There are three late 13c. funeral slabs in the chapter house, whose glazed tiles are the only known examples of their kind in Normandy. The D104 continues to the sea at the point known as the Chaos, from the spectacular jumble of broken rock, the result of falls from the friable chalk and clay of the cliffs.

Turn left into the main road for **Port-en-Bessin**, a splendidly typical fishing port – there are lively auctions of the catches early in the morning on Mondays, Wednesdays and Thursdays – with two basins driving deep into the valley of the Dromme, so that port and town are one. At the harbour mouth scalloped cliffs rise on either hand; the outer harbour is protected by two curving granite jetties which at high tide have a stable population of sea anglers. From their extremities you survey the whole coast of the Bessin. Once bronze was manufactured here, from copper shipped from Brittany and tin from Cornwall.

In the 17c. there was a plan to turn the harbour into a naval base. Vauban's tower on the east cliff bears witness to it, but the project was never carried out, though the idea was revived in the 18c., and again in the 19c. Port-en-Bessin's nearest approach to a military function was to be during the 20c: for the first weeks after the Allied landings it was used considerably, particularly as a petrol port. There are cliff paths to the east and west; the latter can be followed for 3½ kilometres to Sainte Honorine des Pertes.

The road continues through Huppain, whose 12–13c. church

once belonged to the Abbey of Cerisy, to **Colleville-sur-Mer**. Here we are approaching the area which saw some of the bitterest fighting of 6 June 1944. Colleville marks the eastern end of Omaha Beach, the stretch of shore extending westward to Vierville where the Americans lost half of their troops before they were able to establish a bridgehead. The church, with a superb Romanesque spire, is virtually a post-1944 reconstruction; it was around it that the last Germans in Colleville held out until 7 June. A right-hand turning beyond the church leads to the U.S.A. military cemetery above the beach, where the 9386 crosses of white Carrara marble are ranked behind a memorial gateway on whose walls are inscribed the names of the 15,057 soldiers who have no known grave. The allegorical bronze figure is by Donald de Luc.

At Saint-Laurent-sur-Mer the historically inclined may like to turn left for **Formigny**, 3 kilometres inland. Here, on 18 April 1450, was fought the battle which saw the English finally driven out of Normandy. According to the viewpoint, it was won by the French, under the Comte de Clermont, who had the advantage of superior numbers, or lost by the over-confidence of the English commander, Sir Thomas Kiriel, who was a veteran of Agincourt. A memorial to the battle was set up in 1903 at the junction of the N13 and the N814C. About half a kilometre along the former, going west, is the little Chapel of Saint Louis, which the Comte de Clermont built to commemorate the victory. It was restored during the 19c., through the concern of Louis Philippe, and is now the property of the Orléans family. Relics of the battle are preserved in the church.

Returning to **Saint-Laurent**, turn right into the loop road which follows the line of the shore from Les Moulins to **Vierville-sur-Mer**. This was the site of the ill-fated Mulberry A; at the end of the boulevard was the deadly 'Dog Green', a sector where A Company of the 116th Regiment of the US Army lost 70 per cent of its strength, including all its officers and N.C.O.s, within minutes of landing. There are four monuments along the boulevard: in order, a French memorial to U.S. soldiers; a stele below the level of the road marking the temporary burial place of the first U.S. soldiers to fall on French soil; another, half-way up the cliff, to the 6th Engineers Special Brigade; and a monument mounted on a blockhouse to the National Guard of the U.S.A. who fought in France during two World Wars.

Vierville's 13c. church, like the village itself, has been largely rebuilt since 1944. Half a kilometre south-west of it is the **Château de Vaumicel**, a 16c. manor house with corner towers (exterior visits only).

There are two more châteaux in the neighbourhood of Englesqueville-la-Percée: **Beaumont**, a medieval fortress remodelled in the 17c. and **Englesqueville**, just beyond the village, with twin round towers, which is late 16c. The village church is 12–13c. A couple of kilometres further on the little church of **Saint-Pierre-du-Mont**, with a 13c. choir and an 11c. nave, has elements from an earlier period, notable Carolingian sculpture which probably came from the Abbey of Deux-Jumeaux, 5 kilometres west of Formigny, which was demolished at about the time the church was built.

There is a Renaissance château near the church; beyond it a road turns off on the right for the Pointe du Hoc, the one spot in Normandy which, more than thirty years on, still looks like a battlefield. This was the position which the 2nd Battalion of the U.S. Rangers stormed at first light on 6 June 1944, after scaling the cliffs with the help of rope ladders and extendible ladders provided by the London Fire Brigade. It had previously been the target of saturation bombing and shelling from the cruiser *Texas*: the craters and mounds of torn earth, now half-choked with brambles, remain; also the ruined blockhouses. At the end of the point a granite pillar commemorates the Commandos of the 116th Regiment of the U.S. Infantry.

Grandcamp is another fishing port and small holiday resort where low tides uncover a fearsome barrier of reefs, 8 kilometres long. The 13c. church here is remarkable for the fine panelling of the choir, dating from the 18c.

Isigny is a name familiar far beyond Normandy. The small town which is the centre of the richest milk-producing area in a province noted for its dairy cattle – though for quantity of milk production Normandy has recently had to yield first place to Brittany – gives its name to the butter which is sold all over France. Traditionalists may abhor the pestilential little pasteurized packets which now appear on one's breakfast tray instead of the former yellow slab, pearled with moisture, but this is the price of economic progress. The Laiterie Co-operative d'Isigny, which handles 200,000 litres of milk daily, is open to visitors on weekdays and Saturday mornings at 10, 11 (the most interesting time), 14.30 and 15.30.

The town has been largely rebuilt, but there is a pleasing 18c. Hôtel de ville which was once a château. Four or 5 kilometres north and north-west of Isigny the Baie des Veys, into which the Vire and the Douve drain, is a miniature Baie du Mont Saint-Michel: here, too, fertile polders are being reclaimed from what was once a marshy delta. Bird-watchers will find the area of the bay interesting in the spring and autumn; it is a stage on the annual migration routes.

Carentan, a prosperous market town, sleek with well-being – dairying again – with a splendid church and a sideline in breeding hackneys for trotting races, is a pleasant stop on the way up the east side of the Cotentin. Here we are in the low-lying belt of marshland which forms the neck of the peninsula which, if the sea were to rise ten metres, would be an island. Once, indeed, there was a possibility that it would become a man-made one, when Napoleon envisaged driving a canal from the Baie des Veys north-west to Carteret, to avoid the rough north-west passage by the Nez de Jobourg and the Raz Blanchard.

Carentan was luckier during World War II than during previous centuries, when, besides enduring a number of sieges, it was burned by Edward III, en route for Crécy, in 1346, and in 1679 suffered a fire which destroyed five hundred of its houses. The wide Place de la République has a row of old, arcaded houses, more or less touched up during the 19c., but the glory of the town is the church of **Notre-Dame**, whose spire is a landmark. A church was built on the site in the late 12c. If the contemporary ecclesiastical historian, Orderic Vitalis, is correct in saying that Henry Beauclerc heard Easter mass here in 1106 it must have succeeded an earlier one.

The west front of the present building, which incorporates a doorway from the 12c. church, carved with lozenges and zig-zags, as well as part of the original wall, is in sober contrast to the 14–15c. work of the rest of the exterior, whose peak is the elegantly luxurious decoration of the south porch. The statue of Notre-Dame-de-Carentan in the *trumeau* dates from 1950. An airy balustrade encircles the building, running below the flying buttresses of the choir, and the roofs of choir and nave are populated by carved figures, on pinnacles, and gargoyles, on the weather moulding of windows – angel musicians, a spectacled reader, a fox preaching. A dolls' house perched high on the south side of the nave, whose chimney and gable bring the eye to an incredulous halt, was added in the 18c. to lodge the sacristans. The pinnacled 14c. tower rests on a late 12c. bay.

Inside, a carved wooden Renaissance screen divides the nave, the lower part of whose pillars are from the 12c. church, from a soaring late 15c. choir, which is marred by a disastrously inappropriate retable dating from the late 17c. The word of choice for this is 'loutish'. Both in choir and crossing the carvings are as interesting as those outside the church, though in a different spirit. The coat of arms in the vault of the choir is that of Guillaume de Cérisy, *a grand bailli* of the Cotentin and Vicomte de Carentan, whose munificence paid for the rebuilding of the choir.

Behind the church, one turn to the right and another to the left leads to the little harbour which is linked to the sea by 8 kilometres of canal. It no longer does any trade, and is transforming itself, not very dramatically, into a haven for pleasure sailing. Meantime the path beside the canal, pillared by elms, which appears to extend into infinity, is a haven of tranquillity; you feel you have got into a landscape by Hobbema.

On the south side of the town, near the railway station, the oldest part of the Hôtel de Ville, the Louis XIII left wing in brick and stone, has been restored after its wartime damage. The remaining two blocks of the three set round an enormous court, which are stone-built, were added early in the present century. Opposite is a memorial to the 101st Airborne Division, but the small museum which recorded their campaign has now been closed.

North of Carentan the flat country between the N13 and the sea is an old U.S. battle ground. Sainte-Mère-Église was the centre for the landings of the U.S. 82nd Airborne Division on the night of 5-6 June 1944; the coastal strip between La Madeleine and the Dunes-de-Varreville was Utah Beach, where the 4th U.S. Division landed on 6 June, to make its liaison with the airborne troops on the evening of the following day.

Saint-Come-du-Mont has an 11c. church with a notably fine apse, which has remained virtually untouched through nine hundred years. Just before Saint-Come, the N13D turns right for Sainte-Marie-du-Mont, passing on the way the 11c. church of Vierville. Sainte-Marie, the more imposing for being set on what, in this plain, passes for high ground, is worth a stop to see how happily the architectural styles of several centuries have coalesced, particularly in the tower.

We reach the sea at **La Madeleine**, where a monument built on an old blockhouse commemorates the 1st Engineers Special Brigade, and a stele and memorial crypt the 4th Division of U.S. infantry. There is a small *Musée du Débarquement* (visits 9–12, 14–19 from Easter to 1 November; in winter, Sundays and public holidays only, 10–12, 14–19) with a diorama. The sandy beaches on this side of the peninsula extend beyond Saint-Vaast. After La Madeleine, a line of dunes cuts off the view of the sea from the so-called 'route des Alliés', the section of the road which follows the line of Utah Beach. At Varreville, its northern extremity, an opening in them reveals a monument of red granite, in the shape of the prow of a ship, emblazoned with the Cross of Lorraine. It marks the landing place of General Leclerc and the 2nd Armoured Division on 1 August 1944. Here turn inland for **Sainte-Mère-Église**.

This small town, a peacefully prosperous centre of cattle and horse breeding, was the focal point of the U.S. airborne landings. It was finally taken by the Allies on 7 June, after fierce street fighting. The building in the form of a parachute in the Place de l'Église is the **Museum of the Airborne Troops** (open daily, 9–12, 14–17 from Easter to All Saints; winter, Sunday and public holidays only, 10–12, 14–17). The sturdy, saddle-backed tower of the church was the post of the last group of German snipers to hold out in the town. Rather surprisingly, the building, which is basically 13c., with pillars from an earlier church surviving at the crossing, and some additions and modifications from the 14c. and 15c., suffered only minor damage. A window commemorates the landings. There is an impressive eagle lectern from the 18c. and statues from the 14c., 16c and 17c. The so-caled 'Way of Liberty' begins at Sainte-Mère-Église: the first of the stones with which the U.S. Army marked its path across Europe is set up in front of the Hôtel de Ville.

Montebourg, 10 kilometres along the main road to Valognes, was a strategic defensive position and was nine-tenths destroyed when the retreating Germans fired most of the buildings which remained after twelve days of intensive fighting. The 14c. church, with an octagonal spire rising above a pinnacled tower, has been effectively restored. In the dark interior – the nave has no high windows – there is an 11c. font decorated with interlaced carvings, with masks at each corner, and, at the entrance to the choir, an English alabaster statue of Saint Jacques also from the 11c.

From Montebourg, a short detour will take in **Le Ham**, 5 kilometres to the south-west. The 11–13c. church here, whose saddle-backed tower has an outside stairtower, is all that remains of a Bénédictine abbey. There are interesting statues, some as early as the 13c. and 14c., and, in the churchyard, a fine Calvary of a type more often seen in Brittany than Normandy. Continue for rather more than a kilometre beyond Le Ham to pick up the D24 and turn right for **Valognes**.

Here, too, there was extensive damage in 1944. If Valognes has kept more of the atmosphere of Barbey d'Aurevilly's 'aristocratique petite ville' than would seem possible for a town which is 75 per cent new-built, it is because much of its character derives from the number of fine grey stone houses of the 17–18c., many set in large gardens, which were less vulnerable than narrow streets of timbered buildings. The aristocracy is not fanciful, though legend may have somewhat embellished reality. In the 18c. there were a hundred noble families in Valognes, which became a centre of that provincial fashion which is happy in its own conceit. The 18c. novelist and playwright, Alain René Lesage, conveyed the mild ridicule of the larger world when, in his *Turcaret*, he made a character say 'qu'il faut bien trois mois de Valognes pour achever un homme de cour'. Valognes remained oblivious, contented with its round of *salons* which won it the name of 'little Versailles'. There have been schools here since the end of the 13c.; towards the end of the 18c. there were twenty-one girls' schools, with five hundred pupils between them, and the boys' college, now the *lycée national*, had upwards of seven hundred, with more than a hundred of them in 'philo', which was the equivalent of the sixth form. According to tradition, between sixty and a hundred priests stayed on in the town after the Revolution, living in private houses and continuing their ministry. The register shows that seventeen really did so. Barbey d'Aurevilly captures the atmosphere of that time in *Le Chevalier des Touches*, a story of the Chouan rising in the Cotentin, in which the author, against all the evidence, seems to have persuaded himself that his own family had taken part. He spent some years of his childhood as well as of his adult life at Valognes, staying with his uncle, Dr Pontus de Méril. Dr de Méril had ample opportunity of studying the local *noblesse* for, though his advanced opinions aroused the hostility of good society, he was recognized to be a skilful physician, so, as it was said, 'quand elle avait à choisir entre lui et l'extrême onction', good society swallowed its principles and called him in.

The church of **Saint Malo**, in the Place Vicq-d'Azyr, the town's centre, is itself an amalgam of the old and new Valognes. The pre-war building, whose distinctive feature was a lantern tower crowned with a dome in the form of an imperial helmet, which was claimed to be unique in France, included elements from the 13c. to the 17c., so the *Monuments Historiques* had history on their side when, faced with restoring the wreck, they decided to reconstruct only the choir in the original style. A modern lantern tower was built over the crossing, and a simple four-sided spire replaced the octagonal one of the 17c. above the tower on the north side of the choir. Some carvings from the old building have been incorporated into the new west front.

Inside, a nave which is wholly contemporary in both material and design has been grafted on to the Flamboyant east end, with a surprisingly happy result. The windows are attractive, particularly those of the south transept, where radiant blues predominate.

Before starting on a tour of the town, visit the Syndicat d'Initiative, which, in season, operates in the wide Place du Château, behind the west end of the church, to check opening times for the Cider Museum and the Hôtel de Beaumont. (Out of season, neither hôtel nor museum is likely to be open). Then return to the church and, from the east end, walk down the Rue de l'Officialité to the Rue du Petit Versailles. The **Cider Museum** occupies the oldest dwelling in Valognes, a grey stone house with mullioned windows set over the little River Merderet. It is a perfect setting in which to display a process which, in its essentials, did not change from the earliest times until our own day, when cider-making became an industrial process. The equipment, of course, did evolve over the centuries; there are examples here from the *lanlaires*, or great half-moons of stone which represented the most primitive method of crushing apples, through the more sophisticated presses – two wooden ones from the first half of the 18c. are shown – to the later *pressoir roulant*, which made the rounds of households. With them are specimens of the great terracotta vessels which held the end-product. Country people once believed that cider, drunk in sufficient quantity, offered a protection against kidney stones. Today one sometimes hears among them a suggestion that it may predispose to cancer, but the current falling-off in consumption is thought to be more probably due to the general availability of cheap red wine.

A left turn out of the Rue du Petit Versailles leads to the finest of Valognes's many fine houses, the splendid **Hôtel de Beaumont** (visits, 14–18, Tuesday, Thursday, Saturday and Sunday, from 1 July to 15 September). It was built a little after the mid-18c. The sixty metres of its façade are broken by a slender wrought iron balcony above a gracious architrave. The arms in the twin shields carved in the tympanum were effaced during the Revolution. The interior has a splendid staircase with a double ramp. Opposite there is a small manor house of the 15c.

After the Hôtel the first left turn leads into the Rue des Religieuses, a tranquil street of old houses. Barbey lived for some years at No. 34, the Hôtel de Grandval-Coligny. A right turn leads to the old **abbey** of the Bénédictine nuns, a 17c. building which is now the town's hospital. There is a calmly beautiful cloister on the south side of the abbey church, which is now the hospital chapel.

This has a raised sanctuary, with an imposing retable. Note the *trompe-l'œil* paintings of Notre-Dame de la Protection and Saint Vincent de Paul, and look up to see the wreaths of many coloured flowers painted in fresco which surround the roof bosses.

A street which opens out of the Rue des Religieuses, almost opposite the Hôtel de Grandval-Coligny, crosses the Boulevard de Verdun to the Rue du Vieux Château. Its name does not refer to the castle which stood at Valognes from the 11c. to the 17c., though it is doubtful whether the young Duke William, the future Conqueror, was living in it when he had to flee from the town to escape murder during an insurrection by his rebellious barons. Like almost all of medieval Valognes, the castle has vanished. The Vieux Château at the end of the narrow road is the remaining fragment of a bath-house, a relic of the Gallo-Roman town of Alauna, or Alaunia, which was the predecessor of Valognes. A road on the left of the bath-house leads to the suburb of Alleaume, which now occupies the site. The 14c. church here has a little Romanesque arcade and low relief on the exterior of the south side, at the angle of the choir and crossing. In the Rue des Capucins, facing the church, is the Louis XIII façade of the old Capuchin convent, now occupied by Bénédictine sisters.

Back in the town, walk past the church into the Boulevard Leclerc and turn left into the Rue Henri Cornat. The old theatre, at No. 25, now houses a **library** whose nucleus was the books owned by Julien de Laillieu, *curé* of Valognes during the 18c. and Superior of the Seminary. It possesses 250 incunabula and 200 MSS, including bibles from the 13c. and 14c. and a volume from the first press of Paris, dated 1473. Among the antiquities is a Gallo-Roman altar from the Bénédictine priory of Ham. The massive block of stone, marked with crosses at the centre and corners, bears an inscription recording the dedication by Fromond, Bishop of Coutances, in 676.

Further to the north-west, in the Rue Thiers, the great gateway before the 17c. buildings of the state *lycée*, its pediment carved with angels bearing a monstrance, recalls the earlier history of the *lycée* as a seminary and college conducted by the Eudists.

Just past the half-way mark of the 10-kilometre run to Cherbourg a left turn leads to the village of Brix, which gives a last reminder of the Norman roots of so much British history. This was the domain of the Bruce family who, 240 years after the Conquest, gave Scotland one of its most illustrious kings. Their castle was demolished in the 13c., and the process was completed during the 14c., when its stones were used to build the village church.

Appendix

CLIMATE AND SEASON

Approximately, the climate of Normandy is that of southern England, except that, well inland, you are likely to enjoy more really hot summer days. It is obvious that so verdant a countryside must have its share of rain, and there is usually a concentration of it during October. September rivals April and May as a holiday month, depending on whether you prefer orchards bowed with fruit or incandescent with blossom. For seaside holidays August is to be avoided if at all possible: the prices go up as the crowds come in. July or September are infinitely preferable. June, though the sea may still be cool, can be ideal. In most resorts the high season is surprisingly short, not starting until mid-July and ending smartly in mid-September. Out of it, some châteaux and small museums may revert to their winter opening times; apart from that there is everything to be said for avoiding this period.

SYNDICATS D'INITIATIVE

These, the local tourist offices, should be a first call wherever you intend to spend any time. Addresses of the larger ones are given in this book; elsewhere, if they are not obvious, the place to make inquiries is the *mairie*. The Syndicats can supply, along with maps, guides and classified lists of hotels in their region, the current opening times of places of interest. These can be variable, particularly in smaller places: times given in the text should be checked.

HOTELS

These, especially in the country, may be better than their classification would suggest, assuming that the traveller has an appreciation of the kind of comfort that is not machine-turned. In my quite considerable experience of wandering about country Normandy, cleanliness can be relied on.

FOOD

Normany is regarded as an area of good eating even by the French, who take food with proper seriousness. The foundation of the regional cuisine is the abundance of first-class raw materials, pre-eminently butter and cream, which are used lavishly. They are the basis of the voluptuously velvety sauces which accompany many superb fish dishes, though there is a school of thought which holds it a sacrilege to do anything with a perfect sole other than grill it and squeeze a few drops of lemon juice over it. The Normandy coast is an excellent place to acquire a taste for shellfish if you have not already done so, working up from the delectable *moules marinières* by way of oysters to the beautifully composed platters of *fruits de mer*, fronded with seaweed and glittering with ice.

You may be lucky enough to find a farmyard fowl as opposed to the plastic kind, and to eat the renowned ducklings of the Duclair region. You will be unlucky if, near the coast, you do not encounter the *agneau vert pré*, roast lamb whose incomparable flavour comes from the grazing of the salt marshes. Of the two regional specialities, *tripes à la mode de Caen* and the *canard au sang* of Rouen, one need say only that appreciation of the first depends on whether you do or do not like tripe, in whatever mode, and that one should not let the common English aversion to underdone meat prevent one from even trying the second.

The cheeses are many and memorable. Camembert, in its home, is a far different thing from the commonplace commercial product, and ideally Pont l'Évêque should be eaten as well as made in the Pays d'Auge. The novelty for many travellers is likely to be Livarot, a splendid cheese whose flavour is less pungent than its smell.

After the cheese, not, as in England, before it, comes the *tarte aux pommes* which one finds everywhere in France, but the definitive version of which is native to Normandy. Should you be there during the autumn, it is worth looking around market stalls for the old varieties of dessert apples which are not produced on a large scale. Everywhere you will find the *Reine des reinettes*, the one eating apple that rivals a Cox's Orange. The pears also are excellent, particularly when they have been picked at the peak of ripeness a few hours before sale.

A note for those who may have trouble in finding quick, cheap stopgap meals for hungry children. Baked beans and/or tinned spaghetti on toast are not – yet – to be found in France. Small restaurants will probably do egg and chips, as may café bars. The latter will usually provide sandwiches of about half a *baguette*, generously stuffed with ham, pâté or Camembert.

The wine of the country is cider, draught or bottled, the latter blessedly un-gassy. It is often served with *crêpes*, a combination which has little but its unfamiliarity against it. In the pear-growing area around Domfort you will find perry *(poiré)*. Have a care – it goes down as smooth as silk but is far from innocuous. Calvados, apple brandy, is the local equivalent of cognac. Muscadet, the dry, fresh white wine of the Nantes region, which is normally drunk with seafood, is a pleasant enough accompaniment to most summertime meals.

AMUSEMENTS

There has been a proliferation of sailing schools along the Normandy coast in recent years. If the expansion of riding schools does not quite match it, many exist, and in many areas there is a network of bridle paths. Fishing, in sea, lake or river, is widely available. The Syndicat d'Initiative can give details of local possibilities, and of the licences needed for fresh water fishing.

Even small resorts are likely to have a casino, though only the larger ones will offer the full range of roulette, baccarat, boules, black jack, trent et quarante, and chemin de fer. Apart from galas at Deauville, and possibly the exceptional gala night at one or two other places, evening dress is not stipulated, merely 'tenue convenable' which, at the seaside, means little more than 'clean and decent'. In season there are concerts and theatrical performances at the more fashionable resorts.

Rouen's Théâtre des Arts occasionally stages opera.

TRANSPORT

Towns, with three exceptions, are best explored on foot. A car makes the giantism of Le Havre slightly less rebarbative. In both Rouen and Caen, where distances may be tiring, the in-town bus services – Caen's is outstandingly convenient – are a better option than battling with the problems of town traffic and parking. Details and timetables from the Syndicat d'Initiative.

PUBLIC HOLIDAYS AND CLOSING TIMES

First-time visitors should remember that France has some public holidays which are not observed in England – Ascension Day (14 July), the Feast of the Assumption (15 August) and All Saints (1 November) – when shops close, except that bakers' and food shops usually open in the morning. Conversely, as on Sundays, museums and places of interest are usually open. Tuesday is a common closing day for these.

Banks keep roughly British hours but may close at lunch time. In country towns with a Saturday market they commonly open on that day and close on Mondays.

MAPS AND BOOKS

The Michelin sheets for the area are Nos. 52, 54, 55, 59 and 60. Travellers will find that the maps, here and there, have not kept up with changes in road numbering. Provided you are clear about the general direction of your route this is no more than a minor inconvenience.

For those wanting more detailed information, the *Guide Bleu* is comprehensive, though it cannot be classed as light reading. Visitors seriously interested in the church architecture of Normandy will scarcely need to be referred to Volume IV of the *Dictionnaire des Églises de France*, though its bulk classes it with books which one consults before setting out or after returning. More recently published, and more portable, are the two volumes of Lucien Musset's *Normandie Romane*, in the Zodiac edition, which deals with every Romanesque church in the province. The many illustrations are of consistently high quality and the essentials of the text are given in English.

Hachette's *Merveilles des Châteaux de Normandie*, pre-eminently a picture book, contains rather more historical than architectural detail, but is sufficiently informative for non-specialists.

The Michelin *Green Guide*, available in English translation, is a useful adjunct to this book.

Index

Index

361